Managing and Improving Schoo and Behaviour

This new book on school attendance and behaviour brings an international flavour to the field, with contributions on some of the latest empirical research and thinking from around the world. It includes contributions from Canada and the USA, Hong Kong, Europe, the United Kingdom and Ireland. Some of the interesting, wide-ranging, and often unique topics covered in the book include: truancy and well-being, disaffection, pupil absenteeism, social mediation, aggression in primary schools, bullying, emotional barriers to learning, behaviour management training, exclusion, reintegration, the role of educational psychologists, and ethnic diversity and classroom disruption in the context of migration policies.

The book should prove both helpful and useful for a wide range of professionals, students, and academics, across a wide range of educational, care, and social policy disciplines.

This book was originally published as a special issue of *Educational Studies*.

Ken Reid is widely regarded as one of the leading international experts in the field of school attendance, truancy, and behaviour. He was the Chair of the Welsh Government's National Behaviour and Attendance Review (NBAR), which reported in 2008. He is the author or co-author of numerous books on education, research reports, and academic articles in leading journals, and is a much sought after public speaker, professional trainer, and educational commentator within media circles. His most recent books (all published by Routledge) include: *Managing School Attendance* (2014), *An Essential Guide to Improving Attendance in Your School* (2014), *Better Behaviour through Home-School Relations* (with Gill Ellis and Nicola Morgan, 2013), and *Tackling Behaviour in Your Primary School* (with Nicola Morgan, 2012). He was awarded an OBE in the Queen's Birthday Honours List in June, 2010.

Managing and Improving School Attendance and Behaviour

New approaches and initiatives

Edited by
Ken Reid

Routledge
Taylor & Francis Group

LONDON AND NEW YORK

First published 2016
by Routledge

2 Park Square, Milton Park, Abingdon, Oxfordshire, OX14 4RN
711 Third Avenue, New York, NY 10017

Routledge is an imprint of the Taylor & Francis Group, an informa business

First issued in paperback 2017

British Library Cataloguing in Publication Data
A catalogue record for this book is available from the British Library

ISBN 13: 978-1-138-11978-9 (hbk)
ISBN 13: 978-1-138-30926-5 (pbk)

Typeset in Times
by RefineCatch Limited, Bungay, Suffolk

Publisher's Note
The publisher accepts responsibility for any inconsistencies that may have
arisen during the conversion of this book from journal articles to book chapters,
namely the possible inclusion of journal terminology.

Disclaimer
Every effort has been made to contact copyright holders for their permission to
reprint material in this book. The publishers would be grateful to hear from any
copyright holder who is not here acknowledged and will undertake to rectify
any errors or omissions in future editions of this book.

Contents

CONTENTS

Citation Information

The chapters in this book were originally published in *Educational Studies*, volume 41, issues 1–2 (February–May 2015). When citing this material, please use the original page numbering for each article, as follows:

Chapter 5
Rebuilding attendance practices with youth: the role of social mediation
Renira E. Vellos and Jennifer A. Vadeboncoeur
Educational Studies, volume 41, issues 1–2 (February–May 2015) pp. 91–108

Chapter 6
Aggression in primary schools: the predictive power of the school and home environment
Ana Kozina
Educational Studies, volume 41, issues 1–2 (February–May 2015) pp. 109–121

Chapter 7
Constructing bullying in Ontario, Canada: a critical policy analysis
Sue Winton and Stephanie Tuters
Educational Studies, volume 41, issues 1–2 (February–May 2015) pp. 122–142

Chapter 8
Working with schools in identifying and overcoming emotional barriers to learning
Poppy Nash and Annette Schlösser
Educational Studies, volume 41, issues 1–2 (February–May 2015) pp. 143–155

Chapter 9
Some possible effects of behaviour management training on teacher confidence and competence: evidence from a study of primary school teachers in Hong Kong
Paul Cooper and Zi Yan
Educational Studies, volume 41, issues 1–2 (February–May 2015) pp. 156–170

Chapter 10
Promoting resilience through adversity: increasing positive outcomes for expelled students
Nadia Coleman
Educational Studies, volume 41, issues 1–2 (February–May 2015) pp. 171–187

Chapter 11
Factors affecting successful reintegration
David Vittle Thomas
Educational Studies, volume 41, issues 1–2 (February–May 2015) pp. 188–208

Chapter 12
The relationship between ethnic diversity and classroom disruption in the context of migration policies
Gert-Jan M. Veerman
Educational Studies, volume 41, issues 1–2 (February–May 2015) pp. 209–225

For any permission-related enquiries please visit:
http://www.tandfonline.com/page/help/permissions

Notes on Contributors

Gaynor Attwood is an Assistant Vice Chancellor at the University of the West of England, Bristol, UK, where she is also a Professor of Education. She has published in the fields of truancy and disaffection from school, competence-based assessment, and information and communication technology in schools.

H.C.M. (Tim) Carroll retired in 2007 from the School of Psychology, Cardiff University, UK, where he was a Senior Lecturer in Educational Psychology and a Course Director of the MSc programme of initial training for educational psychologists. His research interests have been in the fields of the professional training of educational psychologists, special education, and pupil absenteeism. His publications in the latter area include an edited book, a jointly anchored book, chapters in books, and a number of journal articles. Since his retirement, he has continued with his research on pupil absenteeism and is in the process of publishing his findings.

Haiping Chen is a PhD student in the School of Social Work at Indiana University, Bloomington, IN, USA, whose areas of research interest includes youth development, the civic engagement of older adults, and inter-generational volunteering. She received her bachelor's and master's degrees from Xiamen University, China. Whilst there, she worked on developing a volunteer-support network in urban communities, exploring opportunities for community social workers, and developing a home-based community care programme for older adults.

Nadia Coleman is a member of the Educational Leadership and Policy Studies team at the University of Denver, Colorado, USA. She has taught expelled students in the Denver area since 2009. Her primary focus is on supporting expelled students and their families during and after expulsion. Her research aims to include students' voices in the debate surrounding exclusionary discipline.

Paul Cooper is the Chair and a Professor of Socio-Emotional Development and Education in the Department of Special Education and Counselling at The Hong Kong Institute of Education. Previously, he held the Chair at the University of Leicester, UK, and was for several years the Editor of *Emotional and Behavioural Difficulties*, which is published by Routledge. His main research interests are in the fields of the social-emotional aspects of educational engagement and interventions for promoting positive social and emotional engagement in schools.

Paul Croll is a Professor of Education at the University of Reading, UK. He has researched and published in the fields of truancy and disaffection from school, special educational needs, educational disadvantage, and classroom interaction. His most recent book, written with Gaynor Attwood (above), is *Children's Lives and Children's Futures* (2010). He was an Editor of the *British Journal of Educational Studies* from 2001 to 2009 and is an academician of the Academy of Social Sciences.

Merike Darmody is a Research Officer at the Economic and Social Research Institute (ESRI) and an Adjunct Assistant Professor at the Department of Sociology, Trinity College, Dublin, Ireland. Her key area of interest is in the field of the sociology of education. However, she also has interests in the broader issues on the relationship between an individual and society. Her most recent work includes studies on the ethnic, cultural, and religious diversity in Irish primary and secondary schools. She has also published on schooling contexts, on student outcomes and the experiences of children and young people in primary, secondary, and higher education.

Carolyn Gentle-Genitty is an Assistant Professor and Interim Director of the undergraduate Bachelor of Social Work Programme, on the Indianapolis Campus, at Indiana University, Bloomington, IN, USA. She brings over 20 years of expertise in the fields of youth antisocial behaviour (truancy and gangs), social bonding assessment, teaching, and model and curriculum development, and in related theoretical studies. She is an international speaker, published book and journal author, and app developer ("101 Theory"; Guide to Social Work).

Issac Karikari is a budding research scholar and doctoral student in the School of Social Work at Indiana University, Bloomington, IN, USA. He is actively engaged in the fields of international development, multicultural studies, and civil society organisations. He is generally interested in child welfare issues, and his current unit of interest is children involved in child labour practices.

Jangmin Kim is a PhD student in the School of Social Work at Indiana University, Bloomington, IN, USA. His research interests include school-community collaboration, youth-participatory action research, and civic engagement, as well as social justice-orientated interventions for educational equity and student development.

Ana Kozina is the Head of the Centre for Evaluation Studies at the Educational Research Institute in Slovenia. She has been involved in several previous national and international research projects. She is currently working on a postdoctoral project entitled 'The Development of Guidelines for Aggression Reduction on a School-Level Basis', which involves the production of an anxiety-aggression reduction model in Slovenian primary schools between years 2007 and 2011. Her specific research interest is in the development of models to combat aggression and anxiety, their interplay, and on such inter-related factors at the individual and community levels, as well as on appropriate intervention methods. As an Assistant Professor, she is also engaged in university teaching at the University of Maribor, Slovenia, in the areas of developmental psychology, motivation and emotion, and in the factors of human development.

Poppy Nash is a Lecturer in Education, and is involved in the Psychology in Educational Research Centre in the Department of Education, at the University of York, UK. She has developed various school-based interventions for enhancing resilience in vulnerable learners.

Ken Reid is widely regarded as one of the leading international experts in the field of school attendance, truancy, and behaviour. He was the Chair of the Welsh Government's National Behaviour and Attendance Review (NBAR), which reported in 2008. He is the author or co-author of numerous books on education, research reports, and academic articles in leading journals, and is a much sought after public speaker, professional trainer, and educational commentator within media circles. His most recent books (all published by Routledge) include: *Managing School Attendance* (2014), *An Essential Guide to Improving Attendance in Your School* (2014), *Better Behaviour through Home-School Relations* (with Gill Ellis and Nicola Morgan, 2013), and *Tackling Behaviour in Your Primary School* (with Nicola Morgan, 2012). He was awarded an OBE in the Queen's Birthday Honours List in June, 2010.

Annette Schlösser is an Academic Tutor for the Clinical Training Course at the University of Hull, UK. She also engages in clinical practice in North Lincolnshire CAMHS, working with children, adolescents, and families. She has a particular interest in looked-after children.

David Vittle Thomas has been teaching since 1996 and has worked in both mainstream education settings as a geography teacher and subsequently, in an alternative education setting within a pupil referral unit in Wales. He has specialised in teaching difficult and disadvantaged pupils across the full spectrum of the curriculum, working with pupils with additional learning needs and those with challenging behaviour, including those with social and educational and behavioural difficulties, especially those within the KS2–KS3 age range (8–14 year-old pupils).

Maeve Thornton holds a PhD in Psychology and currently works as a Research Fellow on the national project Growing Up in Ireland Study. Previously, she worked on the Youth Development Study in Northern Ireland, a longitudinal-based study on the risk and protective factors associated with adolescent drug use. During this period, she was also involved in the implementation and management of the Youth Development Study Family Survey, which was a related study focusing on a sample of the original cohort families. Her main areas of interest are in exploring outcomes for the child, especially with regard to the family environment, including family resources, family structure, intra-familial processes, and the socio-historical context in which these operate.

Stephanie Tuters is a doctoral candidate at the Ontario Institute for the Study of Education at the University of Toronto, Canada. Her doctoral research examines the experiences of elementary teachers engaging in equity work and what helps and hinders them in doing this work. She is also the Project Manager for two SSHRC funded research projects, the first, with Dr Jim Ryan, is an investigation into the micro-politics of social justice leadership. The second, with Dr John Portelli, investigates educational equity and inclusion in Neoliberal times.

Jennifer A. Vadeboncoeur is an Associate Professor of Human Development, Learning and Culture at the University of British Columbia, Vancouver, Canada. Her research includes learning from young people about their experiences engaging in informal learning settings, as well as in rethinking learning and teaching relationships with educators. Her most recent publications include *Learning in and Across Contexts: Reimagining Education* (2014), and *Re-Constructing the Adolescent Cultures: Sign, Symbol and Body* (2005).

Gert-Jan M. Veerman is a Lecturer in Education at the Ede Christian University of Applied Sciences, The Netherlands. He is also a PhD student in the Department of Sociology and Anthropology at the University of Amsterdam, The Netherlands. He has published a number of articles in academic journals. In 2011, he received a doctoral grant for teachers from the Netherlands Organisation for Scientific Research (NWO). His main research interests include ethnicity and school performance. Previously, he worked for over 10 years as a primary teacher in schools in Holland.

Renira E. Vellos is a PhD candidate in Human Development, Learning and Culture at the University of British Columbia, Vancouver, Canada. Her research areas include early school leaving, youth in alternative education contexts, re-engagement, educational leadership, and administration and educational policy. Her research interests include how conceptions of social actors in education, like students and administrators, are constructed through discourses that position people differently within educational systems.

Eric Wilka is the Homeless Management Information System specialist at the Coalition for Homelessness Intervention and Prevention Centre in Indianapolis, IN, USA. He works with homelessness data to inform community planning, conduct federal reporting, and promote a data-driven response to homelessness in Indianapolis.

Sue Winton is an Associate Professor at York University, Toronto, Canada. Her research examines influences on policy processes and the implications of education policy and policy processes for critical democracy. Her previous studies include comparative critical policy analyses of US and Canadian safe schools and character education policies, an examination of new media's impact on the theory of political spectacle and education policy, and a rhetorical analysis of a school district's education policy. She is a former elementary school teacher and has taught in Mexico, Canada, and the USA.

Zi Yan is an Assistant Professor in the Department of Curriculum and Teaching at The Hong Kong Institute of Education. His main research interests are in Rasch measurement, and educational and psychological assessment.

Managing and improving school attendance and behaviour: new approaches and initiatives

Ken Reid

Background

At the previous annual *Educational Studies* (ES) Board Meeting held in Exeter in July 2013, it was decided to introduce periodic special editions (SE) of the Journal at the ratio of approximately one for every two years. It was also agreed that given the national and international interest in the field, the focus of a new first SE should be on Managing and Improving School Attendance and Behaviour: New Approaches and Initiatives with hopefully, contributions from around the world.

Subsequently, the protocols to be followed for the SE, including the timescale, length and formatting processes were agreed. It was also decided that the SE would become the first edition of ES in 2015, thereby creating Volume 41, 1. However, in the event, given the unexpectedly high interest in the SE and the subsequent volume and quality of the possible contributions, it was eventually agreed to produce a one-off double edition of the SE, thereby becoming Volume 41, 1 and 2, as well as producing a special edited book containing all the contents.

Process

After the initial publicity for the SE was sent out, some 55 expressions of interest in writing for the SE were received mostly by email, although a few oral requests were also received. Potential contributors were asked to submit a detailed abstract focusing upon the scope of their paper. Of these, a substantial number could be readily dismissed as being unlikely to reach the required standard or because their content lay well outside the remit for the SE.

In the event, an abstract and brief summary were requested from potential authors by no later than 31 December 2013. Subsequently, some 26 potential authors were invited to develop their articles for consideration in the SE. This included two or three international standard authors in the field who subsequently decided not to submit, although they did subsequently agree to act as referees.

Thereafter, a comprehensive list of reviewers for the SE was created. All papers were read by at least two experienced referees, plus the SE Editor, although two were read by three referees and another by four. Some 28 different referees read the potential contributions, most reading only one paper, although some read and assessed two.

After the initial reviewing process, which followed the end of the first submission date of 31 March 2014, only 17 papers were deemed to be of the requisite standard and within the field of particular interest for the SE. Of the 17 first drafts which did reach the required standard, each one was given its own SE identification number. Thereafter, between 31 March and the end of June 2014, an iterative review process took place in which the reviewers' reports were fed back anonymously to the potential authors and subsequently, they each made their own final amendments and changes to the papers based on the feedback from the referees and the SE Editor.

In the event, of the 17 final and amended papers submitted for final consideration in time for the 10 July deadline, 12 were approved for the SE at the Board Meeting on 18 July 2014. However, it was also decided beforehand that one high-quality paper should be published in a regular edition of the Journal as it did not quite fit in with the scope and remit of the SE. The authors of two of the other draft papers have been asked to complete their amended papers in due course also for possible inclusion in a normal edition of ES. Another author who suffered from a serious and debilitating illness during the process and who was, therefore, unable to complete her paper on time has been encouraged to do so and to submit it in due course for consideration by the Board. Thus, from the original 55 abstracts and expressions of interest submitted by the potential contributors, 12 papers were eventually selected for the SE, the remainder falling by the way side at different points in the process, with four others remaining "fluid", dependent upon satisfactory completion according to the terms of the peer review process.

The contributions

In the event, the contributions have come from around the world and include the USA, Canada, Hong Kong, Europe, the UK and Ireland. The contributions include some instantly recognisable experts in the field as well as some authors who are publishing their first academic paper, albeit these are mostly co-authors who have been "nurtured" by more experienced mentors.

Topics included in the final papers include one or more papers on:

- National cohort studies on truancy, well-being and disaffection;
- Reintegration strategies;
- The role of social mediation;
- Aggression in primary schools;
- Behaviour management training;
- Bullying;
- The role of the educational psychologist;
- Increasing positive outcomes for expelled students;
- Overcoming emotional barriers to learning;
- The relationship between ethnic diversity and classroom disruption.

Acknowledgements

First, I would like to thank the Editorial Board and Routledge for having the confidence to invite me to undertake the lead Editorial role in bringing together this Special Double Edition of *Educational Studies* on the theme of Managing and Improving School Attendance and Behaviour: New Approaches and Initiatives. It is extremely pleasing that we have managed to attract such a wide range of high-quality submissions.

Second, I would like to thank all the contributors and peer review referees for all their hard work throughout the process.

Third, I would like to thank Dr Kevin Downing, the Editor-in-Chief of *Educational Studies* and Ian White of Taylor & Francis for all their help, advice and support.

Finally, I would like to thank Lucy Robertshaw for all her technical support throughout the duration of the different tasks which were required throughout a very demanding and time-consuming process.

Introduction

Ken Reid

This double special edition (SE) of *Educational Studies* is focused upon Managing and Improving School Attendance and Behaviour: New Approaches and Initiatives and presents a number of diverse and innovative papers in these two related fields.

School absenteeism and truancy

There can be little doubt that both persistent school absenteeism and truancy are linked to a wide variety of educational and social pathologies such as underachievement, disadvantage, dysfunctional family life, one parent families, adverse social backgrounds, poverty, criminality, low self-esteem, numeracy and literacy deficiencies, poor teaching and poor schooling (Cabinet Office 1998; Reid 2014a, see especially Chapters 1–5). Often, there are disproportionately more absentees and truants located in schools situated in deprived and disadvantaged areas and those schools whose academic performance of their students is worse than those located in more favourable catchment areas or which are better managed and well led (Rutter et al. 1979); although exceptions abound due to a lot of situation-specific variables and internal iterative processes such as having sound pastoral care systems, effective intervention strategies, good teacher–pupil relations and high-quality teaching and learning in place.

Specifically, truancy, persistent school absenteeism and other forms of pupils' non-attendance are closely linked to:

- The effects of poverty
- Unemployment
- Parents on one or more form of state support
- Single parent families
- Children on free school meals (FSMs)
- Low-quality housing
- Overcrowding
- Second-, third- and fourth-generation "familial truancy"
- Family breakdown, divorce, separation and frequent "partner" changes
- Inconsistent home discipline
- Families with poor or low child-rearing skills
- Families in which the father is often away for long periods of time
- Parents or carers who do not support their children's education or learning
- Parents or carers with anti-school attitudes
- Parents who dislike attending their children's school to attend either meetings or social events

- Parents who had their own poor experiences whilst at school, including those with their own learning, numeracy, reading or speech deficiencies or who were bullied whilst at school
- Homes which do not encourage their children's learning or homework
- Homes in which drugs or alcohol have a disproportionate effect
- Homes which do not ensure that their children do not get a good night's sleep or are not well clothed or nourished
- Families engaged in criminal activity or in other forms of deviant sub-cultures
- Disengaged and anti-social urban or rural communities
- The rise in teenage pregnancies (According to the OECD, for example, the UK has the highest rates in Europe)
- The growth of both disaffected children and adults, the rise of the "gang culture" and in anti-social behaviour
- Parents and children who manifest low self-esteem (see i.e. Reid 1982)
- The growth in the number of parents and/or children with mental health problems
- The rise in the number of pupils with special or additional learning needs
- The increase in the number of parents and/or pupils with either learning or psychological difficulties. These issues might include such aspects as dyslexia, dyspraxia, Asperger's Syndrome et seq
- Attending weak, poor, disadvantaged or low-achieving schools
- Attending a maintained school which has received an extremely poor report from school inspection bodies such as Ofsted or Estyn in, for example, England or Wales
- Schools in which pupils' achievement or attendance league table position are at the lower end of performance profiles and which contain a disproportionate number of pupils who fail to gain five or more GCSE's at A* to C-grade level (in the UK), have behavioural and attendance problems, a higher than average number of school exclusions, and often, above average numbers of pupils on either their FSM's or "at-risk" registers

All the evidence from the published literature (Reid 1985, 1986, 1987, 1999, 2000, 2002, 2014a, 2014b) shows that despite different governments from around the world having a wide range of reforms and intervention strategies in place, no one should ever doubt both the economic and social cost of school absenteeism and truancy both during pupils' childhood and into their later adolescent and adult lives (KPMG 2008; NAO 2005; NPC 2005a, 2005b). Research shows that reducing pupils' non-attendance and truancy can be extremely difficult to achieve and, despite a wide range of intervention strategies being used, these are often not only in their infancy but often applied in unique, indiscriminate, local and unscientific ways (Campbell Collaboration Report 2010; Maynard et al. 2012; Reid 2014a, 5–10).

For example, the Campbell Collaboration Report (2010), which investigated intervention strategies with absentees and non-attendees, through the use of a meta-analysis approach, found that:

(a) Too few studies have considered the non-attendance of ethnic minority pupils, especially using intervention strategies on pupils from a wide range of different ethnic backgrounds.

(b) There is a lack of an agreed consensus about the use of critical definitions in the field; something which Gentle-Genitty et al. discuss in the fourth article in this SE.

(c) Too few studies assess the longer term outcomes of their earlier intervention strategies.

(d) There is a dearth of both effective long-term and longitudinal strategies using appropriate methodologies, not only upon school absenteeism and truancy per se, but also upon related issues like student performance, achievement and school improvement.

(e) There have been far too few studies based upon clinical interventions, a point made by Tim Carroll in his article in this SE.

(f) Too few policy-based research studies which inform practice (see also NBAR 2008), too few studies based on early intervention strategies with elementary or primary-aged pupils (Carroll 2010), too few utilising multidisciplinary and interdisciplinary approaches, and those which link pupils' truancy to either bullying or cyber-bullying, to psychological or mental health disorders, using either clinical or non-clinical samples, and too few which take account of the cost–benefit analysis of implementing different types of intervention strategies.

In fact, the Campbell Collaboration Project (2010) authors concluded that most small-scale and local interventions were often not properly evaluated. Of those which were evaluated, the methodology or evaluation processes used were often described as being inappropriate, insufficiently rigorous or inadequately "tight" and frequently could not demonstrate the long-term effectiveness or positive outcomes of the interventions. Sample sizes tended to vary, a wide variety of intervention strategies were used (e.g. group-based therapies, family therapy and one-to-one techniques), and some of the conclusions often claimed to show a moderate or other improvement in students' school attendance without providing some convincing evidence for making the claim. So, we still have a long way to go in this field.

Behaviour

A similar argument and position could be made in the field of managing school behaviour. Although considerably more research over recent years has been undertaken in the field of school behaviour than school attendance, we also still have a great deal more to learn and evaluate properly.

The study of students' behaviour in schools has moved steadily away from the old notions of control and discipline to the point where pupils' rights and views are becoming increasingly respected and more restorative practices or related concepts are being utilised (McCluskey et al. 2008).The new philosophy incorporates such ideas and concepts as values-based education, multidisciplinary and interdisciplinary practice, inclusivity, diversity, individualised or group approaches such as utilising individualised or group learning plans, ascertaining the gains made by using different kinds of therapies, well-being, respect and peer or adult–pupil relationship policies or strategies, increasing the use and role of school councils, improving home–school links, the creation of appropriate pupil support plans, sharing good practice, and combating bullying and cyber bullying through the use of a variety of appropriate policy strategies, as well as utilising all the research evidence from recent studies into the social, emotional, psychological, behavioural and therapeutic needs of pupils, including those with either special or additional learning needs (Ellis, Morgan, and Reid 2013; Reid and Morgan 2012).

Students, who misbehave in class or those who exhibit different kinds of challenging behaviour within their schools, often have much in common with truants or non-attendees. Indeed, their behaviour is often interlinked. Some persistent absentees are often extremely challenging pupils in school when they do attend (Reid 1981, 1984a, 1984b, 1984c, 1985, 1986, 1987). But, some of these issues remain insufficiently well researched.

There are several reasons for this situation. First, far too many teachers remain insufficiently well trained for their roles in managing pupils' behaviour and attendance (NBAR 2008; Reid 2009a, 2009b, 2009c, 2010a, 2010b, 2010c, 2011a, 2011b, 2011c, 2011d); something which Cooper and Yan elaborate upon further in our tenth article in this SE. This includes staff at all levels within the teaching professional as well as in the support or related professional fields.

Second, far too many pupils fail to have either their attendance or behavioural needs identified soon enough which means that far too many interventions take place much too late or never at all. In fact, in some cases, this leads to pupils being excluded from their regular schools as both Coleman and Thomas point out in articles eleven and twelve in this SE.

Third, there are too few and sound early interventions in place, often due to the high numbers of pupils with these needs as well as professional shortages and unnecessary time delays. Moreover, many pupils with related home background problems or those with literacy or numeracy needs or psychological challenges (e.g. having extremely low self-concepts), never get properly identified or supported which, in turn, leads to adult pathologies, unemployment, frequent job changes, criminality and adverse economic and social consequences for society to overcome and manage.

About the contents

This SE contains some 12 diverse but interrelated articles. The first five are all about school attendance and truancy and are contributed by Gaynor Attwood and Paul Croll, Marike Darmody and Maeve Thornton, "Tim" Carroll, Carolyn Gentle-Genitty et al. and finally, by Renira Vellos and Jennifer Vadeboncoeur. The second seven are about various aspects relating to pupils' behaviour. These have been contributed by Kozina (2013), Sue Winton and Stephanie Tuters, Poppy Nash and Annette Schlosser, Paul Cooper and Zi Yan, Nadia Coleman, David (Dai) Thomas and finally, by Gert-Jan Veerman.

The content on school absenteeism and truancy included in this SE covers the fields of truancy and well-being, disaffection, the role of the educational psychologist (EP) and of social mediation, and charts some of the attempts to find a uniform definition on truancy. The content on pupils' behaviour and behaviour management includes articles on: aggression in primary schools related to the role of the home and school; bullying and attempts to overcome school bullying in Ontario, Canada; working with schools to overcome some of the emotional barriers to learning; and some of the possible consequences of behaviour management training on teacher confidence and competence.

These are followed by two articles on reintegration strategies; a much under-researched field, especially in terms of good practice. Both of these two articles examine the concept of reintegration first, from the position of "expelled" (excluded) students and second, from the position of staff engaged in working with disaffected pupils inside a pupil referral unit. Finally, in another much under-researched and sensitive field, the SE concludes with an empirical study on the relationship between ethnic diversity and classroom disruption.

We will now briefly consider the contents of each article. In the opening two empirical articles, both Professors Gaynor Attwood and Paul Croll followed by Merike Darmody and Maeve Thornton consider the evidence from their national cohort study data bases on truancy and well-being among secondary school pupils in England and upon disaffection on disaffection in Irish primary schools.

The Attwood and Croll paper considers two problematic aspects of the lives of young people: the long-standing issues of truancy from school and more recent concerns about the extent of mental well-being. It uses data from a large-scale survey, the Longitudinal Study of Young People in England (LSYPE). LSYPE provides a very large sample which allows for robust analysis of sub-groups within the population; data from families as well as the young people themselves and a panel design so that characteristics of the young people at one point in time can be related to later outcomes. The results show the extent of truancy among Year 10 pupils with well over one in five reporting truanting but high levels of truancy much less common. The reasons given for truancy mostly revolved around dislike of aspects of either their school or schooling. Truancy, even at low levels, was associated with more negative outcomes such as poor examination results and later unemployment. Data on mental well-being, based on the General Health Questionnaire, showed the extent of feelings of distress and inability to cope with everyday life with more serious levels affecting, perhaps, one in five of the young people. Young women were more likely to report problems of mental well-being than young men and truancy was strongly associated with poorer levels of well-being. The contrast between the way that most truants said that it was important to them to do well at school but also that disliking school was given as a reason for truancy suggests the possibility for subsequent school interventions.

The paper by Merike Darmody and Maeve Thornton suggests that internationally there is now a growing body of research on student school engagement. Much of this research highlights the association of school engagement with a range of social, behavioural and academic outcomes. Less attention is paid to factors predicting disaffection among young children across various dimensions using nationally representative data-sets. This paper addresses this gap in research by exploring factors that are related to school disaffection in Irish primary schools. Drawing on a nationally representative study of nine-year-olds, the multivariate analysis reveals that disaffection is associated with a number of personal and institutional factors. While the data relate to the Irish situation, the paper raises a number of issues also of interest to an international audience.

The third paper by "Tim" Carroll provides an interesting and novel way to analysing pupils' attendance data and the link to the work of the EP. From a review of the literature it is concluded that: (i) each form of pupil absenteeism relates to a heterogeneous group of children; (ii) because of such heterogeneity those who are involved in assessment and intervention in relation to pupil absenteeism are faced with a demanding task; (iii) as a consequence of their education and training EPs have the appropriate knowledge and skills for dealing with pupil absenteeism at both the individual and group level; (iv) with respect to dealing with pupil absenteeism, EPs could make and have made a contribution; (v) EPs have the necessary experience of working at a multi-agency level and, in connection with pupil absenteeism, have worked not only with the children and their parents but also at both whole school and multi-agency levels and (vi) EPs have already demonstrated in the literature that they have much to offer in this important and demanding area.

The fourth paper by Carolyn Gentle-Genitty et al. tackles the extremely complex field of attempting to find a universal definition of truancy; an issue which has blighted the topic over a substantial period of time. Their paper notes that there is no shortage of definitions for truancy. In the USA, for example, one state may house many different definitions and there are a variety of challenges arising from this fact. One of the most important to researchers, policy-makers and educators alike, is that because of the lack of uniformly and consistency, it is difficult to compile and ascertain the totality of the phenomenon. The lack of a consistent definition influences a wide range of outcomes including policy matters, financial resources, and definitive responses and intervention strategies. This manuscript attempts to synthesise the literature through the examination of operational definitions of truancy in the US and in other territories. In addition to these operational definitions, expert opinions from focus groups proposed an enhanced definition of truancy. The study is qualitative and uses focus groups and synthesis of the literature to frame the work. Findings are presented. The goal is to synthesise the literature, not in its entirety, but in an attempt to combine and inform the conversation on a definition of truancy, despite initially seeming to be somewhat unachievable.

Finally, the article by Remira Vellos and Professor Jennifer Vadeboncoeur highlights the experiences of students and educators from a larger sociocultural study of participation and engagement at a senior alternative high school programme in British Columbia, Canada. Drawing on participant observation, active interviews and document analysis, school attendance was remediated as a meaningful social practice as a result of the relationships young people formed with educators and peers, rather than meaningful in and of itself or in relation to academic performance. These findings trouble school attendance policies that locate absenteeism as a problem within individual students and as de-contextualised from their lived experiences. Findings also foreground the importance of examining how school attendance may be interpreted by students. For some students, participation in relationships and communities lies behind school attendance, highlighting the necessity of attending to the role of identity and values alongside of the construction of knowledge as central to the work of schools.

The paper by Dr Ann Kozina, begins the section on behaviour. She analyses the predictive power of home- and school environment-related factors for determining pupils' aggression. The multiple regression analyses are performed for fourth- and eighth-grade pupils based on the TIMSS 2007 ($n = 8394$) and TIMSS 2011 ($n = 9415$) databases for Slovenia. At the national level, the LA aggression scale (Kozina 2013) was administered in both TIMSS cycles. For home environment variables, she included those related to socio-economic status, pupils' educational aspirations and parental activities with their children and pupils' free time activities. The results show that the variables related to socio-economic status, spare time activities and parental activities are significant predictors. The results differ however, in both analysed data-sets. For school environment variables, she included those relating to the school climate, pupils' attitudes towards school and school subjects, and pupils' achievement in mathematics. We find that the variables related to school climate and students' self-confidence are significant predictors. These results are stable in both years. The predictive power of the school characteristics model (including only the school environment variables) is larger (based on the proportion of explained variance) compared with the home characteristics model. The hierarchical linear model of data from 2007 and 2011 shows small differences in aggression between schools. The inclusion of two data cycles collected in two time periods allows us to observe changes in aggression predictors over time. Practical implications are finally included.

Next, the article by Sue Winton and Stephanie Tuters considers the impact of bullying upon schools in Ontario, Canada. Increasingly, both bullying and cyberbullying are being linked increasingly to both pupils' non-attendance and truancy as well as to behaviour (Reid 2008, 2014a). As the prevalence and negative effects of bullying become widely known, people around the world seem desperate to solve the bullying "problem". A sizeable body of research about many aspects of bullying and a plethora of anti-bullying programmes and policies now exist. This critical policy analysis asks: how does Ontario, Canada's bullying policy support and/or undermine critical democracy; and how does it reflect, support and further the interests of neoliberalism and/or neoconservatism. Findings indicate that the policy constructs the problem of bullying as a problem of individuals and a "behaviour for learning" problem. The policy also prescribes standardised responses to bullying incidents. We explore ways in which these constructions are undemocratic and unjust. The findings are particularly concerning because bullying policies are often viewed as innocuous by practitioners. This paper offers more than just critique by providing suggestions for how research and policies can become more just and equitable and how bullying policy may be enacted to support critical democracy.

The following paper from Drs Poppy Nash and Annette Schlosser reports a case study on working closely with a secondary school and to enhance understanding of disruptive behaviour, both through the use of bespoke Continuing Professional Development (CPD) materials. This project evolved from the researchers' previous research on the extent to which teachers believe disruptive pupils can control their behaviour. A notable finding was the sizeable minority of teachers in both primary and secondary schools who appear to be unaware of the psychological underpinnings of disruptive behaviour. That is, that such behaviour frequently communicates unresolved emotional needs, rather than wilful defiance.

The current project aims to develop, implement and evaluate CPD resources developed by the researchers, for a one-day staff training day at a secondary school in north England. Prior to training, school staff completed a questionnaire to "audit" their perceptions of disruptive behaviour in school. Following evaluation, the CPD materials will be made available to other schools. It is anticipated that the materials will enable greater mutual understanding and respect for the ways in which disruptive behaviour is perceived by practitioners and school staff. Moreover, they will provide an urgently needed means of facilitating a shared knowledge base and a shared language for addressing emotional barriers to learning.

Next, the paper from Professor Paul Cooper and Zi Yan in Hong Kong aims to explore the relationships between the extent and perceived quality of teachers' experience of training in behaviour management (BM), and their awareness of the nature and extent of behavioural problems among school students, and their confidence in their own competence to deal with such problems; a subject which is close to my own heart (Reid 2011a, 2011b, 2011c, 2011d, 2012). Teachers ($n = 183$) from Hong Kong primary schools were surveyed. The results showed that gender, age and whether teachers have received training had no significant influence on teachers' awareness, conception and confidence regarding BM. A negative correlation was found between teachers' levels of satisfaction in relation to their training experiences and their perceptions of the level of problematic behaviours among students, and the impact of students' problematic behaviour on their teaching. A positive correlation was found between teachers' levels of satisfaction in relation to their training experiences and their confidence in their own competence to deal with students' problematic behaviour.

The following two articles by Nadia Coleman and Dr "Dai" Thomas examine the complex field of dealing with difficult students such as those which have been either "expelled" or "excluded" (depending upon your international location) or are situated within a specialist pupil referral unit (PRU). These are related to the thorny notion of reintegration, a much neglected field of study and where much more research is required; not least in terms of good practice.

The first article by Nadia Coleman endeavours to increase educators' understanding of the experiences of students who have been expelled from school in order to represent this critical stakeholder group in future policy development and programme implementation. Students' perspectives are presented through thick description in this narrative case study. Findings indicate that expulsion from school can alter the trajectory of a student's life—for better or for worse. Without thoughtful intervention from caring educators, this interruption in students' education may have an irreparable destructive impact on students' futures. Educators must develop interventions focused on bringing forth protective factors that are documented to increase resilience, thus making students less susceptible to the risks inherent in removing them from school.

The second study by Dr David Thomas explores the perspectives of education practitioners towards the process of reintegrating pupils (many of whom display social, emotional and behavioural difficulties – SEBD), from a pupil referral unit (PRU) to mainstream educational provision in a rural bilingual Welsh authority, and examines the barriers and facilitators they identified as evident within their individual schools and catchment area served, with regards to reintegrating and including pupils. The study locates the process within a specific geographical context and discusses whether there are specific reintegration barriers and facilitators inherent within the setting.

Patterns of pupil referral and reintegration between the PRU and mainstream schools were examined and analysed from "pupil tracking data" which tracked pupils throughout an academic year from their arrival at the PRU before the perspectives of education practitioners towards potential reintegration barriers and facilitators were gathered through an initial expert sample and a second landscape sample postal questionnaire. Interviews were subsequently conducted with respondents from Primary, Secondary and PRU settings to drill down into the influence of specific barriers and facilitators identified earlier.

This study suggests that although generic reintegration barriers and facilitators may be evident within all settings, there were specific factors inherent within this geographical context identified by education practitioners who acted in the most part as barriers to successful reintegration and inclusion.

The SE concludes with an important and embryonic study by Gert-Jan Veerman on the relationship between ethnic school composition and classroom disruption in secondary education in the context of migration policies. He measured classroom disruption using the students' reports from 3533 schools in 20 countries provided by cross-national PISA (Programme for International Student Assessment) 2009 data. He then employed the migrant share and the ethnic diversity net of the native share as indicators of the ethnic composition of a school. The MIPEX (Immigrant Integration Policy Index) is used as an indicator of migration policies. His results show a positive association between ethnic school diversity net of the migrant share and classroom disruption. Furthermore, he reveals a negative interaction term of the migration policy and ethnic diversity. Consequently, the results indicate that students in countries with a more inclusive migration policy are at least less harmed by influence of ethnic school diversity regarding classroom disruption. Findings partly support the "contact hypothesis" and reject the "threat hypothesis" in an educational context.

Finally, the Editorial Board of Educational Studies very much hope that you enjoy and benefit from a reading of either the full contents of this SE or from dipping in to read the specialist individual papers which are of most interest to you. We also hope that the papers will make a significant contribution to the future study of both empirical and policy analyses within the fields of both school absenteeism and truancy, and pupils' behaviour and the management of these phenomena.

References

Cabinet Office. 1998. *Truancy and School Exclusion Report, Social Exclusion Unit*. London: Cabinet Office.

Campbell Collaboration Report. 2010. *Interventions Intended to Increase Primary and/or Secondary School Attendance, Part 1: Indicated Interventions*. The Campbell Collaboration Fund.

Carroll, H. C. M. 2010. "The Effect of Pupil Absenteeism on Literacy and Numeracy in the Primary School." *School Psychology International* 31 (2): 115–130.

Ellis, G., N. Morgan, and K. Reid. 2013. *Better Behaviour through Home-school Relations*. London: Routledge.

Kozina, A. 2013. "The LA Aggression Scale for Elementary School and Upper Secondary School Students: Examination of Psychometric Properties of a New Multidimensional Measure of Self-reported Aggression." *Psihologija* 46 (3): 245–259.

KPMG. 2008. *Foundation Report on the Long-term Costs of Literacy Difficulties*. London: KPMG.

Maynard, B. R., K. T. McCrea, T. Pigot, and M. S. Kelly. 2012. "Indicated Truancy Interventions: Effects on School Attendance among Chronic Truant Students." *Campbell Systematic Reviews* 10. doi:10.4073/csr.2012.10.

McCluskey, G., G. Lloyd, J. Kane, S. Riddell, J. Stead, and E. Weedon. 2008. "Can Restorative Practices in Schools make a Difference?" *Educational Review* 60 (4): 405–417.

NAO (National Audit Office). 2005. *Improving School Attendance in England*. London: The National Audit office.

NBAR (National Behaviour and Attendance Review). 2008. *Report into School Behaviour and Attendance in Wales: Chair: Professor K. Reid*. Cardiff: Welsh Government.

NPC (New Philanthropy Capital). 2005a. *The Costs of Truancy and School Exclusion*. London: New Philanthropy Capital.

NPC (New Philanthropy Capital). 2005b. *School's Out*. London: New Philanthropy Capital.

Reid, K. 1981. "Alienation and Persistent School Absenteeism." *Research in Education* 26: 31–40.

Reid, K. 1982. "The Self-concept and Persistent School Absenteeism." *British Journal of Educational Psychology* 52 (2): 179–187.

Reid, K. 1984a. "Some Social, Psychological and Educational Aspects Related to Persistent School Absenteeism." *Research in Education* 31: 63–82.

Reid, K. 1984b. "The Behaviour of Persistent School Absentees." *British Journal of Educational Psychology* 54: 320–330.

Reid, K. 1984c. "Disruptive Persistent School Absentees." In *Disruptive Behaviour in Schools*, edited by N. Frude and H. Gault. Chichester: Wiley.

Reid, K. 1985. *Truancy and School Absenteeism*. London: Hodder and Stoughton.

Reid, K. 1986. *Disaffection from School*. London: Methuen.

Reid, K. 1987. *Combating School Absenteeism*. London: Hodder and Stoughton.

Reid, K. 1999. *Truancy and Schools*. London: Routledge.

Reid, K. 2000. *Tackling Truancy in Schools*. London: Routledge.

Reid, K. 2002. *Truancy: Short and Long-term Solutions*. London: Routledge.

Reid, K. 2008. "The Causes of Non-attendance: An Empirical Study." *Educational Review* 60 (4): 345–357.

Reid, K. 2009a. "The National Behaviour and Attendance Review (NBAR) in Wales: Findings on School Behaviour from the Professional Perspective." *Emotional and Behavioural Difficulties* 14 (3): 165–183.

Reid, K. 2009b. "The National Behaviour and Attendance Review (NBAR) in Wales: Findings on Exclusion Set in Context." *Emotional and Behavioural Difficulties* 14 (1): 3–17.

Reid, K. 2009c. "The National Behaviour and Attendance Review in Wales: Findings and recommendations on school attendance." *Research in Education* 81: 20–42.

Reid, K. 2010a. "The Strategic Management of Disaffected Students in Wales." *The International Journal of School Disaffection* 7 (1): 35–40.

Reid, K. 2010b. "Management of School Attendance in the UK: A Strategic Analysis." *Educational Management Administration and Leadership* 38 (1): 88–106.

Reid, K. 2010c. "Improving Attendance and Behaviour in Wales: The Action Plan." *Educational Studies* 36 (3): 233–247.

Reid, K. 2011a. "The Professional Development Needs of Staff in Wales on Behaviour Management and Attendance: Findings from the NBAR Report." *Educational Studies* 37 (1): 15–30.

Reid, K. 2011b. "Tackling Behaviour and Attendance Issues in Schools in Wales: Implications for Training and Professional development." *Educational Studies* 37 (1): 31–48.

Reid, K. 2011c. "The Implications of the NBAR Report for Wales and Future Outlook." *Welsh Journal of Education* 15: 186–225.

Reid, K. 2011d. "The Strategic Management of Truancy and School Absenteeism: Finding Solutions from a National Perspective." *Educational Review* 64 (2): 196–211.

Reid, K. 2012. "An Analysis of the Future Management of School Attendance in Wales." *Emotional and Behavioural Difficulties* 17 (1): 3–12.

Reid, K. 2014a. *Managing School Attendance: Successful Intervention Strategies for Reducing Truancy*. London: Routledge.

Reid, K. 2014b. *An Essential Guide to Improving Attendance in Your School*. London: Routledge.

Reid, K., and N. Morgan. 2012. *Tackling Behaviour in Your Primary School*. London: Routledge.

Rutter, M., B. Maughan, P. Mortimore, and J. Ouston. 1979. *Fifteen Thousand Hours: Secondary Schools and Their Effects upon Children*. London: Open Books.

Truancy and well-being among secondary school pupils in England

Gaynor Attwood[a] and Paul Croll[b]

[a]Faculty of Arts, Creative Industries and Education, University of the West of England, Bristol, UK; [b]Institute of Education, University of Reading, Reading, UK

The paper considers two problematic aspects of the lives of young people: the long-standing issues of truancy from school and more recent concerns about the extent of mental well-being. It uses data from a large-scale survey, the Longitudinal Study of Young People in England (LSYPE). LSYPE provides a very large sample which allows for robust analysis of sub-groups within the population, data from families as well as the young people themselves and a panel design, so that characteristics of the young people at one point in time can be related to later outcomes. The results show the extent of truancy among year-10 pupils with well over one in five reporting truanting but high levels of truancy much less common. The reasons given for truancy mostly revolved around dislike of aspects of school. Truancy, even at low levels, was associated with more negative outcomes such as poor examination results and later unemployment. Data on mental well-being, based on the General Health Questionnaire, showed the extent of feelings of distress and inability to cope with everyday life with more serious levels affecting perhaps one in five of the young people. Young women were more likely to report problems of mental well-being than young men and truancy was strongly associated with poorer levels of well-being. The contrast between the way that most truants said that it was important to them to do well at school but also that disliking school was given as a reason for truancy suggests the possibility of school interventions.

Introduction

A number of papers in this issue of *Educational Studies* have discussed the issue of truancy and strategies for reducing truancy levels in schools. They have also made it clear how stubborn is the problem of unauthorised absence from school and its resistance to strategies to reduce it. In a recent book on school attendance, Reid draws on wide-ranging evidence to conclude that, "… improving school attendance and reducing truancy can be very difficult to achieve and, according to some reports, has remained little changed over the past thirty or more years" (2014, 3). He also demonstrates that this is not just a UK phenomenon but is repeated in other developed countries, especially the USA. In an earlier article (Attwood and Croll 2006), we quoted a report by the National Audit Office (2005) showing that the very substantial sums of money spent by the UK government on initiatives to reduce truancy had not resulted in any reduction in rates of unauthorised absence.

In our earlier study (Attwood and Croll 2006), we used large-scale survey data from the British Household Panel Survey (BHPS) to study various aspects of truancy based on interviews with a national sample of young people and their parents. This analysis provided extensive evidence on the prevalence of self-reported truanting behaviour and its association with personal characteristics of the young people and various aspects of their experiences of and attitudes to school. Because parents were also interviewed, truancy could also be related to family characteristics such as parental monitoring of the child's education and the socio-economic status (SES) of the family based on occupation. And because the BHPS is a panel study, it was also possible to relate levels of truancy to later outcomes such as examination results, participation in post-compulsory education and employment.

The results showed a steady increase in rates of self-reported truancy through the years of compulsory secondary education. Children reporting truancy at either several times or often increased from just over 1% in year 7 (the first year of secondary school) to just under 10% in year 11 (the last year of compulsory schooling). It was also noticeable that the biggest jump in truancy levels occurred between years 9 and 10. Girls and boys reported similar levels of truanting behaviour. The longitudinal nature of the BHPS study made it possible to look at the association of truancy with later outcomes. These showed a uniform picture of increasing levels of truancy being associated with increasing levels of negative outcomes. At the extremes, the comparison of those reporting never truanting and those reporting often truanting showed that the truants were three times less likely to stay in education post 16, were three times more likely to have no good GCSE passes and were ten times more likely to be unemployed six months after leaving education.

The study also showed a number of personal and family characteristics that were predictors of truancy. Children from families in lower socio-economic groups, children of parents who did not monitor homework, children who had poor relationships with their teachers and children who did not put a high value on school were all more likely to truant than other children. But unlike the results of some other studies (e.g. Kinder, Wakefield, and Wilkin 1996; Reid 1999), concerns over bullying were not associated with truancy. Although these patterns of association were consistent and statistically significant, it was also the case that they were not particularly strong. For example, not monitoring homework was associated with truancy but nevertheless most truants were from families where homework was monitored and over half the children whose homework was not monitored did not truant. Similar patterns of weak association were also apparent for SES and attitudes to teachers and school. These relatively weak associations were in marked contrast to the associations of truancy with later education and employment outcomes. Truancy was a very strong predictor of negative outcomes but background factors associated with truancy were much less good predictors of truanting behaviour.

In the present paper, we use the data from another large-scale panel survey, the Longitudinal Study of Young People in England (LSYPE) to extend our previous analysis in a number of ways. First of all, it enables us to replicate the analysis using a much larger sample size than was available for the BHPS. As well as being a replication it also allows some analyses which were not possible in the earlier paper because the relatively limited sample meant that there were too few young people in certain categories, for example, persistent truants from high SES backgrounds. It is also possible to conduct a more extended analysis of the relation of truancy to academic attainment as the LSYPE data-set can be linked to the National Pupil Database. It should be noted that although we are describing the study as a replication, the way that truancy questions were asked differed slightly across the two studies. However, in both studies, self-reports of truancy could be placed in three categories: none, low level and high level. Obviously, the none category is identical across the studies. But in the earlier study, the low level was a response of "once or twice" and the high category "several times" or "often" to a question about truancy in the previous year. In the current study, the low category was a response of "particular lessons" or "just the odd day or lesson" and the high category a response of "several days at a time" or "weeks at a time".

A further focus of the current study which was not present in the earlier analysis is that of pupil well-being and its relationship to truancy. A concern with well-being and with personal happiness, both among children and in the population more generally, has informed a variety of policy initiatives and academic studies. The government Green Paper, *Every Child Matters* (Department for Education 2003) drew attention to a wide range of problems associated with childhood and stressed the role of schools in promoting well-being. Recently, the Department for Education supported an initiative in three local authorities using an intervention to improve young people's resilience and mental health. This had mixed results and limited long-term impact (Department for Education 2011a). The concern with well-being has been informed by the results of a UNICEF (2007) study which suggested that children in the UK had the lowest levels of personal well-being of 20 advanced societies in the OECD. Further evidence comes from a recent academic study of well-being and young people which refers to the, "… widespread perception that the social and emotional well-being of young people has been in decline …" (Gray et al. 2011, 1). There has been a growth of interest in and studies of subjective measures of happiness and personal satisfaction both in populations generally and specifically in young people, especially associated with the work of the economist Richard Layard. Layard points to the paradox that, "… as Western societies have got richer, their people have become no happier." (2006, 3) and argues for the importance of studying happiness and well-being alongside other more conventional social and economic indicators. The LSYPE data-set includes measures of young people's subjective feelings about themselves which give an indication of mental well-being as described below. These measures make it possible to consider truancy in a wider context of a more general sense of well-being, alongside the other social and educational factors we have described.

Methods: the LSYPE data-set

The research reported here is based on a secondary analysis of the LSYPE (Department for Education 2011b). This is a large-scale government-funded panel survey of young people and their families. The aim of the survey was to support the development and evaluation of education policy, in particular, policies concerned with the transition from education to employment. The survey began in 2004, when the young people were 13/14 and has been repeated every year up to 2010. Information was gathered by means of face-to-face personal interviews which included self-completion of some sensitive items. In addition to the young person's interview, the parent identified as the parent most concerned with the young person's education and designated as the "main parent" was interviewed. In most cases, a "second parent" was also interviewed. Data were collected on the socio-economic and educational background of parents, on many aspects of the attitudes, behaviour and educational intentions of the young person and information was also collected about the school they attended. Young people were sampled through their schools in both the maintained and independent sector. The final sample was of approximately 21,000 young people born between September 1989 and August 1990 and 15,770 of these were successfully interviewed in Wave 1, a response rate of 74%. As with all longitudinal surveys, cumulative attrition means that the final response rate is lower than that at any particular wave and the 8682 Wave-7 interviews represented just 41% of the original sample of 21,000. Weights have been calculated for the sample at each wave to allow for the survey design and for survey attrition. This means that the demographic characteristics of sample used for the analysis, for example, the proportion in different socio-economic categories, is identical across the various waves. The data used in this article come from the young people interviewed at both Wave 2 and Wave 7. LSYPE data can be linked to administrative data such as the National Pupil Database. This means that robust attainment data in NPD can be used in an analysis along with family background data and data on young people's own perspectives and intentions.

The analysis for this paper uses data collected at Wave 2 of the survey when the young people were 14 or 15 and Wave 7 of the survey when they were 20 or 21. Key variables are their answer to the question of whether they had truanted in the last year and, if so, how frequently and for what reasons. The young people were also asked a variety of questions about school: how much they valued school, how they got on with their teachers and whether they had been bullied. Data on parental occupations come from the parent interviews at Wave 2 and these have been used for the classification of socio-economic background. Information on levels of educational attainment come from National Pupil Database. Attainment measures used in this paper are the GCSE examination taken when the young people were aged about 16 and the Key Stage-2 assessments at the age of 11. The Wave-7 interviews, when the young people were aged about 20, provide measures of outcomes such as educational attainment and participation, employment and life satisfaction which can be related to the earlier Wave-2 data.

Wave 2 of the survey also included the 12-item version of the General Health Questionnaire (GHQ), a widely used measure of mental well-being which was discussed earlier. The GHQ was developed by Goldberg and colleagues as a measure of current mental health (Goldberg and Hillier 1979). Despite its title, it is specifically concerned with psychological well-being rather than health more generally and asks people to describe their ability to carry out normal functions and the extent of distressing experiences. Items include self-descriptions of concentration, worry, strain, decision-making and so on. The items used in the present study are listed in Table 5. The original scale consisted of 60 items and there are 30-item, 28-item and 12-item versions. All versions of the scale have high levels of reliability and have been widely validated (Goldberg and Huxley 1980) including validation for use with young people (Banks 1983).

Results

Self-reported truancy: extent and motivation

The young people were asked whether they had played truant in the past year and, if so, how frequently and for what reason. The results of these questions are presented in Table 1 for all pupils and separately for males and females. As the figures in Table 1 show, some degree of truancy was widespread in year 10. Between a fifth and a quarter of the young people said that they had truanted with males and females having very similar levels. However, most of this truanting behaviour was fairly limited. Two-thirds of truants said that their truancy was limited to the odd day or lesson and another fifth said it was limited to particular lessons. These two categories accounted for almost nine-tenths of truanting behaviour. More serious truancy was limited to just over 10% of truants: 7.3% said their truancy involved several days at a time and 4.3% said that it involved weeks at a time. This means that for the whole sample, just two-and-a-half per cent reported truanting for more than the odd day or lesson and the most serious truancy, involving weeks, was limited to just under 1% of the sample. As with truancy overall, there were no gender differences with regard to the more extreme end of truancy.

The main reasons the young people gave for their truanting behaviour are also presented in Table 1. Nearly all of the young people, about 90%, gave a reason to explain their behaviour. For half of the young people, the reason was a specific dislike of some aspect of schools, teachers or lessons. The most common response was a dislike of a lesson or lessons (22.1%), followed by a general dislike of school (14.2%) and a dislike of a teacher or teachers (12.7%). A further 20.2% said that they truanted because they were bored, and about 70% of the sample identified some aspect of school that they disliked or that bored them as a reason for missing school. However, a specific dislike of a teacher or teachers was less common than a dislike of a lesson or lessons or school more generally. Only about one in twenty of the truants said that it was bullying that was the reason for absence. The relatively minor role of bullying matches the results of our earlier analysis of BHPS data (Attwood and Croll 2006) although, as reported above and described by Reid (1999), other authors have found bullying to be related to truancy. The reasons given for truancy varied very little between male and female pupils.

Table 1. Self-reported truancy in year-10 pupils in England.

		Males	Female	All
Whether truanted in past year	Yes	893 (22.1%)	943 (23.5%)	1836 (22.8%)
	N	4041	4012	8053
Frequency of truancy	Weeks at a time	33 (4.0%)	40 (4.6%)	73 (4.3%)
	Several days at a time	69 (8.3%)	56 (6.4%)	125 (7.3%)
	Particular lessons	157 (18.9%)	189 (21.6%)	346 (20.3%)
	Just the odd day or lesson	571 (68.8%)	589 (67.4%)	1160 (68.1%)
	N	830	874	1704
Main reason for truancy	Bullying	35 (3.9%)	64 (6.8%)	99 (5.4%)
	Boredom	201 (22.5%)	169 (17.9%)	370 (20.2%)
	Dislike school	125 (14.0%)	135 (14.3%)	260 (14.2%)
	Dislike teacher(s)	129 (14.4%)	104 (11.0%)	233 (12.7%)
	Dislike lesson(s)	177 (19.8%)	228 (24.2%)	405 (22.1%)
	Other	80 (8.9%)	93 (9.9%)	173 (9.4%)
	N	893	943	1836

Truancy and later outcomes

Of the many reasons to be concerned about truancy, one is the likely effect that missing school will have on educational and, possibly, other outcomes. The panel structure of LSYPE makes it possible to match the earlier data on the young people with data collected when they are older. For the present analysis, we shall relate the Wave-2 data from year 10 to the Wave-7 data when the young people were about 20. In Table 2, truancy in year 10 is related to four types of outcome: failing to gain any GCSE passes at grade C or better, being unemployed at the time of Wave-7 data collection, being in full-time education at Wave 7 and responding negatively to a question on life satisfaction. These outcomes are compared across three groups of young people: those who said that they did not truant, those with lower levels of truancy (the odd day or lesson) and those with higher levels of truancy (several days or several weeks at a time).

It is apparent from Table 2 that truancy is associated with less-favourable later outcomes. This association holds for both higher and lower levels of truancy and outcomes are worse for high-level truants than low-level truants. Some of the associations with outcomes are very strong. As would be expected, the strongest patterns of association are with directly educational outcomes. In the GCSE examination taken at the age of about 16, a grade C is generally regarded as a satisfactory outcome for a subject. For pupils who had not truanted, about one in eight had failed to reach this level in any subject. However, this level was almost double for those who had lower levels of truancy and was more than four times higher for those with higher levels of truancy. Well over half of the higher level truants failed to get even one grade C. It is perhaps not surprising that serious truancy is associated with poor examination outcomes but it is striking that even truanting for the odd day or lesson is associated with much poor outcomes than those of the non-truants. Truanting at age 14 or 15 is also strongly associated with not participating in education at age 20. As Table 2 shows, while nearly a half of the non-truants were still in education at this age, just over a quarter of the lower level truants and only one in eight of the higher level truants were still participating in education.

The LSYPE data also make it possible to look at the association of truancy with non-educational outcomes at a later date, in this case, unemployment and life

Table 2. Truancy and later outcomes.

	No truancy	Low level truancy	High level truancy
No GCSEs grade C	821 (13.2%)	338 (22.8%)	106 (55.8%)
N	6159	1484	190
Unemployed at age 20	394 (6.3%)	179 (11.9%)	49 (24.6%)
N	6217	1506	199
In full-time education at age 20	2941 (47.3%)	406 (27.0%)	25 (12.6%)
N	6159	1506	199
Very or fairly dissatisfied with life so far at age 20	417 (6.8%)	201 (13.4%)	31 (16.0%)
N	6158	1500	194

Table 3(a).   Truancy, later outcomes and socio-economic background: No GCSEs at grade C.

Socio-economic status	No truancy	Low-level truancy	High-level truancy
Professional and managerial	120 (4.8%)	60 (11.8%)	20 (48.8%)
N	2513	507	41
Intermediate	235 (14.7%)	83 (20.2%)	16 (44.4%)
N	1601	410	36
Routine and unemployed	366 (25.2%)	170 (39.4%)	57 (67.9%)
N	1451	431	84

Table 3(b).   Truancy, later outcomes and socio-economic background: Unemployed at 20.

Socio-economic status	No truancy	Low-level truancy	High-level truancy
Professional and managerial	91 (3.6%)	44 (8.6%)	6 (13.0%)
N	2531	511	46
Intermediate	111 (6.9%)	30 (7.2%)	6 (17.1%)
N	1616	416	35
Routine and unemployed	394 (26.8%)	87 (19.2%)	33 (35.1%)
N	1469	454	94

satisfaction. As with the education data, truancy was consistently associated with less-satisfactory outcomes. Table 2 shows that low-level truants were twice as likely to be unemployed at age 20 than non-truants and that high-level truants were four times as likely to be unemployed. The young people in the survey were also asked to say how satisfied they were with their life so far. Only a minority said that they were "very" of "fairly" dissatisfied but the figures for low-level truants were twice as high as those for non-truants and those for high-level truants, more than twice as high. It should be emphasised that most truants were not unemployed and were not dissatisfied with their lives so it is nowhere near the case that truancy always leads to these negative outcomes. But the patterns of association are strong and truants are very much more at risk of such outcomes than other young people.

These patterns of association do not in themselves prove that truancy is the cause of the later negative outcomes and other variables may well be involved. It is particularly important to consider the extent to which the associations reported here may be a reflection of the association of the variables being considered with the SES of the families of the young people. Many studies have shown how SES is associated with truancy; young people from less-advantaged backgrounds are more likely to truant than those from more affluent backgrounds (e.g. Attwood and Croll 2006; Reid 2008, 2014). It is also well established that SES has a strong association with many educational- and employment-related outcomes (e.g. Croll 2008; Croll and Attwood 2013; Patterson and Iannelli 2005). It may, therefore, be the case that SES is influencing both truancy and later outcomes, and that the apparent association between truancy and these outcomes simply reflects their common association with SES. This possibility is investigated in Tables 3(a) and 3(b). First, in Table 3(a), the figures for failing to gain a grade C at GCSE are presented separately for truants and non-truants within three broad socio-economic groupings. Then in Table 3(b), the same analysis is repeated for being unemployed at age 20. The same truancy categories are used as those in Table 2: non-truants, low-level truants and high-level truants. The SES groupings are based on the National Statistics Socio-economic Classification (Rose and Pevalin 2003) and are families in professional and managerial occupations (sometimes called the "service class"), families in intermediate occupations and families in routine occupations or who are unemployed.

The relationship of SES to outcomes can be most easily seen by looking at the first column of each of the two tables. This shows the outcomes among non-truants for children from different SES backgrounds. The figures show a clear gradient with children from professional and managerial families being very much less likely to have unfavourable outcomes than those from routine and unemployed families. For both poor GCSE results and unemployment, less than one in twenty of the children from most-advantaged backgrounds have negative outcomes while over a quarter of those from the least-advantaged backgrounds have such outcomes. In both tables, children from intermediate backgrounds have outcomes between these two extremes.

The situation with regard to the association between truancy and outcomes controlling for SES can be examined by making comparisons across the rows of the tables. This shows the outcomes associated with different truancy levels within socio-economic categories. These results show that there are associations between truancy and outcomes independent of the influence of SES but also show a more complex picture to that of the association of SES and outcomes. In almost all of the rows, the comparison shows that high-level truants had worse outcomes than low-level truants who in turn had worse outcomes than non-truants. This pattern was particularly clear for GCSE results and was especially marked in terms of the difference between high-level truants and other young people. Among the highest SES group, higher level truants were 10 times more likely than non-truants to have no good GCSE results and were twice as likely as non-truants from the lowest SES group to have no good GCSEs. So it is clear that socio-economic advantages cannot compensate for serious truancy levels with regard to examination outcomes at 16. But at less serious levels of truancy, there are indications that SES may be a more powerful influence. For example, occasional truants from high SES families had better outcomes than non-truants from both other groups and occasional truants from intermediate backgrounds had better outcomes than non-truants from routine occupational backgrounds.

The figures for unemployment in Table 3(b) also show an association with truancy within SES groupings but stronger associations with SES than with truancy are clearly apparent. Non-truants from high SES backgrounds are less likely to be unemployed than truants and the same is true for young people from intermediate SES backgrounds. However, among the least-advantaged SES backgrounds, although high-level truants have the highest unemployment levels, low-level truants are less likely to be unemployed than non-truants. Table 3(b) shows marked difference between the two higher SES groups and the young people from the least-advantaged families. All of the young people in the two higher groups, including those reporting more serious truancy, have better unemployment outcomes than any of the low SES group, including the non-truants. For example, high SES, high truancy young people have half the unemployment level of low SES non-truants. So although there remains an association between truancy and unemployment, it is relatively weak compared with the association between socio-economic background and unemployment. As other studies have shown (Heath 1981; Croll 2008), young people from more-advantaged socio-economic backgrounds appear to have a kind of cushion effect in which they do not suffer the negative consequences of poor educational performance which affects those from less-advantaged families. Among more serious truants, this does not occur with regard to GCSE outcomes but is apparent with regard to later risk of unemployment.

Socio-economic and attitudinal factors associated with truancy

We referred at the beginning of this paper to the evidence on the relationship of truancy to various socio-economic, educational and attitudinal variables, and these factors were considered for the LSYPE data. It was evident in Table 1 that there were only very small differences between male and female pupils in truancy. In Table 4, we now consider differences between pupils at different levels of attainment, pupils from different socio-economic backgrounds, pupils who do and do not report being bullied and pupils with different attitudes to the value of school and to their relationships with their teachers.

The figures in Table 4 show that both attainment and SES are associated with levels of truancy, although these relationships are not particularly strong. The attainment figures are from Key Stage-2 assessments at the age of 11, well before the truanting behaviour reported here. The pupils have been placed in three attainment groupings based approximately on the quartiles of the overall KS2 score (with the middle two quartiles combined). Pupils in the highest quartile were less likely to truant than the other pupils and were much less likely to have high levels of truancy. Pupils in the lowest quartile were not more likely to truant than the middle group but were more likely to have high levels of truancy. So, attainment at the end of the primary school is a predictor of truancy in the fourth year of secondary school. But the association is not especially strong and most of the lower attainers do not truant while some of the higher attainers do. The figures for different socio-economic backgrounds show a similar pattern of weak association to those for attainment. In particular, young people from the least-advantaged family backgrounds have higher truancy levels than other young people but, nevertheless, 70% of them do not truant and less than one in twenty have high levels of truancy.

In the discussion of the reasons young people gave for truancy, bullying did not emerge as a major factor and only one in twenty said that it was the main reason for their truancy. The comparison of the truancy levels of those who do and do not say they had been bullied, presented in Table 4, may suggest a slightly greater role for bullying than the young people's own attributions. The figures show quite a widespread experience of bullying with 40% of the young people saying they had been bullied in the previous year. Those reporting bullying were about 12% points higher in reporting truancy and were more than twice as likely to report high levels. But, as with the attainment and SES figures, most of those who had been bullied did not truant.

Stronger patterns of association are apparent with regard to the attitudinal variables relating to the value of school and perceptions of teachers. The biggest difference to emerge in the table is between those young people who disagreed with the statement, "Doing well at school means a lot to me" and other pupils. Of those who did not value doing well at school, half reported truanting and one in ten reported

Table 4.   Factors associated with truancy.

	Key Stage 2			SES		
	High	Medium	Low	High	Medium	Low
Non-truants	1805	2765	1648	2530	1617	1468
	83.6%	75.3%	74.2%	81.4%	77.0%	70.9%
Low-level truants	321	782	405	512	415	453
	14.9%	21.3%	18.2%	16.5%	19.8%	21.9%
High-level truants	17	84	98	43	36	96
	0.7%	2.3%	4.4%	1.4%	1.7%	4.6%
N	2158	3674	2222	3108	2100	2071
No answer frequency	15	43	71	23	32	53

	Bullied in past year		Matters to do well at school		How many teachers treat you unfairly		
	No	Yes	Yes	No	None or hardly any	Some	All or most
Non-truants	3842	2158	5792	285	5022	799	287
	82.5%	69.2%	80.2%	49.1%	82.1%	60.6%	59.9%
Low-level truants	704	766	1200	213	931	420	139
	15.1%	24.6%	16.6%	36.7%	15.2%	31.9%	29.0%
High-level truants	68	118	131	57	97	55	38
	1.5%	3.8%	1.8%	9.8%	1.6%	4.2%	7.9%
N	4655	3112	7219	580	6116	1318	479
No answer frequency	41	70	96	27	66	44	15

high levels of truancy. But it should also be noted that these are a small proportion of the sample; only 7.4% said that it was not important to them to do well at school. So, although not valuing school is a good predictor of truancy, it is also the case that the great majority of truants did think it important to do well at school. Most truants, well over 80%, and most of those with high-level truancy, about 70%, said it was important to do well at school. While not valuing school is associated with truancy, thinking that school is important does not necessarily stop young people from truanting.

A similar although somewhat less strong pattern of association occurs with perceptions of teachers, also presented in Table 4. The young people had been asked how many of their teachers they thought treated them unfairly. The responses have been grouped into a low category of "none" or "hardly any", a medium category of "some" and a high category of "most" or "all". More than three-quarters of the young people perceived very little, if any, unfairness from their teachers. But about one in six said that some teachers were unfair and 6% said that most or all teachers were unfair. Perceiving some or more teachers as unfair is associated with truancy, with more than twice as many of these pupils reporting truanting as other pupils. And seeing most teachers as unfair was particularly associated with high levels of truancy. But, as with the perceptions of the value of school, only a minority of pupils thought that teachers were unfair and most of those who truanted were positive about their teachers. More than six out of ten truants and half of high level truants said no teachers or hardly any teachers were unfair.

Mental well-being

The version of the GHQ used in LSYPE is a 12-item scale in which the young people were asked to respond to a series of questions about how they felt about themselves designed to measure mental well-being. The full list of items are given in Table 5. These include questions about concentration levels and losing sleep, questions about ability to cope with normal life and also feelings of happiness and worthlessness. For each question, the young people were asked to say whether they had felt more like this recently, about the same, less like this or much less like this. The questions include both negative and positive items, so for some items feeling less like it was negative, while for others feeling more like it or the same was negative. Previous studies have shown high reliability levels and this was repeated for the present data-set. The value of Cronbach's Alpha (a reliability measure based on split half reliability) was 0.86.

In Table 5, the percentages of the young people giving negative responses to each item are presented for the sample as a whole and also separately for male and female respondents. The table also shows the proportion of the sample grouped according to the numbers of negative responses: negative responses to no items, to one to three items, to four to six items and to more than six items.

As the figures in Table 5 show, although most young people have few if any negative feelings about themselves, a substantial minority express some negative feelings and, for a small proportion, the scale indicates a degree of distress and inability to cope with the challenges of everyday life. Almost half of the sample give entirely positive responses and report no negative feelings about themselves and their lives. A further third have negative responses to three or fewer of the items. But almost one in five of the young people reported negative feelings for four or more items and a minority of these, amounting to 7.5% of the total sample, reported negative feelings for half or more of the scale items. It is striking that young women in the sample are much more likely to report negative feelings than young men. The males in the sample were less likely to have negative responses at all and were much less likely to

Table 5. Mental well-being: the GHQ-negative responses.

	All %	Male %	Female %
Concentration levels	15.2	11.5	18.9
Lost sleep through worry	19.4	13.5	25.4
Feeling useful	9.5	7.9	11.4
Capable of making decisions	6.4	4.8	8.0
Constantly under strain	27.3	21.5	33.4
Couldn't overcome difficulties	20.4	15.4	25.6
Enjoy normal day-to-day activities	10.3	8.5	12.1
Able to face up to problems	8.5	5.8	11.3
Feeling unhappy and depressed	24.1	16.8	31.7
Losing confidence in yourself	19.0	13.2	25.0
Thinking of yourself as a worthless person	12.1	7.8	16.5
Feeling reasonably happy	11.1	8.4	13.9
No negative responses	48.4	55.2	41.5
1 to 3 negative responses	32.9	32.1	33.8
4 to 6 negative responses	11.2	8.2	14.4
6 or more negative responses	7.5	4.6	10.4
N	8162	4121	4041

report high levels of distress and inability to cope. Young people reporting four or more negative responses were twice as likely to be female as male, and the gender difference is even greater at the more extreme end of the scale with one in ten of the young women having negative feelings on half or more of the items.

Looking at the detailed results for each item on the scale in Table 5 shows that this gender difference is consistently the case for each item. The highest level of response was reporting feeling constantly under strain which was the case for more than a quarter of the total sample and a third of the young women. Other high levels of reported problems were feeling unhappy and depressed, feeling unable to overcome difficulties and losing sleep through worry. Lower levels of reported difficulties were feeling unable to make decisions, feeling able to face up to problems and feeling useful with under one in ten giving negative answers. What seems to be a worryingly extreme response of feeling "a worthless person" was reported by one in eight of the total sample and one in six of the young women. Overall, these results from a very substantial sample of young people support the views discussed above that we should be concerned with the mental well-being of young people. While most of the respondents reported few or no negative feelings about themselves, a minority experienced a number of aspects of their lives as distressing or as creating pressures they could not deal with.

Problems of mental well-being are gender related but do not relate to socio-economic background or attainment levels. The correlations between the GHQ score and measures of attainment at 11 and at 16 are effectively zero: a Pearson product moment coefficient of 0.03 with the overall KS2 score and of –0.01 with the overall GCSE points score. So, well-being or lack of it are evenly spread across different levels of attainment. They are also evenly spread across young people from different socio-economic backgrounds. In Table 6, figures are given for the average number of negative responses on the GHQ. Males and females differ substantially with a much higher average school for young women but pupils from different SES backgrounds are very similar. However, the figures for GHQ levels in Table 6 show considerable differences relating to the experiences of bullying and of truancy. Young people who report being bullied have well over twice the level of negative GHQ responses as those who do not. Similarly, truancy and levels of truancy are strongly related to the well-being measure. Young people who have not truanted have the

Table 6.   Mean GHQ scores by gender, SES, experience of bullying and truancy.

		Mean GHQ	N
Gender	Male	1.28	4121
	Female	2.20	4041
SES	High	1.77	3145
	Medium	1.63	2189
	Low	1.75	2092
Bullying	Yes	2.68	3154
	No	1.10	4706
Truancy	None	1.52	6088
	Low	2.42	1467
	High	3.11	186

Table 7. Truancy and well-being by gender.

GHQ level	Truancy level: males			Truancy level: females		
	None	Low	High	None	Low	High
0	1784	339	30	1373	212	24
	57.8%	47.6%	31.9%	45.8%	28.1%	26.1%
1–3	970	239	41	982	276	30
	31.4%	33.6%	43.6%	32.7%	36.6%	32.6%
4–6	223	82	12	384	145	19
	7.2%	11.5%	12.8%	12.8%	19.2%	20.7%
6–12	110	52	11	261	122	19
	3.6%	7.3%	11.7%	8.7%	16.2%	20.7%
N	3087	712	94	3000	755	92

lowest level of negative responses and those with high levels of truancy have more than twice the levels of negative response than the non-truants.

The relationship between truancy and well-being is explored in more detail in Table 7. Because of the gender differences in well-being, the cross-tabulation of truancy levels and well-being levels is given separately for males and females. The figures show the strong relationship between truancy and well-being which holds both for males and females. Well-being levels are higher for young men than for young women and higher for non-truants than truants, but the form of the relationship of truancy and well-being holds for both groups. Only just under a third of male high-level truants and just over a quarter of female high-level truants have no well-being issues on the GHQ. The well-being issues are at their highest for the high-level truants but it should be emphasised that even low levels of truancy are associated with lower levels of well-being. For example, this group of truants, both male and female, experience twice the level of the most serious well-being problems as equivalent non-truants.

Overview

The paper has used a major longitudinal data resource, the LSYPE to address the long-standing issue of truancy among school pupils and also the more recent concern with the well-being of young people. These data confirm the substantial prevalence of truanting behaviour with well over one in five of the year-10 pupils reporting truancy although only one in forty reported more serious levels of truancy. Most young people explained their truancy in terms of either a generalised dislike of school or a more specific dislike of particular lessons or teachers. Males and females reported similar truancy levels. Truancy was associated with SES and attainment, with those from less-advantaged backgrounds and those with lower attainment levels more likely to be truants. Reporting being bullied was also associated with higher levels of truancy although this was only given as a reason for truancy by a small proportion. But these patterns of association were not particularly strong and attitudinal variables such as not valuing school and thinking teachers unfair had stronger patterns of association with truancy. There is something of a paradox here arising from the fact that only a small proportion of the sample said that it was not important to them to do well at school or that most teachers were unfair. Seeing most teachers as unfair and, even more so, saying doing well at school was not important were very good predictors of truancy. But nevertheless, the great majority of truants did value school and did think that most teachers were fair. The longitudinal nature of LSYPE made it possible to consider the association between truancy in year 10 and longer term outcomes such as GCSE results and employment status at age 20. Truancy, even at low levels, was strongly associated with less-favourable outcomes such a failing to get any good GCSE grades and being unemployed at 20. Coming from an advantaged SES background did not prevent the association of truancy with low GCSE results but did mitigate the association with unemployment. So, although truancy is related to negative outcomes for everyone, the relationship is particularly marked for the less socially and economically advantaged.

The other aspect of young people's lives considered in the paper is that of well-being: the extent to which the young people reported personal distress and inability to cope with ordinary aspects of life. As some of the authors referred to have argued, a minority of young people reported substantial problems of mental well-being. In contrasts to truancy, issues of well-being were gender related, with females more likely to report difficulties. Again in contrast to truancy, well-being issues were not related to academic attainment or to family SES. However, truancy and well-being were clearly related to one another; truants were more likely than non-truants to have mental well-being issues and those with higher levels of reported well-being problems were more likely to truant.

The results show that problems of truancy and mental well-being are both features of the lives of many young people, although neither is characteristic of a majority. But for those who truant, there are serious risks in terms of longer term outcomes and the reported well-being issues are clearly distressing for those who suffer them. The strong association between truancy and well-being shows that for many young people these problems are cumulative. A noteworthy feature of the results reported here is that most truants say that it is important for them to do well at school, even though truancy is associated with not doing well at school, and most truants are not negative about their teachers. But alongside this belief in the value of school, is the dislike of aspects of school which was by far the most common reason given for truancy. This suggests that there may be school-based interventions to reduce truancy as argued by Reid (2014) and others. The results on well-being presented here also suggest that truancy needs to be seen in the context of the many difficulties facing young people and as part of wider issues of social adjustment.

References

Attwood, G., and P. Croll. 2006. "Truancy in Secondary School Pupils: Prevalence, Trajectories and Pupil Perspectives." *Research Papers in Education* 21 (4): 467–484.

Banks, M. 1983. "Validation of the General Health Questionnaire in a Young Community Sample." *Psychological Medicine* 13 (2): 349–353.

Croll, P. 2008. "Occupational Choice, Socio-economic Status and Educational Attainment: A Study of the Occupational Choices and Destinations of Young People in the British Household Panel Survey." *Research Papers in Education* 23 (3): 243–268.

Croll, P., and G. Attwood. 2013. "Participation in Higher Education: Aspirations, Attainment and Social Background." *British Journal of Educational Studies* 61 (2): 187–202.

Department for Education. 2003. *Every Child Matters*. London: The Stationery Office. Cm 5860.

Department for Education. 2011a. *Longitudinal Survey of Young People in England*. www.education.gov.uk/research.

Department for Education. 2011b. *UK Resilience Programme Evaluation Final Report*. DFE-RR097. www.education.gov.uk/research.

Goldberg, D., and V. Hillier. 1979. "A Scaled Version of the General Health Questionnaire." *Psychological Medicine* 9 (1): 139–145.

Goldberg, D., and P. Huxley. 1980. *Mental Health in the Community*. London: Tavistock.

Gray, J., M. Galton, C. McLaughlin, B. Clarke, and J. Symonds. 2011. *The Supportive School: Well-being and the Young Adolescent*. Cambridge: Cambridge Scholars.

Heath, A. 1981. *Social Mobility*. London: Fontana.

Kinder, K., A. Wakefield, and A. Wilkin. 1996. *Talking Back: Pupil Views on Disaffection*. Slough: NFER.

Layard, R. 2006. *Happiness: Lessons from a New Science*. London: Penguin.

National Audit Office. 2005. *Improving School Attendance in England*. London: The Stationery Office.

Patterson, L., and C. Iannelli. 2005. *Social Class and Educational Attainment: A Comparative Study of England, Wales and Scotland*. Edinburgh: Centre for Educational Sociology Working Paper.

Reid, K. 1999. *Truancy and Schools*. London: Routledge.

Reid, K. 2008. "The Causes of Non-attendance: An Empirical Study." *Educational Review* 60 (4): 345–357.

Reid, K. 2014. *Managing School Attendance*. London: Routledge.

Rose, D., and D. Pevalin. 2003. "The NS-SEC Described." In *A Researcher's Guide to the National Statistics Socio-economic Classification*, edited by D. Rose and D. Pevalin, 6–27. London: Sage.

UNICEF. 2007. *An Overview of Child Well-being in Rich Countries*. Florence: Innocenti Research Centre. Report Card 7.

What predicts disaffection in Irish primary schools?

Merike Darmody and Maeve Thornton

The Economic and Social Research Institute (ESRI), Dublin, Ireland

Internationally there is now a growing body of research on student school engagement. Much of this research highlights the association of school engagement with a range of social, behavioural and academic outcomes. Less attention is paid to factors predicting disaffection among young children across various dimensions using nationally representative data-sets. This paper addresses this gap in research by exploring factors that are related to school disaffection in Irish primary schools. Drawing on a nationally representative study of nine-year-olds, the multivariate analysis reveals that disaffection is associated with a number of personal and institutional factors. While the data relate to the Irish situation, the paper raises a number of issues also of interest to an international audience.

Introduction

There is now a growing body of literature on student engagement and its impact on academic achievement. Much of this research focuses on older students, although research on younger children is also building up (Reid 2004, 2012). At primary school level, the engagement of pupils is particularly influenced by social interactions with peers and teachers, and high but realistic expectations of the latter (Furrer and Skinner 2003; Li, Lerner, and Lerner 2010). Many existing studies focus on the impact of school engagement on academic outcomes. Pupils who prepare homework and who feel like they belong to their school tend to do better academically, compared to their less-engaged peers (Fredricks, Blumenfeld, and Paris 2004).

At the opposite end of the spectrum are disengaged or disaffected pupils who tend to associate school with negative experiences. Disaffection encompasses emotional, behavioural and cognitive elements (Fredricks, Blumenfeld, and Paris 2004) and can be perceived as the beginning of a progression that can lead to early school leaving (Finn 1989; Furlong and Christenson 2008). Data from the United Kingdom shows that behaviour in primary schools is worsening with pupils being suspended for inappropriate or disruptive behaviour (see Department for Education statistics for 2010/2011). Pupils more likely to be suspended tend to be boys and those from disadvantaged backgrounds. Lack of engagement with the curriculum and disruptive behaviour can progress to truancy and exclusion from school, and limit the later life chances of young people involved (Hodgson 1999).

Research in the Irish context (see Clerkin and Creaven 2013) shows that disaffection is a problem among a minority of Irish primary school children. It is important to understand the underlying processes of disaffection among the primary school children as earlier studies have indicated that at the age of 11 some students in Irish schools had expressed feelings of "boredom" and had begun to disengage from classroom activity and school (Keogh and Whyte 2007). The figures available from the Department of Education and Skills (2012) show that fewer – only a very small proportion of pupils – left their primary school without going to another primary, secondary or special school within the State. While different authors have highlighted the impact of disaffection on student outcomes, existing research has not sufficiently unpacked the factors leading to disaffection at primary school level. This study aims to fill this gap in research by attempting to answer the following question: What micro (individual and family) and meso (school) level factors are associated with school disaffection among young children?

This study is unique in Ireland in that for the first time it enables researchers to take into account information from three different sources: the child, his/her parents and teachers. Detailed analyses enable us to look at the simultaneous effect of different factors that impact on student engagement or disaffection. In this paper, we have adopted a quantitative multivariate analytical approach to study school disaffection because this phenomenon is simultaneously affected by various individual, social and institutional variables. The following section gives a short overview of existing empirical studies on disaffection. The paper then moves on to the description of the Irish context. Section four presents data and methodological approach, followed by the presentation of research results. The discussion section concludes the paper.

Previous research on school disaffection

School disaffection is a major concern for education practitioners and policy-makers across different jurisdictions as it has been found to be strong predictor of poor grades, low test scores and early school leaving (Skinner, Wellborn, and Connell 1990). Although present in the educational and sociological literature since the 1970s, "disaffected students" can be considered a somewhat contested term, since it seems to imply to the alienation of young people themselves from formal education, whereas increasing evidence suggests that disaffection is a result of a complex interplay between institutional and individual decision-making and criteria (Williamson 1999), and not just a result of individual factors. Considering its complex and multidimensional nature, school disaffection is not an easy construct to define but generally refers to children and young people who do not engage with formal education. In educational research it has often been used as an "umbrella term", describing a number of different behaviours and attitudes that can be broadly seen as elements of disaffection (Holroyd and Aramour 2003). Osler and Starkey suggest that,

> disaffection is used as an explanatory term to account for a range of behaviours, including low attainment, persistent disruption, truancy and other forms of self-exclusion. Disaffection implies behaviour that is reactive to the school as an institution, though this is usually treated as an individual rather than a group phenomenon. (2005, 199)

Researchers have argued that the causal factors of disaffection can be divided into three broad domains: cognitive (low expectations; and lack of goals and aspirations), behavioural (truancy, absenteeism, aggressive behaviour, passivity and withdrawal from participation in learning) and affective (low self-esteem and feelings of alienation) (see Heathcote-Elliott and Walters 2000; Skinner et al. 2008). Heathcote-Elliott and Walters (2000) argue that "it is the interaction between these factors and other variables (e.g. personality, behavioural dispositions) which are at the roots of severe disaffection" (6). Skinner et al. (2008) also highlight the importance of an emotional component in disaffection, manifesting itself in feelings of boredom, anxiety and frustration in the classroom (Skinner et al. 2008). The latter has received less attention in research although emotions may play an important role in developing disaffection over time (Roeser, Strobel, and Quihuis 2002). Because of a range of definitions, "disaffection" has almost become synonymous with any behaviour that is perceived to deviate from the norm. In general, disaffected students tend to have little interest in school (Kinder et al. 1999; Ofsted 2008).

Over the years, the research focus has shifted from identifying the proportion of disaffected pupils to framing the dimensions of disaffection, including its underlying causes, as well as personal and structural criteria and an interplay between these two spheres. The "disaffected" are by no means a homogenous group. However, some groups of children in particular are more likely to disengage: boys, children from ethnic minority groups and those from low SES backgrounds (Wigfield et al. 2006). Disaffection is also triggered or contributed to by structural factors and social interaction within school (Reid 1986).

Characterisations of disaffection in educational research have focused on absenteeism, bad behaviour and negative attitudes towards school. It is generally acknowledged that unless addressed early, at pre-school level, lack of interest in school and certain perceptions that students have about themselves and the world around them may result in fractured progression through compulsory education and limited life chances later on (Bronfenbrenner 1986; Skinner et al. 2008). These young children are likely to become increasingly disaffected over time. Disaffection often arises when pupils find lessons boring, irrelevant or overly stressful (Kinder et al. 1995). The negative impact of ability grouping on students' self image as learners has been highlighted by many authors (see Boaler 2005). Skinner et al. (2008) found that competence made the strongest contributions to behavioural disaffection manifested by withdrawal from work in the class and increased anxiety. Interpersonal relationships with teachers are also important. Where students reported teacher support, behavioural and emotional disaffection was found to decline over time (Skinner et al. 2008). In addition, disaffection is associated with social interaction with peers. The feeling of victimisation was found to be the strongest factor influencing pupil disaffection in a study by Wolke et al. (2000). It is important to consider bullying and victimisation issues among young children before their experiences become ingrained. Finally, as demonstrated in previous literature (e.g. Massoni 2011), extra-curricular activities have also been shown to have an effect on feelings about school. Positive effects include better behaviour, better grades and school completion, among others, probably due to the fact that organised activities tend to require certain levels of discipline which can then impact on behaviour in the school setting.

Disaffection can have many forms. Heathcote-Elliott and Walters (2000) have conceptualised a "continuum of disaffection" reflecting levels varying between active and passive and mild and severe. This study defines "school disaffection" as a multidimensional construct involving behavioural, cognitive, affective spheres, but also child, family and school factors. It is argued in the paper that only by exploring the simultaneous effect of all these spheres will a clearer understanding of disaffection among primary school pupils be reached.

Irish context

Irish education system

In Ireland, children attend primary school from around the age of 4 or 5 years until they are 12 or 13 years of age even though the compulsory schooling starts at the age of 6. The youngest classes in the primary school system incorporate much of what would be considered "pre-schooling" in other countries. The primary school cycle lasts for eight years generally starting with two years of infant classes, followed by class 1 to class 6. The Irish primary education sector consists of state-funded primary schools (an overall majority), special schools and private primary schools. State-funded schools include religious schools, multidenominational schools and Gaelscoileanna, which are schools that teach the curriculum through the Irish language.

Attendance and behaviour among Irish primary school pupils

Attendance and behaviour is a problem among a small but significant number of primary school pupils in Ireland. In general, schools catering for greater proportions of "disadvantaged" students have lower attendance rates (Darmody, Smyth, and McCoy 2008). According to Millar (2013), approximately 11% of primary school pupils were absent for 20 days or more during the school year 2010–2011. However, this equates to 56,500 primary school students. Non-attendance is significantly higher in special schools and in ordinary schools with special classes. In addition, non-attendance is a greater problem in urban as opposed to rural areas, particularly in terms of the "absent 20 or more days" category. This figure has remained stable over time. Since 2000 a statutory framework for addressing school absenteeism has been provided by the Education Welfare Act (2000). Parents or guardians are generally responsible for ensuring that children attend school. The National Educational Welfare Board (NEWB) is responsible for developing and implementing a single, strategic approach to attendance, participation and retention in schools to meet the needs of children who are at risk of early school leaving or of developing attendance problems. The integrated service brings together expertise and knowledge of four services – Home School Community Liaison, Educational Welfare Service, School Completion Programme and the Visiting Teacher Service for Travellers. The NEWB also collects data on school absenteeism, suspensions and expulsions in primary and secondary schools. Comparative data reveals that absenteeism among primary school children in Ireland was higher compared to NI, England and Scotland, but lower than that of Wales (see Table 1).

It should be noted, that the absenteeism rates in Ireland may not reveal the full picture as they do not take account of attendance trends of children between the ages of 4–6. It is important to establish good attendance patterns from the moment the children are enrolled into school.

School expulsions are relatively rare in Ireland at the primary school level with 16 pupils being expelled in 2010–2011. The rate of suspensions is equally low at 0, 2% in the same academic year (Millar 2013). The newly established Child and

Table 1. % of absenteeism among primary school pupils in Ireland and the UK (2010/2011).

	Unauthorised[a]	Overall
Ireland	–	6.1
Northern Ireland	1.4	5.1
England	0.7	5.1
Scotland	1.2	5.2
Wales	0.9	6.7

Source: Millar (2013).
[a]Ireland does not differentiate between authorised and unauthorised absences.

Family Agency is responsible for supporting families and their children in combating poor school attendance. In addition, the NEWB's intervention model One Child, One Team, One Plan has a central role in addressing issues around attendance and behaviour.

Research on primary school children

Clerkin and Creaven (2013) drawing data from PIRLS and TIMSS examine the attitudes of Irish primary pupils towards school and compare it to the findings from other countries. According to their analysis a majority (74%) of Irish pupils liked being in school, however, this finding is lower than the international averages in the two studies. Irish pupils were somewhat more likely to report not liking school compared to their peers in other countries (13% vs. 6% among TIMSS countries, and 7% among PIRLS countries). Consistent with previous research (e.g. McCoy, Smyth, and Banks 2012), boys expressed much more negative views than girls about school and were less likely to feel that they belonged at their school and that they felt safe there, a trend similar to other countries. Interestingly, pupils in Urban Band 1 schools (i.e. those identified as having the highest concentrations of socio-economically disadvantaged pupils, and in receipt of the greatest additional support) were most likely to *agree a lot* that they like being in school, possibly reflecting the importance of social sphere for these children. Irish boys and migrant children were most likely to have experienced bullying.

Disruptive behaviour in the classroom was reported as being a serious problem for the teachers of 10% of pupils in Ireland and 12% of pupils across all PIRLS countries. For the majority of pupils in Ireland, their teachers said that disruptive behaviour was a problem *to some extent* (43%; compared to PIRLS average, 53%) or *not at all* (47%; compared to PIRLS average, 35%). Home environment appeared to have impact as well: in Ireland over half of pupils (62%) were taught by teachers who said that their teaching was limited *to some extent* or *a lot* because pupils were not getting enough sleep, higher than the PIRLS (48%) and TIMSS (47%) averages.

Thornton, Darmody, and McCoy (2013) showed that persistent absenteeism was a problem among a minority of Irish primary school pupils. The study indicated that attendance was linked to a number of factors including parental. However, some "hidden" factors also impact attendance. For example, children living with a mother who suffers from depression or witnessing parental conflict were more likely to miss school. Disaffection was also associated with a number of school-level factors. Research by Keogh and Whyte (2007) indicated that for children who were struggling academically, there were very few opportunities to experience achievement in the primary classroom context. Subsequently, these children started disengaging by the end of the primary school.

Methods and data source

This article reports the results of a survey of Growing Up in Ireland – a national longitudinal study of children. The main aim of the study is to paint a full picture of children in Ireland and how they are developing in the current social, economic and cultural environment. The analysis draws on the first wave of this longitudinal study of 8568 nine-year-olds. The study combines information from parents, school principals, teachers and children themselves. In doing so it provides valuable and detailed information about the home environment of these children, their family, their school and their engagement with the schooling process.

There were two main components to the fieldwork: school-based and household-based. The school-based fieldwork involved a self-completion questionnaire for the school principal and two self-completion questionnaires for the child's teacher. The principal questionnaires recorded school-level details on school characteristics including size, challenges and ethos, along with some personal details about the principal. The teacher-on-self questionnaire recorded class-level details such as class size, curriculum and teaching methods, and some personal details about teachers themselves. The teacher-on-child questionnaire recorded child-level details on the child's behaviour, academic performance and school preparedness.

The informants in the household-based component of the fieldwork were the nine-year-old child, their primary caregiver (defined as the person who provides most care to the child – in most cases, the child's mother) and, if resident in the household, the spouse/partner of the child's primary caregiver (usually, but not always, the child's father). Detailed information was collected from nine-year-old children on their perceptions of school and their teachers. In addition, parents were asked about their involvement in their child's school.

As with all cross-sectional data, caution is therefore required in attributing causality when factors are measured at the same time point. However, the broad range of information gathered in the study, acknowledging proximal and distal contexts in the child's life, allows for a more nuanced analysis of the data in terms of exploring individual pathways and trajectories.

Analytical approach

As a first step, and relying on previous research evidence, exploratory analyses were carried out using cross-tabulations to ascertain which factors were of most interest when looking at school disaffection. As the literature points to several important aspects of disaffection, cross-tabulations were run for a number of variables pertaining to behavioural, cognitive, affective, individual, and family and school factors. On the basis of these analyses, it was then decided which variables to include in the multivariate model. Due to small cell counts some variables could not be included in the multivariate analysis. These included school variables such as the Irish-speaking status of the school, the religious denomination of the school and whether the school was private or not.

Regression models were then developed to run with the sample using SPSS. Because the dependent variable in this case was dichotomous, logistic regression was deemed the most suitable method for carrying out the multivariate analysis. Logistic regression also enabled the simultaneous estimation of the relationship between the independent (or predictor) variables and the dependent variable, in this case school disaffection, allowing for a more comprehensive analysis than would have been possible using only bivariate descriptive analyses (for example, cross-tabulation). In accordance with some prior assumptions for logistic regression, checks were made for adherence to details such as minimum number of cases per independent variable, as well as ratio of valid cases to independent variables, and multicollinearity between independent variables. The current models satisfied these assumptions.[1]

The models in the analysis were then run in four steps, including sets of: behavioural variables; cognitive and affective factors; child characteristics; and family and school characteristics.

Measures used

School disaffection

School disaffection was based on the child's report of liking school. They were asked "Do you like going to school" and answer categories were *always, sometimes and never*. Those who responded that they never liked school (*n* = 577) were categorised as being disaffected with school.

Individual characteristics

Child's temperament was measured using the EAS Temperament scale (Buss and Plomin 1984) which has subscales for shyness, emotionality, activity and sociability.

School achievement

At age 9 the children completed the Drumcondra Maths and Reading tests. Scores from these tests were standardised to account for different class (age) groups and scores split into quartiles. This analysis uses the lowest quartile maths and reading scores.

Child's behavioural characteristics

The *Behavioural Adjustment* subscale of the Piers-Harris self-concept scale was used as a self-reported measure of the child's own behavioural self-concept. This contained general items around behaviour such as "I do many bad things" and "I behave badly at home", as well as some school-related items such as "I am well behaved in school" and "I am good at my schoolwork". The subscale scores on the Piers-Harris are standardised and divided into categories – *very low, low, low average, average and high average*. Here we look at those who are *low average or below* in their behavioural adjustment, in keeping with the previously highlighted link between it and disaffection in the research literature (e.g. Skinner, Wellborn, and Connell 2008).

Family characteristics

Household social class was grouped into four categories – *professional/managerial; non-manual/skilled manual; semi-skilled/unskilled manual; and unemployed* and maternal education was grouped into three categories – *lower secondary or primary education; higher secondary education; and degree or postgraduate degree.*

School characteristics

Delivering Equality of Opportunity in Schools (DEIS) is the Action Plan for Educational Inclusion, and remains the Department of Education and Skills policy instrument to address educational disadvantage. There are four DEIS statuses – *Urban band 1, Urban band 2, rural DEIS and non-disadvantaged.*

Research findings

Descriptive analysis

Findings showed that behavioural adjustment as reported by the child him or herself was associated with school disaffection. For example, 12% of those who rated themselves as low average or below in terms of their behavioural adjustment also reported never liking school, compared to 4% of those who rated themselves as average or above. Teacher report of emotional or behavioural problems limiting the child's activity were also associated with disaffection, with 14% of those who were reported as having problems also being disaffected with school compared to 6% who weren't. Furthermore, the primary caregiver report of the child's behaviour (often starts fights or bullies others) was also associated with attitudes towards school (12% of those who were reported as fighting or bullying others compared to 4% of those who didn't). Other aspects of the child's behaviour that may be linked to motivation about school included homework completion and absenteeism. Where the teacher reported occasional or regular incompletion of homework, disaffection was higher (10%) compared to 5% of those who always did their homework, and high levels of absenteeism (i.e. 20 or more days) were also associated with higher levels of disaffection. Involvement in extra-curricular activities such as a sports/fitness club (8% compared to 6%) or cultural activities (e.g. music, dance and drama) (9% compared to 4%) seemed to have a negative association with disliking school, whereas belonging to a youth club had a positive association (10% compared to 6%). Reading for pleasure was associated with liking school in that only 6% of those who read for pleasure on a regular basis disliked school compared to 12% of those who read less often, although it is very likely that these are related to other factors such as household social class.

In terms of school achievement, being in the bottom quartile for maths or reading scores was associated with higher levels of school disaffection (10 and 11%, respectively) compared to 6% of those in higher quartiles (for both maths and reading). Apart from actual performance though, perceptions of how one was doing in school were also important. It was found that 36% of those who thought they were doing poorly were also more likely to dislike school, compared to 9% of those who thought they were doing average/ok and just 5% of those who thought they were doing well.

Furthermore, for nine-year-olds in *Growing Up in Ireland*, liking their teacher was strongly associated with school disaffection. A large proportion of children (30%) who didn't like their teacher also reported never liking school. This compared to 8% of those who sometimes liked their teacher and 3% who always liked their teacher.

In terms of the child's individual characteristics, 10% of boys reported never liking school compared to 4% of girls. Aspects of the child's temperament were also associated with attitudes towards school in that those with a shy temperament were more likely to dislike school, as were those with a more emotional temperament.

Contrary to previous literature, however, findings here showed that children with a chronic illness were no more likely to dislike school than other children, although this may be due to the fact that the measure of chronic illness used here does not include mental or behavioural disorders. These have been explored through the use of other measures in our analyses, namely through the child's own report of

Table 2. Descriptive analysis of selected factors associated with school disaffection among primary school children[a].

	Number of children with behavioural/ cognitive/affective problems	% of children with behavioural/ cognitive/affective problems who are disaffected	Number of children who are disaffected	% of children who are disaffected and have behavioural/cognitive/ affective problems
Behavioural adjustment (child report)				
Below average	2842	12	346	64
Average or above	5281	4	193	36
Homework completion				
Occasionally/ regularly not done	2313	10	232	40
Ref: never not done	6255	6	345	60
Fights or bullies other children (parent report)				
True	398	14	54	9
Ref: false	8170	6	523	91
Behavioural/emotional problems (teacher report)				
Yes	288	14	40	7
Ref: no	8280	6	537	93
Performance in maths				
Lowest quartile	2104	11	220	38
Ref: rest	6464	6	357	62
Performance in reading				
Lowest quartile	2085	11	238	41
Ref: rest	6483	5	339	59
Likes teacher				
Never	510	30	152	27
Sometimes	3433	8	263	47
Ref: always	4409	3	146	26

[a]The table is used to illustrate the figures for a selection of the variables under consideration, namely those pertaining to some of the behavioural, cognitive and affective aspects of school disaffection.

behavioural adjustment and the teacher report of emotional/behavioural problems which have a limiting effect on the child's activities.

Finally, both household social class and maternal education were associated with school disaffection while immigrant children were slightly less likely to dislike school (5%) compared to 7% of non-immigrants. The DEIS (disadvantaged) status, principal perception of there being an adequate number of teachers in the school and school size were also correlates of school disaffection.

While these results point to a clear association between some negative behavioural, cognitive and affective factors and disaffection with school, Table 2 adds some perspective to these findings. For example, while the majority of children who were doing poorly in reading and maths were much more likely to be disaffected, being disaffected did not make them more likely to perform worse in school. And although the table does show that a majority of disaffected children rate themselves as below average in terms of their behaviour (60% compared to 40%), it also highlights that, in terms of parent and teacher reports of the child's behaviour, the majority of disaffected children do not fight or bully other children (9% compared to 91%), and are not limited in their activities by emotional or behavioural problems (7% compared to 93%).

Multivariate analysis

This section looks at all of the different factors discussed above simultaneously and their association with the level of disaffection among Irish primary school children. Multivariate modelling allowed us to explore more nuanced insights into the processes involved. A logistic regression model (see Table 3) was used because a binary outcome was considered – never liking school compared to all others ($n = 577$). Odds ratios (ORs) were used as a measure of effect size to describe the strength of association between the binary data values.

The results of these analyses indicate that the biggest single factor associated with school disaffection was the child's feelings about their teacher. Only sometimes liking their teacher resulted in a more than twofold increase in not liking school (OR = 2.47, $p < 0.001$) compared to always liking them, while never liking their teacher resulted in a 10-fold increase (OR = 10.15, $p < 0.001$). Conversely, where children reported that their teacher was someone they would turn to if they had a problem, the chances of not liking school were much lower (OR = 0.69, $p < 0.01$) than for those who did not cite their teacher as someone they would turn to. This may point to the importance of the levels of positivity or negativity in this relationship for the child, arising in the possibility of it acting as either a risk or protective factor in terms of the child's feelings about school.

In terms of some of the behavioural variables used in the models it was apparent that a number of factors held significance in relation to school disaffection. For example, the child's self-reported behavioural adjustment (which included some school-related behaviour) was highly correlated with school disaffection (OR = 1.91, $p < 0.001$), as was the teacher report of child emotional/behavioural difficulties (OR = 2.21, $p < 0.01$), although as can be seen from Table 3, this only became statistically significant when the child's characteristics were entered in the model. For example, we know that boys are more likely to have behavioural/emotional problems than girls, as was the case here (5% were reported as having problems compared to 2% of girls), while those identified as having such problems by their

Table 3. Multivariate analysis of factors predicting school disaffection among primary school children.

	Model 1	Model 2	Model 3	Model 4
Behavioural				
Behavioural adjustment (child report)				
Below average	2.75***	1.99***	1.95***	1.91***
Ref: average or above				
Absent				
20+ days	1.83<	1.96<	2.02<	2.11*
Ref: <20 days				
Homework completion				
Occasionally/regularly not done	1.55***	1.38**	1.36**	1.29*
Ref: Never not done				
Fights or bullies other children				
True	1.68**	1.79**	1.61*	1.60*
Ref: false				
Behavioural/emotional problems (teacher report)				
Yes	1.03	1.52	1.83*	2.21**
Ref: no				
Extracurricular activities				
Reading for pleasure	0.60***	0.72**	0.78*	0.80<
Sports	0.95	0.92	0.80<	0.85
Cultural	0.51***	0.58***	0.74*	0.78<
Youth club	1.44*	1.59*	1.64**	1.50*
Cognitive				
Performance in maths				
Lowest quartile		1.26<	1.30*	1.27<
Ref: rest				
Performance in reading				
Lowest quartile		1.41*	1.43**	1.34*
Ref: rest				
Affective aspects				
Talk to teacher about problems				
Yes		0.75*	0.72*	0.68**
Ref: no				
Likes teacher				
Sometimes		2.56***	2.37***	2.47***
Never		11.22***	9.65***	10.15***
Ref: always				
Perception of school performance				
Doing poorly		3.58***	3.88***	3.21**
Doing average/ok		1.28*	1.28*	1.27*
Ref: doing well				
Child characteristics				
Gender				
Male			2.15***	2.32***
Ref: female				
Temperament				
Shyness (continuous)			1.18*	1.14<
Emotionality (continuous)			1.09	1.08

(*Continued*)

Table 3. (*Continued*).

	Model 1	Model 2	Model 3	Model 4
Family factors				
Social class				
Non-manual/skilled manual				1.11
Semi-skilled/unskilled manual				1.12
Unemployed				2.08***
Ref: professional/managerial				
Maternal education				
Lower secondary/primary				1.52*
Higher secondary				1.68**
Non-degree				1.43
Ref: degree or above				
Parent–teacher meeting				
Yes				0.58*
Ref: no				
Gets on with siblings				
Sometimes				1.18
Never				2.14**
Ref: always				
School characteristics				
Adequacy of number of teachers				1.76**
Poor				
Ref: fair/good/excellent				
DEIS status				
Urban band 1				0.8
Urban band 2				1.25
Rural deis				0.53*
Ref: non-disadvantaged				
School size (continuous)				1.00*

*Signifies < 0.05; **signifies < 0.01; ***signifies < 0.001; < significance < 0.10.

teacher were also significantly more likely to be shy or have a more emotional temperament. The parent report of the child's behaviour (in terms of often fighting or bullying other children) was an indication of a more general association between behavioural characteristics and school disaffection ($OR = 1.60$, $p < 0.01$), in line with previous research. Analysis of school specific behaviours indicated that those who occasionally or regularly did not do their homework were about 30% more likely than other children to be disaffected with school ($OR = 1.29$, $p < 0.05$), while those who were absent 20 days or more were more than twice as likely ($OR = 2.11$, $p < 0.05$) to exhibit disaffection. There was some indication that extracurricular activities, including regularly reading for pleasure, were associated to some extent with school disaffection, indicating perhaps that it may be the *motivation* to engage in other activities extends to school or perhaps vice versa. However, it was notable that while those who took part in cultural activities outside of school were less likely to feel disaffected, those who belonged to a youth club at age 9 were actually about 50% more likely to dislike school ($OR = 1.50$, $p < 0.05$). However, it is likely that these differences are at least partially driven by socio-economic factors. For example, while those in the higher social groups were more likely to go to a sports/fitness club or partake in cultural activities, those in the lowest social group were more likely than others to belong to a youth club.

Previous research indicates that it is not just actual achievement, but also *perception* of how we are doing that is highly salient. For example, scoring in the lowest quartile for reading or maths was positively associated with school disaffection (Reading – OR = 1.34, $p < 0.05$; Maths – OR = 1.27, $p = 0.09$). However, when looking at children's perception of how well they were doing in school, there was a relatively strong correlation, and those who thought that they are doing poorly were more than three times more likely to be disaffected with school than those who thought they were doing well (OR = 3.21, $p < 0.01$). This affective aspect to the child's performance is an important one given that 60% of those in the bottom quartile for maths regard themselves as *doing well in their schoolwork*, 38% as doing *average/ok* and only 2% thinking that they are doing *poorly*. The corresponding figures for those in the lowest reading quartile were the same. Not surprisingly, boys were more than twice as likely as girls to be in the disaffected group (OR = 2.32, $p < 0.001$), while having a shy temperament also remained a significant factor (OR = 1.14, $p = 0.08$), an important finding in its own right in that temperament may be a more difficult factor to change or modify.

Finally, we looked at the more general contexts of the home and school environments. We found, for example, that children living in the lowest social class households were more than twice as likely as those in the highest social group to be disaffected with school (OR = 2.08, $p < 0.001$), while maternal education was also associated with children's feelings about school. Children whose mother had a lower secondary/primary education, or an upper secondary level qualification were significantly more likely to be disaffected compared to those whose mothers had a degree or higher qualification (lower secondary/primary – OR = 1.52, $p < 0.05$; upper secondary – OR = 1.68, $p < 0.01$). Attending parent–teacher meetings was also highlighted as a potential buffer against disaffection as there was a negative correlation between parents attending parent–teacher meetings and the child's feelings about school (OR = 0.58, $p < 0.05$). Family social climate variables, such as parental conflict and the parent–child relationship were not significantly associated with school disaffection in the multivariate model (not shown here), although sibling relationships were (OR = 2.14, $p < 0.01$). Immigrant status was also not found to be associated with disaffection in the multivariate analysis.

The DEIS status of the school was associated with disaffection in that children in rural DEIS schools were less likely to be disaffected than those in non-disadvantaged schools, (OR = 0.53, $p < 0.05$), although there was no significant association with disaffection for those attending urban DEIS schools. The overall size of the school was also important with bigger schools associated with more disaffection. This effect was small but significant (OR = 1.00, $p < 0.05$). Finally, where principals reported inadequate (poor) numbers of teachers, the odds of school disaffection were about 75% higher than for schools where teacher numbers were perceived to be adequate or good (OR = 1.76, $p < 0.01$).

Discussion and conclusion

There is now an extensive body of literature on school disaffection and the different components of this phenomenon. Willms (2000) notes that across the OECD countries, about one in four students are classified as having a low sense of belonging, and about one in five students has very low participation, both indicators of disaffection. Less is known about the situation among younger children although a growing body of research literature indicates that the processes leading to disaffection and alienation from school start early, and that the phenomenon is triggered by a complex interplay between personal, family and institutional factors. This paper has considered factors predicting school disaffection among primary school pupils in Ireland. In doing so, it drew on data from the national longitudinal study *Growing Up in Ireland.*

Given the importance of attachment to school in terms of students' academic performance and future outcomes, identifying those factors that have a negative effect on students' feelings about school is most important. As has been demonstrated in the current paper, disaffection is a multidimensional phenomenon and while there are common denominators that have persisted through the decades, such as gender and social class, we have attempted to shed light on additional variables that are not always considered when studying school disaffection. The current work has built upon both international and Irish research to further highlight the importance of exploring the effects of behavioural, cognitive and affective, family background and school-related factors, as well as the complex interplay between them. Using a multivariate approach and drawing on a nationally representative sample of nine-year-old children, the article contributes towards establishing a profile of disaffected children.

Not surprisingly, and in line with previous research, pupils with behavioural problems, as reported by the child, their teacher and their parent, were also more likely to be disaffected with school, as were those with higher levels of absenteeism (>20 days) and higher rates of homework incompletion. However, our findings indicated that for young Irish children the biggest single factor associated with school disaffection was linked to the child's feelings about their teacher, in line with existing research (Slater, Davies, and Burgess 2012). One plausible reason for this could be that children who were not doing so well at school (in terms of maths and reading) were more likely to report "never" liking their teacher compared to other students. This supports previous Irish research showing that students with lower mathematics and reading scores were more likely to report negative interaction with teachers, compared to their better performing peers (Smyth, McCoy, and Darmody 2004). Interestingly though, lower performing students were also more likely to "always" like their teacher compared to others, which highlights the potential of this very salient relationship to be either a risk *or* a protective factor for younger children.

Furthermore, while academic progress itself was important, perception of academic progress also mattered. These findings highlight the importance of the affective aspects of the child's experience, which may not be as obvious to teachers or parents, but nonetheless must be recognised in order to deal with disaffection. While behavioural problems may be more easily recognisable, disaffected children can often be withdrawn or uninterested and so greater care may be needed in order to recognise potential issues.

The results also confirm previous studies that the socio-economic background of the pupil is also strongly associated with disaffection and alienation (e.g. Ofsted 2008; Willms 2000). These children often come from families characterised by unemployment and lower levels of maternal education. Another family factor includes children who are dealing with emotionally difficult situations at home who may also experience greater difficulties in coping with school life (Macleod, McAllister, and Pirrie 2010). This possible "spillover effect" was found in relation to persistent absenteeism among Irish primary school children (Thornton, Darmody, and McCoy 2013), where the parental relationship was associated with absenteeism. In the current work, it was children who reported never getting on with siblings who were much more likely to dislike school compared to those who "always get on", an area so far relatively unexplored in school engagement research.

The persistent gender effect is also a matter of concern. Over the decades, boys and, in particular, working-class boys have been found more likely than girls to disengage from school, suggesting possible lack of alternatives to academic activities available to them at school. On the other hand, and contrary to previous studies (e.g. Willms 2000), migrant children in Irish schools have been found to be somewhat less disaffected compared to native students. This could be explained that migrants in Ireland are generally highly educated and place a great value on education (Darmody, Byrne, and McGinnity 2012). In line with previous studies migrant children in Ireland are often victims of bullying Clerkin and Creaven (2013) but their positive disposition towards school (Darmody, Byrne, and McGinnity 2012) seems to override this experience.

Participation in extracurricular activities also emerged as a correlate of school disaffection in the current research, although this is very likely to be driven by socio-economic factors. For example, Lareau (2002) observes that middle-class children tend to be involved in high levels of extracurricular activities, usually involving structured activities that often have to be paid for. Working-class children, on the other hand, tend to have more "self-directed" and unstructured leisure time. Similarly, in the current research we found that children with higher SES were more likely to participate in sports or cultural activities, which often have to be paid for, compared to those from the lowest social class, who were much more likely to belong to a youth club where activities are much less likely to be structured or organised.

This study showed that while pupils' liking of their teacher and being able to talk to him/her when experiencing problems was significantly linked to disaffection, other contextual factors seemed to have less of an impact. For example, the analysis did not uncover any statistically significant link between urban disadvantaged (DEIS) and non-disadvantaged schools, contrary to our expectations. It is possible that additional resources from the government to combat educational disadvantage in these schools have acted as a protective factor. What seemed to matter however was the adequacy of the number of teachers in the school as reported by the principal. It is reasonable to assume therefore that there may be more stress on teachers in terms of time management and that there would be fewer teachers available to whom pupils could go to when experiencing problems. Future research could explore links between teacher stress and school disaffection among students.

These findings have important implications for educational policy indicating that the phenomenon is associated with a range of individual, relational and structural factors. Although social class remains a significant element in children's disposition towards school, schools have an important role to play in supporting the children in their care. This article suggests that policies directed at attendance and behaviour need to consider students' sense of belonging to the school as well as their home background. The NEWB has pointed to evidence that a whole school approach that draws together school policies on areas of school life such as student involvement, curriculum, behaviour and relationships have the potential to make a difference to how children feel about their school. A whole school approach to disaffection should ensure that policies exist at school level regarding how best to encourage school engagement. To achieve this, schools must have sufficient number of staff available to support students. Recent cuts in the education budgets in various jurisdictions is likely to put schools under strain in providing vulnerable students with adequate support, including access to quality extracurricular activities for all pupils.

It is important to acknowledge, however, that schools cannot tackle the issue of disaffection on their own. Results from research in the UK (Ofsted 2008) indicate that regular and effective communication with students and their families, including their involvement in the development of support strategies, proves very effective. Policies to combat disaffection need to confront the following challenges as identified by Ofsted (2008): an unwillingness on the part of parents to work with the school; external influences and attractions that are more compelling for the students than school; and weaknesses in the provision made by the schools and other services for their students (4–5). In its new remit, the NEWB has committed to offering "a cohesive and integrated support service to children, families and schools".

Essentially there is a demonstrated need at primary level to monitor academic, personal and social progress consistently and regularly so that students at risk of disaffection are identified early and intervention strategies can be implemented before more serious problems take hold. Furthermore, there is clearly no one solution to preventing school disaffection, but enhancing current knowledge of factors associated with this phenomenon will hopefully be of benefit to policy-makers in Ireland, and elsewhere, in targeting limited resources in a constricted economy. Considering the prevalence of school disaffection among some students there is, perhaps, a need to re-evaluate programmes currently targeting disaffected students in terms of their helpfulness. Finally, the study has implications for the professional development of teachers. Better understanding of factors associated with disaffection should also be considered in initial teacher education as well as in continuing professional development. Considering the complexity of factors involved, disaffected young people should not be regarded in a uniform manner; rather parents, schools and other relevant organisations need to work together to provide the support according to the specific needs of the pupils.

Note

1.   For a guide to Logistic Regression see Hosmer and Lemeshow (2000).

References

Boaler, J. 2005. "The 'Psychological Prison' from Which They Never Escaped: The Role of Ability Grouping in Reproducing Social Class Inequalities." *FORUM* 47 (2): 135–144. doi: 10.2304/forum.2005.47.2.2.

Bronfenbrenner, U. 1986. "Alienation and the Four Worlds of Childhood." *Phi Delta Kappan* 67: 430–436.

Buss, A., and R. Plomin. 1984. *Temperament: Early Developing Personality Traits*. Hillsdale, NJ: Erlbaum.

Clerkin, A. and A.-M. Creaven. 2013. "Pupil Engagement." In *National Schools, International Contexts: Beyond the PIRLS and TIMSS Test Results*, edited by Eivers and Clerkin. http://www.erc.ie/documents/pt2011_ch3.pdf.

Darmody, M., E. Smyth, and S. McCoy. 2008. "Acting Up or Opting Out? Truancy in Irish Secondary Schools." *Educational Review* 60 (4): 359–373.

Darmody, M., D. Byrne, and F. McGinnity. 2012. "Cumulative Disadvantage? Educational Careers of Migrant Students in Irish Secondary Schools." *Race Ethnicity and Education* 17 (1): 25–48.

Department of Education and Skills. 2012. *Statistical Report*. www.education.ie.

Finn, J. D. 1989. "Withdrawing from School." *Review of Educational Research* 59: 117–142.

Fredricks, J. A., P. C. Blumenfeld, and A. H. Paris. 2004. "School Engagement: Potential of the Concept, State of the Evidence." *Review of Educational Research* 74: 59–109.

Furlong, M. J., and S. L. Christenson. 2008. "Engaging Students at School and with Learning: A Relevant Construct for All Students." *Psychology in the Schools* 45: 365–368.

Furrer, C., and E. A. Skinner. 2003. "Sense of Relatedness as a Factor in Children's Academic Engagement and Performance." *Journal of Educational Psychology* 95: 148–162.

Heathcote-Elliott, C., and N. Walters. 2000. *Combating Social Exclusion Occasional Paper 9: ESF Objective 3 Disaffected Youth*. Accessed April 9, 2014. http://www.surrey.ac.uk/Education/cse/paper9.doc

Hodgson, A. 1999. "Analysing Education and Training Policies for Tackling Social Exclusion." In *Tackling Disaffection and Social Exclusion*, edited by A. Hayton, 126–152. London: Kogan Page.

Holroyd, R., and K. Aramour. 2003. "Re-engaging Disaffected Youth through Physical Activity Programs." Paper presented at the British Educational Research Association Annual Conference, Heriot-Watt University, Edinburgh, September 11–13.

Hosmer, D. W., and S. Lemeshow. 2000. *Applied Logistic Regression*. New York: Wiley.

Keogh, A., and J. Whyte. 2007. *What is Smart? An in-Depth Study of Children's Concepts of Intelligence*. Children's Research Centre, TCD. https://www.tcd.ie/childrensresearchcentre/assets/pdf/Publications/What_is_Smart.pdf.

Kinder, K., J. Harland, A. Wilkin, and A. Wakefield. 1995. *Three to Remember: Strategies for Disaffected Pupils*. Slough: NFER.

Kinder, K., S. Kendall, K. Halsey, and M. Atkinson. 1999. *Disaffection Talks*. Slough: NFER.

Lareau, A. 2002. "Invisible Inequality: Social Class and Childrearing in Black Families and White Families." *American Sociological Review* 67 (5): 747–776.

Li, Y., J. V. Lerner, and R. M. Lerner. 2010. "Personal and Ecological Assets and Academic Competence in Early Adolescence: The Mediating Role of School Engagement." *Journal of Youth and Adolescence* 39 (7): 801–815.

Massoni, E. 2011. "Positive Effects of Extra Curricular Activities on Students." *ESSAI* 9, Article 27. http://dc.cod.edu/cgi/viewcontent.cgi?article=1370&context=essai.

McCoy, S., E. Smyth, and J. Banks. 2012. *The Primary Classroom: Insights from the Growing up in Ireland Study*. Dublin: NCCA/ESRI.

Macleod, G., J. McAllister, and A. Pirrie. 2010. "Emotional Education as Second Language Acquisition?" *The International Journal of Emotional Education* 2 (1): 34–48.

Millar, D. 2013. *Analysis of School Attendance Data in Primary and Post-primary Schools 2010/11*. Dublin: Educational Research Centre.

Ofsted. 2008. *Good Practice in Re-engaging Disaffected and Reluctant Students in Secondary Schools*. http://dera.ioe.ac.uk/9213/1/Good%20practice%20in%20re-engaging%20disaffected%20and%20reluctant%20students%20in%20secondary%20schools.pdf.

Osler, A. and H. Starkey. 2005. "Violence in Schools and Representations of Young People: A Critique of Government Policies in France and England." *Oxford Review of Education*, 31 (2): 195–215.

Reid, K. 1986. *Disaffection from School*. London: Routledge.

Reid, K. 2004. "The Views of Head Teachers and Teachers on Attendance Issues in Primary Schools." *Research in Education* 72: 60–76.

Reid, K. 2012. *Tackling Behaviour in Your Primary School*. London: Routledge.

Roeser, R., K. R. Strobel, and G. Quihuis. 2002. "Studying Early Adolescents' Academic Motivation, Social–Emotional Functioning, and Engagement in Learning: Variable- and Person-Centered Approaches." *Anxiety, Stress and Coping* 15: 345–368.

Skinner, E., C. Furrer, G. Marchand, and T. Kindermann. 2008. "Engagement and Disaffection in the Classroom: Part of a Larger Motivational Dynamic?" *Journal of Educational Psychology* 100 (4): 765–781.

Skinner, E. A., J. G. Wellborn, and J. P. Connell. 1990. "What It Takes to Do Well in School and Whether I've Got It: A Process Model of Perceived Control and Children's Engagement and Achievement in School." *Journal of Educational Psychology* 82: 22–32.

Slater, H., N. M. Davies, and S. Burgess. 2012. "Do Teachers Matter? Measuring the Variation in Teacher Effectiveness in England." *Oxford Bulletin of Economics and Statistics* 74: 629–645.

Smyth, E., S. McCoy, M. Darmody. 2004. *Moving up: The Experiences of First Year Students in Post-Primary Education*. Dublin: ESRI/Liffey Press.

Thornton, M., M. Darmody, and S. McCoy. 2013. "Persistent Absenteeism among Irish Primary School Pupils." *Educational Review* 65 (4): 488–501.

Wigfield, A., J. S. Eccles, U. Schiefele, R. Roeser, and P. Davis-Kean. 2006. "Development of Achievement Motivation." In *Handbook of Child Psychology*, edited by W. Damon (Series) and N. Eisenberg (Volume), 6th ed., Vol. 3, 933–1002. New York: John Wiley.

Williamson, H. 1999. *'Disaffected' Youth: Background Research, Political Recognition and Policy Development*. Wales Youth Agency. http://www.youthworkwales.org.uk/creo_files/upload/files/Disaffection.pdf.

Willms, D. 2000. *Student Engagement at School – A Sense of Belonging and Participation. Results from PISA 2000*. Paris: OECD.

Wolke, D., S. Woods, L. Bloomfeld, and L. Karstadt. 2000. "The Association between Direct and Relational Bullying and Behaviour Problems among Primary School Children." *Journal of Child Psychology and Psychiatry* 41 (8): 989–1002.

Pupil absenteeism and the educational psychologist

H.C.M. (Tim) Carroll

School of Psychology, Cardiff University, Cardiff, UK

From a review of the literature, it is concluded that (i) each form of pupil absenteeism relates to a heterogeneous group of children; (ii) because of such heterogeneity, those who are involved in assessment and intervention in relation to pupil absenteeism are faced with a demanding task; (iii) as a consequence of their education and training, educational psychologists (EPs) have the appropriate knowledge and skills for dealing with pupil absenteeism at both the individual and group level; (iv) with respect to dealing with pupil absenteeism, EPs could make and have made a contribution; (v) EPs have the necessary experience of working at a multi-agency level and, in connection with pupil absenteeism, have worked not only with the children and their parents but also at both whole school and multi-agency levels; and (vi) EPs have already demonstrated in the literature that they have much to offer in this important and demanding area.

Introduction

With a view to determining whether the educational psychologist (EP) has a role to play in relation to the problem of pupil absenteeism, answers will be given to the following questions.

(1) What is pupil absenteeism?
(2) What is an EP?
(3) With respect to dealing with pupil absenteeism, in what ways could EPs make a contribution and in what ways have they made a contribution?
(4) With whom have EPs worked when dealing with pupil absenteeism?
(5) To what extent have EPs been involved in the problem of pupil absenteeism?

In order to obtain answers to these questions, the following databases were explored up to the end of December, 2013: Educational Resource Information Centre, British Education Index and PsycINFO, and the following journals, up to March, 2014: DECP Debate, Educational and Child Psychology, EP in Practice, The Psychologist, and The Psychology of Education Review.

What is pupil absenteeism?

In order to answer this question, overviews will be provided in relation to the following three forms of pupil absenteeism: truancy, school phobia/school refusal and attendance at or below/absence at or above a specific value.

Truancy

Up until 1941, the only types of pupil absenteeism, other than absence from school for reasons to do with illness, which were of concern to schools and local authorities were truancy, post-registration truancy and parentally condoned absence. These three types of absenteeism take the following forms. Truancy: "unlawful absence from school without the parents' knowledge or permission" (Hersov 1960, 130); post-registration truancy: a form of absence "in which a pupil is marked present on the register but is not present at an individual lesson or lessons during the course of the day" (Stoll and O'Keefe 1989, 10); and parentally condoned absence: "unauthorised school absence in which the parents keep the child home for reasons of their own" (Thambirajah, Grandison, and De-Hayes 2008, 14).

The literature on truancy has indeed grown over the years, thanks in part to Reid, the UK's most prolific researcher and writer on truancy and non-school attendance, whose most recent books include, for example, "An Essential Guide to Improving Attendance in your School: Practical Resources for All School Managers" (Reid 2014a) and "Managing School Attendance: Successful Intervention Strategies for Reducing Truancy" (Reid 2014b). However, rather than refer to Reid's work per se, reference will be made in this part of this article to just two relatively recent articles, namely those of Attwood and Croll (2006) and Maynard et al. (2012). They have been selected in order to provide support for the view that truants constitute a heterogeneous group and that, furthermore, some of the more frequently occurring problems associated with truancy are present in relation to children who do not become truants.

Attwood and Croll's study was based on data taken from the British Household Survey (BHS) and interviews relating to the school experience of 17 adolescents who had been absent from school one or more days per week during the year. However, in view of the smallness of the sample, the interview results will not be considered here. With respect to the BHS study, the data collected took the form of information elicited by interview from young people and their parents. As a consequence of the former being asked when they were aged 16 years a question relating to skipping school without an excuse during the last year, it was possible for Attwood and Croll to come to the following conclusions based upon making comparisons on various variables between those who reported truanting several times or often and those who reported truanting once or never. "Coming from families of low socio-economic status, parents not monitoring home work, negative attitudes towards teachers and the value of education are all associated with higher levels of truancy. However, the majority of young people in those situations do not truant and there are many truants who do not have these characteristics" (Attwood and Croll 2006, 467).

The study conducted by Maynard et al. involved a sample of 1646 12–17 year olds, all of whom had been interviewed at home, drawn from the US 2010 National Survey on Drug Use and Health. The sample comprised four groups of what the researchers described as truants, namely those who, during the 30 days prior to being interviewed, had admitted missing school because they had "skipped or 'cut' or just didn't want to be there" (Maynard et al. 2012, 1674). On the basis of the participants' responses to questions relating to "five indicator variables: school engagement, participation in school-based activities, grades, parental academic involvement and the number of days skipped during the previous 30 day period" (Maynard et al. 2012, 1674), each respondent was, by means of latent profile analysis and multi-nominal regression, assigned to one of four groups: achievers, moderate students, the academically disengaged and chronic skippers. The respective group sizes and average number of days skipped per group were as follows: 470, 400, 673 and 103; 1.58, 2.17, 2.12 and 12.96 days. On the basis of statistically comparing the four groups in terms of those five key indicator variables, five demographic variables (age, gender, race/ethnicity, family income and father in the home) and five externalising behaviours (alcohol use, marijuana use, theft > \$50, drug sales and fighting), Maynard et al. concluded: "Results from the present study suggest that truant youth are not a homogenous group, but rather present with different risk profiles as they relate to key indicators, demographic characteristics and externalising behaviour" (Maynard et al. 2012, 1671).

School phobia/school refusal

In 1941, Johnson et al. published the first article specifically on school phobia, "a type of emotional disturbance associated with great anxiety that leads to serious absence from school" (Kahn, Nursten, and Carroll 1981, 28). However, in 1957, Johnson published an article in which she reported on her discussion of a 1955 workshop on school phobia and, in that article, she stated that "School phobia is a misnomer. Actually, it is separation anxiety which occurs not only in early childhood but also in later years" (Johnson 1957, 307). Post-1957 other writers, e.g. Hersov (1960), Elliott (1999) and Thambirajah, Grandison, and De-Hayes (2008), have preferred the term school refusal to school phobia or separation anxiety whilst others, e.g. Berg (1980), have used the terms school phobia and school refusal interchangeably. The picture has become even more complicated as a result of further subcategories of school refusal being identified. Atkinson et al. (1989) subjected 100 school refusers' clinic files to various forms of statistical analysis and came up with three clusters, namely one containing "children who feared separation from dependent overprotective mothers", a second comprising children who "were perfectionistic and depressed" and a third containing "extensively disturbed children from multiproblem families, who had suffered early separation or loss, and who were fearful and depressed" (Atkinson et al. 1989, 191). In a later article, King and Bernstein (2001), on the basis of reviewing the literature, concluded that "there appears to be support for three primary, distinguishable clinical groups of school refusers: phobic school refusers, separation-anxious school refusers, and anxious/depressed school refusers" (King and Bernstein 2001, 199). Not surprisingly, there is indeed overlap between the groups identified by Atkinson et al. and those proposed by King and Bernstein.

Truancy and school phobia/school refusal

The following study conducted by Bools et al. (1990) involved a non-clinical sample of 100 persistent absentees who had been referred by education welfare officers to a local education authority attendance committee. Given the source of the sample, one would have expected it to have comprised traditional truants and no school phobics/school refusers. However, on the basis of information collected from the children's parents (mostly the mothers on their own) by one of two child psychiatrist using a semi-structured interview schedule which had been designed for the investigation, it was found that "the pattern of school non-attendance, irrespective of the presence of any psychiatric disorder", as judged by the interviewing psychiatrist, fell into one of four groups: "'school refusal', 'truancy', a 'mixed pattern' or 'neither'" (Bools et al. 1990, 172), with the respective numbers of children falling into each group being 24, 53, 9 and 14. Thus, contrary to expectation, approximately, a quarter of the persistent absentees were classified as school refusers. In addition to allocating each child to one of the four non-attendance groups, each psychiatrist also judged whether each child was considered to have a conduct disorder, an emotional disorder, a mixture of both the aforesaid disorders or no disorder. Interestingly, only 49% of the truants and 50% of the school refusers were rated as having a conduct disorder and an emotional disorder, respectively. Furthermore, 47% of the truants and 38% of the school refusers were considered to have no disorder. The researchers also subjected their data to cluster analysis and this gave rise to three groups of children, namely: (i) those "with the features of "school refusal" who often had generalised neurotic disorders"; (ii) those "with the features of "truancy" all of whom had conduct disorders"; and (iii) those "who were usually "truants" but less often psychiatrically disturbed" (Bools et al. 1990, 171). On the basis of briefly reviewing four empirical studies, namely that of Bools et al. above, that of Atkinson et al. referred to in the previous paragraph and two others (Kolvin, Berney, and Bhate 1984; Berg et al. 1985), Kearney (2003) concluded that there was both considerable overlap across the four studies and important differences between them. For this reason and for other reason to do with the lack of agreement about the different aspects of pupil absenteeism, he went on to argue at the end of his literature review that there was a need to replace all the other terms which had been used before with a single term, "school refusal behaviour", which he and Silverman had first used in 1996. According to Kearney (2003, 59), the term refers to "a child-motivated refusal to attend school or difficulty remaining in classes for an entire day" and covers "prior descriptions of this population, including truancy, psychoneurotic truancy, school refusal, school phobia, and separation anxiety".

Attendance at or below/absence at or above a specific value

On the basis of their review of the literature on truancy and school refusal, Lyon and Cotler (2007, 552) drew attention to the fact "that the criteria used to identify students for inclusion in research are often inconsistent and frequently overlap. This is particularly true when the severity of nonattendance (i.e., school days missed) is used". They supported this statement by referring to two truancy and five school refusal studies for which the criteria ranged from 10 to 40% of school days missed. Galloway (1982) used an even more extreme criterion, namely an absence rate of at least 50% in his study of persistent unauthorised absentees. By way of justifying his own research, he correctly pointed out in the introduction to his article that "Although psychologists and psychiatrists have devoted a great deal of attention to school phobia and truancy … there is a surprising lack of systematic information about the 'silent majority' of absentees who are never referred for specialist advice". (Galloway 1982, 317). Given that the focus of his research was unauthorised absentees and that the studies referred to above in this paragraph were about truants and school refusers, it is relevant to point out that there have been even fewer studies which have simply employed attendance data as a basis for identifying participants for research. To date, the only researchers who have adopted such an approach appear to be Reid and the author.

The study by Reid (1982) is unique because, surprisingly, it is still the only one on the self-concepts and self-esteem of persistent absentees. In his study, they were adolescents, all of whom had absence rates of 65% or more. Comparisons of them with two control groups, one of which comprised pupils matched for age and gender in the same class, and the other, similarly matched, but from the "A" stream, showed that, as a group, the persistent absentees: (i) "came from more deprived, less stable and lower socioeconomic backgrounds than the other two control groups" (Reid 1982, 184), though not all pupils from problem homes had poor attendance records; (ii) had significantly below average intelligence and did less well academically at both primary and secondary levels; and (iii) compared with both control groups, had significantly lower self-concept and lower self-esteem scores, though, as revealed by the standard deviations for the three groups, a minority of the persistent absentees had either higher self-concept scores or higher self-esteem scores than a minority of those in the control groups.

In a series of six articles, Carroll compared primary school pupils with attendance rates of 80% or less at both 7 and 11 years of age with those of pupils with normal attendance records and found that such poor primary school attendance appeared to be linked to the following:

- living in council-rented accommodation; being in an overcrowded home; sharing a bedroom, sharing a bed; having a father in a manual occupation; the father being unemployed or there being no father in the home; having a mother who was not in paid employment; being eligible to receive free school meals; being in a one-parent family; being in a family having more than three children; and, based on the criteria of Wedge and Prosser (1973), being disadvantaged (Carroll 2000);
- parental education which was minimal; with respect to reading, the parent providing his/her child with a poor model; with respect to the parent's attitude to the child's education, a lack interest; problems of a marital kind; paternal management of the child which was inadequate; and, with respect to the child, "overdependence on the mother, irritability, misery and, at the age of 11, undue worrying about things" (Carroll 1986, 210);
- being born in May, June, July or August (Carroll 1992b);
- poorer attainments, particularly in mathematics (Carroll 2010, 2012);
- having fewer friends (Carroll 2011); and
- having emotional and behavioural difficulties which took the form of either "neurotic" or "antisocial" disorders (Carroll 2013).

From the above findings, it is not possible to conclude either that environmental factors cause poor school attendance or that within child factors are either the cause or the result of poor attendance. Furthermore, for each of the negative factors which appears to be related to poor attendance, it was the case that some of those with poor attendance did not experience one or more of the negative factors and that some of those with normal attendance had experience of one or more of the negative factors. Finally, it is perhaps not surprising that there are certain similarities between the above results and those arising from the truancy and school phobia/school refusal studies, e.g. with respect to home background factors and emotional and behavioural difficulties.

Given that, as revealed in the preceding literature review, neither truants, school phobics/school refusers nor those who had attendance at or below/absence at or above a specific value were found to constitute a homogenous group, and given the problems relating to the terms truancy and school phobia/school refusal which were pointed out by Kearney in his 2003 article, there is clearly a need for an alternative term to cover these, to some extent, different forms of school attendance problems. Unfortunately, Kearney's term, "school refusal behaviour" suffers from the fact that Kearney means by it a child-motivated refusal to attend school or a lesson(s). As a consequence, the label does not apply to that grey area when it is not clear whether the school absence is motivated. Kearney's label also suffers from its obvious association with the label "school refusal", which is meant to be encompassed by Kearney's "umbrella" label. Since 1986, this author has used the term "pupil absenteeism" to cover all forms of pupil absence, irrespective of cause. For the reasons just given, he considers it to be a more useful term than Kearney's. He prefers it to such labels as truancy and school phobia/school refusal because "it does not carry with it the connotations commonly associated with either of the two labels, e.g. that the problem is "in the child", but instead draws attention to the problem of absenteeism itself, and makes it more likely that it will be seen to be not just about the child but to do with" her/his "home, school, neighbourhood in which she/he lives and society itself" (Carroll 1986, 206). It should be noted that other EPs have chosen to use other equally neutral labels, e.g. chronic non-attendance (Lauchlan 2003) and extended school non-attendance (Pellegrin 2007). However, like Lauchlan and Pellegrini, this author considers that each form of pupil absenteeism relates to a heterogeneous group of children with the result that, with respect to both assessment and intervention, those who deal with pupil absenteeism are faced with a far more demanding task than would be the case if each form of pupil absenteeism related to a homogeneous group of children for which there exists accepted approaches to assessment and well tried methods of treatment/intervention.

What is an EP?

An EP is a person who, as an adult, will have studied psychology to a level which makes her/him eligible for the Graduate Basis for Chartered Membership (GBC) of the British Psychological Society (BPS). Up until 2009 a person living in England, Northern Ireland or Wales who had achieved eligibility for the BPS's Graduate Basis for Registration (GBR) (the title which preceded GBC) and who wished to become a Chartered EP would have to have: (i) qualified as a teacher; (ii) taught for a minimum of two years; (iii) gone on to train as an EP, normally on a full-time, one-year course/programme leading to an academic qualification in the practice of educational psychology; and (iv) worked for one year as an EP under the supervision of a Chartered EP. Before the 1970s the qualification in educational psychology would have been a diploma in educational psychology but from the 1970s onwards it would have been a master's degree in educational psychology, e.g. an M.Ed.Psy., an M.Sc. or an M.Ed. In 2006 a very important change in the training of EPs took place and one which was in keeping with developments in higher education throughout the European Union. Instead of training as a teacher, teaching for two years and obtaining a master's degree, a person holding a qualification in psychology which gave eligibility for GBR was able to apply in 2006 for entry onto a three-year, full-time university programme leading to a doctorate in educational psychology and also to eligibility for both Chartered Membership of the BPS and membership of the Division of Educational and Child Psychology of the BPS. However, such was the competition for places on the fourteen programmes that only the minority of applicants were successful and those who were would, between obtaining eligibility for GBR and taking up a place on a programme, have gained additional experience relevant to their future role as an EP.

The BPS's publication, "Accreditation through partnership handbook: Guidance for undergraduate and conversion programmes in psychology" (British Psychological Society 2013a) provides full details of what is required of a programme which, when successfully completed by an individual, makes her/him eligible for GBC. The actual syllabus for such a programme has the following core domains: biological psychology, cognitive psychology, developmental psychology, individual differences, social psychology, conceptual and historical issues in psychology, and research methods. Successful completion of an accredited programme having these seven core domains provides a necessary initial basis, which is then built on during the three year programme, for achieving various learning outcomes for a doctorate in educational psychology, some of which relate to the following: "psychological assessment, intervention and evaluation"; "collaboration with the interacting systems of families, schools, communities and other agencies"; conducting "research and evaluation"; and transferring "knowledge and skills to new settings and situations" (British Psychological Society 2013b, 17). Given its implications for evidence-based practice (Frederickson 2002), it is relevant to mention that, fundamental to all BPS programmes, whether undergraduate or postgraduate, is the fact that psychology is a scientific discipline.

Aside from the small number of EPs who are in private practice, most EPs are employed by local authorities and function within educational psychology services. According to the British Psychological Society in an undated publication which includes a brief description of each of the eight branches of applied psychology, EPs work in a variety of ways. For example, they deal with "learning difficulties, social and emotional problems, issued around disability as well as more complex developmental disorders". Their work takes a variety of forms including, for example, "observation, interviews and assessments" and offering "consultation, advice and support to teachers, parents, the wider community as well as the young people concerned" (British Psychological Society +2006, 18). Although the BPS's brief description is sufficient for the purposes of this paper, the interested reader will find far fuller accounts on the role of the EP in Cameron (2006), Farrell et al. (2006), Frederickson and Miller (2008) and Fallon, Woods, and Rooney (2010).

With respect to dealing with pupil absenteeism, in what ways could EPs make a contribution and in what ways have they made a contribution?

Given the heterogeneity of pupil absenteeism in terms of what it is, its possible causes and possible effects, it follows that, with respect to dealing with it, what is required is a team approach in which at least one member of the team has a well based understanding of child development, cognitive development, individual differences, the behaviour of groups and people within groups – in particular, families and schools – methods of intervention in order to deal with pupil absenteeism at different levels, and the ability to conduct research. From the preceding section it will be apparent that such a person is a qualified EP. That EPs can make a contribution to dealing with pupil absenteeism follows from two publications by Miller and Todd (2002) and Abrams (2006). In both publications it was shown that EPs can make an important contribution to helping schools deal with problem behaviour in schools. Although neither publication made reference to pupil absenteeism per se, the arguments made in relation to problem behaviour would apply equally to that of pupil absenteeism.

Fundamental to effective intervention is arriving at an appropriate description of the presenting problem and an examination of its possible causes. As Elliott (1999, 1003) observed in his scholarly practitioner review on school refusal: "The heterogeneous nature of school refusal is such that a detailed assessment is necessary in order to identify the most appropriate form of intervention (King, Ollendick, and Tonge 1995)". By the same token pupil absenteeism is also deserving of detailed assessment. According to Hallam and Rogers (2008, 252) "It is now accepted that each child's case should be considered individually, focusing on developing a functional analysis of non-attendance (Kearney and Sims 1997)". That such an approach is advocated by EPs is evident in that, in their respective literature reviews on dealing with chronic non-attendance/extended school non-attendance, Lauchlan (2003) and Pellegrin (2007), who are both EPs, described functional analysis in detail. According to Kearney and Silverman (1999) functional analysis: (i) is based on their claim that children miss school for four main reasons; and (ii) takes the form of conducting an assessment which is in part based on a scale devised by Kearney and Silverman (1993) which gives rise to both child and parent rating. The results of the assessment are then used for deciding on the main reason why the child is missing school, and then implementing the form of treatment which is appropriate for the reason identified. In their article Kearney and Silverman (1999) actually specified the treatment which is required for each of the four reasons. In a later article Kearney (2007) claimed that he had demonstrated the utility of functional analysis by showing in an empirical study that, compared to basing the treatment on what he described as the form of behaviour, e.g. truancy or school refusal, it was more successful in predicting the number of school days missed in a school year.

Although functional analysis has much to offer, it is constrained by the facts that: (i) it is based on the claim referred to above and (ii) the form of treatment is predetermined. Fortunately, in the view of this author, the way in which today's EPs are trained to approach problems has far greater potential for dealing successfully with pupil absenteeism. One such approach, the Constructionist Model of Informed Reasoned Action (COMOIRA) which takes the form of "a new flexible model of professional practice designed to integrate theory and practice" has been developed by Gameson and was first described in Gameson et al. (2003, 96). Full details of the model and how it can be used by EPs and trainee EPs are given in the 2003 article and two subsequent ones (Gameson et al. 2005; Rhydderch and Gameson 2010). Unfortunately space does not permit further description of COMOIRA other than to say that "Within COMOIRA psychological theory is integrated into a framework of decision points that examines and promotes change" (Rhydderch and Gameson 2010, 127). With respect to pupil absenteeism, the desired change could be, for example that of: (i) getting a child back to school and dealing with those factors which prevented the child from attending school; or (ii) improving the overall pupil attendance rate for a school. As for the route to bringing about such changes, it would not be prescribed in the way that Kearney and Silverman (1999) described but instead, informed by appropriate psychological theory/theories, would involve "visiting" that combination of COMOIRA decision points which would lead to the desired change being achieved.

As the following quotations imply, with respect to the literature on treatment/ intervention approaches for dealing with the various aspects of pupil absenteeism, there is far more on school phobia/refusal than on other forms of pupil absenteeism: "Compared with the extensive literature on the treatment of school refusal, there is a remarkable absence of published work on the treatment of other forms of absence" (Galloway 1985, 84); and "little research has been conducted to identify effective methods of truancy reduction, particularly among elementary-aged students" (McCluskey, Bynum, and Patchin 2004, 214).

From the following references it may be seen that behavioural treatments, with their foundations in learning theory, were particularly popular with EPs in the 1970s/1980s for treating school phobics/school refusers: Lowenstein (1973), Galloway and Miller (1978), Bowdler and Johns (1982), Galloway (1985) and Blagg (1987). More recently, cognitive behaviour therapy (CBT) as a way treating school phobia/school refusal has grown in popularity. As is shown in the following articles, CBT is clearly a method of intervention which has its basis in psychological theory and, as revealed by Majors and Sykes (2008), is also being taught to trainee EPs: Moffitt et al. (2003), Doobay (2008), and Heyne et al. (2011).

To the extent that the family has a part to play in dealing with all types of school attendance problems, family therapy, with its foundations in systems theory, could also be used by EPs to tackle non-school attendance. However, but two relevant reference were identified, one of which had to do with using family therapy with adolescent school refusers (Bryce and Baird 1986) and the other was a book edited by two former EPs, Downing and Osborne (1985) which, though it contains only a few references to family therapy, has the same theoretical basis as family therapy and provides a valuable basis for engaging in family therapy in relation to pupil absenteeism.

In keeping with the earlier observation about the lack of published research on interventions aimed at truancy and forms of absence other than school phobia/school refusal, a thorough search of the data bases identified but one intervention approach with a psychological basis, namely one which involved adolescents in a group situation and which used a combination of "intrinsic motivational stimulation strategies, motivational interviewing and solution-focused counselling" (Enea and Dafinioiu 2009, 185) for dealing with truancy. However, there are other group-based interventions with a psychological basis which could be used by EPs to deal with certain aspects of pupil absenteeism, e.g. family therapy (Goldenberg and Goldenberg 2013), social skills training (Spence, Donovan, and Brechman-Toussaint 1999) and "Circle of Friends" (Newton, Taylor, and Wilson 1996), though to date there do not appear to be any articles describing their use for this purpose,

With respect to adopting a whole school approach in order to bring about an improvement in attendance, the need for such an approach was demonstrated by Reynolds and Murgatroyd (1977) and Carroll (1992a) at the secondary and primary school levels respectively. In both studies it was demonstrated that there were certain schools with attendance rates which were below what could be expected from the home circumstances of the pupils in the schools. Several EPs have written about working at a whole school level, e.g. Gregory (1980), Bowdler and Johns (1982),

O'Hara and Jewell (1982), Gupta (1990), Moore et al. (1993) and Lewis (1995). With respect to the theoretical basis for their approaches, that described in the first three articles and that of Moore et al. was influenced by Burden (1978) who had argued that EPs should extend their role to one of working with schools as a whole and should do this by adopting a systems-based approach. In terms of what the EPs were attempting to achieve, Gregory (1980), Moore et al. (1993) and Lewis (1995) were working with the schools to reduce truancy whilst the other EPs were trying to help the schools to improve school attendance. Further details of using a whole school approach for dealing with attendance problems are given in the book by Hallam and Rogers (2008) which also has a chapter on dealing with persistent absentees.

With whom have EPs worked when dealing with pupil absenteeism?

At the time when EPs worked in child guidance clinics (CGCs) i.e. before educational psychology services (EPSs) became the norm, this would have been an easy question to answer. In a typical CGC the EP was part of a team comprising a child psychiatrist (who normally headed the team), a social worker/psychiatric social worker and an EP. Referrals to the CGC were dealt with by the team, with the EP having responsibility for liaising with the school, the social worker with the family and the psychiatrist with the GP and the medical services. In relation to cases of school phobia referred to a CGC, an article by Chazan (1962) implies that one of the contributions of the EP in the CGC in which Chazan worked as an EP was that of arranging a change of school in certain cases.

As for the EP who works in an EPS, a report for the DFEE written by Kelly and Grey (2000) who conducted the research, reveals that the modal EP in 1998/9 was employed by an LEA, was part of an EPS which was staffed by a team of six to twelve EPs, worked in a patch of schools (secondary and their feeder primaries) with a total pupil population in the patch of 4 to 5000, and spent about half of her/his time in schools where she/he worked with individual pupils, their teachers and parents, SEN co-ordinators, other teachers and head teachers. With respect to multi-agency work, according to the report at least 50% of EPs had worked with social services staff, health service staff and staff in the higher education sector. Furthermore, EPs expressed a need for greater involvement in multi-agency work. That EPs are likely to be involved in the twenty-first century in even more multi-agency work, particularly in response to the *Every Child Matters* agenda and the establishment of Children's Services, is reflected in the following four articles: Farrell et al. (2006), Gaskell and Leadbetter (2009), Fallon, Woods, and Rooney (2010) and Greenhouse (2013).

With respect to the answer to the question posed, only one directly relevant article was found which deals specifically with multi-agency work in relation to pupil absenteeism. According to Grandison (2008) who is a senior EP and one of the co-authors of the book on school refusal by Thambirajah, Grandison, and De-Hayes (2008), her work in relation to cases of school refusal involved her in working with "the headteacher of the pupil referral unit (PRU) for pupils with medical needs, a child and adolescent psychiatrist and an educational welfare officer (EWO)" (Grandison 2008, 21). However, from the publications referred to in the last four paragraphs of the preceding section of this article, it may be inferred that, in dealing with pupil absenteeism, the EPs would have worked with parents, teachers, heads of years, PRU staff, EWOs, head teachers and child psychiatrists.

To what extent have EPs been involved in the problem of pupil absenteeism?

Although this question has to some extent been answered in the two preceding sections, it has not been fully answered: hence this final section. Aside from cases of truancy referred to by Britain's first EP, Burt (1925), in his book, "The Young Delinquent", and three article by Tyerman (1958), Chazan (1962) and Lowenstein (1973), the first piece of hard evidence on the practical involvement of EPs with pupil absenteeism emerged from a large scale questionnaire survey conducted in 1977 of the kind of problems which EPs in England and Wales dealt with in their daily work. The survey revealed that 93.5, 91.5, 79.2 and 64.2% of EPs were involved with behaviour problems, poor school attainment, ESN(M) children, and school attendance problems respectively (Division of Educational and Child Psychology 1978). Despite the fact that, in 1977, the majority of EPs dealt with pupil absenteeism, both before and since 1977 the number of publications by practising EPs on their involvement in pupil absenteeism has been relatively small.

With respect to truancy, the first text specifically on the subject written by an EP was an article by Tyerman (1958). Since then a number of EPs have written about truancy, e.g. Gregory (1980), Galloway (1985), Moore et al. (1993) and Lewis (1995). Both school phobia and school refusal have also received the attention of EPs, namely Chazan (1962), Lowenstein (1973), Galloway and Miller (1978), Bowdler and Johns (1982), Galloway (1985), Blagg (1987), Elliott (1999), Grandison (2008) and Miller (2008). Finally, various EPs, e.g. Carroll (1977, 1996), Dawson (1982), O'Hara and Jewell (1982), Galloway (1985), Lauchlan (2003), Pellegrin (2007), Nuttall and Woods (2013) and Gregory and Purcell (2014), have published articles or books on one or more of the following: absenteeism, pupil absenteeism, persistent absenteeism, chronic non-attendance, extended school non-attendance, non-attendance and school refusal behaviour. In keeping with the growing awareness that pupil absenteeism is a complex problem and one which should not be viewed in simplistic terms, as reflected by the labels "truancy" and "school phobia/school refusal", the EP of the twenty-first century has a far broader perspective on the subject and believes that the problem should be tackled in a variety of ways and within an appropriate multi-agency context.

References

Abrams, D. 2006. "British Psychological Society Submission to the Ministerial Stakeholders' Group on Pupil Behaviour and Discipline." *DECP Debate* 121: 12–17.

Atkinson, L., B. Quarrington, J. J. Cyr, and F. V. Atkinson. 1989. "Differential Classification in School Refusal." *The British Journal of Psychiatry* 155: 191–195.

Attwood, G., and P. Croll. 2006. "Truancy in Secondary School Pupils: Prevalence, Trajectories and Pupil Perspectives." *Research Papers in Education* 21 (4): 467–484.

Berg, I. 1980. "School Refusal in Early Adolescence." In *Out of School: Modern Perspectives in Truancy and School Refusal*, edited by L. Hersov and I. Berg, 231–251. Chichester: John Wiley.

Berg, I., G. Casswell, A. Goodwin, R. Hullin, R. McGuire, and G. Tagg. 1985. "Classification of Severe School Attendance Problems." *Psychological Medicine* 15: 157–165.

Blagg, N. 1987. *School Phobia and Its Treatment*. London: Croom Helm.

Bools, C., J. Foster, I. Brown, and I. Berg. 1990. "The Identification of Psychiatric Disorders in Children Who Fail to Attend School: A Cluster Analysis of a Non-clinical Population". *Psychological Medicine* 20: 171–181.

Bowdler, D., and P. Johns. 1982. "Non Attendance at School: Three Approaches in Manchester." *AEP Journal* 5 (8): 32–37.

British Psychological Society. +2006. *Your Journey into Psychology*. www.bps.org.uk/careers.

British Psychological Society. 2013a. *Accreditation through Partnership Handbook: Guidance for Undergraduate and Conversion Programmes in Psychology*. Leicester: British Psychological Society.

British Psychological Society. 2013b. *Accreditation through Partnership Handbook: Guidance for Educational Psychology Programmes in England, Northern Ireland and Wales*. Leicester: British Psychological Society.

Bryce, G., and D. Baird. 1986. "Precipitating a Crisis: Family Therapy and Adolescent School Refusers." *Journal of Adolescence* 9 (3): 199–213.

Burden, R. L. 1978. "Schools' Systems Analysis: A Project Centred Approach." In *Reconstructing Educational Psychology*, edited by B. Gillham, 113–131. London: Croom Helm.

Burt, C. 1925. *The Young Delinquent*. London: University of London Press.

Cameron, R. J. 2006. "Educational Psychology: The Distinctive Contribution." *Educational Psychology in Practice* 22 (4): 289–304.

Carroll, H. C. M. 1977. *Absenteeism in South Wales*. Swansea: Faculty of Education, University College of Swansea.

Carroll, H. C. M. 1986. "Parental Factors in Primary School Pupil Absenteeism and Their Possible Implications for Educational Psychologists." *Educational and Child Psychology* 3 (3): 202–212.

Carroll, H. C. M. 1992a. "School Effectiveness and School Attendance." *School Effectiveness and School Improvement* 3 (4): 258–271.

Carroll, H. C. M. 1992b. "Season of Birth and School Attendance." *British Journal of Educational Psychology* 62: 391–396.

Carroll, H. C. M. 1996. "The Role of the Educational Psychologist in Dealing with Pupil Absenteeism." In *Unwillingly to School*, edited by I. Berg and J. Nursten, 4th ed., 228–241. London: Gaskell.

Carroll, T. 2000. "Pupil Absenteeism in the Primary School." In *Combatting Educational Disadvantage: Meeting the Needs of Vulnerable Children*, edited by T. Cox, 53–64. London: Falmer Press.

Carroll, H. C. M. (Tim). 2010. "The Effect of Pupil Absenteeism on Literacy and Numeracy in the Primary School." *School Psychology International* 31 (2): 115–130.

Carroll, H. C. M. (Tim). 2011. "The Peer Relationships of Primary School Pupils with Poor Attendance Records." *Educational Studies* 37 (2): 6197–6206.

Carroll, H. C. M. (Tim). 2012. "Corrigendum to the Article 'the Effect of Pupil Absenteeism on Literacy and Numeracy in the Primary School'." *School Psychology International* 33 (2): 240.

Carroll, H. C. M. (Tim). 2013. "The Social, Emotional and Behavioural Difficulties of Primary School Children with Poor Attendance Records." *Educational Studies* 39 (2): 223–234.

Chazan, M. 1962. "School Phobia." *British Journal of Educational Psychology* 32: 209–217.

Dawson, R. 1982. "Non-attendance: The Barnsley Approach." *AEP Journal* 5 (10): 50–51.

Division of Educational and Child Psychology. 1978. "Psychological Services for Children." *Bulletin of the British Psychological Society* 31: 11–15.

Doobay, A. F. 2008. "School Refusal Behavior Associated with Separation Anxiety Disorder: A Cognitive-behavioral Approach to Treatment." *Psychology in the Schools* 45 (4): 261–272.

Downing, E., and E. Osborne. 1985. *The Family and the School: A Joint Systems Approach to Problems with Children*. London: Routledge & Kegan Paul.

Elliott, J. G. 1999. "Practitioner Review: School Refusal: Issues of Conceptualisation, Assessment, and Treatment." *Journal of Child Psychology and Psychiatry* 40 (7): 1001–1012.

Enea, V., and I. Dafinioiu. 2009. "Motivational/Solusion-focused Intervention for School Truancy among Adolescents." *Journal of Cognitive and Behavioral Psychotherapies* 9 (2): 185–198.

Fallon, K., K. Woods, and S. Rooney. 2010. "A Discussion of the Developing Role of Educational Psychologists within Children's Services." *Educational Psychology in Practice* 26 (1): 1–23.

Farrell, P., K. Woods, S. Lewis, S. Rooney, G. Squires, and M. O'Connor. 2006. *A Review of the Functions and Contribution of Educational Psychologists in England and Wales in Light of "Every Child Matters: Change for Children"*. Manchester: School of Education, University of Manchester.

Frederickson, N. 2002. "Evidence-based Practice and Educational Psychology." *Educational and Child Psychology* 19 (3): 96–111.

Frederickson, N., and A. Miller. 2008. "What Do Educational Psychologists Do?" In *Educational Psychology: Topics in Applied Psychology*, edited by N. Frederickson, A. Miller, and T. Cline, 1–24. London: Hodder Education.

Galloway, D. 1982. "A Study of Persistent Absentees and Their Families." *British Journal of Educational Psychology* 52: 317–330.

Galloway, D. 1985. *Schools and Persistent Absentees*. Oxford: Pergamon Press.

Galloway, D., and A. Miller. 1978. "The Use of Graded in Vivo Flooding in the Extinction of Children's Phobias." *Behavioural Psychotherapy* 6: 7–10.

Gameson, J., G. Rhydderch, D. Ellis, and H. C. M. Carroll. 2003. "Constructing a Flexible Model of Integrated Professional Practice: Part I, Conceptual and Theoretical Issues." *Educational and Child Psychology* 20 (4): 96–115.

Gameson, J., G. Rhydderch, D. Ellis, and H. C. M. Carroll. 2005. "Constructing a Flexible Model of Integrated Professional Practice: Part II, Process and Practice Issues." *Educational and Child Psychology* 22 (4): 41–55.

Gaskell, S., and J. Leadbetter. 2009. "Educational Psychologists and Multi-agency Working: Exploring Professional Identity." *Educational Psychology in Practice* 25 (2): 97–111.

Goldenberg, H., and I. Goldenberg. 2013. *Family Therapy: An Overview*. 8th ed. Belmont, CA: Brook/Cole.

Grandison, K. 2008. "A Community-based Multi-agency Response to School Refusal." *DECP Debate* 128: 21–23.

Greenhouse, P. M. 2013. "Activity Theory: A Framework for Understanding Multi-agency Working and Engaging Service Users in Change." *Educational Psychology in Practice* 29 (4): 404–415.

Gregory, P. 1980. "Truancy: A Plan for School-based Action-research." *AEP Journal* 5 (3): 30–35.

Gregory, I. S., and A. Purcell. 2014. "Extended School Non-attenders' Views: Developing Best Practice." *Educational Psychology in Practice* 30 (1): 37–50.

Gupta, Y. 1990. "A Study in the Improvement of School Attendance in a Comprehensive School." *Link* 16: 11–16.

Hallam, S., and L. Rogers. 2008. *Improving Behaviour and Attendance at School*. Maidenhead: Open University/McGraw-Hill Education.

Hersov, L. A. 1960. "Persistent Non-attendance at School." *Journal of Child Psychology and Psychiatry* 1: 130–136.

Heyne, D., F. M. Sauter, B. M. Van Widenfelt, R. Vermeiren, and P. M. Westenberg. 2011. "School Refusal and Anxiety in Adolescence: Non-randomized Trial of a Developmentally Sensitive Cognitive Behavioral Therapy." *Journal of Anxiety Disorders* 25: 870–878.

Johnson, A. M. 1957. "School Phobia: Workshop, 1955: Discussion." *American Journal of Orthopsychiatry* 27: 307–309.

Johnson, A. M., E. L. Falstein, S. Szurek, and M. Svendsen. 1941. "School Phobia." *American Journal of Orthopsychiatry* 11: 702–711.

Kahn, J., J. P. Nursten, and H. C. M. Carroll. 1981. *Unwillingly to School: School Phobia or School Refusal: A Psycho-social Problem*. Oxford: Pergamon Press.

Kearney, C. A. 2003. "Bridging the Gap among Professionals Who Address Youths with School Absenteeism: Overview and Suggestions for Consensus." *Professional Psychology: Research and Practice* 34 (1): 57–65.

Kearney, C. A. 2007. "Forms and Functions of School Refusal Behavior in Youth: An Empirical Analysis of Absenteeism Severity." *Journal of Child Psychology and Psychiatry* 48 (1): 53–61.

Kearney, C. A., and W. K. Silverman. 1993. "Measuring the Function of School Refusal Behavior: The School Refusal Assessment Scale." *Journal of Clinical Child Psychology* 22: 85–96.

Kearney, C. A., and W. K. Silverman. 1999. "Functionally Based Prescriptive and Nonprescriptive Treatment for Children and Adolescents with School Refusal Behavior." *Behavior Therapy* 30: 673–695.

Kearney, C. A., and K. E. Sims. 1997. "Anxiety Problems in Childhood: Diagnostic and Dimensional Aspects." In *Clinical Management of Anxiety*, edited by J. A. den Boer. New York: Marcel Dekker.

Kelly, D., and C. Gray. 2000. *Educational Psychology Services (England): Current Role, Good Practice and Future Directions*. Nottingham: DfEE.

King, N. J., and G. A. Bernstein. 2001. "School Refusal in Children and Adolescents: A Review of the Past 10 Years." *Journal of the American Academy of Child and Adolescent Psychiatry* 40 (2): 197–205.

King, N., T. H. Ollendick, and B. J. Tonge. 1995. *School Refusal: Assessment and Treatment*. Needham Heights, MA: Allyn & Bacon.

Kolvin, I., T. P. Berney, and S. R. Bhate. 1984. "Classification and Diagnosis of Depression in School Phobia." *The British Journal of Psychiatry* 145: 347–357.

Lauchlan, F. 2003. "Responding to Chronic Non-attendance: A Review of Intervention Approaches." *Educational Psychology in Practice* 19 (2): 133–146.

Lewis, C. 1995. "Improving Attendance-reducing Truancy: A School Based Approach." *Educational Psychology in Practice* 11 (1): 36–40.

Lowenstein, L. F. 1973. "The Treatment of Moderate School Phobia by Negative Practice and Desensitization Procedures." *Association of Educational Psychologists Journal* 3: 46–50.

Lyon, A. R., and S. Cotler. 2007. "Toward Reduced Bias and Increased Utility in the Assessment of School Refusal Behavior: The Case for Diverse Samples and Evaluations of Context." *Psychology in the Schools* 44 (6): 551–565.

Majors, K., and G. Sykes. 2008. "Trainee Educational Psychologists' Experience of Working with Cognitive Behaviour Therapy (CBT). 2008." *DECP Debate* 128: 16–18.

Maynard, B. R., C. P. Salas-Wright, M. G. Vaughn, and K. E. Peters. 2012. "Who are Truant Youth? Examining Distinctive Profiles of Truant Youth Using Latent Profile Analysis." *Journal of Youth and Adolescence* 41: 1671–1684.

McCluskey, C. P., T. S. Bynum, and J. W. Patchin. 2004. "Reducing Chronic Absenteeism: An Assessment of an Early Truancy Initiative." *Crime & Delinquency* 50 (2): 214–234.

Miller, A. 2008. "School Phobia and School Refusal: Coping with Life by Coping with School?" In *Educational Psychology: Topics in Applied Psychology*, edited by N. Frederickson, A. Miller, and T. Cline, 215–234. London: Hodder Education.

Miller, A., and Z. Todd. 2002. "Educational Psychology and Difficult Behaviour in Schools: Conceptual and Methodological Challenges for an Evidence-based Profession." *Educational and Child Psychology* 19 (3): 82–95.

Moffitt, C. E., B. F. Chorpita, and S. N. Fernandez. 2003. "Intensive Cognitive-behavioral Treatment of School Refusal Behavior." *Cognitive and Behavioral Practice* 10: 51–60.

Moore, L., H. Clarke, S. Corfield, L. Edwards, S. Evans, F. Farino, G. Pasternicki, A. Pratten, J. Robertson, and D. Wakefield. 1993. "A School-based Action Research Project on Truancy." *Educational Psychology in Practice* 8: 208–213.

Newton, G., G. Taylor, and D. Wilson. 1996. "Circles of Friends." *Educational Psychology in Practice* 11 (4): 41–48.

Nuttall, C., and K. Woods. 2013. "Effective Intervention for School Refusal Behaviour." *Educational Psychology in Practice* 29 (4): 347–366.

O'Hara, M., and T. Jewell. 1982. "Non Attendance at School: A Behavioural Approach in Oldham." *AEP Journal* 5 (8): 28–32.

Pellegrini, D. W. 2007. "School Non-attendance: Definitions, Meanings, Responses, Interventions." *Educational Psychology in Practice* 23 (1): 63–77.

Reid, K. 1982. "The Self-concept and Persistent School Absenteeism." *British Journal of Educational Psychology* 52: 179–187.

Reid, K. 2014a. *An Essential Guide to Improving Attendance in Your School: Practical Resources for All School Managers*. Abingdon: Routledge.

Reid, K. 2014b. *Managing School Attendance: Successful Intervention Strategies for Reducing Truancy*. Abingdon: Routledge.

Reynolds, D., and S. Murgatroyd. 1977. "The Sociology of Schooling and the Absent Pupil: The School as a Factor in the Generation of Truancy." In *Absenteeism in South Wales*, edited by H. C. M. Carroll, 51–67. Swansea: Faculty of Education, University College, Swansea.

Rhydderch, G., and J. Gameson. 2010. "Constructing a Flexible Model of Integrated Professional Practice: Part 3 – The Model in Practice." *Educational Psychology in Practice* 26 (2): 123–149.

Spence, S. H., C. Donovan, and M. Brechman-Toussaint. 1999. "Social Skills, Social Outcomes, and Cognitive Features of Childhood Social Phobia." *Journal of Abnormal Psychology* 108 (2): 211–221.

Stoll, P., and D. O'Keefe. 1989. *Officially Present: An Investigation into Post-registration Truancy in Nine Maintained Schools*. Warlingham: Education Unit, Institute of Economic Affairs.

Thambirajah, M. S., K. J. Grandison, and L. De-Hayes. 2008. *Understanding School Refusal*. London: Jessica Kingsley.

Tyerman, M. J. 1958. "A Research into Truancy." *British Journal of Psychology* 28: 217–225.

Wedge, P., and H. Prosser. 1973. *Born to Fail*. London: Arrow Books.

Truancy: a look at definitions in the USA and other territories

Carolyn Gentle-Genitty, Isaac Karikari, Haiping Chen, Eric Wilka and Jangmin Kim

Indiana University School of Social Work, Indianapolis, USA

There is no shortage of definitions for truancy. One state may house many different definitions and there are a variety of challenges arising from this fact. One of the most important to researchers, policy-makers and educators alike, is that because of the lack of uniformity and consistency, it is difficult to compile and ascertain the totality of the phenomenon. The lack of a consistent definition influences a wide range of outcomes including policy matters, financial resources and definitive responses and intervention strategies. This manuscript attempts to synthesise the literature through the examination of operational definitions of truancy in the USA and in other territories. In addition to these operational definitions, expert opinions from focus groups proposed an enhanced definition of truancy. The study is qualitative and uses focus groups and synthesis of the literature to frame the work. Findings are presented. The goal is to synthesise the literature, not in its entirety, but in an attempt to combine and inform the conversation on a definition of truancy.

Why should we care about truancy? Truancy is a social problem around the world (Maynard et al. 2012). In our view, it is riddled with multiple challenges. Most of all, there is a battle to determine whose role it is to respond to children identified as not attending school when authorities and/or their parents believe they should be attending. Unclear also is the appropriate response to such behavior. The USA has placed tremendous value on education as a way of equalising persons from various backgrounds, classes and cultures but the system has been constantly criticised (Levin 1972). The major critique is that many persons, who do not succeed or fail to take advantage of the equalisation opportunity provided by the American educational system, have limited participation. Subsequently, those with little education and already disadvantaged are further alienated from society (Toby 1957).

Levin reported that

> when some citizens received considerably poorer education than the norm for the society, not only will those persons suffer [and be excluded from the main stream, due to a lack of participation in the legal economy], but the larger society will suffer too. (4)

Sadly, students who are truant are likely to engage in delinquent behaviors and deviant practices, making it a social problem and a public health concern. School connectedness – or lack thereof – is also a factor in truancy (Barry, Chaney, and

Chaney 2011; Reid 1999, 2005), resulting in students' disengaging from formal systems, like school (Barry, Chaney, and Chaney 2011; Lawrence et al. 2011; Maynard et al. 2012; Reimer and Dimock 2005). Disengaged from the formal school system, students engaged in deviant activities are educated on the streets (McDonald Brown, and Birrane 1994) which becomes an expensive burden to tax payers[1] (Bachman, Green, and Wirtanen 1971).

Policy-makers and school personnel have relied heavily on the law and its definitions to guide their response to truancy. The categorisation however, has been inconsistent, in both the USA and other territories (Maynard et al. 2012; Reid 2014. American academic and political scientist James Q. Wilson and economist, Glenn Loury, both suggest that this issue provides evidence of administrative deficiencies. Administrative systems have failed truant children and we must begin to make amends (Wilson and Loury 1987).

Chambers (2000) explains that understanding the structure of a social problem is best understood through the boundaries of the problem's goals, objectives, service delivery and administration systems. A definition provides the goals, objectives and rules for operation. This manuscript attempts to synthesise the literature through the examination of operational definitions of truancy in the USA and other territories and expert opinions to propose a common definition of truancy.

Context of the problem

Truants do not live or operate in a vacuum. They affect and are affected by the environment around them and the outcomes outside of school (Attwood and Croll 2006; Epstein and Sheldon 2002; Reid 2010). There is no shortage of definitions for truancy and its related factors (see: Appendix 1 – Truancy definitions). Admittedly, definitional concerns include more than truancy and absenteeism but also interventions and strategies used to respond to students who are constantly not in attendance (Reid 2014).

In fact, the discussions calling for common terminology or more inclusivity in the definitions of truancy are dated (Maynard et al. 2012) but the attempt to synthesise and present one such inclusive definition is new. In the state of Indiana for example, there is one official legal definition of truancy, considered "habitually truant" if he or she has accumulated 10 or more unexcused absences in a single school year. However, in a research conducted with 99 principals from similarly numbered schools in Indiana, it was evident that each school also had (their) its own unofficial definition of truancy (Gentle-Genitty 2009) see: Appendix 2 – Definitions of truancy in one Midwestern state.

This situation creates an absence of a standardised response with consequences for teachers and students alike (Reid 2014). For instance, if the child is labelled as a truant by the school and the services and programmes to respond to the social problem are limited only to the school, this will impede the ability of society to address the root cause of problems such as family, discipline, relational, financial, disorganisation, environmental, lack of resources, supervision and more (Chambers 2000; Gentle-Genitty 2009; Reid 1999). A standardised truancy definition is thus the first step in facilitating better comparisons among schools and states, researchers and authors, and statistical reporting. As Maynard and colleagues (2012) report the magnitude of the problem, currently, is based on indicators used some suggesting increases, others suggesting decreases. The definition of truancy – at least one that aims to be comprehensive – must take into consideration more than the number of absences and have the potential to yield accurate accounts of the frequency of the behaviour and the number of students. It must be specific and should address the problem of truancy and non-attendance.

Government and various school districts continue to make great investments in efforts to standardise truancy noting that the early intervention helps avoid or reduce the costs associated with corrective measures (Garry 1996; Joftus and Maddox-Dolan 2003; Katz 1976; McCluskey, Bynum, and Patchin 2004). Defining truancy is the complexity of the problem and ascertaining the aspect needed for a unified, comprehensive definition is a multifaceted endeavour. Without an adequate definition of the problem and the categories or types of the problem, it is hard to assess a problem's direct impact. It is important to use an integrated theory approach (Bryson 2004) as research urges the need to merge knowledge of the problem and the etiology of the behaviour to infiltrate the problem (Catalano et al. 1998). Given the variety of methods used to track chronic truancy, conducting comparison studies may be difficult, to say the least. However, synthesising literature to tell a story of how truancy has been defined in the USA and other territories can inform our next steps in such work.

Purpose of present study

The purpose of the study was twofold. It was first to attempt to consolidate and or synthesise the massive amount of literature on the operational definitions of truancy. Second, it was to ground the literature with real persons engaged in the work of truancy in schools in the USA and other territories through focus groups.

The two research questions were (1) what are the operational definitions of truancy in the USA and other territories, evident from the literature? (2) Can we produce a unified definition by using truancy experts in a focus group? To attempt a response to these two questions, a study design and methodology was chosen as was a convenient study sample.

Method

Two methods were used: synthesis of the literature and focus groups. To navigate the literature to find operational definitions of truancy in the USA and other territories, the authors spent three years conducting a review of the literature. The database used included EBSCO Host, Academic Search Premier, SocINDEX with Full Text, Social Work Abstracts, ERIC, Education Research Complete, Educational Administration Abstracts and Professional Development Collection. The keywords used in the search were first "truancy", followed by "school non-attendance", "drop-outs", "adolescents" and "youth". The terms were searched individually and using "AND" as a Boolean. The last search was conducted in the fall of 2012. Two of the authors were involved in the search and selection of studies. These same two persons were involved in the data extraction process. There was no extraction form. The first person extracted any type of definition found in the literature and the second person reviewed the articles and operational definitions extracted for accuracy. A table was formed to capture the author, year of publication and definition extracted. The screening method was used to determine the eligibility of articles which met the inclusion/exclusion criteria.

Data analysis was conducted in 2013. We understood there were multiple search terms that could have been used for this study and thus recognised the limitations with the search terms used. The decision was made to limit these terms for brevity in starting to assess the work. Although dropout can be a result of truancy, it was used because it is common for researchers and authors to speak about and define truancy as they discuss dropout. This is because truancy is a symptomatic behavioural outcome of dropout. References from each truancy article were examined and any relevant articles found, were also researched. This search was carried out until there was saturation or repetition of the same articles and authors, as determined by the authors' review. The researchers found 226 articles with the search term truancy. The articles found were then combed to ascertain criteria for inclusion and exclusion. *Inclusion criteria*: Articles included were those which were both research and conceptual, and had at least some semblance of a definition of truancy for the USA or other territories. By semblance, we meant any statement that read as if it intended to define truancy or define characteristics of its sample. *Exclusion criteria*: Those conceptual and research based articles were excluded which *did not* have any semblance of a definition of truancy. There was not a specific search done for *these criteria*.

The second method that informed this work was feedback from an in-person and an online focus group conducted by the lead researcher. For the focus groups, a convenient sample was used. The primary researcher began exploring this area in 2007 and was invited to present on the topic at the International Truancy and Dropout Prevention Association (IATDP)[2] in 2012. To complement the work, she used the one hour and a half presentation session to host a focus group on the topic of coining a common definition of truancy. Because the group was international in scope, in operation since 1911, hosting this particular focus group was ideal. Following the session, a draft definition of truancy resulted. As an additional step it was suggested that hosting of an online focus group could get the participation of the 250 active members registered on the Association's listserve to give their input on the definition. A call went out to the entire listserve asking for feedback on the definition. The result was a 28 member online focus group composed of education workers, government officials, judges, and truancy expert stakeholders with multiple years of experience in educational settings. These persons agreed to take the draft definition and voluntarily coin a comprehensive definition of truancy. After the first round of suggestions was made, the data downloaded from all emails sent to the listserves were analysed. One of the authors sieved through the responses and identified any changes needed to the previous definition. Once completed, the definition was cleaned up and amended as suggested. The third step was resending the definition again for vote and agreement. Each member who participated was invited to vote "yes" or "no" to the definition. There was 100% acceptance of the definition by all 28 persons. The resulting definition was "truancy is a student's act of non-attendance evidenced by missing part or all of the school day without it being legitimately excused by school or per state law".

Results

Synthesised literature results

The summary of the operational definitions of truancy in the USA are presented below followed by definitions in other territories.

Operational definition of truancy in USA: non-attendance and absenteeism

For the operational definition of truancy, we used only the results from the eight databases noted in the methods section with search term "truancy." The result was 226 articles. Of the 226, 137 were automatically excluded as the abstracts did not discuss truancy in detail and offered no semblance of a definition of truancy. Of the remaining articles, 89 were read but another 26 were excluded for lack of relevancy or despite keywords listed as truancy the key word tags did not have anything to do with Truancy. Of 63 articles on truancy extracted and reviewed in an attempt to synthesise available literature, the findings stressed the point of non-attendance and absenteeism when defining or explaining truancy (i.e. Claes, Hooghe, and Reeskens 2009; Darmody, Smyth, and McCoy 2008; Dube and Orpinas 2009; Epstein and Sheldon 2002; Fantuzzo, Grim, and Hazan 2005; Gastic 2008; Gleeson 1992; Goldberg 1999; Kearney 2008; Lawrence et al. 2011; Lehr, Sinclair, and Christenson 2004; McIntyre-Bhatty 2008; Newsome et al. 2008; Pritchard and Williams 2001; Reid 2003b, 2004; Rhodes et al. 2010; Ventura and Miller 2005). These authors used the word absent, absenteeism or non-attendance in their definitions or explanations.

The review of the literature, using the database above, suggests that there already existed one comprehensive definition. This definition used currently by various truancy reduction programmes was coined by the Office of Juvenile Justice and Delinquency Prevention (OJJDP). It defined truancy as a person "who misses 20% or more of school days within a six week period" (1996, 1). This definition was not found to be used in territories other than the USA.

Other singular definitions include Wilson et al. (2008) who identified truancy as an absence, of which pupils themselves indicated would be unacceptable to teachers. Another definition defined truancy as students distancing themselves from school and issues related to rates of daily student attendance (Epstein and Sheldon 2002). Hendricks et al. (2010) looked at truancy in terms of the percentage of hours students spent in school per semester. Other organisations like the Boston Urban Youth Foundation in the USA[3] define truancy as lateness to class and excused *absences* for long periods – i.e. not showing up to class for more than three days (Rodríguez and Conchas 2009). In contrast to how the Boston Urban Youth Foundation determined truancy and habitual lateness, an Early Truancy Intervention study conducted in a southern school district in the USA, classified students as truants if they were absent for 15 or more times (Lawrence et al. 2011). The instances and examples mentioned above are illustrations from the literature that there is no single or common standard operational definition for determining what constitutes truancy or classification of truancy (Attwood and Croll 2006).

Berg (1997) presents another dimension of school absenteeism known or referred to as school refusal. The criteria for determining school refusal are when a child:

(1) Seeks the comfort and security of home, preferring to remain close to parental figures, especially during school hours;
(2) Displays evidence of emotional upset when faced with the prospect of having to attend school, although this may only take the form of unexplained physical symptoms; and
(3) Manifests no severe antisocial tendencies, apart from possible aggressiveness, when attempts are made, to force school attendance; and
(4) Does not attempt to conceal the problem from parents (Berg 1997, 90).

Unlike typical truancy, school refusal cannot be said to be more peculiar to people of any one particular social class or status (Reid 2014). Additionally, it does not have any direct relationship with a student's capacity or ability for learning. It is however more likely to occur as children grow and move from the primary or elementary level of school to higher levels (Berg 1997). According to Kearney (2006, 2007), school refusal represents the overarching concept of school avoiding behaviours which include truancy. Common themes from the literature also indicate that, in the USA, the definitions tended to be influenced by the school's view of the problem as unacceptable behaviour compared to students' perspectives as distancing from the school environment (Reid 2014) (See Table 1). This discovery may suggest to us that as we aim to coin a unified definition in the long-term, beyond the scope of this manuscript, we may have to speak to the view of the school and the view of the student. Truancy is part of that collective. It is necessary to note that school absence and truancy are not entirely the same. In essence not every unexcused absence should be labelled truancy (Darmody, Smyth, and McCoy 2008; Gleeson 1992). Some school policies (such as those pertaining to holidays) may set the stage or result in instances of unexcused absences (Darmody, Smyth, and McCoy 2008).

Different definitions of truancy in other territories

Truancy is a global phenomenon. School non-attendance is a subject that has attracted a lot of interest both locally and internationally. It is a subject on which much research continues to be conducted; as well as, a phenomenon that is very complex. Part of this complexity becomes evident in the lack of a common universal definition (Claes, Hooghe, and Reeskens 2009; Lawrence et al. 2011). Yet, it is widely acknowledged as a problem (Mounteney, Haugland, and Skutle 2010; Pathammavong et al. 2011). In fact, what has created a lot of challenges in researching the topic and problem of truancy is the usage of many informal terminologies to classify, categorise, report and respond to truancy. With no data-set being the same, any comparison study on truancy is suspect and automatically flawed. Attempts to curb the problem have been futile. Failure to do so is an injustice to students everywhere. The operational definitions found for truancy in other territories are only a small indication that the problem is not US based but world-wide.

Reid (2005, 2010, 2014) has multiple definitions of truancy, types and categories in describing the phenomena of truancy and labels absences as unacceptable by teachers and local education authorities. Similarly, Lawrence and colleagues (2011) identified some informal terms and slangs for truancy in six countries across the world. For example, in Australia, it may be commonly referred to as either *wagging* or *bludging;* in South Africa, *bunking* or *jippo*; in Ireland and the UK it is referred to as *mitching*; in India, *skipping*; in England as *twagging,* and in the USA as either *sloughing, ditching* or *hooky*. It must also be noted that other slang terms may exist, yet they may not have been documented. Lack of documentation of terms used is a growing concern in other territories.

The most comprehensive study found was by Claes and colleagues (2009). They conducted a 28 nation comparative study. Claes, Hooghe, and Reeskens (2009) presented truancy as absence without authorisation. Though these researchers claim a

Table 1. Studies in the USA.

Category	Author(s) and year	Definition(s) and conception(s) of truancy
School perspectives: unacceptable behaviour	Barry, Chaney, and Chaney (2011), Henry (2007, 2010), McNeal Jr. (1999)	• Skipping or cutting school/ classes • Intentional absence from school; intentionally leaving school early, or intentionally missing classes • School non-attendance
	DeSocio et al. (2007), Fantuzzo, Grim, and Hazan (2005), Lehr, Sinclair, and Christenson (2004), McCray (2006), Newsome et al. (2008), Rhodes et al. (2010), Sinha (2007)	• Unexcused absences from school or classes • Unexcused absences from school; chronic unexcused • School absenteeism • Staying away without permission • Unexcused absence from school; absenteeism • Chronic absenteeism; any unexcused absence including missing specific classes • Unexcused absence of students from school
	Gastic (2008), Henry, Thornberry and Huizinga (2009), Henry and Thornberry (2010), Rhodes and Reiss (1969), Ventura and Miller (2005), Zhang et al. (2007, 2010)	• Unexcused absences from school for the entire day or a particular extracurricular activity • The study also discussed thoughts of intentionally missing school as playing a role in truancy • Skipping school without a valid excuse • Physical withdrawal from school and labelled it as active avoidance • Absenteeism from school • Habitual engagement in unexcused absences from school
	Dube and Orpinas (2009)	• Absent without knowledge of parents; excessive absenteeism
	Kearney (2006, 2007, 2008)	• Part of a collective of school avoiding behaviours considered to be problematic. Manifestations of such behaviour include anxiety while in school, skipping

(*Continued*)

Table 1. (*Continued*).

Category	Author(s) and year	Definition(s) and conception(s) of truancy
		some classes and not attending school • School refusal behaviour is the overarching concept of such behaviour • Illegal, unexcused absence from school; absenteeism without parents knowledge; excessive absenteeism marked by child anxiety as well absence from school correlated with deviant behaviour and academic problems, family-related problems and socio-economic disadvantage
Student perspective: distance from school	Epstein and Sheldon (2002)	• Focuses on students distancing themselves from school; and issues related to rates of daily student attendance
	Fallis and Opotow (2003), Hallfors et al. (2002), Walls and ERIC Clearinghouse on Urban Education (2003)	• Class cutting • Presents it as a deliberate act in an effort to avoid certain people or courses • Makes an important observation that "cutting is the slow-motion process of dropping out made class-by-class and day-by-day in students' daily lives" (104) • Skipping school; cutting classes • Truancy is an indicator of low school attachment • Always late to class; not showing up to class for more than 3 days

common definition was used in the study, they also referenced countries in their study such as Great Britain that has no clear statutory definition of truancy (Davies and Lee 2006). Practices such as going on holidays or shopping trips and visiting relatives when school is in session may count as truancy. Consequentially, Claes, Hooghe, and Reeskens (2009) note that definitions of truancy are contextual and may vary from one setting to another as determined by the existing rules in a country or state. Mounteney, Haugland, and Skutle (2010) equally point out the impact of local and international laws in determining truancy; yet their study of truancy in

Table 2. Some operational definitions in other territories.

	Author(s) and year	Country	Definition(s) and conception(s) of truancy
Comparison study	Claes, Hooghe, and Reeskens (2009)	28 nation comparative study: Australia, Belgium, Bulgaria, Chile, Colombia, Cyprus, Czech Republic, Denmark, Estonia, Finland, Germany, Greece, Hong Kong, Hungary, Italy, Latvia, Lithuania, Norway, Poland, Portugal, Romania, Russia, Slovak Republic, Slovenia, Sweden, Switzerland, the UK, the USA	• Any unexcused or undocumented absence from school. Definitions are contextual and may be determined by the existing rules in a country or state • Forms of truancy: encompasses pupils that arrive late in a systematic manner and those who do not arrive at school at all
One nation study	Darmody, Smyth, and McCoy (2008)	Republic of Ireland	• Unauthorised and illegitimate absences; intentional absence from specific classes; chronic absenteeism • School absence and truancy are not entirely the same -not every unexcused absence should be labelled truancy. Some school policies (such as those pertaining to holidays) may set the stage or result in instances of unexcused absences
	Attwood and Croll (2006), Davies and Lee (2006), Gleeson (1992), McIntyre-Bhatty (2008), Reid (2003a, 2003b, 2004, 2005, 2006, 2008, 2010), Southwell (2006), Wardhaugh (1990), Wilson et al. (2008)	The UK	• Unauthorised absenteeism from school. Absence from specific classes • Typologies of truancy: "blanket truancy", (children not turning up at school) and "post-registration truancy" (pupils missing particular lessons) • Total or partial avoidance of school • No statutory definition of truancy; however, practices such as going on

(*Continued*)

Table 2. (Continued).

Author(s) and year	Country	Definition(s) and conception(s) of truancy
		holidays or shopping trips and visiting relatives when school is in session may count as truancy
		• School non-attendance; also discusses truancy as a form of social exclusion; further notes that school absenteeism does not necessarily constitute truancy
		• Interesting quote, "In other words compulsory education and school non-attendance constitute two faces of the same coin: it would be inconceivable to imagine otherwise where education for all is required by law" (Gleeson 1992, 438)
		• Intentional absence from school; A form of absenteeism
		• A form of self-exclusion for girls (Osler et al. 2002, as cited in Reid 2003b)
		• A persistent school absentee
		• Much truancy and other forms of non-attendance are caused by schools themselves
		• Deliberately missing school without good cause
		• Absence without a valid or legitimate reason is considered truancy
		• Absent from school, including absent from a particular class, with or without the parents knowledge

(*Continued*)

Table 2. (Continued).

Author(s) and year	Country	Definition(s) and conception(s) of truancy
		• An illegal absence without parental consent or knowledge • Unauthorised absences; school non-attendance • Absences which pupils themselves indicated would be unacceptable to teachers (3)
Goldberg (1999)	Cambodia	• Unexcused absences – "staying out of school without obtaining permission; going to school, then leaving without obtaining permission before the day is over" (3) • The article further looks at unexcused absences, as lack of a written note from a parent or teacher or some official document from a doctor explaining a student's absence
Pathammavong et al. (2011)	Canada	• Skipping class; missing entire days of school without parental consent
Mounteney, Haugland, and Skutle (2010)	Norway	• Being absent from school without permission, taking into the account the local and national rules and regulations

Norway revealed the phenomenon is generally similar to what has been presented in places such as the USA and Britain. Pathammavong and colleagues (2011) in their Canada study presented similar notions. For example, Mounteney and colleagues (2010) and Pathammavong and colleagues (2011) mentioned skipping class as indicative of truancy.

In Cambodia, truancy can generally be referred to as unexcused absences (Goldberg 1999). Furthermore, absences are considered to be unexcused, if there is no written note from a parent or teacher or some official document from a doctor explaining a student's absence (Goldberg 1999). See Table 2 for operational definition in other territories.

Sub-categories of truancy in the US and other territories

Beyond the operational definitions of truancy several scholars called for distinctions among student absences and non-attendance, noting that absences could be either authorised or unauthorised – i.e. unexcused absences (Attwood and Croll 2006; Hartnett 2007; O'Keefe and Stoll 1994). Maynard and colleagues (2012) refer to the need of such distinctions in interventions too. For instance, Walls and ERIC Clearinghouse on Urban Education (2003) presents two types, those who cut or miss class, and those who miss full days. Claes, Hooghe, and Reeskens (2009) likewise point out typologies of truancy framed differently from O'Keefe and Stoll's (1994). According to Claes, Hooghe, and Reeskens (2009), truanting students may be categorised as those "pupils that arrive late in a systematic manner" and those who do not come at all (124). Hendricks et al. (2010) identified three levels of truancy – severe (students with less than 79% of hours present during the baseline semester), moderate (79–87% hours present) and mild (88–90% hours present).

Reid's 1985 work also offers four categories of truancy which captures different patterns and characteristics of non-attendance. In what he termed "categories of persistent absence", the four categories were: traditional or typical absentee, institutional absentee, psychological absentee and the generic absentee (48). The traditional or typical absentees are usually from unsupportive backgrounds with unfavourable and troubling social circumstances. They are likely to have issues related to low self-concept such as low self-esteem and feelings of inadequacy. The institutional absentee, unlike the traditional or typical absentee, may not have any self-concept-related problems. Their backgrounds may play into the reason for their truancy but institutional absentees generally miss school for educational reasons. They may avoid particular lessons or classes or school days. In some cases, they may miss class periods but still remain on the school premises. The psychological absentee avoids school for psychologically based reasons or a general fear of school. This may be as a result of factors such as physical disabilities that put them at a disadvantage as well as encounters with bullies. The generic absentee is one who misses school for any of the aforementioned reasons. These categories by Reid (1985) reflect some of the earliest attempts at delineating the peculiar characteristics of truants and the nature of student absence. They are, however, broad.

Other scholars have mentioned forms of persistent absence or truancy which may previously have been subsumed under Reid's (1985) categories. O'Keefe and Stoll (1994) conducted a study investigating the causes and the scale truancy problems among pupils in years 10 and 11, covering 150 schools and a total number of

37,683 pupils. In their study, truancy was divided into two broad forms namely post-registration truancy (PRT) and blanket truancy (BT). They defined BT as "unjustified absence from school of pupils who have not registered in school" (O'Keefe and Stoll 1994, 29). PRT basically entails absence from lessons after registration. O'Keefe and Stoll (1994), further dichotomised PRT into offsite and onsite truancy to differentiate between cases where students leave the school premises and cases where they still remain in school even though they do not go to class. Looking at the description for PRT, and its two forms, the point can be made that it was previously subsumed under Reid's (1985) category of the institutional absentee. Reid (2005, 2010) further elaborates on PRT by stating that a student may still be on the school premises and yet not attends classes and when such students do attend class, whether coerced or compelled, they may be physically present, but mentally absent, thereby furthering the achievement gap in education.

In explaining the patterns and trends of truancy, some scholars mention the intentionality behind students' avoidance of particular lessons and leaving school early. In other words, students deliberately skip school or cut classes (Barry, Chaney, and Chaney 2011; Darmody, Smyth, and McCoy 2008; DeSocio et al. 2007; Fallis and Opotow 2003; Hallfors et al. 2002; Henry 2007, 2010; Kearney 2006, 2007; Reid 2003a, 2003b; Spencer 2009). Others mention persistent absence from school (Darmody, Smyth, and McCoy 2008; Dube and Orpinas 2009; McIntyre-Bhatty 2008; Rhodes et al. 2010), which reveals why truancy and chronic absenteeism are often used interchangeably (Lawrence et al. 2011; Lehr, Sinclair, and Christenson 2004; McCray 2006).

Also, what may sometimes be noted as other forms of truancy and absenteeism such as specific lesson absence, parentally condoned absence, near truancy (psychological absence), school refusal and school phobia (Reid 1999, 2005, 2010, 2014) are in some cases reiterations or the further breaking down of previously noted forms. The motive for skipping school or cutting classes may sometimes be a deliberate act not just to avoid certain courses or lessons but certain people as well (Fallis and Opotow 2003), such as a particular teacher or a classmate. Beyond normal school hours and conventional academic activities, students can also be considered truants for unexcused absences or deliberately avoiding particular extracurricular activities (Gastic 2008) or failure to comply with policy. In fact, in some school districts in the USA (such as the North Thurston, Mead, Seattle and Spokane School Districts in the state of Washington), the attendance policy requires students to submit a note signed by a parent or guardian confirming their absence from school. Students 18 years of age are exempt from this requirement (Hartnett 2007). Hartnett (2007) reveals how elaborate some of the policies regarding attendance can be; a case in point is that of the state of Washington. In situations of repeated illness, a note may be required from a doctor. When absenteeism continues for 20 days in succession, a student may lose his or her place in school, which means the school will cut them off. Hartnett (2007) also identifies some of the limitations of the policy. For instance, the policy does not give consideration to students whose absence may be necessitated by a need to help at home. Again, consideration is not given to those whose absence may be occasioned by their parents' inability to take them to school. Congruously, in the state of Wisconsin, accumulating five or more illegal absences in a semester is considered habitual truancy (Henry, Thornberry, and Huizinga 2009). Illegal absences thus refer to absences that are not endorsed by the school or a student's parents. Some of these concerns also occur in other territories.

Results from the online focus group and in-person sessions

To ground the synthesis of the literature, it was important to speak with persons who were currently working in the field of truancy. Two focus groups were conducted. A summary of the focus group concerns was generated from an in-person and online focus group.

In general, truancy was a concern for all persons in the focus groups. More specifically, in the review of the transcripts from the online focus group and notes from the in-person focus group to generate a common definition, there were four concerns. These included the need for a uniform definition as there are various definitions from state to state and country to country. Second, they noted that most definitions and laws lacked properties to respond to children who do not live with their parents or who were not enrolled at all. The third concern was the discussion that most definitions did not differentiate between excused and excusable absences. Lastly, they noted that definitions currently do not attempt to respond to the missed opportunities for learning. Despite some observations highlighted below, both groups lamented on concerns for the need of a definition but that it was complex. However, after the hour and a half long discussion in the face-to-face group, they determined that the definition needed to be broad, include who is responsible, and the number of days. In addition, some members and one in particular wanted to use the word student instead of child. She writes "Works for me. I would just replace child with student so it fits all grade levels. I know how folks in upper grades don't like being thought of as children."

The participants noted that no definition was conclusive but that it would be a start to allow for persons around the world to have a common definition on which to hang their hat and inform their special context. They lauded the idea that some places viewed truancy as illegal when in fact the child, often truant, is in fact underage and under the care of his or her parents. Concerns like these, they stated, should be responded to using policy and revised legislation. In attacking legislation, the age of the truant child must also be re-established so that a person will know who is included and not included when they mention a truant child.

In general, the definitions shared were very different and many thought other aspects should be included in their own respective state definitions. One respondent suggested that it goes beyond just the truancy definition but the words excused and unexcused should be included.

> Here's the problem I have with using the word "excused" or "excusable" in the definition of truancy: parents will always argue that any time they produce a note with a reason for their student's absence it is/should be excused. We must, therefore, further define what we mean by "excused" or "excusable" in order to more clearly and comprehensively define truancy. (Person 5)

Because of it being a status offence and vary by state, person 8, a local District Attorney wrote

> for now, in terms of excusable and inexcusable, we need to look towards our own State laws to guide us on that. Maybe that segment should be included [in our uniform definition is] legitimately excused per State law, city ordinance.

In addition, person 7 went on to say

> I would also add that the word "truant" itself tends to have a connotation referring to kids that are "delinquent." In our schools, officials have a hard time with calling elementary age students "truants". This is why we went toward nonattendance.

Another concern was that of having a uniform definition. Many spoke out about it being important and two respondents shared that "it would be remarkable if we could come to a consensus as an organisation. We all agree that the definition of truancy is very important" (Persons 1 and 4). Spotlighting a very different concern that results from this discussion was what person 3 wrote "there also is the issue of those students that never enrol. Technically they aren't absent because of non-enrollment". However, the concern of not having a dropout age was also a concern for some (Persons 1, 2 and 4).

Lastly, another concern was that even if a uniform definition could not be found, there should be some agreement on the compulsory age for education and the persons who hold responsibility. In regard to the concern of responsibility, Person 2 remarked that

> what I don't understand in our district is that you can "drop out" without parental permission. But then we have kids who want to come back to school who let's say parents can't get off work, or even worse, don't care, the student can't re-enrol without a parent.

The concept of having a uniform definition is touted as being important by several respondents. For instance, Person 4 said "as an international organisation, we may need to ensure that the age is the same from state to state." Person 8 emphasised school age as being important in her definition, "truancy is the act of a school aged student being ..." In addition, person 5 added that the

> Texas statutes actually address students who are of compulsory attendance age but not enrolled in school and who are known to live within district boundaries. The problem with those students is that we rarely become aware of them unless a neighbour or concerned citizen reports them for being outside during the school day. In our district, our attendance administrators make a home visit and are generally told the student is being home schooled. In Texas, we then have no further educational jurisdiction over the student.

These are the concerns that do not clearly identify responsibility and response. On average, the participants included persons who had education levels of no less than a bachelor's degree and no more than a doctoral degree. They ranged from judges, social workers, truancy experts, researchers, pupil attendance officers, supervisors, executive directors, teachers, community outreach coordinators and teen court coordinators.

Discussion

From literature

There is a need for a common definition. Challenges in comparative assessments have been flawed with the absence of a consistently used definition of truancy. Maynard et al. (2012) in their systemic study of interventions found that the numerous gaps and deficiencies in the literature must change and doing the same thing expecting different results is simply not enough. Clear in this review is that much of the same continues and we were far from having a common definition. The OJJDP definition came closest but lacked some aspects. For instance, though this definition could potentially have students missing much more than 10 days over a school year, it can encourage principals to have an earlier identification and intervention point with truants. Thus, we need to incorporate some way of not just collecting and storing data on absences, but also various categories and typesets, like those presented herein, with no intention of purposely labelling students, but to effectively respond to the variations in truancy. As the definition is revised and standardised, the tracking methods would be improved. Today many schools use attendance registers held by teachers; however, this option of tracking is often flawed, despite its convenience and cost-effectiveness. Students often leave the school system and are dropped from registers with little to no verification of their whereabouts (Montecel, Cortez, and Cortez 2004). For instance, the review of the literature noted that there can be lesson-absence, post-registration and parental-condoned truancy types (Reid 1999, 2005, 2014). The OJJDP found that there were four correlates of truancy: the family situation, school performance, economic indicators and individual student variables (Baker, Sigmon, and Nugent 2001). In addition, awareness of various categories of truants, such as traditional, psychological, institutional, recreational and lifestyle can help us develop programme-specific responses for truants (Bonikowske 1987; Reid 1999). This latter portion also presents a concern about the many informal ways of referring and discussing truancy thereby impacting the study of the area comprehensively. In addition, it must be noted that school non-attendance and truancy may further be compounded by the immigration status of families, and adherence to religious conventions among other things. These are factors that may require further exploration. We [researchers and authors of this article] agree there are some legal aspects but it has now spanned the scope of a societal problem and not just one for the truant officers, case workers and the courts.

In some cases, there were differences between absences and non-attendance but very little on the differentiation between excused and excusable absences. This seemed to vary when we categorised by student perspectives and the school's view of truancy. This was cloudy even more when the many informal terminologies were infused. As a result, it would be fair to say that because the search terms were limited to the formal terminology a lot of data were not included because informal terms were not known and hence absent from the search. More work and collaborative approaches are needed to respond to defining and tracking truancy so that our report is effective in scope.

From focus group

The organisation used for the study, IATDP, provided a platform to reach persons around the world. However, there were immediate limitations. First and foremost, not many international persons were present at the conference that year. Secondly, most participants spoke from their vantage point, considering only their units. This further excluded international contexts. The most notable concern was that this was the first forum of its kind known to the authors. As a result, many of the participants valued participating and sharing their viewpoints, but also had other concerns they wanted to address. Thus, the forum was unable to respond to all the concerns and forum needs. For instance, someone posted that

> I am so excited to see and know that the Open Forum dialogue continues. The defini-
> tion of truancy is very important. However, I would also like a national "drop out
> age". As an International organisation, we may need to ensure that the age is the same
> from state to state. Please share your thoughts!

As this was out of the scope of the work, the concern was not addressed. Another
respondent shared

> My thoughts are; I agree it would be remarkable if we could come to a consensus as
> an organisation. We all agree that the definition of truancy is very important. I think a
> national "Drop out age" would be tremendous! I think we may want to remember the
> reason for trying not being so specific is because of the various definitions from state
> to state. Thanks so much for all of your help to get us were we want to be.

The final definition the group crafted was "Truancy is a student's act of non-attendance evidenced by missing part or all of the school day without it being legitimately excused by school or per state law." Consequentially, given the complexity
of truancy as a phenomenon, some aspects were absent from this definition. It was
reworked by the authors to read … Truancy is a non-home school student's act of
non-attendance evidenced by missing part or all of the school day without it being
authorised by medical practitioner or sanctioned by parent(s) and/or legitimately
excused by school or per state law. The aspects emphasised were to characterise that
it does not include children who were home-schooled, that it was the act and not the
person, the differentiation between part and whole days, making sure to remove
excused and excusable absences such as those characterised by a doctor's note or
those with parent or school permission and state law. Of course, this is the first itera-
tion and needs much refining using a collaborative approach.

Conclusion

The authors of this article know there are flaws in every definition and by no means
are we requesting that this be the specific definition endorsed. As researchers, however, someone or some entity needs to take charge rather quickly to coin a definition
of truancy. The outcome can be the development and use of consistent benchmarks
for systematic measurement and comparison nationally. Yes, this is only but one
attempt to find a way to effectively measure and track truancy and there are other
forms of school refusals. Berg (1997) points out that school absenteeism known or
referred to as school refusal is more likely to occur as children grow and move from
the primary or elementary level of school to higher levels, and school refusal too is
likely to occur after some prolonged absence from school as a result of illness or
holidays. However, school refusal in general is not new and policy-makers, educators and administrators, social workers and researchers will continue to have ways
of capturing what it involves and by such extension difficulty defining it …

The effort was made to craft a common uniform definition for truancy; one that
seeks to be comprehensive in scope and simple in nature. It was hoped that this uniform definition or something similar, could be adopted by schools and data sources
to enable comparisons and data collection across states and school systems. Only
when such is in place, will policy-makers, educators and administrators, social workers and researchers be better able to address and curb this global phenomenon. It is
a social plight that is personally and socially counterproductive and debilitating to
the economy and our society. The work herein aimed to respond to an important

aspect of truancy and to synthesise the literature and find consensus on a definition of truancy. We agree that continued discussion and debate about truancy and how truancy is defined is important.

Acknowledgements

We thank the IATDP Executive and Membership for their support. Special editorial thanks to Eun Hye Yi, Sisters Mary Serra, Mary Rose, Liz, and Carol.

Notes

1. According to Mendel (2000), in reference to a study of the cost of dropping out and engaging in a life of delinquency and drugs, the total cost to the American tax payer is $470,000–$750,000 per child annually with a total lost, on average, ranging from $1.7 to $2.3 million annually.
2. The IATDP is a body comprising education workers, government officials and other stakeholders working jointly to address truancy and reduce student attrition. It has been in existence since 1911 (IATDP, n.d.). The group, IATDP was chosen because the primary author was invited to conduct a session on defining truancy at their 102nd conference.
3. The Boston Urban Youth Foundation is a community-based organisation with a focus on helping Black and Hispanic youth towards a more secure academic future (Rodríguez and Conchas 2009).

References

Attwood, G., and P. Croll. 2006. "Truancy in Secondary School Pupils: Prevalence, Trajectories and Pupil Perspectives." *Research Papers in Education* 21 (4): 467–484.

Bachman, J. G., S. Green, and I. D. Wirtanen. 1971. *Dropping out – Problem or Symptom. Youth in Transition*. Vol. III. Ann Arbor, MI: Institute for Social Research, University of Michigan.

Baker, M. L., J. N. Sigmon, and M. E. Nugent. 2001. *Truancy Reduction: Keeping Students in School*. Washington, DC: Office of Juvenile Justice and Delinquency Prevention.

Barry, A. E., B. Chaney, and J. Chaney. 2011. "The Impact of Truant and Alcohol-related Behavior on Educational Aspirations: A Study of Us High School Seniors." *Journal of School Health* 81 (8): 485–492.

Berg, I. 1997. "School Refusal and Truancy." *Archives of Disease in Childhood* 76 (2): 90–91.

Bonikowske, D. 1987. *Truancy: A Prelude to Dropping out*. Bloomington, IN: National Education Service.

Bryson, J. M. 2004. *Strategic Planning for Public and Non-profit Organizations: Guide to Strengthening and Sustaining Organizational Achievement*. 3rd ed. San Francisco, CA: Jossey-Bass.

Catalano, R. F., H. L. Berglaund, J. A. M. Ryan, H. S. Lonczak, and J. D. Hawkins. 1998. *Positive Youth Development in the United States: Research Findings on Evaluations of Positive Youth Development Programs*. Social Development Research Group: University of Washington. Accessed March 16, 2006. http://aspe.hhs.gov/hsp/PositiveYouthDev99/index.htm

Chambers, D. E. 2000. *Social Policy and Social Programs: A Method for the Practical Public Policy Analyst*. 3rd ed. Boston, MA: Allyn and Bacon.

Claes, E., M. Hooghe, and T. Reeskens. 2009. "Truancy as a Contextual and School-Related Problem: A Comparative Multilevel Analysis of Country and School Characteristics on Civic Knowledge among 14 Year Olds." *Educational Studies* 35 (2): 123–142.

Darmody, M., E. Smyth, and S. McCoy. 2008. "Acting up or Opting out? Truancy in Irish Secondary Schools." *Educational Review* 60 (4): 359–373.

Davies, J., and J. Lee. 2006. "To Attend or Not to Attend? Why Some Students Chose School and Others Reject It." *Support for Learning* 21 (4): 204–209.

DeSocio, J., M. VanCura, L. A. Nelson, G. Hewitt, H. Kitzman, and R. Cole. 2007. "Engaging Truant Adolescents: Results from a Multifaceted Intervention Pilot." *Preventing School Failure* 51 (3): 3–9.

Dube, S. R., and P. Orpinas. 2009. "Understanding Excessive School Absenteeism as School Refusal Behavior." *Children & Schools* 31 (2): 87–95.

Epstein, J. L., and S. B. Sheldon. 2002. "Present and Accounted for: Improving Student Attendance through Family and Community Involvement." *The Journal of Educational Research* 95 (5): 308–318.

Fallis, R., and S. Opotow. 2003. "Are Students failing School or Are Schools failing Students? Class Cutting in High School." *Journal of Social Issues* 59 (1): 103–119.

Fantuzzo, J., S. Grim, and H. Hazan. 2005. "Project Start: An Evaluation of a Community-wide School-based Intervention to Reduce Truancy." *Psychology in the Schools* 42 (6): 657–667.

Garry, E. M. 1996. *Truancy: First Step to a Lifetime of Problems*. Washington, DC: US Department of Justice: Office of Juvenile Justice and Delinquency Prevention.

Gastic, B. 2008. "School Truancy and the Disciplinary Problems of Bullying Victims." *Educational Review* 60 (4): 391–404.

Gentle-Genitty, C. 2009. *Tracking More than Absences: Impact of Schools' Social Bonding on Chronic Truancy.* Saarbrücken, Germany: Lambert Academic Publishing.

Gleeson, D. 1992. "School Attendance and Truancy: A Socio-historical Account." *Sociological Review* 40 (3): 437–490.

Goldberg, M. E. 1999. "Truancy and Dropout among Cambodian Students: Results from a Comprehensive High School." *Social Work in Education* 21 (1): 49–63.

Hallfors, D., J. L. Vevea, B. Iritani, H. Cho, S. Khatapoush, and L. Saxe. 2002. "Truancy, Grade Point Average, and Sexual Activity: A Meta-analysis of Risk Indicators for Youth Substance Use." *Journal of School Health* 72 (5): 205–211.

Hartnett, S. 2007. "Does Peer Group Identity Influence Absenteeism in High School Students?" *High School Journal* 91 (2): 35–44.

Hendricks, M. A., E. W. Sale, C. J. Evans, L. McKinley, and S. DeLozier Carter. 2010. "Evaluation of a Truancy Court Intervention in Four Middle Schools." *Psychology in the Schools* 47 (2): 173–183.

Henry, K. L. 2007. "Who's Skipping School: Characteristics of Truants in 8th and 10th Grade." *Journal of School Health* 77 (1): 29–35.

Henry, K. 2010. "Skipping School and Using Drugs: A Brief Report." *Drugs: Education, Prevention & Policy* 17 (5): 650–657.

Henry, K. L., and T. P. Thornberry. 2010. "Truancy and Escalation of Substance Use during Adolescence." *Journal of Studies on Alcohol & Drugs* 71 (1): 115–124.

Henry, K. L., T. P. Thornberry, and D. H. Huizinga. 2009. "A Discrete-time Survival Analysis of the Relationship between Truancy and the Onset of Marijuana Use." *Journal of Studies on Alcohol & Drugs* 70 (1): 5–15.

International Association of Truancy and Dropout Prevention (IATDP). n.d. "Mission Statement and Goal." http://www.iatdp.org/mission.php.

Joftus, S., and B. Maddox-Dolan. 2003. *Left out and Left behind: NCLB and the American High School.* Washington, DC: Alliance for Excellence in Education.

Katz, M. S. 1976. *A History of Compulsory Education Laws. Fastback Series, No. 75. Bicentennial Series.* http://files.eric.ed.gov.ezproxy.lib.utah.edu/fulltext/ED119389.pdf.

Kearney, C. A. 2006. "Dealing with School Refusal Behavior: A Primer for Family Physicians." *Journal of Family Practice* 55 (8): 685–692.

Kearney, C. A. 2007. "Forms and Functions of School Refusal Behavior in Youth: An Empirical Analysis of Absenteeism Severity." *Journal of Child Psychology and Psychiatry* 48 (1): 53–61.

Kearney, C. 2008. "An Interdisciplinary Model of School Absenteeism in Youth to Inform Professional Practice and Public Policy." *Educational Psychology Review* 20 (3): 257–282.

Lawrence, S. A., W. Lawther, V. Jennison, and P. Hightower. 2011. "An Evaluation of the Early Truancy Intervention (ETI) Program." *School Social Work Journal* 35 (2): 57–71.

Lehr, C. A., M. F. Sinclair, and S. L. Christenson. 2004. "Addressing Student Engagement and Truancy Prevention during the Elementary School Years: A Replication Study of the Check & Connect Model." *Journal of Education for Students Placed at Risk* 9 (3): 279–301.

Levin, H. M. 1972. *The Costs to the Nation of Inadequate Education. in Select Committee on Equal Educational Opportunity United States Senate. the Effects of Dropping out.* Washington, DC: U.S. Government Printing Office.

Maynard, B. R., K. T. McCrea, T. Pigott, and M. S. Kelly. 2012. "Indicated Truancy Interventions: Effects on School Attendance among Chronic Truant Students." *Campbell Systemic Reviews* 10, doi:10.4073/csr.2012.10.

Maynard, B. R., C. P. Salas-Wright, M. G. Vaughn, and K. E. Peters. 2012. "Who are Truant Youth? Examining Distinctive Profiles of Truant Youth Using Latent Profile Analysis." *Journal of Youth and Adolescence* 41 (12): 1671–1684.

McCluskey, C., T. S. Bynum, and J. W. Patchin. 2004. "Reducing Chronic Absenteeism: An Assessment of an Early Truancy Initiative." *Crime & Delinquency* 50 (2): 214–234.

McCray, E. D. 2006. "It's 10 a.m.: Do You Know Where Your Children Are?" *Intervention in School & Clinic* 42 (1): 30–33.

McDonald Brown, C., and K. A. Birrane. 1994. "What's Happening to Our Children?" *Maryland Journal* 27 (3): 35–39.

McIntyre-Bhatty, K. 2008. "Truancy and Coercive Consent: Is There an Alternative?" *Educational Review* 60 (4): 375–390.

McNeal Jr, R. B. 1999. "Parental Involvement as Social Capital: Differential Effectiveness on Science Achievement, Truancy, and Dropping out." *Social Forces* 78 (1): 117–145.

Mendel, R. A. 2000. *Less Hype, More Help: Reducing Juvenile Crime, What Works – What Doesn't*. Washington, DC: American Youth Policy Forum.

Montecel, M. R., J. D. Cortez, and A. Cortez. 2004. "Dropout-prevention Programs: Right Intent, Wrong Focus, and Some Suggestions on Where to Go from Here." *Education and Urban Society* 36 (2): 169–188.

Mounteney, J. J., S. S. Haugland, and A. A. Skutle. 2010. "Truancy, Alcohol Use and Alcohol-related Problems in Secondary School Pupils in Norway." *Health Education Research* 25 (6): 945–954.

Newsome, W., D. Anderson-Butcher, J. Fink, L. Hall, and J. Huffer. 2008. "The Impact of School Social Work Services on Student Absenteeism and Risk Factors Related to School Truancy." *School Social Work Journal* 32 (2): 21–38.

Office of Juvenile Justice and Delinquency Prevention and Office of Elementary and Secondary Education. 1996. *Truancy: Creating Safe and Drug-Free Schools: An Action Guide*. Washington, DC: US Department of Justice and US Department of Education.

O'Keefe, D., and P. Stoll. 1994. *Truancy in English Secondary Schools: A Report Prepared for the DFE*. London: DfEE.

Osler, A., C. Street, M. Lall, and K. Vincent. 2002. *Not a Problem? Girls and Social Exclusion*. London: National Children's Bureau.

Pathammavong, R., S. T. Leatherdale, R. Ahmed, J. Griffith, J. Nowatzki, and S. Manske. 2011. "Examining the Link between Education Related Outcomes and Student Health Risk Behaviours among Canadian Youth: Data from the 2006 National Youth Smoking Survey." *Canadian Journal of Education* 34 (1): 215–247.

Pritchard, C., and R. Williams. 2001. "A Three-year Comparative Longitudinal Study of a School-based Social Work Family Service to Reduce Truancy, Delinquency and School Exclusions." *Journal of Social Welfare & Family Law* 23 (1): 23–43.

Reid, K. 1985. *Truancy and School Absenteeism*. London: Hodder and Stoughton.

Reid, K. 1999. *Truancy and Schools*. New York: Routledge.

Reid, K. 2003a. "A Strategic Approach to Tackling School Absenteeism and Truancy: The PSCC Scheme." *Educational Studies* 29 (4): 351–371.

Reid, K. 2003b. "Strategic Approaches to Tackling School Absenteeism and Truancy: The Traffic Lights (TL) Scheme." *Educational Review* 55 (3): 305–321.

Reid, K. 2004. "A Long-term Strategic Approach to Tackling Truancy and Absenteeism from Schools: The SSTG Scheme." *British Journal of Guidance & Counselling* 32 (1): 57–74.

Reid, K. 2005. "The Causes, Views and Traits of School Absenteeism and Truancy." *Research in Education* 74: 59–82.

Reid, K. 2006. "The Views of Education Social Workers on the Management of Truancy and Other Forms of Non-attendance." *Research in Education* 75: 40–96.

Reid, K. 2008. "The Causes of Non-attendance: An Empirical Study." *Educational Review* 60 (4): 345–357.

Reid, K. 2010. "Finding Strategic Solutions to Reduce Truancy." *Research in Education* 84: 1–18.

Reid, K. 2014. *Managing School Attendance: Successful Intervention Strategies for Reducing Truancy*. Oxon: Routledge.

Reimer, M. S., and K. Dimock. 2005. *Truancy Prevention in Action: Best Practices and Model Truancy Programs*. Clemson, SC: Clemson University National Dropout Prevention Center/Network.

Rhodes, A. L., and A. J. Reiss Jr. 1969. "Apathy, Truancy and Delinquency as Adaptations to School Failure." *Social Forces* 48 (1): 12–22.

Rhodes, J. F., J. M. Thomas, C. M. Lemieux, D. S. Cain, and C. C. Guin. 2010. "Truancy Assessment and Service Centers (TASC): Engaging Elementary School Children and Their Families." *School Social Work Journal* 35 (1): 83–100.

Rodríguez, L. F., and G. Q. Conchas. 2009. "Preventing Truancy and Dropout among Urban Middle School Youth: Understanding Community-based Action from the Student's Perspective." *Education & Urban Society* 41 (2): 216–247.

Sinha, J. 2007. "Youth at Risk for Truancy Detour into a Faith-based Education Program: Their Perceptions of the Program and Its Impact." *Research on Social Work Practice* 17 (2): 246–257.

Southwell, N. 2006. "Truants on Truancy – A Badness or a Valuable Indicator of Unmet Special Educational Needs?" *British Journal of Special Education* 33 (2): 91–97.

Spencer, A. M. 2009. "School Attendance Patterns, Unmet Educational Needs, and Truancy: A Chronological Perspective." *Remedial & Special Education* 30 (5): 309–319.

Toby, J. 1957. "Social Disorganization and Stake in Conformity." *Journal of Crime Law & Criminology* 48: 12–17.

Ventura, H. E., and J. Miller. 2005. "Finding Hidden Value through Mixed-methodology: Lessons from the Discovery Program's Holistic Approach to Truancy Abatement." *American Journal of Criminal Justice* 30 (1): 99–120.

Walls, C., and ERIC Clearinghouse on Urban Education, N. Y. 2003. "New Approaches to Truancy Prevention in Urban Schools." *ERIC Digest.*

Wardhaugh, J. 1990. "Regulating Truancy: The Role of the Education Welfare Service." *Sociological Review* 38 (4): 735–764.

Wilson, J. Q., and G. C. Loury, eds. 1987. *Families, Schools, and Delinquency Prevention.* New York: Springer-Verlag.

Wilson, V., H. Malcolm, S. Edward, and J. Davidson. 2008. "'Bunking Off': The Impact of Truancy on Pupils and Teachers." *British Educational Research Journal* 34 (1): 1–17.

Zhang, D., A. Katsiyannis, D. E. Barrett, and V. Willson. 2007. "Truancy Offenders in the Juvenile Justice System: Examinations of First and Second Referrals." *Remedial and Special Education* 28 (4): 244–256.

Zhang, D., V. Willson, A. Katsiyannis, D. Barrett, J. Song, and W. Jiun-Yu. 2010. "Truancy Offenders in the Juvenile Justice System: A Multi-cohort Study." *Behavioral Disorders* 35 (3): 229–242.

Appendix 1. Definitions around the USA

State	Definition of Truancy	Definition of Habitual Truancy
Arizona	Truancies are unexcused absences for at least one class period during the school day (Ariz. Rev. Stat. § 15-803)	Habitually truant students are truant for at least five school days within a school year (Ariz. Rev. Stat. § 15-803)
California	Any pupil subject to compulsory full-time education or to compulsory continuation education who is absent from school without valid excuse three full days in one school year or tardy or absent for more than any 30-min period during the school day without a valid excuse on three occasions in one school year, or any combination thereof, is a truant and shall be reported to the attendance supervisor or to the superintendent of the school district (Cal. Educ. Code § 48,260) Any pupil who has once been reported as a truant and who is again absent from school without valid excuse one or more days, or tardy on one or more days, shall again be reported as a truant to the attendance supervisor or the superintendent of the district (Cal. Educ. Code § 48,261)	A student is deemed a habitual truant if the student has been reported as a truant three or more times in one school year. No student will be deemed an habitual truant unless an appropriate district officer or employee has made a conscientious effort to hold at least one conference with a parent or guardian of the pupil and the pupil himself, after the filing of either of the reports required by Cal. Educ. Code § 48,260 or Cal. Educ. Code § 48,261 (Cal. Educ. Code § 48,262)
Colorado		A student between seven and 16 years old having four unexcused absences from public school in any one month or 10 unexcused absences from public school during any school year is habitually truant. Absences due to suspension or expulsion are considered excused (Colo. Rev. Stat. § 22-33-107)
Connecticut	Truants are children age 5–18, enrolled in a public or private school with four unexcused absences from school in any month or 10 unexcused absences from school in any school year (Conn. Gen. Stat. § 10-198a)	Habitual truants are children age 5–18, enrolled in public or private schools, with 20 unexcused absences within a school year (Conn. Gen. Stat. § 10-200)
Delaware	Truant means a student who has been absent from school without valid excuse for more than three school days during a school year (Del. St. ti. 14, § 2721)	
Florida		A habitual truant is a student who has 15 unexcused absences within 90 calendar days with or without the knowledge or consent of the student's parent and is subject to compulsory

(Continued)

Appendix 1. (*Continued*).

State	Definition of Truancy	Definition of Habitual Truancy
Idaho		school attendance (FLA. REV. STAT. § 1003.01) An habitual truant is a student who – in the judgment of the board of trustees – has repeatedly violated the attendance regulations established by the board, or any child whose parents or guardians have failed or refused to cause the child to comply with the state's compulsory attendance law (IDAHO CODE § 33-206)
Illinois	A truant is a child subject to compulsory school attendance and who is absent without valid cause for a school day or portion thereof (ILL. REV. STAT. CH. 105, PARA. 5/262A)	A child subject to compulsory school attendance and who is absent without a valid excuse from school for 10% or more of the previous 180 regular attendance days is a chronic or habitual truant (ILL. REV. STAT. CH. 105, PARA. 5/262A)
Kentucky	Any student who has been absent from school without valid excuse for three or more days, or tardy without valid excuse on three or more days, is a truant. Being absent for less than half of a school day is regarded as being tardy (KY. REV. STAT. ANN. § 159.150)	Any child who has been reported as a truant two or more times is a habitual truant (KY. REV. STAT. ANN. § 159.150)
Louisiana		Any child who has been found by the juvenile court to have been reported as a truant two or more times during a one-year period is a habitual truant (KY. REV. STAT. ANN. § 600.020) Per annotations. "While "habitual truant" is defined differently in KY. REV. STAT. ANN. § 159.150 and KY. REV. STAT. ANN. § 600.020, the statutes may be reconciled in their application by district courts and pupil personnel directors." A student shall be considered habitually absent or habitually tardy after (1) all reasonable efforts by the principal and the teacher have failed to correct the condition after the fifth unexcused absence or fifth unexcused tardy within any month or (2) if a pattern of five absences a month is established (LA. REV. STAT. ANN. § 17:233)
Maine	A person required to attend school or alternative instruction under Maine's compulsory school attendance law is truant when an absence of a half day	A person is habitually truant if they are required to attend school or alternative instruction and have attained the equivalent of 10 full days

(Continued)

Appendix 1. (*Continued*).

State	Definition of Truancy	Definition of Habitual Truancy
	is not excused (ME. REV. STAT. ANN TIT. 20-A, 3272)	of unexcused absences or seven consecutive school days of unexcused absences during a school year (ME. REV. STAT. ANN TIT. 20-A, 3272)
Minnesota		An habitual truant is a child under the age of 16 years who is absent from school without lawful excuse for seven school days – if the child is in elementary school – or for one or more class periods on seven school days if the child is in middle, junior high or high school. A child who is 16 or 17 years of age who is absent from school without excuse for one or more class periods on seven school days and who has not lawfully withdrawn from school is an habitual truant (MINN. REV. STAT. § 260C.007)
Nevada	A pupil who has one or more unapproved absences from school is considered truant (NEV. REV. STAT. ANN. § 392. 130)	Any child who has been declared truant three or more times within one school year will be declared a habitual truant (NEV. REV. STAT. ANN. § 392.140)
New Mexico	Truant means a student who has accumulated five unexcused absences within any 20-day period (N.M. STAT. ANN § 22-12-9)	A student who has accumulated the equivalent of 10 or more unexcused absences within a school year is a habitual truant (N.M. STAT. ANN § 22-12-9)
Pennsylvania		Habitually truant means absence for more than three school days or its equivalent following the first notice of truancy given under PA. STAT. ANN. TIT. 24, § 13-1354 (PA. STAT. ANN. TIT. 24, § 13-1333)
Texas		A student commits an offence if he is required to attend school under Texas' compulsory school attendance law and fails to attend school on 10 or more days or parts of days within a six-month period in the same school year or on three or more days or parts of days within a four-week period (TEX. EDUC. CODE ANN. § 25.094)
Utah	Any school-age minor who is subject to the state's compulsory education law, and who is absent from school without a legitimate or valid excuse, is truant (UTAH CODE ANN. § 53A-11-101)	Any school-age minor who has received more than two truancy citations within one school year from the school in which they are or should be enrolled and eight absences without a legitimate or valid excuse or who, in defiance of efforts on the part of school authorities to resolve a

(*Continued*)

Appendix 1. (*Continued*).

State	Definition of Truancy	Definition of Habitual Truancy
		student's attendance problem, refuses to regularly attend school or any scheduled period of the school day is an habitual truant (UTAH CODE ANN. § 53A-11-101)
Wisconsin	Truancy means any absence of part or all of one or more days from school during which the school attendance officer, principal or teacher has not been notified of the legal cause of the absence by the student's parent or guardian. It also means intermittent attendance carried on for the purpose of defeating the intent of Wisconsin's compulsory school attendance law (WIS. REV. STAT. § 118.16)	A student who is absent from school without an acceptable excuse for part or all of five or more school days during a school semester is considered habitually truant (WIS. REV. STAT. § 118.16)
Wyoming	An unexcused absence is the absence – as defined in the policies of the local board of trustees – of any child required to attend school when such absence is not excused to the satisfaction of the board of trustees by the parent or guardian (WYO. STAT. ANN. § 21-4-101)	Any child with five or more unexcused absences in any one school year is a habitual truant (WYO. STAT. ANN. § 21-4-101)
Territory		
Guam	Truant means a student found to be absent from school without a reasonable and bona fide excuse from a parent (GUAM CODE ANN. § 6401)	A student that has incurred 12 or more unexcused absences in a school year, and is of compulsory attendance age, is a habitual truant (GUAM CODE ANN. § 6402)

Resources: ECS State Policy Database: http://www.ecs.org/ecs/ecscat.nsf/WebTopicView?OpenView& RestrictToCategory=Attendance–Truancy.
Kyle Zinth (2005). Researcher in the ECS Information Clearinghouse, updated this report.

Appendix 2. Definitions of chronic truancy in one Midwestern state

1. Missing school for a reason that is not state approved
2. Over 16 days
3. Parents unaware absence
4. A student absent 7 or more times within the course of the school year
5. The act of unauthorised absence from school or class for any period of time or leaving school proper
6. 10+
7. 3 or more truancies (absent from school without parental authorisation)
8. Multiple unverified absences
9. 3 or more unexcused absences per semester
10. 2 or more truancies
11. 10 absences
12. 2 or more
13. Repeated absence w/o parent notification to the school
14. Truancy is the failure to report to assigned classes or absences that occur without the knowledge or
15. 3 or more consecutive days absent without notification
16. 4 truancies (12 unexcused absences or any truancy event absent without parent knowledge that would e
17. After 15 absences
18. Missing more than 5 days unexcused
19. 3 truancy incidents
20. On several or more occasions being willfully out of school without the knowledge and/or the approval
21. 10 or more unexcused absences
22. No defined "habitual" truancy
23. 10–15 unexcused absences
24. 3 days truant
25. More than ten days
26. 12 or more absences
27. A student who is truant three times during any semester
28. 8 unexcused days of absence
29. 6 or more days
30. 3 or more unexcused absences in a row
31. 5 tardies in a trimester

44. Ten or more unexcused absences
45. We do not have a specific definition
46. 2 or more unexcused absences in a row
47. 9 unexcused absences
48. Child being absent and neither the parent of school is aware of, or the reason for the absence
49. 15 absences
50. Any unexcused absence
51. Absent for more than 10 days without an excuse
52. Absence without just cause
53. Third truancy
54. Continuing to miss school after repeated warnings
55. More than 10 Absences
56. 4 days of an absence without parental contact
57. An absence that is not excused and without parental knowledge
58. 3 separate truancy offences
59. 5 days or more
60. Two or more
61. 10 or more
62. Unverified absence or being somewhere other than directed by school personnel
63. Students may not miss more than 10 unexcused days of school
64. 10 days
65. 12 or more absences without a medical
66. We do not really have a definition, but it would be a student who repeatedly misses school so that l
67. Willfully refuses to attend in defiance of parent authority, having 3 incidents of such
68. A student who has more than five unexcused absences in a semester
69. More than 11
70. 3 unexcused absences as determined by the admin
71. More than three times
72. More than two truancy infractions
73. 3 or more misses without notification
74. More than 10 absences of concern

(Continued)

Appendix 2. (*Continued*).

32. Willful refusal to attend school in defiance of parental authority	75. 2nd incident of unexcused absence
33. Unexcused/unreported absence on a "regular" basis	76. 13 unexcused absences in one year
34. None	77. Three or more truancies
35. Same as state's	78. A student who is chronically absent by having unexcused absences from school for more than ten (10)
36. Three reports unofficially (not stated in handbook)	79. More than 10 days missed
37. The same as the state of Indiana	80. Habitual truancy designation will be applied to any student who is at least 13 years of age but less
38. Absent without permission and notification to proper school authorities	81. No parent contact and missing 5+ days
39. More than 8 unexcused absences/semester	82. A student who is truant 3 or more times
40. Missing more than 5 days each six weeks	83. Over 20 days
41. Absent with 3 or more unexcused absences	84. 10 or more days in a semester
42. 10 or more days without a Dr's note	85. 2 or more Undocumented absences
43. 3 or more unexcused absences	86. No clear definition

Appendix 3. Verbatim focus group quotes

Respondents	Data – Verbatim quotes
(Person 1)	My thoughts are; I agree it would be remarkable if we could come to a consensus as an organisation. We all agree that the definition of truancy is very important. I think a national "Drop out age" would be tremendous! I think we may want to remember the reason for trying not being so specific is because of the various definitions from state to state
(Person 2)	I am new also. I work in two states as far as Truancy, in Mo. and in KS. But in Ks. St law is 3, 5, and 7
	K.S.A. 72-1113 A student is truant when he she is inexcusably absent from school a significant part of the school day. 3 consecutive days- 5 days in a school semester-7 days in a school year
	I work as a Drop Out Specialist looking for students who have dropped out. I go look for them and try to get them back in (enrolled) and when I do I hit a barrier. What I don't understand in our district is that you can "drop out" without parental permission. But then we have kids who want to come back to school who let's say parents can't get off work, or even worse, don't care, the student can't re-enrol without a parent. I'm talking high school age
	We have kids who don't live with their parents, but can't re enrol without a parent, silly!!!!!
	I slid off track here, but it should be 18. That way if the student decides to drop out, they can re-enrol if they want with or w/o a parent
	Mandatory school age is -every child who is enrolled and or 7–18 years of age. Significant part of the day is= one third of the day
(Person 3)	There also is the issue of those students that never enrol. Technically they aren't absent because of non-enrollment. Just a thought to add to the definition. Thanks

(Continued)

Appendix 3. (*Continued*).

Respondents	Data – Verbatim quotes
(Person 4)	The definition of truancy is very important. However, I would also like a national "Drop out age". As an International organisation, we may need to ensure that the age is the same from state to state
(Person 5)	Texas statutes actually address students who are of compulsory attendance age but not enrolled in school and who are known to live within district boundaries. The problem with those students is that we rarely become aware of them unless a neighbour or concerned citizen reports them for being outside during the school day. In our district, our attendance administrators make a home visit and are generally told the student is being home school. In Texas, we then have no further educational jurisdiction over the student
	Here's the problem I have with using the word "excused" or "excusable" in the definition of truancy: parents will always argue that any time they produce a note with a reason for their student's absence it is/should be excused. We must, therefore, further define what we mean by "excused" or "excusable" in order to more clearly and comprehensively define truancy
(Person 6)	Works for me. I would just replace child with student so it fits all grade levels. I know how folks in upper grades don't like being thought of as children
	"Truancy is the act of a student missing any part or all of the school day without a legitimate, documented excuse or reason."
(Person 7)	I'm new to the group but wanted to throw out our definition of truancy. Our county has expanded the scope to include nonattendance. We did this as it was discovered that MANY students were missing school with multiple excused absences. We redefined our language as "nonattendance". The results were similar as those who were unlawful; missed opportunities for learning
	Definition of truancy/nonattendance:
	When a child misses school or class without an excuse from his or her parent/guardian, leaves school without permission of the teacher or principal, or is consistently late for school
	I would also add that the word "truant" itself tends to have a connotation referring to kids that are "delinquent". In our schools officials have a hard time with calling elementary age students "truants". This is why we went toward nonattendance
(Person 8)	"Truancy is the act of a school aged student being absent without any excusable reason from any part of a required school day."
	"Truancy is the act of missing any part of school without permission"
	"Truancy is the act of a school aged student being absent without any excusable reason from any part of a required school day."
(Group of 8 Teachers)	"Truancy is the act of missing any part of school without permission."
(Person 9)	I would prefer to use non-attendance and excessive absenteeism as opposed to truant as well. For now in terms of excusable and inexcusable, we need to look towards our own State laws to guide us on that. Maybe that segment should be included "legitimately excused per State law, city ordinance" whatever you are adhering to

Rebuilding attendance practices with youth: the role of social mediation

Renira E. Vellos and Jennifer A. Vadeboncoeur

Human Development, Learning, & Culture, Department of Educational & Counselling Psychology, and Special Education, Faculty of Education, The University of British Columbia, Vancouver, Canada

This article highlights the experiences of students and educators from a larger sociocultural study of participation and engagement at a senior alternative high school programme in British Columbia, Canada. Drawing on participant observation, active interviews and document analysis, school attendance was remediated as a meaningful social practice as a result of the relationships young people formed with educators and peers, rather than meaningful in and of itself or in relation to academic performance. These findings trouble school attendance policies that locate absenteeism as a problem within individual students and as decontextualised from their lived experiences. Findings also foreground the importance of examining how school attendance may be interpreted by students. For some students, participation in relationships and communities lies behind school attendance, highlighting the necessity of attending to the role of identity and values alongside of the construction of knowledge as central to the work of schools.

Introduction

Across research traditions, absenteeism has been accepted as a problem in schools by mental health professionals, public health officials and educators alike, and is alleged to signal risk factors for substance use, psychiatric disorders, economic deprivation and various types of criminal behaviour (e.g. Alexander 2012; Barton 2006; Carnes 1976; Reid 2005; Suh and Suh 2007). Absenteeism plays a role in the process of disengagement and early school leaving for youth in high school and, therefore, an understanding of absenteeism may contribute to efforts to re-engage students so they complete graduation requirements (e.g. Alexander, Entwisle, and Horsey 1997; Bond and Beer 1990). However, absenteeism and what it means to be absent from school varies depending on the definition used, the consequences for absence and the perspectives of participants in context. Definitions also shape descriptions and explanations of absenteeism, as well as recommendations from research. Although LeCompte and Dworkin (1991) challenged researchers to attend to both individual and social factors in their research identifying early school leaving as a process, much of the research on absenteeism still focuses on either individual or social factors, and little of it takes a process approach.

Psychological theories tend to focus on individual factors and use internalising explanations for absenteeism, including school phobia, separation anxiety, school refusal and school refusal behaviours (e.g. Hanna, Fischer, and Fluent 2006; Kearney and Silverman 1996; Tyrrell 2005). These theories often seek to identify child-motivated absences and provide advice for the treatment and skill building of the individual student who is referred by teachers or administrators to counsellors or mental health professionals. Results from these investigations tend to lead to various types of short-term interventions to help address student anxiety issues and social skills or offer individual support through group training (Sambonsugi 2011; Steinberg 1999). These theories locate explanations for students' absenteeism in individual students and suggest interventions or treatments for individual students as a method to reduce absenteeism.

Social perspectives tend to emphasise the social conditions that seem to explain absenteeism, including, poverty, racism and gender issues (e.g. Costen 2012; Gregory, Skiba, and Noguera 2010). These perspectives add to the conversation the location of explanations for students' absenteeism in social conditions. Social perspectives suggest attention to addressing these social conditions – for example, the impact of poverty and housing instability – as a key component of programmes that seek to reduce absenteeism. Without this macro-level emphasis, it is likely that interventions that focus only on individual students will not provide them with the necessary enabling conditions to work within challenging social environments, and short-term interventions are likely to show short-term improvements. Some long-term research programmes are contributing works that attend to both individual and social factors (Reid 1985), and it is here that our work contributes as well.

Building on these perspectives, we advance a sociocultural perspective that locates absenteeism and attendance in the social practices constituted by students and teachers in school environments; a perspective that is explicitly social, relational and dialectical (see Gutiérréz 2002; Lave and Wenger 1991). This article presents findings from a larger qualitative study of reengagement at one alternative senior high school programme, identified as "Mountain High",[1] in an urban school district in British Columbia (BC), Canada (see Vellos 2009). The study was designed to address the research question: How do youth and educators co-construct an engaging learning context? While the larger study highlighted the ways in which student engagement was socially constructed in relationships between youth and educators, this article focuses on the construction of school attendance as a specific social practice that was mediated by educators. Absenteeism was related to student disengagement from mainstream schooling; however, attendance in the alternative programme was understood to be an intentionally mediated practice through which youth rebuilt trust in and recognition from educators in the process of becoming participants in a community.

This article is divided into four sections. The first section describes the theoretical framework, the context and the methodology. The second section describes three activities that contributed to the social practice of attending school at Mountain High. The third section provides a discussion of these activities as markers of community building. Finally, the fourth section offers a brief summary and notes the significance of shifting from behavioural consequences for "absent individuals" to a sociocultural perspective on attendance defined as a process of mediating the increasing participation of students in communities of practice.

Theoretical framing, context and methodology

The sociocultural perspective advanced here draws upon research into learning as participation in communities of practice (Lave and Wenger 1991). Becoming a participant is an evolving process that begins peripherally and – mediated by more experienced community members – the contributions of each participant become more central to the social practices of the community over time. Both individual and community are in dialectical relationship, mutually constitutive and conceptualised as dynamic: learning includes involvement in new tasks, developing new understandings and coming to know in new ways; and the changes enabled by learning entail new "living relations" between persons, positions and participation in practice (Lave and Wenger 1991, 53). Therefore, learning always also involves the construction of identities and values, as well as the construction of knowledge (Vadeboncoeur, Vellos, and Goessling 2011), and becoming a participant in a community of practice is likely to require negotiations around knowing, becoming and valuing that may challenge or support the positions of institutions, educators and students in different ways. From this perspective, absence from school occurs in relation to the social practices co-constituted by students and teachers in school environments and, therefore, attendance needs to be addressed in the way these practices are constituted as well.

The concept of social practice is defined as a repertoire of actions that includes roles, language and expectations for participation that reflect the culture of an institution, like a school or a context, like a classroom (Gutierréz 2002; Holland and Cole 1995). Particular practices have become identified with mainstream schooling, such as scheduled classes that take place for a specific amount of time and that are initiated by the ringing of a bell or buzzer; beginning the class with a "roll call" or taking attendance; having lessons followed by some form of assessment, such as a quiz or test; and having students sit for provincial exams and/or standardised tests. As described by Gutierréz (2002), social practices offer both stability and gaps for improvisation and transformation. The tension between continuity and change is what allows a practice to be both recognisable to and learnable by novice participants (continuity), and responsive as the presence of new participants becomes an occasion for negotiation and new goals emerge (change).

The tension between continuity and change was at the heart of the work of educators at Mountain High: "doing school" in ways consistent with the requirements of the school district and yet, "doing school" in new ways that enabled negotiations with students in order to foster attendance and participation. Unique to this study was the shared perspective of the educators to go beyond deficit models of youth to examine the ways in which students and educators could rebuild attendance practices, as students were becoming more experienced participants, and through which attendance was becoming a regular form of participation in school. Student–educator relationships were at the centre of this process as students became more experienced participants in the community of practice at Mountain High.

Perspectives and experiences of students in alternative programmes and Mountain High

In 2008, the McCreary Centre Society published a report based on a survey of 339 youth between 13 and 19 years old from 34 alternative education programmes in BC (Smith et al. 2008). Of the youth, 49% were female and 51% were male; 57% identified as having European ancestry and 36% identified as Aboriginal. Entitled *Making the Grade: A Review of Alternative Education Programmes in British Columbia* (2008), this report documented the challenges that youth in alternative schools face in relation to attending school. These included the impact of poverty, such as unstable housing (41% in transitory housing, 51% had left home, 37% had been told to leave home) and insecure income (32% legally employed, 20% illegally employed or earning from street performance activities). In addition, students had experienced forms of abuse and exploitation (51% physical abuse, 44% sexual abuse of females and 10% of males), mental health issues (issues with anger 22%, depression 21%, ADHD, 18%) and issues with drug use and abuse (78% had first drink by the age of 14, 69% had smoked marijuana in the past month), as well as multiple challenges to school engagement (48% had been enrolled in three or more schools, 34% had been held back a grade).

For many of the youth responding to the survey, alternative schools became opportunities to re-engage because they offered support services not available in mainstream schools (30% noted the flexible programme, 43% noted the teaching style). Teachers and youth service workers were perceived as supportive and encouraging. They respected students and provided opportunities for connecting to school through positive relationships (43% responded that teachers respect student abilities, 41% responded that teachers and staff respect all students, 39% responded that teachers and staff understand my situation). Youth surveyed also reported that they had friends who encouraged them to continue attending school (39%). Peer relationships helped them improve their attendance at alternative school over their attendance at their previous mainstream school (45% did not skip, and of those who skipped, 47% of students reported skipping less than when at their previous school).

Mountain High was a small alternative programme situated on a different site than the mainstream high school to which it was attached. It served just over 115 youth from throughout the city. Many of the students in this alternative programme had been referred to the programme after not meeting attendance requirements at their mainstream high schools. Some students were born in countries other than Canada, for example, Bosnia and Japan, but the majority of the students were of Canadian ancestry. Mountain High had seven full-time teachers and three Youth and Family Workers (YFW). Mountain High did not have an onsite principal, however, one of the teachers was assigned the role of "Head Teacher" and split duties between teaching and administration. The number of educators available to students depended on school board funding, and the school board had suffered substantial budget cuts in recent years. As a senior high school programme, Mountain High was designed for grade 11–12 students (16–19 years of age); in some instances, there were allowances made for youth to enter if they were missing one or two grade-10 courses.

In general, the McCreary Society Centre report reflected the range of experiences of students at Mountain High. Students at Mountain High had complicated educational histories: the majority were living on their own, had part- and full-time jobs (i.e. as cashiers, prep cooks and street performers), had a history of enrolment in multiple schools and were more likely to enrol in adult continuing programmes than return to mainstream schooling to graduate. They had their share of personal and social issues that compounded their educational experiences. Students experienced family issues that impacted their education: as youth with single parents or parents who were separated, youth in foster care, youth with parents with depression. One teacher at Mountain High described students as "vulnerable" youth who "take on behaviours that are distracting, that seem like bad ass behaviours", yet "there are signs that those behaviours are linked to traumas" (Linda, Ln 166–168). For Linda, these behaviours indicated that they did not feel comfortable in mainstream environments and felt their experiences were too different from the norm to belong and succeed in schools. Youth in the McCreary study did not want to return to mainstream schools (44%). Students at Mountain High also expressed "hating regular school", in part, because in mainstream schools there was only one way to do things or better said, two ways, the right way and the wrong way. Yet, like youth in the McCreary Society Centre survey, students at Mountain High wanted to graduate, wanted to develop job skills (40% McCreary, 100% Mountain High) and planned to continue on to college, technical school or university (32% McCreary, 100% Mountain High).

Perspectives and policies of schools

In Canada, provincial governments are responsible for articulating educational policies for each separate province. In BC, the Ministry of Education ensures every child an education up to age 18 in *The School Act* (1996). School boards articulate attendance policy in broad terms that are then taken up by individual school administrators as the basis for school policies and procedures. All school policies are consistent with the Ministry and are approved by school boards, but they vary.

The attendance policy for Mountain High (1995) was stated on the first page of the *Handbook*, as follows:

> We expect our students to enrol in a full academic programme leading to graduation. We also expect our students to attend classes at a high level, with a minimum attendance for credit of 85%. We have a large waiting list, and this makes us eager to have students who prove their desire to be at Mountain High by attending and participating fully in the programme. (1)

Several aspects of this statement are interesting to note. At the same time that it provides detail about a required attendance level of 85% to receive credit for taking a course, it also positions students as potential members of a community ("our students" is repeated twice), and it identifies educators as "eager" to work with "students who prove their desire to be at Mountain High by attending and participating fully in the programme" (1). In practice, while the teachers reminded students repeatedly that the importance of attending school and being in class was because they could learn, the percentage level itself did not appear to be significant to teachers. The Head Teacher noted that the intention was to work with students to address attendance and/or other concerns so that each student could be successful. What was important was that students showed an improvement in attendance over time.

If this is juxtaposed with four additional mainstream high school attendance statements, a difference in tone seems to surface. Policy for Schools 1 and 2 were written in second person addressing the reader as you/your in the majority of statements. School 1 addressed its policy to parents and guardians and School 2 addressed its policy to students as noted below.

School 1: Please phone the school's Early Warning system at 604-111-1234 if your son or daughter is going to be absent or late with an excuse. If we don't hear from you by 9:00 am, a parent volunteer will call you at home or work to find out about your child's absence. Unexplained absences will result in a … message from our automated messaging system. If there is a perceived error in your child's attendance, please discuss this with your child and then contact the school to update your child's attendance report.

School 2: The most important responsibility of Brighton students is to attend classes on time. If you miss class for any reason, it is your responsibility to account to the teacher for your absence. A phone call must be made to the office by a parent the morning of your absence, and a written explanation is required, signed by parent or guardian. Parents will be contacted and students with poor attendance habits will face discipline. Senior students with chronically poor attendance will be withdrawn.

While there is some flexibility in how to interpret the policies of Schools 1 and 2, both policies assume a relational chain between students and parents or guardians, and between parents or guardians and schools. In addition, they assume that absences can always be predicted the morning of, and identified in advance of the behaviour. These qualities – communicated by parents or guardians in advance – form the basis for the distinction between "excused" and "unexcused" absences.

Both Schools 3 and 4 emphasised their responses to absence in general terms that reflected to some extent the influence of "zero-tolerance" approaches that, ironically, lead students inexorably to suspension and, in some cases, early school leaving. However, the language contains flexibility in interpretation as well.

School 3: Truancy: Definition: Absence from class(es) without reason or permission; leaving campus without checking out; cumulative each semester. 1st Offence (1–3 truancies): Teacher will meet with student to review expectations and assigns a classroom consequence; teacher contacts parents. 2nd Offence: Teacher refers student to counsellor and assigns classroom consequence; counsellor contacts parents. 3rd Offence: Teacher refers student to VP; VP meets with student and assigns an office consequence; VP contacts parents. ON GOING: Teacher refers student to VP; VP assigns in or out of school suspension of 1–3 days; VP meets with parents and student; final warning given. CHRONIC (Over 16): may be withdrawn from classes.

School 4: The staff and administration at Valley High believe the responsibility for attendance lies mainly with students and their parents; however, if they do not assume this responsibility, the school will do everything possible to enforce attendance according to the School Act and our school policy. Truancy will result in a referral to the administration. Parents will be notified and disciplinary action may follow. Excused absences: When a student has been absent, a note from a parent explaining the reason for the absence may be required. This note will allow the student the opportunity to make up any missed work. Parents are asked to call the school prior to 9:00 am if a student is absent from the school. In this case, a note is not required. … Truancy is defined as absence from the class or school without valid reasons. When a student has been truant, the student may be suspended from school. The parents will be contacted.

As attendance policies become more directive, they run the risk of positioning absenteeism as a criminal behaviour. Indeed, school-related behaviours, like absenteeism, are oftentimes used as predictors of future criminal behaviour for students, and in the US, have been associated with the term "school-to-prison" pipeline, which speaks to assumptions about students who are absent, as mostly students of colour who during their absences engage in criminal behaviour that alienates them from school and connects them to the criminal system (Alexander 2012). Research has demonstrated that when used in combination with the influence of "zero-tolerance"[2] approaches, attendance policies run the risk of focusing on absenteeism as a self-fulfilling predictor of criminal behaviour (Gregory, Skiba, and Noguera 2010).

Policies on absenteeism defined through theories that criminalise absence from schools have also served to alienate families from schooling. This is demonstrated when decisions about consequences for student absenteeism are made without parental consultation, yet in consultation with the juvenile system (Hoyle 1998). These policies may serve to further disconnect students from schools by offering school removal as punishment for not attending school, as well as offering this consequence to certain categories of students more than others (see Hoyle 1998), for example, research suggests absenteeism is more common for students from working-class backgrounds (e.g. Reid 1985, 2005, 2012; Tyerman 1968; Vellos and Vadeboncoeur 2013).

Methodology

This study used qualitative methods, including participant observation, active interviews and document analysis during a six-week period at Mountain High. A total of 50 h of participant observation were recorded. Observations were carried out using a participation framework that focused on identifying social practices through five features of learning contexts: location, relationships, content, pedagogy and assessment/ evaluation (Vadeboncoeur 2006). As relationships evolved with the first author, students took more active roles in identifying aspects of the context that were important to them and the first author recorded ongoing informal dialogues with students that allowed them to share their stories outside of the more formal active interview interaction. Participant observation (Patton 2002) became even more important than originally expected because of the way that the students volunteered information regarding their lives and experiences in mainstream schools.

Eight active interviews (Holstein and Gubrium 2004) were carried out: four with educators, teachers and a Youth and Family Worker, and four with students. Active interviews position the interview as a co-construction between two participants who contribute to and learn from the outcome of the interview. In interviews with the students and educators at Mountain High, students currently enrolled had specific kinds of experiences at mainstream schools that led to their disengagement from schools. This disengagement was manifested through behaviours that put them at risk for not graduating. These behaviours included smoking, using drugs, cutting class, being late, avoiding homework and in general, not fitting in with the school community. Youth at Mountain High compared their previous schools and their present alternative school and found differences. These differences included, smaller classes, blocked sessions that allowed for four courses at a time, teachers that cared and motivated them, and educators that recognised their strengths and helped them build upon these.

Document analysis included the *Mountain High School Handbook* (1995), and attendance policies across three school districts and four schools within those districts. A constant comparative analysis (Glaser 1965) was conducted concurrently with data collection and categories were developed with specific attention to the development of relationships and social practices that enabled the participation of students. The lens used for this article was attendance, defined as being present for class.

Co-constructing attendance: a relational practice of students and educators

Attendance played a specific role in the process of disengagement from schooling in mainstream schools, as well as a role in the process of participation at Mountain High. Many students in this alternative programme had been referred due to their accumulated absences at their mainstream high schools; they had not conformed to the expected practice of attending school. Data that support the mediation of attendance is presented in this section: (1) explaining a late arrival or absence, (2) belonging through a relational dyad and (3) leaving mainstream behind: new rituals, new community. These sorts of activities were intentionally constructed with students in an effort to rebuild a rationale for attendance.

Explaining a late arrival or absence: excused or unexcused

Attendance policies are often based on the assumption that the first step to a successful academic performance is being present in class when lessons are taught. These policies suggest that attendance is an important component to participation and that participation is an important component of academic performance. Often, what constitutes "attendance" and "academic performance" – the beginning and end-point of the assumed educational trajectory – is defined, while participation is less clearly defined. The Head Teacher of Mountain High, Jane, agreed with this perspective and stated, "many have great attendance, but many continue to struggle with attendance and we, over the course of the history of the school … have encouraged them to attend because obviously there is a correlation between attendance and success" (Ln 100–103). She was also quick to add, however, that there were several ways in which she and her colleagues had begun to structure participation to encourage attendance, including "on time quizzes", participation credit for social responsibility, tardy sheets, and relationships with a Youth and Family Worker. These counted as participation in this community and were seen as valued and valuable. Findings from this study, however, suggested that academic performance was not a significant motive for participation and, interestingly, for some students, there was not a relationship between attendance and academic performance.

Linda, an experienced teacher of 18 years, stated, "In order to learn from this class you need to be here, straight up" (Obs 8, Ln 106). Her emphasis was on engaging students in learning, rather than merely performance goals. She introduced youth to her version of a tardy sheet on the first day. Linda explained how she wanted them to fill it out, the information she wanted and how she would use it to determine if tardiness was "the nature of the beast" (Obs 11, Ln 157). Linda explained that if she noticed a pattern to their tardiness, then she would impose a 5% loss on their grade point average. The tardy sheet was a quarter cut piece of blue paper that included a space for the student to write their name, how late they were and the reason for being late. This form was picked up upon entering the classroom, completed by the students in the hall and placed in a basket on Linda's desk. During the course of the lesson, Linda walked around the room. Eventually, she arrived to her desk, picked up the sheets and read them to herself as she continued walking and conversing with the class members. During the observations, Linda reminded the class of the tardy sheets when students walked in without filling them out, but did not mention anything written on tardy sheets or call attention to specific students for their late arrivals. One day, after reading the note from one of the students, Linda assigned the class a task and then disappeared briefly. At the end of the class session, one Youth and Family Worker waited at the door, signalled to the student, and they walked together to her office.

Students were also engaged in making decisions about when assessments should be scheduled. Patterns of attendance indicated that Monday and Friday were days that students were more likely to be absent. This pattern was discussed in class with students as they decided when learning assessments would be done. Linda used a democratic process of voting for test days giving students a choice for when tests would be held. The options for test days included Tuesday through Thursday, and students voted for Wednesday test days. By eliminating Mondays and Fridays, students provided reasons for their possible absence: working extra hours on weekends, having to make trips to visit family in the interior of BC many hours away and some simply stated they had a hangover on Monday mornings.

Despite acknowledging their absences from school, in interviews, Mountain High students were adamant that what mattered was learning and that absences should not be counted toward their grade. For example, Jenny emphasised,

> This my perfect learning environment, like its awesome, 'cause I can sit here, and I can, you know, whatever … And you know I actually, I actually do think … cause like I was never interested in politics or anything like that before, now Im totally, you know, I'm at home, on Wikipedia, like you know, scrolling, typing in all this stuff, and just learning. (Ln, 100–106)

Dee, a recent graduate of Mountain High who had left home at age 17, explained that while enrolled in mainstream high school, she lived two bus rides, one Skytrain ride and one Seabus ride away from her mainstream high school. This was over two hours of commuting daily. Dee also worked night and weekend shifts to earn money and this made getting up on time for school a challenge. Despite her challenges with attendance, Dee did not want her grades in high school to be affected, so she devised an attendance system: she showed up on assessment days, but was regularly absent on other days. Dee claimed that her grades on tests and reports were exemplary and made up for marks lost from pop quizzes and participation points; she was convinced that her grades should be unaffected by her school absences because she was learning the material.

When probed further about her absences, Dee explained that she felt no one at the school noticed her absence, no one asked her why she was absent or asked how she was doing, and she used this apparent disconnect with people at the mainstream school to justify her continued absences. Dee's arrival at Mountain High happened when the mainstream school in which she was enrolled finally noticed she had been repeatedly absent without an excuse and referred her to Mountain High. The relationship between attendance and academic performance was not clear-cut for Dee. Rather, students like Dee found ways around this policy that balanced both (1) the complexity of their lives and (2) a desire to learn and complete high school. That is, until it caught up with them.

"Belonging" through a relational dyad

Youth at Mountain High were either referred by school personnel or requested to transfer in, but they could not be accepted into the programme unless one of the YFW supported their application. YFWs had to agree to support each student through their time at Mountain High, both academically and personally. With this commitment, students were enrolled in the school. Everyone knew which YFW was working with which student, and it was not unusual for a youth to be identified as "belonging" to a particular YFW. It was common knowledge which YFW to check in with if a student was late, absent or did not seem to be himself or herself. Being part of the acceptance process provided each YFW with significant information about students and their educational histories. As a result, they were the primary link between school and home. When something happened in the home or in the school life of a student, the YFW was the one who knew. Though the role of the YFW was critical to the success of this alternative programme, it was not a position made available in mainstream schools or in all alternative schools in this school district.

The daily first period "check-in" by the YFW served both an administrative and a relational purpose. Students knew the YFW would drop by to make sure they had arrived safely. They were aware that the YFW check-in was an administrative task monitoring their attendance. They also knew, however, that the YFWs looked forward to saying hello to them and that hello reassured them that someone at the school was waiting for them. Compared to the experiences youth reported about not feeling like anyone had missed them or noticed how they were doing in mainstream school, the visit by the YFW was confirmation that they mattered in this particular community. It was an important aspect of the relationship between YFW and student, a ritual that emphasised on a daily basis the importance of attending and the value of being a member of this community.

The "check-in" activity with students sometimes led to additional actions: calling home if something was out of the ordinary, calling the youth personally if they had not shown up to school, and decision-making on the basis of students' personal and sometimes financial challenges. Interestingly, the relationship between student and YFW obliged students to take responsibility for their actions knowing that it affected someone else. For example, Dee's attendance practices at Mountain High improved simply because she felt that her YFW would have to assume the responsibility for her absence. Dee's transformation from a student who, in mainstream schools, did not feel cared about or noticed, to one who showed up to school out of concern for her YFW was a radical departure from her previous lack of connection and recognition in school.

The sense of shared responsibility between students and YFWs surfaced in the interviews, and was observed informally through participant observation. Students engaged in normative practices of schooling, like attending and being on time, in part, not to make their YFW worry. Dee continued to visit her YFW after graduation for two reasons: (1) she missed MJ and wanted to keep in touch, and (2) MJ made time to chat with Dee although she had already graduated, an action that communicated that she cared for Dee in return. For students like Dee, whose experiences in mainstream schools had led her to Mountain High and who were now at university, the relationship with her YFW provided her with a stability and continuity that she lacked in her personal life.

Students at Mountain High respected their YFWs and often sought their council on a wide range of matters. For example, when Jon was making academic decisions, he made sure to ask his YFW to recommend classes and teachers to take. Dee met with her YFW for advice about academic matters even after she graduated and was attending a post-secondary institution. Donald sought his YFW's advice about what to do when his cell phone disappeared and reappeared in the hands of one of his peers. During observations, he said he wanted to confront this peer, but on the advice of his YFW, he let the Head Teacher, his YFW and the other student's YFW address the situation. In another instance, a student's father, whom the YFW mentioned had been in and out of rehabilitation centres, had contacted the YFW to see the student. The first author learned that the student had been placed in care for "good reason", and was currently living on his own. The student was relieved when his YFW did not press him to visit with his father and, instead, allowed him to make the decision. According to the student, his YFW kept his father "in his place" (Obs 6, Ln 75).

Leaving mainstream behind: new rituals, new community

In interviews and observations, students at Mountain High admitted to feeling that their presence in mainstream school went unnoticed by teachers and that, this contributed to feeling that their absence would go equally unnoticed. For example, Dee spoke about missing class, returning to school and then going to the office for a note to re-enter class as a practice that appeared to be without consequences. She did this without fear of "going to the office", and answering questions of administrators about why she had been absent. It was so habitual that she was completely surprised when she received a letter from the school saying that she had been "referred out". Another student, Jon, reported that he went to class "baked all the time" (under the influence of marijuana) (Ln 48), and that the teachers never said anything. However, in addition to feeling that teachers did not notice their presence or absence, peers also had an impact in how youth experienced school. Jenny described that she tried, "to make friends and I tried to fit in, and, but I could never really, you know, ... trying to put myself into the box" (Ln 89–91). Her inability to make friendships suggested to her that she did not belong at that school.

Reasons for why youth at Mountain High felt they did not fit in mainstream schools often became the reasons youth felt they belonged at Mountain High. At Mountain High

> everyone's kinda the same right, they didn't work out in public schools, and that's either cause they smoked too much weed or they skipped classes, or didn't do their homework, so we can all kinda relate to each other in that sense we're all screw-ups. (Jon, Ln 114–117)

At Mountain High, "everyone, you know, talks to each other, everyone gets along" (Jon, Ln 107–108), and "you are very close to all the students cause there's only like a hundred of us" (Dee, Ln 159–160). The size of Mountain High allowed students to be recognised by educators and peers and get to know each other.

The kind of attention students received when they returned after an absence signalled both that they were missed and that, they were expected to attend and participate. On one occasion, a student who was absent on Monday was teased as soon as he walked in the following Tuesday morning. His peers offered many excuses for his absence including the "drunken weekend", "running away with a girl" or "the weekend in gaol" excuse. With a smile on his face, he brushed off most of these and accepted the drunken weekend excuse provided by his peers. Later that day, however, in a smaller circle of friends he explained he had been kicked out of his rental, and had to find a new place to live. Nobody in the group laughed or chided him about this situation, they simply asked about his new place. Given the small size of the school and the many people involved in the daily lives of students – including teachers, YFWs and peers – there were few if any opportunities for youth to be absent without being noticed. It was visibly more difficult for students to enter class without undergoing a version of a "welcome back to school" cheer.

Students at Mountain High openly discussed differences between teachers at Mountain High and ones they had met in mainstream schools. Jon appreciated that teachers at Mountain High were "down for discussion": "like its not just taking notes from the teachers' lectures, its easier to get in [the discussion] and express yourself", as a result, "kids are more down to talk about what's going on and put in their opinions and stuff" (Ln 134–138). Linda had also offered to help him with his essay writing after class. Jenny suggested that the teachers were flexible and that everyone should go to schools that were small and alternative where teachers know you: "whatever I'm thinking about, I can say it here" (Ln 103). Donald emphasised that, "kids don't skip because they want to … but because class (in mainstream) is so bad" (Ln 150–152). Donald highlighted that Mountain High teachers were different "they care and know how to teach … they do a fantastic job. I stay in school the whole time, never skip cause I don't need to skip" (Ln 146–148). In addition to the impact of teachers, Dee cited her motivation to attend Mountain High as stemming from her relationship with her YFW, MJ. As Dee explained,

> the whole attendance thing, I would try to come to school for her [MJ], more than for myself, because I knew she was going to get in [trouble] from the Head Teacher because I wasn't coming and I was part of her [group]. (Dee, Ln 280–285)

The trouble that Dee alluded to was the result of the shared responsibility MJ had agreed to when she agreed to support Dee's application to Mountain High.

While the students often teased each other, their camaraderie impacted their relationship to schooling in a positive way. On the one hand, it allowed them to be more open about what they knew or did not know in terms of academics and, on the other, though they teased each other relentlessly about topics from their school abilities to their fashion sense, the teasing was always amicable and acknowledged them as belonging at this school. There were also unspoken boundaries around topics for teasing; teasing was not appropriate for housing issues or family illnesses, but was kept to lighter topics that were considered shared issues. The act of being teased publically gave students the opportunity to feel noticed and accepted, an experience that they had lacked in mainstream schooling. They no longer worried about whether they fit in school and focused instead on what becoming a "student" at Mountain High entailed.

Discussion: attending differently

Students felt that Mountain High was different than mainstream school though, through observation, many of these differences were barely identifiable. Indeed, many of the social practices at Mountain High appeared very "mainstream". Participant observations identified expected school practices like schedules, assignments, IRE questioning sequences (teacher initiation, student reply, teacher evaluation) (Mehan 1979) and provincial exam preparation. Mountain High followed school board policies, including those related to attendance, so what made the experience of Mountain High so different initially seemed elusive. One obvious difference was the intentional mediation of attendance by educators resulting in attendance patterns that improved over time. For example, Monday morning first classes averaged the highest numbers of late students. By the fourth week, attendance averaged 13 of 16 students present, and though seven students were late, only two had been late twice during that term. Observations were that students at Mountain High began the programme by coming in a bit late and being absent here and there, but this diminished rapidly. Educators consistently and genuinely engaged students as responsible and valued participants who belonged to their community.

The tardy sheet was one method of allowing students to take responsibility for their actions. It allowed them to ask for help without "going to the office" to get a note, and miss further lessons. This practice was dependent on the relationship between the student and the teacher, since each note was written for a specific teacher; students provided thoughtful responses because these responses potentially impacted their relationship with the teacher. As the observations noted, Linda read these notes calmly and took them seriously. Her actions emphasised the students' presence, rather than judging their behaviour. The fostering of relationships is consistent with the positive experiences of schooling that Davis (2002) identified as important to youth's decisions to stay in school, as well as the significance of relationships for attending programmes after school as noted by Vadeboncoeur and Rahal (2013). Allowing students to provide their own reasons for their absence without the necessity of signed parental consent demonstrated a level of respect for them and the decisions they made. While Epp and Epp (2001) noted that rigid school policies that require written parental consent may sometimes lead to disengagement from school, acknowledging that youth have complex lives may provide encouragement for participation. This was particularly fitting because many students at Mountain High were senior high school students, some of whom lived on their own.

The daily check-in for each student by YFWs was the physical equivalent of a thread that linked YFW–student dyads. It established the dedication of a YFW to a student and confirmed the student's value regardless of academic performance. Youth in this study were sure that their YFW had their best interests at heart and would continue to support them even after graduation. Students at Mountain High saw themselves and their lived experiences as different, but their differences were not barriers to learning in a context like Mountain Hill given the role of "their" YFW. Croninger and Lee (2001) found that youth who reported feeling that their teachers, or in this case, YFWs, were a significant source of guidance on both school and personal matters, were more engaged in school.

At Mountain High, the relationships that students formed with peers and educators were central to their continued engagement in the programme and grounded their belonging to this particular community. It could have been argued that there is little to expect from students who belonged to peer groups of self-identified "screw-ups" while in mainstream schools. Yet, on the contrary, being with other students who had also had difficult experiences in mainstream schooling, and who had also faced complicated family and social lives provided the enabling and engaging conditions. These same youth, who now had the emotional and social supports offered at Mountain High, wanted to be at school. Finding a commonality in the "poor fit" they had experienced in mainstream schools, enabled youth at Mountain High to bond over those experiences and participate in school with redefined conceptions of the kinds of peer groups that are popular in mainstream and media depictions of high school peer culture. Eckert (1989) and Hartnett (2007/8) reported that relationships with peers at school impact the experiences of youth in school. In this situation, relationships with educators and peers were the basis of "doing school" differently as part of a community.

Concluding thoughts

This article highlights the experiences of students and teachers participating in a senior high school alternative programme, and suggests that much can be learned about attendance as a socially mediated practice. When conceived of as a community built upon the practices of more-experienced participants mediating the participation of novice participants, the significant role and responsibility of educators is highlighted. Different activities were created to rebuild the practice of school attendance: the tardy sheet, check-ins and community building were highlighted here. It is important to note that we do not think that the use of tardy sheets, check-ins and community building rituals can simply be taken up across different school contexts as ways to "fix kids" or "fix attendance". What is significant is that these activities were built for a specific purpose in a specific learning context and, as such, they made sense to and were perceived as relevant to the educators who utilised them.

Alternative schools can be conceptualised as communities where participation is valued and the contributions of novice participants become occasions for rebuilding community practices, enabling both continuity and change. This conception of learning includes a recognition of learning as a process of becoming and valuing, as well as coming to know: having access to and coming to know particular curricular content shapes the way students see themselves and how others see them, as well as values for thinking, feeling and acting in the world (Vadeboncoeur, Vellos, and Goessling 2011). We often emphasise the epistemic experience of schooling and fail to recognise the ways in which schooling as a process contributes to the shaping of identities of students, identities that are deemed more or less appropriate and valued accordingly. Knowing the effects of leaving school early, we must be more mindful of the institutional bias toward pushing students out, when the more appropriate response for both students and society is likely to be to retain and/or recreate a relationship with them.

The lack of more familiar and explicit disciplinary consequences to being late and/or absent may seem counter to the experience of many people who have lived through mainstream schooling; however, for youth who attended Mountain High, breaking the association between absenteeism and behavioural consequence found in mainstream schools allowed students to rebuild the practice of school attendance, to rebuild a rationale for attending school and to rebuild their identities and values in the process. Youth were able to think about being present in school as coming to a place where they mattered. As Donald noted, one "purpose of school is having responsible citizens, continuing in their lives, and contributing to the place they're living in" (Ln 467–468). Becoming a responsible citizen, one that lives and makes contributions to one's community, became so important that students adjusted their other responsibilities in order to attend school. And what is, perhaps, even more significant: the educators at Mountain High were willing to recognise this change through their relationships with the students, to see the students as growing participants and to allow their relationships to evolve accordingly with more trust and more responsibility.

Based on the experiences shared by students and educators at Mountain High, we highlight the importance of shifting to building community, rather than emphasising ever clearer behavioural consequences for defined infractions. For example, what becomes possible if we:

(1) *Reduce the size of schools and classes* so that the value of each young person and adult, and the relationships between them, is recentred?

(2) Focus on *the presence of students* by enabling each student to participate, to feel a sense of belonging and community, especially through peer-mediated supports, like mentor students?

(3) Designate *an adult for each student*, one who is mindful of the well-being of the student, who can be familiar with the life challenges of that student and who can identify what an absence might signify?

(4) Hold *high expectations for student learning based on participation in the community*, allowing students to identify through their contributions to the community, large and small, as they become increasingly proficient as a member of a school community(ies)?

These recommendations are in line with a vision of schools as places where students feel welcomed and where they will be missed if they are absent, where they develop a sense of responsibility as a member of a community in relation to a community that includes members who are responsible for them: a vision that is more in line with a world where participation in equitable social practices is emphasised, along with our social relationships.

Further research in alternative learning contexts – a large-scale study or international research – could, perhaps, examine more deeply: (1) the relationships between how attendance policies are written and the extent to which they support the kinds of relationships that students and educators need to learn and teach together (this may play out differently in different policy contexts); (2) the supports that teachers need to build communities with youth, create learning opportunities and focus on learning and teaching (this may play out differently given different versions of enacted community and the cultural values attached); and (3) the effects on learning when educators recognise the lived experiences of youth in making decisions that impact future educational opportunities, as well as recognise youth themselves as dynamic and developing learners.

As noted by one of the YFWs at Mountain High, "rules without relationships don't work" (MJ, Notes). While in policy there is a tendency to develop more prescriptive rules when we want to influence students, the educative aspect of these rules only applies if relationships are already in place. Though attendance at Mountain High was considered of central importance, it was neither considered to be more important than the student – and therefore a reason to expel a student from school – nor considered as separate from the lived experiences of each student. For students, especially youth for whom the rules of mainstream schooling did not work, it was the relationships they formed in practices mediated by educators that allowed them to define anew goals for themselves and each other.

Notes

1. The name of this school and the names of all participants are pseudonyms.
2. Zero-tolerance policies that outline mandatory behavioural consequences for infractions have not taken hold in Canada. Since the time of this study, in 2008, the Ontario Human Rights Commission challenged the Ontario school board's *Safe Schools* (1999) code of conduct for creating a list of infractions that explicitly led to suspension or expulsion. The list of infractions was divided into (1) infractions that required a mandatory expulsion or suspension and (2) infractions that were left up to the discretion of the principal and included, for example, persistent truancy. Ontario's newer Safe and Caring Schools Policy (Revised April, 17, 2013), the *Provincial Code of Conduct and School Board Codes of Conduct* (2012), no longer contains these sections. In BC, the language about attendance was also revised to comply with *BC Safe and Caring Schools* (2012). Since 2012, the emphasis in policy has been on promoting safe and caring school environments and moving away from policies that focus on behavioural consequences, although variability does exist.

References

Alexander, M. 2012. *The New Jim Crow: Mass Incarceration in the Age of Colorblindness.* New York: New Press.

Alexander, K. L., D. R. Entwisle, and C. S. Horsey. 1997. "From First Grade Forward: Early Foundations of High School Dropout." *Sociology of Education* 70: 87–107.

Barton, P. E. 2006. "The Dropout Problem: Losing Ground." *Educational Leadership* 63 (5): 14–18.

BC Ministry of Education. 1996. *School Act*. Governance and Legislation Branch. Revised Statutes of British Columbia, August 1, 2013.

Bond, K., and J. Beer. 1990. "Dropping Out and Absenteeism In High School." *Psychological Reports* 66: 817–818.

Carnes, E. 1976. "Factors Responsible for Dropouts." *Journal of the International Association of Pupil Personnel Workers* 20: 81–85.

Costen, R. 2012. "First Choice for a Second Chance: Factors Supporting Temporary Dropouts Who Re-enroll in High School." Unpublished PhD thesis, University of Southern Mississippi.

Croninger, R., and V. E. Lee. 2001. "Social Capital and Dropping out of High School: Benefits to At-risk Students of Teachers; Support and Guidance." *Teachers College Record* 103: 548–581.

Davis, W. E. 2002. *Students at Risk: Who Are They? What Do We Know About Them? How Can We Help Them? Institute for the Study of Students at Risk*. Orono, MN: University of Maine.

Eckert, P. 1989. *Jocks and Burnouts: Social Categories and Identity in High School*. New York: Teacher's College Press.

Epp, J. R., and W. Epp. 2001. "Easy Exit: School Policies and Student Attrition." *Journal of Education for Students Placed at Risk* 6: 231–247.

Glaser, B. G. 1965. "The Constant Comparative Method of Qualitative Analysis." *Social Problems* 12 (4): 436–445.

Gregory, A., R. Skiba, and P. Noguera. 2010. "The Achievement Gap and the Discipline Gap: Two Sides of the Same Coin." *Educational Researcher* 39: 59–68.

Gutierréz, K. D. 2002. "Studying Cultural Practices in Urban Learning Communities." *Human Development* 45: 312–321.

Hanna, G. L., D. J. Fischer, and T. E. Fluent. 2006. "Separation Anxiety Disorder and School Refusal in Children and Adolescents." *Pediatrics in Review* 27: 56–63.

Hartnett, S. 2007. "Does Peer Group Acceptance Influence Absenteeism in High School Students?" *The High School Journal* 91 (2): 35–44.

Holland, D., and M. Cole. 1995. "Between Discourse and Schema: Reformulating a Cultural Historical Approach to Culture and Mind." *Anthropology and Education Quarterly* 26: 475–489.

Holstein, J. A., and J. F. Gubrium. 2004. "The Active Interview." In *Qualitative Research: Theory Method and Practice*, edited by D. Silverman, 140–161. Thousand Oaks, CA: Sage.

Hoyle, D. 1998. "Constructions of Pupil Absence in the British Education Service." *Child and Family Social Work* 3: 99–111.

Kearney, C. A., and W. K. Silverman. 1996. "The Evolution and Reconciliation of Taxonomic Strategies for School Refusal Behavior." *Clinical Psychology: Science and Practice* 3: 339–354.

Lave, J., and E. Wenger. 1991. *Situated Learning: Legitimate Peripheral Participation*. Cambridge: Cambridge University Press.

LeCompte, M. D., and A. G. Dworkin. 1991. *Giving Up on School: Student Dropouts and Teacher Burnouts*. Newbury Park, CA: Corwin Press.

Mehan, H. 1979. "'What Time is It, Denise?': Asking Known Information Questions in Classroom Discourse." *Theory into Practice* 18 (4): 285–294.

Patton, M. Q. 2002. *Qualitative Research and Evaluation Methods*. 3rd ed. Thousand Oaks, CA: Sage.

Reid, K. 1985. *Truancy and School Absenteeism*. London: Hodder & Stoughton.

Reid, K. 2005. "The Causes, Views and Traits of School Absenteeism and Truancy." *Research in Education* 74: 59–82.

Reid, K. 2012. "The Strategic Management of Truancy and School Absenteeism: Finding Solutions from a National Perspective." *Educational Review* 64 (2): 211–222.

Sambonsugi, N. 2011. "Factors That Are Responsible for High School Dropouts in the U.S. and Impact of High Stakes Testing Policy." Unpublished PhD thesis, Southern University and A & G College.

Smith, A., M. Peled, M. Albert, L. Mackay, D. Stewart, E. Saewyc, and The McCreary Centre Society. 2008. *Making the Grade: A Review of Alternative Education Programs in British Columbia*. Vancouver, BC: McCreary Centre Society.

Steinberg, L. 1999. *Adolescence*. 5th ed. Boston, MA: McGraw-Hill.

Suh, S., and J. Suh. 2007. "Risk Factors and Levels of Risk for High School Dropouts." *Professional School Counseling* 10: 297–306.

Tyerman, M. J. 1968. *Truancy*. London: University of London Press.

Tyrrell, M. 2005. "School Phobia." *Journal of School Nursing* 21: 147–151.

Vadeboncoeur, J. A. 2006. "Engaging Young People Learning in Informal Contexts." *Review of Research in Education* 30: 239–278.

Vadeboncoeur, J. A., and L. Rahal. 2013. "Mapping the Social Across Lived Experiences: Relational Geographies and After-school Time." *Banks Street Occasional Paper Series* 30: 1–15.

Vadeboncoeur, J. A., R. E. Vellos, and K. P. Goessling. 2011. "Learning as (One Part) Identity Construction: Educational Implications of a Sociocultural Perspective." In *Sociocultural Theories of Learning and Motivation: Looking Back, Looking Forward*, edited by D. M. McInerney, R. A. Walker, and G. A. D. Liem, 223–251. Charlotte, NC: Information Age.

Vellos, R. E. 2009. "Re-engagement in Learning Contexts: Negotiations Between Adults and Youths in the Zone of Proximal Development." Unpublished Master's thesis, University of British Columbia.

Vellos, R. E., and J. A. Vadeboncoeur. 2013. "Alternative and Second Chance Education." In *Sociology of Education*, edited by J. Ainsworth, 35–38. Thousand Oaks, CA: Sage.

Aggression in primary schools: the predictive power of the school and home environment

Ana Kozina

Educational Research Institute, Ljubljana, Slovenia

In this study, we analyse the predictive power of home and school environment-related factors for determining pupils' aggression. The multiple regression analyses are performed for fourth- and eighth-grade pupils based on the Trends in Mathematics and Science Study (TIMSS) 2007 ($N = 8394$) and TIMSS 2011 ($N = 9415$) databases for Slovenia. At the national level, the *Lestvica agresivnosti* aggression scale was administered in both TIMSS cycles. For home environment variables, we included those related to socio-economic status, pupils' educational aspirations, parental activities with their children and pupils' free time activities. The results show that the variables related to socio-economic status, spare time activities and parental activities are significant predictors. The results differ in both analysed data-sets. For school environment variables, we include those related to the school climate, pupils' attitudes towards school and school subjects and pupils' achievement in mathematics. We find that the variables related to school climate and students' self-confidence are significant predictors. These results are stable in both years. The predictive power of the school characteristics model (including only the school environment variables) is larger (based on the proportion of explained variance) compared with the home characteristics model. The hierarchical linear model of data from 2007 to 2011 shows small differences in aggression between schools. The inclusion of two data cycles collected in two time- periods allows us to observe changes in aggression predictors over time. Practical implications are finally included.

Aggression is behaviour that aims to cause harm to oneself or another person or actually causes it (Flannery, Vazsonyi, and Waldman 2007). Aggressive behaviour has negative outcomes, both short-term and long-term ones, for children and adolescents that are aggressive (e.g. anxiety, exclusion, low educational achievement) as well as for the victims of their aggressive acts (e.g. anxiety, depression, lower educational achievement, low self-esteem) (Flannery, Vazsonyi, and Waldman 2007; Huesmann 1994). Both aggressors and victims are present in schools and both groups need help and intervention.

In schools, aggressive behaviour disrupts the process of learning and affects the school climate. Aggression is significantly related to a negative school climate (Malm and Löfgren 2006; Popp 2003), frequent aggressive behaviour at school (Archer and Coyne 2005; Boxer et al. 2003; Ybrandt and Armelius 2010), a low level of school connectedness (Brookmeyer, Fanti, and Heinrich 2006) and absenteeism (Vitaro, Brendgen, and Barker 2006). It is also related to students having negative attitudes towards school (Kozina 2007; Malm and Löfgren 2006), negative attitudes towards school subjects (Krall 2003) and lower educational achievements (Brown, Anfara, and Roney 2004; Green et al. 1980; McEvoy and Welker 2000; Wentzel and Asher 1995; Zhou, Main, and Wang 2010).

Moreover, a large body of evidence shows that achievement and aggression are negatively correlated (Flannery, Vazsonyi, and Waldman 2007; Huesmann 1994; Krall 2003; Marjanovič Umek and Zupančič 2004; Schwartz et al. 2006). Research shows that aggressive behaviour in early childhood serves as a significant predictor of negative attitudes towards school, which is also strongly related to lower school achievement (Huesmann 1994). Furthermore, the associations between the aggression and the school climate (Flannery, Vazsonyi, and Waldman 2007) as well as between aggression and achievement (McEvoy and Welker 2000) are significant even when socio-economic status (SES) is controlled for. Indeed, these variables often reinforce one another. For instance, pupils who exhibit more aggression at an early age also develop a negative attitude towards school, which results in lower achievement (Zhou, Main, and Wang 2010), and they are more commonly rejected by their peers (Flannery, Vazsonyi, and Waldman 2007; Huesmann 1994). Rejection by one's peers is significantly and consistently associated with lower connectedness to the class, which is followed by low involvement in class and school activities (Buhs, Ladd, and Herald 2006; Ladd, Kochenderfer, and Coleman 1997; Wentzel and Asher 1995), which ultimately significantly predicts low-educational achievement (Buhs, Ladd, and Herald 2006; Ladd, Kochenderfer, and Coleman 1997; Vandell and Hembree 1994). Peer group is thus one of the strongest factors of social development and social behaviour. Being surrounded by aggressive peers is an important predictor of aggressive behaviour being developed in non-aggressive students (Flannery, Vazsonyi, and Waldman 2007; Huesmann 1994). Therefore, early intervention is supported.

Studies have also shown that programmes for aggression reduction, both in Slovenia (Mugnaioni Lešnik et al. 2008) and in other countries (Huesmann 1994), are for the most part unsuccessful. Therefore, it makes sense to place extra focus on the possible predictors of aggressive behaviour in the school setting by developing ways in which to influence those characteristics in order to influence aggression.

Of home-related characteristics, the most strongly related to aggression is SES (Connor 2002; Guerrero et al. 2006; Huesmann 1994), both at the individual and at the community levels (Flannery, Vazsonyi, and Waldman 2007; Krall 2003), and this finding has also proven to be the case in Slovenia (Dekleva 2000). Longitudinal studies (Connor 2002) have shown that when comparing the effects of family and community SES on aggression, a low family SES is an important predictor of aggressive behaviour for both children and adolescents, even when community SES is controlled for. Also significantly associated with high levels of aggression are the low-educational level of parents (Overton 2004), low-educational aspirations (Finn and Frone 2003; Kozina 2007), negative familial relationships (Guerrero et al. 2006; Overton 2004; Reis, Trockel, and Mulhall 2007; Scott 1998; Tanaka, Raishevich, and Scarpa 2010) and the frequency of watching TV (Baron and Richardson 1994; Kozina 2007).

In the present study, we focus on the predictive power of selected variables related to the school and home environment for determining students' aggression. Variables that form a part of the Trends in Mathematics and Science Study (TIMSS) studies are included. We divided the set of predictors into two groups: home and school in order to compare the predictive value of both environments. Home environment variables include those related to SES (e.g. migration status, parents' education, occupation, number of books at home), pupils' educational aspirations, parental activities with their children and pupils' free time activities. School environment variables include those related to the school climate, pupils' attitude towards school and school subjects and pupils' achievements (maths and science achievements and reading literacy). In addition to the analysis of the predictive power of school factors for aggression, possible differences in the levels of aggression at the school level are also analysed by using the hierarchical modelling of TIMSS data from 2007 to 2011. The inclusion of data from both these years enables the greater generalisability of the findings.

Method

Participants

For the 2007 data, we used the TIMSS 2007 national study sample (for Slovenia).[1] For the 2011 data, we used the TIMSS 2011 study sample. Sampling was multi-level and stratified (regions within Slovenia were set as strata). In total, 148 and 209 primary schools in Slovenia were sampled randomly in 2007 and 2011, respectively (school enrolment and region were taken into consideration). Within the selected schools, fourth- and eighth-grade classes were selected randomly (one or two per school). Random sampling was conducted by using WinW3S software (IEA DPC, v. 2006). If parental permission was given, the selected school classes were included in the study as a whole (Table 1).

Instruments

The *Lestvica agresivnosti* (LA) aggression scale (Kozina 2013) consists of 18 self-evaluation items measuring four components of aggression (physical, verbal, inner and aggression towards authority) in the population of primary school pupils and upper-secondary school students. Considering the significant correlation between components, a second-order PCA for testing the existence of a higherorder component was performed both on a sample of primary school pupils ($0.31 < r < 0.48$) and on a sample of upper-secondary school students ($0.22 < r < 0.38$). The sums of the components were used as input data. The second-order PCA showed that in the

Table 1. Sample characteristics.

Grade	2007				2011			
	Male	Female	Total	Age (SD)	Male	Female	Total	Age (SD)
Fourth	2621	2663	4351	9.8 (0.326)	2347	2158	4674	9.9 (0.344)
Eighth	2545	2569	4043	13.8 (0.405)	2274	2173	4741	13.9 (0.351)

Notes: 2007: 86.3% of eighth grade students and 81.6% of fourth-grade students had a mother who was born in the country. 2011: 86.9% of eighth grade students had a mother who was born in the country. Further, 18.8% had a mother with at least ISCED 5a degree, 13.2% with ISCED 5b, 23.2% with ISCED 4, 15.9% with ISCED 3, 5.5% with ISCED 2 and 0.6% with ISCED 1; 81.6% of fourth grade students had a mother who was born in the country, 17.8% had mother with at least ISCED 5a degree, 18.2% with ISCED 5b, 49.5% with ISCED 4, 7.1% with ISCED 3, 0.5% with ISCED 2 and 0.2% with ISCED 1.

background of the structure there is a general aggression component, which is highly loaded with all principal first-order components both in the sample of primary school pupils (0.729; 0.865; 0.854; 0.842) and in the sample of upper-secondary school students (0.753; 0.613; 0.798; 0.814). In the sample of primary school pupils, it explains 67.94% and in the upper-secondary school students sample 56.07% of the total variance of first-order components. This means that we can use the sum of components as a general aggression score. The four-factor hierarchical structure was confirmed with CFA on samples of pupils (RMSEA = 0.067; CFI = 0.912; TLI = 0.897; SRMR = 0.047) and students (RMSEA = 0.079; CFI = 0.895; TLI = 0.876; SRMR = 0.049). The scale thus proved to be psychometrically adequate on the samples of pupils (reliability: $0.724 < \alpha > 0.839$; sensitivity: $r_{average} = 0.56$; validity: $r_{LA-BDHI} = 0.69$) and students (reliability: $0.702 < \alpha > 0.805$; sensitivity: $r_{average} = 0.43$).

TIMSS background questionnaires are designed to measure the characteristics of students' home and school environments. In the analyses, the following variables and internationally developed indexes were used:

- SES; books in the home;
- Migration status; use of language at home;
- Parental educational level;
- Spare time activities (only in 2007);
- Parental support (only in 2011);
- Index of early numeracy – activities and tasks (only in 2011);
- Index of home educational resources (only in 2011);
- Index of students' positive affect towards mathematics/index of students that like maths;
- Index of students' positive affect towards science/index of students that like science;
- Indexes of students' valuing mathematics and science;
- Indexes of students' self-confidence in learning mathematics and science;
- Index of students' perception of being safe at school/index of students being bullied at school;
- School climate; and
- Maths achievement.

For detailed information on the TIMSS variables, see the TIMSS international reports (Martin et al. 2012; Mullis, Martin, and Foy 2008) and TIMSS national reports (Japelj Pavešič, Svetlik, and Kozina 2012; Japelj Pavešić et al. 2008).

Procedure

The administration of the LA aggression scale took place after the administration of the TIMSS (on the same day but not within the TIMSS study). The procedure for the TIMSS study is set in accordance with a precisely specified international sche-dule. After completing the TIMSS questionnaires, participants were given the LA aggression scale, both in 2007 (administration: April 2006) and in 2011 (administra-tion: April 2010). As was the case in the entire TIMSS study, identification codes (randomly assigned combinations of numbers) were used to ensure anonymity. To assure data compatibility, students used the same identity codes in TIMSS and in

LA administration so that afterwards the databases could be merged. The time allotted for completing the LA was not limited. Data were gathered for analysing aggression predictors and not measuring the aggression of individual children; therefore, cut-off points for aggression were not calculated and extra attention was not given to individuals regarding their aggression (owing to the anonymity procedures, this was not possible).

Results

In 2007, the aggression of fourth-grade students can be predicted by the amount of time students devote to spare time activities. The students that watch TV, play computer games or spend time on the Internet are more likely to report higher aggression. On the contrary, the more time they spend on helping in the household or reading books for enjoyment, the less aggression they report. Students who come from migrant families and speak the test language at home less frequently report higher levels of aggression. The model as a whole explains 9% of the variance. In 2011, the aggression of fourth-grade students can be significantly predicted only by one variable. If parents check the homework of students often, students report higher aggression. The amount of explained variance by the model is therefore low (1%) (Table 2).

Similarly, eighth-grade students' aggression can be explained by the amount of time students spend on homework in their spare time. When students spend more time on homework, they report higher aggression. Students that come from families with lower SES also report higher levels of aggression (Table 3).

In 2011, the less frequently eighth-grade students speak the test language at home, the more aggressive they are, whereas students with mothers that have a

Table 2. Predictive power of selected home environment characteristics for fourth-grade pupils' aggression.

	b (SE)	β (SE)	$t\,(b)$	$t\,(\beta)$	R^2	R^{2*}
2007						
Constant	21.08 (3.16)		6.67			
Language at home	1.73 (0.42)	0.09 (0.02)	4.10	4.29		
Spare time – TV	1.25 (0.33)	0.10 (0.03)	3.81	3.77		
Spare time – computer games	1.54 (0.32)	0.13 (0.03)	4.85	4.81		
Spare time – housework	−0.84 (0.22)	−0.07 (0.02)	−3.77	−3.71		
Spare time – read book for enjoyment	−1.21 (0.28)	−0.10 (0.02)	−4.33	−4.43		
Spare time – internet	0.89 (0.27)	0.08 (0.02)	3.30	3.35		
Immigration status – student	2.28 (0.93)	0.05 (0.02)	2.45	2.44	0.09	0.09
2011						
Constant	79.15 (4.25)		18.63			
How often parents check your homework	−0.84 (0.34)	−0.06 (−0.02)	−2.46	−2.48	0.01	0.01

Notes: Owing to the nested sampling design, data were weighted (House Weight). To increase the possibility of generalisation, we used corrected R^2. Multiple regression was conducted (forced entry method) on IDB Analyzer (IEA DPC, v.3.1). The assumption of multicollinearity was tested on both data sets and was not violated (the VIFs were lower than 10 (Myners 1990) (in 2007 VIF varied between 1.048 and 1.718 and in 2011 between 1.060 and 1.482). Linearity assumption was not violated – based on scatter plots.

higher education report lower levels of aggression. In addition, students that have higher educational expectations are more aggressive. By contrast, when parents spend more time on talking with their children about their school work and when they make sure that students have set aside enough time for homework, students report lower levels of aggression (Table 3).

Both in 2007 and in 2011, students that feel safe at school, evaluate the school climate as more positive and feel more confident regarding school and school subjects report lower levels of aggression (Table 4).

As in the fourth grade, both in 2007 and in 2011 students that feel safe at school, that evaluate the school climate as more positive and that feel more confident regarding school and school subjects report lower levels of aggression. There are two exceptions: (i) in 2007, students that value science more report higher aggression and (ii) in 2011, students that value Earth Science more report higher aggression (Table 5).

We were interested in whether the predictors of student aggression vary between schools. Hence, a hierarchical linear model was used to statistically analyse the data where students (level 1) were nested within schools (level 2). For level 1, House Weight was used. For level 2, School Weight was used. The intercept only model (null model) in 2011 showed an ICC of 0.06 for fourth-grade students (and 0.05 for eighth-grade students). Thus, 6% of the variance in fourth-grade students' aggression and 5% of that in eighth-grade students' aggression can be explained by differences between schools. Since the percentage of explained variance between schools is low, the hierarchical analyses would not give significantly different results to those presented above.

Table 3. Predictive power of selected home environment characteristics for eighth-grade pupils' aggression.

	b (SE)	β (SE)	$t(b)$	$t(\beta)$	R^2	R^{2*}
2007						
Constant	20.05 (3.23)					
Spare time- homework	1.13 (0.32)	0.09 (0.02)	3.51	3.63		
SES	0.60 (0.18)	0.08 (0.02)	3.32	3.37	0.01	0.01
2011						
Constant	68.08 (3.12)		21.84			
Language at home	−1.30 (0.42)	−0.08 (0.02)	−3.11	−3.30		
Educational level - mother	−0.45 (0.13)	−0.07 (0.02)	−3.36	−3.39		
Educational expectations - student	0.79 (0.22)	0.09 (0.03)	3.57	3.57		
Talking with parents about school	−1.45 (0.33)	−0.11 (0.02)	−4.42	−4.41		
Parent make sure students have enough time for homework	−1.05 (0.24)	−0.09 (0.02)	−4.38	−4.42	0.06	0.05

Notes: Owing to the nested sampling design, data were weighted (House Weight). To increase the possibility of generalisation, we used corrected R^2. Multiple regression was conducted (forced entry method) on IDB Analyser (IEA DPC, v.3.1). The assumption of multicollinearity was tested on both data sets and was not violated (the VIFs were lower than 10 (Myners 1990) (in 2007 VIF varied between 1.072 and 1.371 and in 2011 between 1.082 and 1.942). Linearity assumption was not violated – based on scatter plots.

Table 4. Predictive power of selected school environment characteristics for fourth-grade pupils' aggression.

	b (SE)	β (SE)	t (b)	t (β)	R^2	R^{2*}
2007						
Constant	24.07 (2.67)		9.00			
Index of students' positive affect towards maths	1.84 (0.44)	0.10 (0.02)	4.19	4.17		
Index of students' positive affect towards science	1.39 (0.38)	0.08 (0.02)	3.67	3.68		
Index of students' self-confidence about learning maths	0.89 (0.43)	0.04 (0.02)	2.04	2.05		
Index of students' self-confidence about learning science	0.94 (0.38)	0.04 (0.02)	2.46	2.48		
Index of students' perception of being safe at school	4.28 (0.32)	0.24 (0.02)	13.22	13.92		
School climate	2.65 (0.32)	0.20 (0.02)	8.39	7.98	0.17	0.17
2011						
Constant	91.64 (1.36)					
Index of students being bullied at school	5.24 (0.40)	0.30 (0.02)	67.19			
Index of students liking learning maths	1.43 (0.47)	0.08 (0.03)	13.22	13.49		
Index of students liking learning science	1.30 (0.44)	0.07 (0.02)	3.02	3.05		
Index of students confident in learning maths	1.55 (0.46)	0.08 (0.02)	2.97	3.01		
Index of students confident in learning science	1.98 (0.53)	0.11 (0.03)	3.40	3.36		
School climate	2.45 (0.35)	0.18 (0.03)	3.70	3.71	0.23	0.23

Notes: Owing to the nested sampling design, data were weighted (House Weight). To increase the possibility of generalisation, we used corrected R^2. Multiple regression was conducted (forced entry method) on IDB Analyser (IEA DPC, v.3.1). The assumption of multicollinearity was tested on both data sets and was not violated (the VIFs were lower than 10 (Myers 1990) (in 2007 VIF varied between 1.014 and 1.371 and in 2011 between 1.037 and 1.558). Linearity assumption was not violated – based on scatter plots.

Discussion

As far as home-related predictors are concerned, the data from both 2007 and 2011 showed different predictors. Despite the fact that the predictor variables differed in these years (e.g. the TIMSS questionnaire in 2011 did not include spare time activities, while that in 2007 did not include parental activities), we decided to include all variables possible in both measured years. In this way, we can ascertain a comprehensive picture of how the different activities and characteristics of the home environment are related to students' aggression.

In 2007, spare time activities are related to students' aggression in both the fourth and the eighth grades. In the fourth grade, the more time students spend on passive (Gril 2006) forms of spare time activities (e.g. videogames, TV, Internet), the more aggressive they are. Our results are in line with the positive relationship established in different research designs across studies (Connor 2002; Huesmann 1994).

Table 5. Predictive power of selected school environment characteristics for eighth-grade pupils' aggression.

	b (SE)	β (SE)	t (b)	t (β)	R^2	R^{2*}
2007						
Constant	25.17 (2.78)		9.04			
School climate	2.69 (0.25)	0.22 (0.02)	10.72	10.75		
Index of students' positive affect towards maths	0.95 (0.29)	0.07 (0.03)	3.27	3.21		
Index of students' positive affect towards science	1.33 (0.36)	0.10 (0.02)	3.70	3.73		
Index of students valuing maths	1.07 (0.47)	0.05 (0.02)	2.31	2.33		
Index of students valuing science	−1.01 (0.35)	−0.07 (0.02)	−2.92	−2.91		
Index of students' self-confidence learning maths	1.20 (0.37)	0.07 (0.02)	3.21	3.18		
Index of students' self-confidence learning science	0.83 (0.38)	0.05 (0.02)	2.19	2.20		
Index of students' perception of being safe at school	3.23 (0.36)	0.18 (0.02)	9.02	9.24	0.19	0.19
2011						
Constant	88.35 (4.38)		20.16			
Index of students being bullied at school	4.07 (0.40)	0.21 (0.02)	10.19	10.18		
Index of students liking learning maths	1.43 (0.45)	0.07 (0.02)	3.18	3.24		
Index of students liking learning biology	1.82 (0.48)	0.10 (0.03)	3.83	3.82		
Index of students valuing Earth Science	−1.39 (0.50)	−0.08 (0.03)	−2.77	−2.81		
Index of students' self-confidence in learning maths	1.70 (0.54)	0.09 (0.03)	3.13	3.17		
Index of students liking learning Earth Science	1.16 (0.49)	0.07 (0.03)	2.36	2.38		
School climate	2.54 (0.35)	0.20 (0.03)	7.28	7.01	0.19	0.19

Notes: Owing to the nested sampling design, data were weighted (House Weight). To increase the possibility of generalisation, we used corrected R^2. Multiple regression was conducted (forced entry method) on IDB Analyser (IEA DPC, v.3.1). The assumption of multicollinearity was tested on both data sets and was not violated (the VIFs were lower than 10 (Myers 1990) (in 2007 VIF varied between 1.031 and 1.981 and in 2011 between 1.062 and 2.553). Linearity assumption was not violated – based on scatter plots.

Nevertheless, the relationship between watching TV and aggressive behaviour is not straightforward and is mediated by personality and temperament traits (e.g. aggressive individuals tend to watch more TV) (Huesmann 1994). The influence of TV watching on aggression is higher in childhood compared with adolescence (Connor 2002); therefore, early intervention in the form of the promotion of active spare time activities (e.g. sports) is supported. Gril (2006) reported that two-thirds of Slovenian primary school students spend their free time in passive ways (e.g. watching films) and one-quarter behind a computer. This could be worrying information for Slovenia and it brings into focus the process of influencing and offering children and adolescents more possibilities for active spare time use. Our results also show that students who read books for enjoyment or help with household chores report lower aggression. This finding is in line with self-determination theory (Ryan and Deci 2009), which proposes giving responsibilities and choices to children and adolescents as a key competence for developing positive self-esteem.

Our results are also congruent with the research literature that has established that aggressive behaviour is more frequent in students from immigrant families and in families of lower SES. We can find several explanations of these types of relationships in the research literature. For instance, some studies (Gorman-Smith and Tolan 1998, cited in Matthews, Dreary, and Whiteman 2009; Perkins and Borden 2003) mostly suggest that aggressive behaviour is one of the many adaptation difficulties (also reported by immigrant families; see Kraševec Ravnik 1996) that individuals of low SES face. Individuals with lower SES more frequently report feeling threatened and perceive neutral events as more threatening compared with individuals of higher SES. This cognitive appraisal can lead to more aggressive reactions (Matthews, Dreary, and Whiteman 2009). Low SES families more frequently report negative patterns of relationships, which again can lead to more aggressive behaviour (Matthews, Dreary, and Whiteman 2009).

The patterns of parental behaviour (individual activities related to schoolwork) were included in TIMSS 2011. In 2011, parental activities served as a significant predictor of students' aggression. When parents check students' homework more frequently, students report higher aggression. The relationships and types of analyses conducted do not allow us to ascertain a causal interpretation. For instance, the relationship could be mediated by a third variable such as low-educational achievement. Aggression is related to lower achievement at school, while parents of more aggressive students that are less successful at school must spend more time on homework (checking, encouraging, etc.). On the contrary, this could also show the lack of confidence that parents have in their children, which could also result in their higher aggression.

Vallerand, Fortier, and Guay (1997) studied the specific contextual and motivational predictors of high dropout rates. The study indicated that students who perceived their parents (and teachers) as allowing them to be more autonomous saw themselves as more confident related to schoolwork and they were less likely to quit school. Both conclusions are at this point only preliminary and they still need more in-depth analyses of the relationship between parenting styles and student achievement. In Slovenia, similar analyses have shown a significant positive relationship between educational achievement and students' perceived autonomy (Rutar Leban et al. 2009).

Students that have higher autonomy from their parents and teachers show higher confidence regarding school subjects. Confidence is one of the most significant predictors of aggression in our school characteristics regression model. The results are congruent in both years and both grades. Again, supporting autonomy is recommended, as self-confidence is positively related to achievement (Martin et al. 2012). In the expectancy–value model (Pintrich 2003), three general components are important for the learning achievement: belief in one's ability or skill to perform the task (expectancy components); belief in the importance, interest and utility of the task (value components); and feelings about the self or emotional reactions to the tasks (affective components). We used all these components (TIMSS indexes) as possible predictors of students' aggression. Overall, we found that the strongest predictors of aggression are expectancy components in the form of self-confidence about certain subject matters. The results showed that by increasing students' self-confidence, we can expect their aggression level to decrease. Schools could thus focus on building students' confidence by positive appraisal, individualisation and a supportive learning environment.

In general, as school-related factors are congruent in both years and for both grades, this enables us to draw more stable conclusions. Students' aggression can be significantly predicted by the perception of a negative school climate (with more frequent bullying at school), positive attitudes towards school and students' self-confidence regarding school subjects. A positive relationship between students' reports of their own aggressive behaviour and frequency of overall aggressive behaviour is expected. This is in line with the finding that being surrounded by aggressive peers is one of the strongest predictors of aggressive behaviour being developed in non-aggressive students (Archer and Coyne 2005; Boxer et al. 2003; Conner 2002; Flannery, Vazsonyi, and Waldman 2007; Huesmann 1994; Wienke-Totura et al. 2009). The frequency of aggressive behaviour at school is an indicator of a negative school climate (Freiberg 1999); therefore, early intervention in the form of school climate changes is supported. Special focus should be placed on providing clear and consistent sanctions for aggressive behaviour (e.g. clear rules, emotional and social learning) and creating an environment that fosters positive attitudes towards school subjects (e.g. relating subject matters to everyday life and the interests of students).

In comparison to the home characteristics regression models, the school characteristics regression models explain larger parts of fourth- and eighth-grade students' aggression. School context, as measured in our study, has a larger predictive value for pupils' aggression, indicating that schools can play a significant role in aggression prevention and reduction. As far as home environment predictors are concerned, special attention should be paid to immigrant students and the promotion of active spare time activities.

Although the study offers important insights into some of the characteristics related to pupils' aggression in large representative samples at two time points, it is not without limitations. One of the biggest limitations of the study is the limited selection of the predictor variables, which are not nearly all the variables that could predict pupils' aggression and therefore our conclusions are limited. The percentages of explained variances by the regression models (especially home related models) are low and therefore the conclusions are limited. Future studies should focus more thoroughly on one or two characteristics such as confidence regarding school subjects and the autonomy process regarding aggressive behaviour.

Note

1. The study used TIMSS study samples in order to assure greater representativeness and the joint use of TIMSS databases.

References

Archer, J., and S. M. Coyne. 2005. "An Integrated Review of Indirect, Relational, and Social Aggression." *Personality and Social Psychology Review* 9: 212–230.

Baron, R. A., and D. R. Richardson. 1994. *Human Aggression.* New York: Plenum.

Boxer, P., L. Edwards-Leeper, S. E. Goldstein, D. Musher-Eizenman, and E. F. Dubow. 2003. "Exposure to "Low-Level" Aggression in School: Associations with Aggressive Behaviour, Future Expectations, and Perceived Safety." *Violence and Victims* 18 (6): 691–704.

Brookmeyer, K. A., K. A. Fanti, and G. C. Heinrich. 2006. "Schools, Parents, and Youth Violence: A Multilevel, Ecological Analysis." *Journal of Clinical Children and Adolescence Psychology* 35: 504–514.

Brown, K. M., V. A. Anfara, and K. Roney. 2004. "Student Achievement in High Performing, Suburban Middle Schools and Low Performing, Urban Middle Schools: Plausible Explanations for the Differences." *Education and Urban Society* 36 (4): 428–456.

Buhs, E. S., G. W. Ladd, and S. L. Herald. 2006. "Peer Exclusion and Victimization: Processes that Mediate the Relation between Peer Group Rejection and Children's Classroom Engagement and Achievement?" *Journal of Educational Psychology* 98: 1–13.

Connor, D. F. 2002. *Aggression and Antisocial Behaviour in Children and Adolescents Reserach and Treatment.* New York: Guilford Press.

Dekleva, B. (2000). "Šola, Mladi, Nasilje [School, Youth, Violence]." In *Prestopniško in odklonsko vedenje mladih – vzroki, pojavi, odzivanje* [Deliquency in Youth - Reasons, Types and Interventions], edited by V. A. Šelih, 137–141. Ljubljana: Bonex.

Finn, K. V., and M. R. Frone. 2003. "Predictors of Aggression at School: The Effect of School-Related Alcohol Use." *NASSP Bulletin* 87 (363): 38–54.

Flannery, D. J., A. T. Vazsonyi, and I. D. Waldman. 2007. *The Cambridge Handbook of Violent Behavior and Aggression.* Cambridge: Cambridge University Press.

Freiberg, H. J. 1999. *School Climate: Measuring, Improving, and Sustaining Healthy Learning Environments.* London: Falmer Press.

Green, K. D., R. Forehand, S. J. Beck, and B. Vosk. 1980. "An Assessment of the Relationship among Measures of Children's Social Competence and Children's Academic Achievement." *Child Development* 51: 1149–1156.

Gril, A. 2006. *Prosti čas mladih v Ljubljani* [Youths' Spare Time in Ljubljana]. Ljubljana: Pedagoški inštitut.

Guerrero, A. P. S., E. S. Hishinuma, N. N. Andrade, S. T. Nishimura, and V. L. Cunanan. 2006. "Correlations among Socioeconomic and Family Factors and Academic, Behavioral, and Emotional Difficulties in Filipino Adolescents in Hawai'i." *International Journal of Social Psychiatry* 52 (4): 343–359.

Huesmann, L. R. 1994. *Aggressive Behaviour – Current Perspectives.* New York: Plenum Press.

Japelj Pavešič, B., K. Svetlik, and A. Kozina. 2012. Znanje matematike in naravoslovja med osnovnošolci v Sloveniji in po svetu, izlsedki raziskave TIMSS 2011 [Slovenia in TIMSS 2011 Study]. Ljubljana: Pedagoški inštitut.

Japelj Pavešić, B., K. Svetlik, A. Kozina, and M. Rožman. 2008. *Matematični dosežki Slovenije v raziskavi TIMSS 2007* [Slovenian Math Achievement in TIMSS 2007 study]. Ljubljana: Pedagoški inštitut.

Kozina, A. 2007. *Measurement of Students' Aggressive Behaviour in School Settings. V: ECER. 2007. Contested Qualities of Educational Research.* Ghent: EERA.

Kozina, A. 2013. "The LA Aggression Scale for Elementary School and Upper Secondary School Students: Examination of Psychometric Properties of a New Multidimensional Measure of Self-reported Aggression." *Psihologija* 46 (3): 245–259.

Krall, H. 2003. "Mladina in nasilje: teoretične koncepcije in perspektive pedagoškega ravnanja [Youth and Violence: Theoretical Concepts and Perspectives in Educational Process]." *Sodobna Pedagogika* 54 (2): 10–25.

Kraševec Ravnik, E. 1996. *Varovanje zdravja posebnih družbenih skupin v Sloveniji* [Health Issues in Marginal Groups in Slovenia]. Ljubljana: Inštitut za varovanje zdravja Republike Slovenije in Slovenska fondacija.

Ladd, G. W., B. J. Kochenderfer, and C. C. Coleman. 1997. "Classroom Peer Acceptance, Friendship, and Victimization: Distinct Relational Systems that Contribute Uniquely to Children's School Adjustment?" *Child Development* 68: 1181–1197.

Malm, B., and H. Löfgren. 2006. "Teacher Competence and Students' Conflict Handling Strategies." *Research in Education* 11 (1): 62–73.

Marjanovič Umek, L., and M. Zupančič. 2004. *Razvojna psihologija* [Developmental Psychology]. Ljubljana: Znanstvenoraziskovalni inštitut Filozofske fakultete.

Martin, M. O., I. V. S. Mullis, P. Foy, and G. M. Stanco. 2012. *TIMSS 2011 International Science Results*. Boston, MA: TIMSS&PIRLS International Study Center.

Matthews, G., I. J. Deary, and M. C. Whiteman. 2009. *Personality Traits*. Cambridge: Cambridge University Press.

McEvoy, A., and R. Welker. 2000. "Antisocial Behavior, Academic Failure, and School Climate: A Critical Review." *Journal of Emotional and Behavioral Disorders* 8 (3): 130–140.

Mugnaioni Lešnik, D., A. Koren, V. Logaj, and M. Brejc. 2008. *Nasilje v šolah: Konceptualizacija, prepoznavanje in modeli preprečevanja in obvladovanja* [Violence in Schools: Concepts, Identifications, Models of Prevention and Intervention]. Ljubljana: Šola za ravnatelje.

Mullis, I. V. S., M. O. Martin, and P. Foy. 2008. *TIMSS 2007 International Mathematics Report: Findings from IEA's Trends in International Mathematics and Science Study at the Fourth and Eighth Grades*. Chestnut Hill, MA: TIMSS & PIRLS International Study Center, Boston College.

Myners, R. 1990. *Classical and Modern Regression with Implications*. 2nd ed. Boston, MA: Duxbury.

Overton, W. F. 2004. *Trajectories of Physical Aggression from Toddlerhood to Middle Childhood*. Oxford: Blackwell.

Perkins, D. F., and L. M. Borden. 2003. "Positive Behaviours, Problem Behaviours, and Resiliency in Adolescence." In *Handbook of Psychology, Developmental Psychology*, edited by V. R. M. Lerner, M. A. Easterbrooks, and J. Mistry, 373–395. Hoboken, NJ: John Wiley and Sons.

Pintrich, P. R. 2003. "Motivation and Classroom Learning." In *Handbook of Psychology, Educational Psychology*, Vol. 7, edited by I. B. Weiner, 103–122. Hoboken, NJ: John Wiley and sons.

Popp, U. 2003. "Nasiljev šoli in koncepti njegovega preprečevanja [Violence in School and Concept of Prevention]." *Sodobna Pedagogika* 54 (2): 26–41.

Reis, J., M. Trockel, and P. Mulhall. 2007. "Individual and School Predictors of Middle School Aggression." *Youth & Society* 38 (3): 322–347.

Rutar Leban, T., T. Vršnik Perše, A. Kozina, and Z. Pavlović. 2009. "Elementi vzgojnega sloga staršev in dosežki mladostnikov [Elements of Parental Style and Students' Achievement]." *Šolsko Polje* 20 (3/4): 87–103.

Ryan, R. M., and E. L. Deci. 2009. "Promoting Self-Determined School Engagement: Motivation, Learning, and Well-Being." In *Handbook on Motivation at School*, edited by K. R. Wentzel and A. Wigfield, 171–196. New York: Routledge.

Schwartz, D. J., A. H. Gorman, J. Nakamoto, and T. McKay. 2006. "Popularity, Social Acceptance, and Aggression in Adolescent Peer Groups: Links with Academic Performance and School Attendance." *Developmental Psychology* 42 (6): 1116–1127.

Scott, S. 1998. "Aggressive Behaviour in Childhood–Fortnightly Review." *British Medical Journal* 316: 202–206.

Tanaka, A., N. Raishevich, and A. Scarpa. 2010. "Family Conflict and Childhood Aggression: The Role of Child Anxiety." *Journal of Interpersonal Violence* 20 (10): 1–17.

Vallerand, R. J., M. S. Fortier, and F. Guay. 1997. "Self-Determination and Persistence in Real-Life Setting: Towards a Motivational Model of High Dropout." *Journal of Personality and Social Psychology* 72: 1161–1176.

Vandell, D. L., and S. E. Hembree. 1994. "Peer Social Status and Friendship: Independent Contributors to Children's Social and Academic Adjustment." *Merrill-Palmer Quarterly* 40 (4): 461–477.

Vitaro, F., M. Brendgen, and E. D. Barker. 2006. "Subtypes of Aggressive Behaviours: A Developmental Perspective." *International Journal of Behavioural Development* 30 (1): 12–19.

Wentzel, K. R., and S. R. Asher. 1995. "The Academic Lives of Neglected, Rejected, Popular, and Controversial Children." *Child Development* 66: 754–763.

Wienke-Totura, C. M., C. MacKinnon-Lewis, E. L. Gesten, R. Gadd, K. P. Divine, S. Dunham, and D. Kamboukos. 2009. "Bullying and Victimization among Boys and Girls in Middle School: The Influence of Perceived Family and School Contexts." *Journal of Early Adolescence* 29 (4): 571–609.

Ybrandt, H., and K. Armelius. 2010. "Peer Aggression and Mental Health Problems: Self-Esteem as a Mediator." *School Psychology International* 31: 146–163.

Zhou, Q., A. Main, and Y. Wang. 2010. "The Relations of Temperamental Effortful Control and Anger/Frustration to Chinese Children's Academic Achievement and Social Adjustment: A Longitudinal Study." *Journal of Educational Psychology* 120 (1): 180–196.

Constructing bullying in Ontario, Canada: a critical policy analysis

Sue Winton[a] and Stephanie Tuters[b]

[a]Faculty of Education, York University, Toronto, Canada; [b]LHAE, Ed Admin, University of Toronto, Toronto, Canada

As the prevalence and negative effects of bullying become widely known, people around the world seem desperate to solve the bullying "problem". A sizeable body of research about many aspects of bullying and a plethora of anti-bullying programmes and policies now exist. This critical policy analysis asks: how does Ontario, Canada's bullying policy support and/or undermine critical democracy; and how does it reflect, support and further the interests of neoliberalism and/or neoconservatism? Findings indicate that the policy constructs the problem of bullying as a problem of individuals and a "behaviour for learning" problem. The policy also prescribes standardised responses to bullying incidents. We explore ways in which these constructions are undemocratic and unjust. The findings are particularly concerning because bullying policies are often viewed as innocuous by practitioners. This paper offers more than just critique by providing suggestions for how research and policies can become more just and equitable and how bullying policy may be enacted to support critical democracy.

What can be done to stop bullying? As the widespread prevalence and negative effects of bullying on youth and society become widely known, researchers, teachers, parents and government officials around the world appear desperate to solve the bullying "problem". Their concern has given rise to a sizeable body of knowledge about characteristics, behaviours and effects of bullies, victims and bystanders; new laws and policies; and a plethora of anti-bullying programmes. Not aiming to minimise concerns about bullying on youth, the critical policy analysis (CPA) described in this article asks a different question: how does Ontario, Canada's current bullying policy support and/or undermine critical democracy? More specifically, it examines Ontario's approach to addressing bullying in schools to understand if and how it reflects, supports and furthers the interests of neoliberalism, neoconservatism and/or critical democracy.

We begin by locating our study in the field of CPA. We then briefly review the contemporary global education policy context and highlight how neoliberalism and neoconservatism, as political rationalities (Brown 2006), have influenced education policy in Ontario and beyond. Next, we review how bullying is typically conceptualised in research and policy and discuss critiques of their dominant discourse around bullying. We then explain how we conducted a critical discourse analysis of key

Ontario bullying policy texts. Finally, we present findings from our analysis and demonstrate that Ontario's bullying policy serves the interests of neoliberalism and neoconservatism in three main ways: (1) by constructing bulling as an individual (as opposed to a social/systemic) problem; (2) by constructing bullying as a "behaviour for learning" problem (Ball, Hoskins et al. 2011)[1]; and (3) by adopting a standardised approach.

Critical policy analysis

This article draws on findings from a larger study located in the field of CPA and adopts a critical understanding of policy. Unlike traditional conceptions that view policy exclusively as authoritative decisions written in official texts (Rizvi and Lingard 2010), a critical perspective sees policy as involving practices, power, struggles and compromises (Ball 1994; Bowe, Ball, and Gold 1992). Policy is understood as complex, inherently political and infused with values rather than as a linear process that parallels a rational model of decision-making (Bowe, Ball, and Gold 1992; Stone 2002). CPA emphasises the importance of examining policy within its historical, social, economic, cultural and political contexts (Rizvi and Lingard 2010; Taylor 1997; Vidovich 2007; Winton 2012a, 2012b). Further, CPA understands that policy problems, like the social world, are social constructions, and it views language as playing a central role in creating and disseminating these constructions (Edelman 1988; Scheurich 1994; Winton 2013). It recognises that how a policy problem is constructed affects the possibilities for how the problem is addressed. Finally, CPA aims to challenge inequalities by understanding the role policies play in producing and maintaining them (Winton 2013).

Grounded in the assumptions and concerns of CPA, the study conceptualises policy as a cycle comprised of three contexts: influence, text production and practices (Bowe, Ball, and Gold 1992). The context of influence includes public and private arenas wherein discourses are constructed, key concepts are defined and struggles over meaning take place (Bowe, Ball, and Gold 1992). The context of text production includes texts representing policy such as official policy documents, legislation, speeches, web sites, news reports, reports and research related to the policy issue (Bowe, Ball, and Gold 1992). Policy texts are both text and discourse (Ball 1994; Gale 1999). As texts they attempt to represent ideas and influence what people do (Ball 1994). As discourses, policy texts construct and reconstruct the social world (Bacchi 2000). Policy discourses permeate all three contexts of the policy cycle (Gale 1999). The context of practice includes actions taken in the name of policy (Koyama 2013) as well as actions organised by policy decisions even if they are not recognised as such. These actions produce outcomes and effects (Ball 1994). The contexts of influence, text production and practice continuously affect one another.

Policy cycles exist at all levels of policy activity, and cycles influence one another. Their relationships can be conceptualised as existing within a web wherein the policy contexts of one cycle influence cycles at the same level as well as cycles at other levels. Policy webs are themselves embedded in international influences (Vidovich 2007; Winton 2012b). This article focuses on the relationship between the context of influence, which include neoliberal and neoconservative ideologies dominant nationally and internationally, and the context of text production in Ontario's bullying policy cycle and discusses how the first two contexts have and may continue to influence the context of practice.

Ontario education policy in the contemporary global context

Contemporary education policies are designed within a global policy field (Rizvi and Lingard 2010). Ideas travel through transnational policy networks via global academic and political meetings; intergovernmental organisations; multinational corporations; policy entrepreneurs; rapid communication technologies; international students and programmes; movement of people across borders; and the media (Ball 1998; Rizvi and Lingard 2010). Rizvi and Lingard (2010) describe a global convergence around neoliberal ideas and values in education policy.

Neoliberalism is committed to the "essential fairness and justice of markets" (Apple 2006, 35) and promotes a global market economy with limited but strategic state intervention (Bencze and Carter 2011; Winton 2008). Neoliberal ideology, which celebrates competition, entrepreneurialism, private ownership, accountability, consumer choice and the individual, has transformed social, economic and political policy globally in part through initiatives such as privatisation, deregulation, regressive tax reforms, campaigns of state debt and deficit reduction, attacks on trade unions, opening doors to foreign investment and the dismantling of social services (Ball 1998; Baronov 2007; Carpenter, Weber, and Schugurensky 2012; Carroll and Shaw 2001; Davies and Bansel 2007; Larner 2000). Neoliberal subjects' "desires, hopes, ideals and fears have been shaped in such a way that they desire to be morally worthy, responsibilised individuals, who, as successful entrepreneurs, can produce the best for themselves and their families" (Davies and Bansel 2007, 251). Individuals' choices, indeed all social behaviour, are conceived as outcomes of rational choices (Davies and Bansel 2007).

A second key influence on contemporary education policy in Canada, the USA and the UK is one operating in connection with neoliberalism: neoconservatism (Apple 2006; Bencze and Carter 2011; Pinto 2012; Winton 2008). Neoconservative ideology includes both social and political attitudes (Nevitte and Gibbins 1984). Politically, neoconservatives want to reduce the size, influence and spending of government and see it better supporting the private sector (Nevitte and Gibbins 1984). Important social components of neoconservatism include a fear of diversity, desire for greater control and predictability, standardisation and celebration of the moral authority of tradition (Apple 2006; Winton 2012b). Neoconservatives advocate schools with "traditional, uncontestable curriculum" (Pinto 2012, 24) and "get tough" approaches to crime.

Critics of neoliberal and neoconservative influences on education contend they contradict principles of critical democracy. Critical democracy is an ideal that values equity, diversity, dialogue, inclusion, reasoned choices, social justice and citizens' participation in decisions that affect their lives (Pinto 2012; Solomon and Portelli 2001). Rather than a form of government, critical democracy is a way of life (Dewey 1966). It prioritises social justice above individual liberty (Pinto 2013). Not only do the tenets of neoliberalism and neoconservatism conflict with the beliefs and commitments of critical democracy, they lay the groundwork for "profoundly anti-democratic political ideas and practices to take root in the culture and the subject" (Brown 2006, 702).

In Canada, each province and territory is responsible for providing and governing education for its citizens; there is no national education policy. Successive governments in Ontario since the mid-1990s have introduced a number of education policies supporting and reflecting neoliberal and neoconservative values and goals.

These policies include: the creation of an office responsible for coordinating standardised provincial testing of students; a standardised provincial curriculum for Kindergarten-12; the development of standards for the teaching profession; a provincial *Code of Conduct;* Safe Schools legislation; and the Character Development Initiative (Carpenter, Weber, and Schugurensky 2012; Winton 2012b).

Among other outcomes, Ontario policies grounded in neoliberal and neoconservative values have resulted in: a narrowed curriculum that prioritises numeracy and literacy above all other subjects (Joshee 2012; Westheimer 2010); the redefinition of school success as high achievement on standardised tests and of equity as narrowing gaps in achievement on these tests (Joshee 2012); reduced professional autonomy for teachers (Carpenter, Weber, and Schugurensky 2012; Westheimer 2010); increased reliance on parents to raise funds for schools; disproportionate rates of school exclusion for racial minority students, students with special needs, poor students, and academically failing, White students (Bhattacharjee 2003; Daniel and Bondy 2008); the prioritisation of preparing students for the workplace (Joshee 2012); decreased emphasis on promoting students' critical thinking (Westheimer 2010); reduced funding for classrooms (Carpenter, Weber, and Schugurensky 2012); and, ultimately, the exacerbation of social inequalities and the erosion of democracy in education (Carpenter, Weber, and Schugurensky 2012; Solomon and Portelli 2001).

Bullying research

Research and popular interest in bullying at school have increased over the past few decades as the prevalence and negative effects of bullying on youth and society become widely known. While prevalence is difficult to determine, Limber (2002 as cited in Sherer and Nickerson 2010) report that one in five children are victims of bullying. One in three children are bullies, victims or both (Nansel et al. 2001 as cited in Sherer and Nickerson 2010). A 2003 Canadian study found that 29% of students had experienced bullying once or twice during the past school term (Mishna et al. 2010). Members of minoritised groups are particularly vulnerable to bullying (Mishna et al. 2010, 45).

Much research focuses on individuals' behaviour (Walton 2005). Research on bullying aims to: define bullying; identify bullies, bystanders and victims; and develop and evaluate anti-bullying initiatives in efforts to reduce bullying and its consequences. Despite some variations, bullying is often defined along the following lines (Walton 2005):

> a student is being bullied or victimized when he or she is exposed, repeatedly and over time, to negative actions on the part of one or more other students. It is a negative action when someone intentionally inflicts, or attempts to inflict, injury or discomfort upon another – basically what is implied in the definition of aggressive behaviour. (Olweus 1994, 1173)

Thus, bullying is understood to involve intentional and repeated behaviour of one individual towards another; further, a power imbalance of some kind exists between the bully and the victim (Dake, Price, and Telljohann 2003). This power imbalance may be attributed to size, perceived strength, sexual orientation, class, socio-economic status and other factors. Efforts to identify bullies suggest that boys are more frequent instigators of bullying, particularly physical bullying, and that girls bully less than boys but engage in more relational bullying than physical bullying (Berger 2007; Farrington 1993). Bullies are described as aggressive and power seeking (Berger 2007; Salmivalli 2010) and are often perceived as popular by their peers even if they are not (Dijkstra, Lindenberg, and Veenstra 2008; Poyhonen, Juvonen, and Salmivalli 2010; Salmivalli 2010). Bullies feel less connected with their teachers and their schools than non-bullies (Berger 2007). Victims are identified as either weak or vulnerable compared to their peers in some way or they are aggressive yet socially outcast (Berger 2007).

Research on bullying behaviour identifies three forms: physical, verbal and social (Law et al. 2012). Bullying may involve physical altercations, verbal exchanges such as threats or insults, facial or other obscene gestures, or any form of intentional exclusion from social or group activities (Pornari and Wood 2010). Incidents of bullying can involve issues of race, class, sex, sexual orientation, gender and ability. Bullying can occur in person or through the use of texts or technology.

Finally, research has aimed to understand the effects of bullying. Significant relationships have been found between bullying behaviours and the physical, psychological and social well-being of children (Dake, Price, and Telljohann 2003). Students who have been bullied experience higher levels of suicidal and depressed thoughts, anxiety, low self-esteem, absence and fear of school (among other things) (Dixon 2011; Nishina 2004; Olweus 1994). These effects are long lasting. For instance, children who experienced bullying at age 8 were found to have symptoms of clinical depression at age 15 (Dake, Price, and Telljohann 2003). Additional negative outcomes include: low academic achievement; physical and psychological difficulties in adulthood, including depression, low self-esteem and suicidal ideation; higher rates of antisocial acts; greater likelihood of dropping out of school; and higher risk of arrest as an adult (Jacobs 2008). Being a bystander is associated with perceiving the school climate to be unsafe, being afraid of being bullied, decreased school attendance and refusing to use the washroom for fear of bullying (Berger 2007; Furlong, Sherer, and Nickerson 2010; Jacobs 2008; Nishina 2004; Poyhonen, Juvonen, and Salmivalli 2010).

Researchers acknowledge that bullying must be considered within context even as their research focuses on individuals. Indeed, bullying is often described using ecological systems theory which acknowledges that bullying is complex phenomenon with multiple influences, causes and correlates (Atlas and Pepler 1998 as cited in Mishna et al. 2010, 44). Nevertheless, the emphasis in much bullying research remains on individuals and their behaviour rather than on social or cultural elements and outcomes (Walton 2005, 2011).

Policy responses to bullying

In addition to research attention, bullying has received an increasing amount of political attention over the last 15 years. Many European countries have laws regarding bullying in schools, including Finland, France, Ireland, Luxembourg, Malta, Sweden and the UK (Dixon 2011, 25). In the United States, all 50 states have bullying laws, policies or (US Department of Health and Human Services n.d.). In Canada, most provinces and territories have policies regarding bullying and some, like Ontario, have recently changed their legislation to make their policies law. Quebec, Manitoba, New Brunswick and Alberta have introduced bullying legislation since 2012. The different Canadian jurisdictions that have bullying policies and programmes vary greatly, however, their approaches are alarmingly similar (Walton 2011). A cursory review of different policy and programme documents highlights their similarities. Manitoba's Bill 18 (Government of Manitoba 2013), for example, defines bullying as behaviour that is

> intended to cause, or should be known to cause, fear, intimidation, humiliation, distress or other forms of harm to another person's body, feelings, self-esteem, reputation or property; or (b) is intended to create, or should be known to create, a negative school environment for another person.

Similarly, New Brunswick's Bill 52 defines bullying as

> systematically and chronically inflicting physical harm or psychological distress on one or more pupils and may involve (a) teasing, (b) social exclusion, (c) threats, (d) intimidation, (e) stalking, (f) physical violence, (g) theft, (h) sexual or racial harassment, (i) public humiliation, or (j) destruction of property. (Government of New Brunswick 2012)

Bullying is a suspendable offence in New Brunswick, and students who are suspended for bullying must "participate in educational programmes highlighting the negative consequences associated with bullying and harassment" (Government of New Brunswick 2012). The bullying prevention legislation in Bill 3 in Alberta is similarly strict. For instance, the Bill's section 31 states that students are required to refrain from, report and not tolerate bullying behaviours; under section 36 students can be suspended for failure to comply with any part of section 31 (Government of Alberta 2012).

Notably, these and other policies across Canada (and beyond) frame and approach bullying as an individualised phenomenon. They focus on the actions of and consequences for "specific" individuals rather than acknowledging the complex and multifaceted nature of bullying and the larger societal and systematic forces at play (Walton 2004, 29). Initiatives often refer to a "bully", "victim" or "bystander" suggesting clear distinctions exist between them. These distinctions oversimplify the nature of bullying and promote the conceptualisation of bullying as a problem of "good" and "bad" individuals (Walton 2005, 94). Oversimplification contributes to the creation of standardised "one-size" fits all policy and programme solutions to bullying. Constructing bullying as a problem of individuals reflects neoliberalism's emphasis on the responsible, rational subject.

Furthermore, research demonstrates bullying often involves issues of marginalisation and exclusion (e.g. racism, classism and homophobia), yet policies and programmes focus largely on bullying in general, avoiding issues such as homophobia (Walton 2004). This standardisation of bullying treats all bullying incidents as though they are the same and therefore require the standardised interventions and solutions (Loutzenheiser 2009). Within standardised approaches certain forms of bullying receive greater attention than others. Bullying that conforms to dominant conceptions of acceptable and unacceptable behaviours, such as physical altercations between a physically superior bully and a smaller victim, receive more attention whereas acts of bullying grounded in discrimination and oppression receive less focus. Bullying motivated by discrimination and oppression creates educational environments that are safer for some students (those who conform to dominant identities) than others (those who experience marginalisation and oppression; Walton 2004).

While paying limited attention to contextual factors that support and perpetuate bullying, policies give considerable attention to how bullying affects school climate. For example, the New York State Education Department states

> Bullying in general and cyberbullying in particular are becoming increasingly important concerns to educators, students, and parents and have created new challenges for school administrators in their efforts to create and maintain safe and secure learning environments. Students need to feel safe in order to maximise their academic and social potential. (1)

Ball et al. (2011) detail the English government's emphasis on the relationship between bullying and academic achievement through various "behaviour for learning" initiatives (2). Below, we demonstrate that Ontario's bullying policy similarly emphasises positive "behaviour for learning". Before turning to this discussion, however, we first describe the approach we used to understand how if and how Ontario's approach to addressing bullying reflects, supports and furthers the interests of neoliberalism, neoconservatism and/or critical democracy.

Methodological approach

As part of a larger CPA, we undertook a critical discourse analysis (CDA) of Bill 13 (Government of Ontario 2012) and PPM 144 (Ontario Ministry of Education 2012b) to understand how these texts construct the problem of bullying and the solutions they mandate for addressing the problem. CDA combines semiotic/linguistic analysis and social analysis to understand "how texts construct representations of the world, social relationships, and social identities" and highlights how practices and texts are shaped by relations of power (Fairclough 2001; Taylor 1997, 432). Many methodological approaches to CDA are used in education research (Rogers et al. 2005) including those described by Fairclough (2001), Gee (2010) and Thomas (2005).

Our approach to CDA draws on Chouliaraki and Fairclough's framework (1999, as cited in Fairclough 2001) and Thomas's (2005) operationalisation of it for CPA. This framework involves five stages. Stage one involves the identification of a social problem; the problem can be a social practice or the construction of a social practice (Thomas 2005). In this component of our CPA, the discursive construction of bullying in official Ontario policy texts was the social problem of interest. Stage two of the framework aims to "reconstruct the relationship between the policy texts and the context in which they are used" (Thomas 2005, 30). Doing so involves analysing the social practices within which the discourse is located as well as analysing the practices in the current discursive moment relative to other social moments (Thomas 2005). Here, we drew on extensive work already completed as part of our larger CPA. That is, we examined relationships between texts in the context of text production of Ontario's safe schools policy web and activities in the contexts of influence and practice. We also constructed an historical narrative of safe schools and bullying policies in Ontario from 1994 to the present. We constructed the policy web and historical narrative based on an extensive analysis of "official" policy texts produced by the Ontario government, Ontario's *Education Act*, government press releases, news articles, reports of Ontario's Safe Schools Action team, scholarly research, and reports and websites produced by government and non-governmental organisations since 1994.

Stage two also involved identifying discourses in Bill 13 and PPM 144 (Ontario Ministry of Education 2012b) to understand the relationship between "linguistic elements and the social" (Thomas 2005, 33). To understand how the texts discursively construct bullying we read Bill 13 (Government of Ontario 2012) and PPM 144 (Ontario Ministry of Education 2012b) line-by-line and highlighted all textual references to bullying, bullies, victims as well as statements describing what principals, schools, school boards, students and parents can, should, or must do in relation to bullying. Highlighted phrases were grouped in categories with like phrases (e.g. supports for bullies, reporting bullying, and parent involvement). Examining the categories individually as well as holistically, we considered what was not represented in the text as well as what was present. For example, when we examined what schools *are* required to implement in schools, we noted that they *are not* required to ensure critical examination of how power over others is exerted by institutions, governments and other groups in society and/or how dominant societal power relationships are reflected in bullying in schools.

Stage three of the framework involved consideration of the ways the discursive construction of bullying functions within current social practices. We asked: whose/ what interests are served by this discourse? How does it reflect and recreate the social world? How does this discourse relate to the current climate of neoliberalism and neoconservatism in Ontario and beyond? And finally, how does this discourse relate to education as a critical democratic process? This stage is intended to help illuminate why the social problem may be resistant to change. In stage four, we identified "possibilities for change in the way social life is organised" (Thomas 2005, 39). We considered how vague language and omissions in Bill 13 (Government of Ontario 2012) and PPM 144 (Ontario Ministry of Education 2012b) as well as other policy texts create opportunities for interpretation and enactment that support alternate constructions of bullying. Finally, in stage five, we reflected on our own social positions and how they may have influenced and limited our analysis. We now turn to a discussion of our findings. We first present a summary of stage five, so readers understand how the subsequent findings may be related to our perspectives and experiences.

Researchers in the research

We are both white, middle-class women, who examine policy through a critical lens and aim to enhance democracy in public education systems. Through our combined experiences working with marginalised youth, in elementary schools, and in Ontario's Ministry of Education, we have come to view all policy as political. Our research (and Winton's teaching in undergraduate and graduate programmes in education) aims to understand the outcomes and effects of policy (Ball 1994) and identify opportunities for democratising policy processes. We are persuaded by our previous research (Tuters 2014; Winton 2012a, 2012b, 2013) and others' scholarship (e.g. Carpenter, Weber, and Schugurensky 2012; Joshee 2012; Pinto 2012; Rizvi and Lingard 2010) that neoliberal and neoconservative ideas and values are important influences on contemporary educational policy processes in Ontario and beyond. Thus, we approached the current study with the question: "*how* are neoliberal and neoconservative interests evident, advocated, and furthered through this policy" rather than "*are* neoliberal and neoconservative interests evident, advocated, and furthered through this policy?" Consequently, we may have overlooked discourses present in Bill 13 (Government of Ontario 2012) and PPM 144 (Ontario Ministry of Education 2012b) that challenge neoliberalism and neoconservatism even though we recognise that policies contain multiple, even contradictory, discourses (Goldberg 2006).

Further, as a student in a doctoral programme (Tuters) in educational administration and a professor of education in a university (Winton), our present connections to the classroom and policy arena are limited. This distance, and our commitments to democratic policy processes and appropriation, may lead us to make recommendations that are not tenable in the social and political realities of Ontario education. Recognising these limitations, we contacted colleagues in the field to provide background information and clarification at various points in the research.

Historical context of Bill 13: Ontario safe schools policy 1994–2012

Bill 13 is the latest in a series of changes to Ontario's Safe Schools strategy. Ontario's first province-wide policy to address school safety was introduced in 1994 as the Violence-Free Schools policy. This policy required that school boards develop and implement policies to prevent and respond to violence. The Violence-Free Schools policy was replaced when changes to the *Education Act* outlined in Bill 81, the *Safe Schools Act*, were introduced in 2000. The *Education Act* is the province's legislation related to public schools. The *Safe Schools Act* outlined specific infractions that would result in automatic suspension or expulsion from Ontario schools. It mirrored many of the zero-tolerance policies introduced throughout the US since the 1990s (American Psychological Association Task Force 2008; Ayers, Ayers, and Dohrn 2002), although it did allow for mitigating factors to be considered and consideration of whether the student's continuing presence in the school created an unacceptable risk to the safety of anyone in the school (Bhattacharjee 2003; Daniel and Bondy 2008). The *Safe Schools Act* was criticised by a range of actors, including Ontario's Human Rights Commission, because of perceptions that it disproportionately impacted racialised groups (Bhattacharjee 2003).

The Liberal government modified Safe Schools provisions of the *Education Act* in 2007 with Bill 212, *the Education Amendment Act*. Changes to the law included the removal mandatory suspensions and expulsions and added the requirement that all school boards "develop and implement policies on bullying prevention and intervention" (Ontario Ministry of Education 2007, 1). Bullying was added to the list of infractions that may lead to suspension. The requirements specific to bullying prevention and intervention were detailed in Policy/Programme Memorandum (PPM) 144 (Ontario Ministry of Education 2007). PPMs are directives to Ontario's district school boards and school authorities that "outline the Ministry of Education's expectations regarding the implementation of ministry policies and programmes" (Ontario Ministry of Education 2014). PPMs are updated as policies and legislation change. PPM 144 addresses bullying prevention and intervention; in 2007 it included the following definition:

> Bullying is typically a form of repeated, persistent, and aggressive behaviour directed at an individual or individuals that is intended to cause (or should be known to cause) fear and distress and/or harm to another person's body, feelings, self-esteem, or reputation. Bullying occurs in a context where there is a real or perceived power imbalance. (Ontario Ministry of Education 2007, 3)

PPM 144 (Ontario Ministry of Education 2007) recognised that bullying takes many forms and can occur through face-to-face interactions or through technology.

The changes introduced through Bill 212 reflect recommendations made by the Safe Schools Action Team – a group established by the provincial government in 2004 to propose ways to "make schools safer through a province-wide bullying pre-vention plan" (Safe Schools Action Team 2005, 2). When introducing the Team, the government explained, "The prevention of bullying and aggressive behaviour in schools has become a growing concern. According to the Centre for Addiction and Mental Health, one-quarter of students are being bullied at school and one-third of students reported having bullied someone" (Ontario Ministry of Education 2004, December 14). The Team's plan suggested changes that would help establish posi-tive school climates that support improved student achievement (Safe Schools Action Team 2005).

Ontario's *Education Act* was again modified June 5, 2009 with Bill 157, the *Education Amendment Act* (*Keeping Our Kids Safe at School*). A new version of PPM 144 (Ontario Ministry of Education 2012b) was released to outline changes related to bullying. These changes included the requirement that board employees respond to "any student behaviour that is likely to have a negative impact on the school climate ... such inappropriate behaviour may include bullying" (Ontario Ministry of Education 2009, 5). Further, any board employee who becomes aware of a student engaging in an activity "for which suspension or expulsion must be considered" (bullying is one such activity) is obligated to report the matter to the principal as soon as possible (Ontario Ministry of Education 2009, 5). The employee must confirm his/her report on a form provided by Ontario's Ministry of Education. The principal must inform the employee whether or not action has been taken and the parent or guardian of the harmed student must be notified. Finally, boards were required to ensure their bullying prevention and intervention policies reflect the prin-ciples of Ontario's *Equity and Inclusive Education Strategy* released earlier that year

Bill 13: An act to amend the education act with respect to bullying and other matters

We turn now to a close examination of Ontario's current approach to addressing bullying in schools. The most recent changes were introduced in Bill 13, *An Act to Amend the Education Act with Respect to Bullying and Other Matters* (Government of Ontario 2012). Bill 13 was introduced in November 2011, passed in June 2012 and came into force 1 February 2013. The additions and changes related to bullying arising from the passing of Bill 13 are many. First, a definition of bullying was defined in law:

"bullying" means aggressive and typically repeated behaviour by a pupil where,

(1) the behaviour is intended by the pupil to have the effect of, or the pupil ought to know that the behaviour would be likely to have the effect of,
  (a) causing harm, fear or distress to another individual, including physical, psychological, social or academic harm, harm to the individual's reputa-tion or harm to the individual's property, or

(b) creating a negative environment at a school for another individual; and

(2) the behaviour occurs in a context where there is a real or perceived power imbalance between the pupil and the individual based on factors such as size, strength, age, intelligence, peer group power, economic status, social status, religion, ethnic origin, sexual orientation, family circumstances, gender, gender identity, gender expression, race, disability or the receipt of special education. (Ontario Ministry of Education 2012b, 4)

This definition is more expansive than earlier definitions provided in early versions of PPM 144 and adds gender identity and gender expression to the list of individual factors that may be targeted by bullying.

In addition, a definition of cyberbullying was included:

(1.0.0.2) For the purposes of the definition of "bullying" in subsection (1), bullying includes bullying by electronic means (commonly known as cyberbullying), including,

(1) creating a web page or a blog in which the creator assumes the identity of another person;

(2) impersonating another person as the author of content or messages posted on the internet; and

(3) communicating material electronically to more than one individual or posting material on a website that may be accessed by one or more individuals. (Ontario Ministry of Education 2012b, 4)

Other changes include the designation of an annual bullying awareness week and the requirement that school boards conduct school climate surveys (with questions that address bullying related to sexual orientation, gender identity and gender expression as well as questions on sexual harassment) with students, parents and staff at least every two years. In addition, principals must suspend a student for bullying and consider referring the student for expulsion for the student if it is not the student's first suspension for bullying and if, in the principal's opinion, the student's presence in the school "creates … an unacceptable risk to the safety of another person" (Ontario Ministry of Education 2012b, 2). A student must also be suspended and considered for expulsion for bullying incidents "motivated by bias, prejudice, or hate based on race, national or ethnic origin, language, colour, religion, sex, age, mental or physical disability, sexual orientation, gender identity, gender expression, or any other similar factor (e.g. socio-economic status, appearance)" (Ontario Ministry of Education 2012b, 2).

Furthermore, the law now requires that school boards "support and maintain a positive school climate in their schools" and have equity and inclusive education policies (Ontario Ministry of Education 2012b, 2). Supports for students who have been bullied, witnessed bullying or engaged in bullying must be provided, and employees must report bullying incidents to principals and principals must now report to parents of students who have engaged in serious incidents including bullying (in addition to parents of students that have been harmed). Their reports must include the nature of the activity, the nature of the harm, any disciplinary measures taken, any steps taken to protect the harmed students and the supports provided to the students. Finally, boards must provide annual training for staff about bullying prevention and creating a positive school climate.

Neoliberalism, neoconservatism and Ontario's Bill 13

Above, we demonstrated that neoliberalism and neoconservatism are political ratio-nalities that are influencing educational purposes, policies and practices in Ontario and beyond; here we are concerned with how they influence and are reinforced by Ontario's Bill 13 and PPM 144 (Ontario Ministry of Education 2012b). Our findings demonstrate that bullying is constructed in a problematic fashion which perpetuates the status quo by serving the interests of neoliberalism and neoconservatism in three key ways: (1) by constructing bullying as an individual (as opposed to a social/systemic) problem; (2) by also constructing bullying as "behaviour for learning" problem; and (3) by adopting a standardised approach that reinforces neoliberal and neoconservative values of control and authority. We present our findings below, fol-lowed by a discussion of how these policy discourses are contradictory to critical democracy.

Bullying: a problem of individuals

Bill 13 (Government of Ontario 2012) and PPM 144 (Ontario Ministry of Education 2012b) construct the problem of bullying primarily as a problem of individuals. A bully is identified as a "pupil" and a "child" who harms "another individual" directly or indirectly (Ontario Ministry of Education 2012b, 3–4). Bullying, according to Bill 13, is intentional. Not only does the Bill's general definition of bullying state that "the behaviour is intended" (Government of Ontario 2012), the Bill also uses verbs that imply conscious choice such as "creating", "impersonating" and "communicat-ing" in its definition of cyberbullying. Its preamble identifies bullies as "students who have engaged in inappropriate behaviour" and explains that they (as well as victims and others) need assistance "in developing healthy relationships, *making good choices*, continuing their learning and achieving success" (emphasis added, Government of Ontario 2012). Construing bullying as the consequence of individu-als' choices reflects the neoliberal conception of the subject as one who exercises rational choices and is responsible for those choices.

The policy's solutions to the problem of bullying, not surprising given the prob-lem's definition, also addresses individuals. While suspensions and expulsions are proposed for bullies alone, most other solutions address bullies, victims and bystand-ers. Examples include providing "supports" for bullies, victims or others affected by bullying (including supports that may be provided by social workers, psychologists, and social and mental health agencies and/or that are linked to curriculum); raising all students' awareness of the consequences of bullying; early intervention; and clear standards of behaviour (Ontario Ministry of Education 2012b). PPM 144 (Ontario Ministry of Education 2012b) explains "If students who are bullied, who bully oth-ers, or who witness bullying receive the necessary support, they can learn effective strategies for interacting positively with others and for promoting positive peer dynamics" (3). This solution suggests bullying is also due in part to individuals' lack of skills, and therefore, can be addressed by teaching these skills. PPM 144 (Ontario Ministry of Education 2012b) states:

> in the course of a day, there are many "teachable moments" when issues appear to arise. Prompt intervention with a few moments of coaching and support at these critical times can help all children and youth, including those who may be at risk, to *develop the skills* and understanding that they need to maintain positive relationships with

others. Such interactions that students have with their teachers, other school staff, and fellow students, as well as with principals, vice-principals, their parents, and others, can be used to help them *improve their social skills.* (emphasis added, 5)

The construction of bullying as an individual problem in Ontario's policy reflects the dominant definition in research and policies more broadly. This construction, however, is simplistic and problematic (Walton 2011). It fails to recognise that "bullying is embedded in cultural norms, values, and social status in the whole community" (Hamarus and Kaikkonen 2008 1). It also ignores historical and systemic hierarchies of power that influence individual interactions, and it negates examination of the related power structures and cultures that privilege certain ways of knowing, being and behaving over other ways and lead to bullying incidents related to membership in a group. Further, decontextualising bullying relieves schools and school systems of the responsibility to engage students, educators and other members of the community in learning about the complex and conflicting nature of human values and interactions as they relate to bullying.

Bullying: a "behaviour for learning" problem

A current policy priority in Ontario is academic achievement, primarily in the areas of math and literacy, for the purposes of creating citizens who are able to compete within and contribute to the growth of the global economy (Ontario Ministry of Education 2012b; Winton 2013). Like English behaviour policies (Ball et al. 2011), Ontario's bullying policy reinforces this focus by constructing bullying as a "behaviour for learning" problem (2). That is, bullying is construed as a problem mainly because it gets in the way of learning and the achievement of high academic standards (Ball et al. 2011). PPM 144 (Ontario Ministry of Education 2012b) explains, for example, that "Schools that have bullying prevention and intervention policies foster a positive learning and teaching environment that supports academic achievement for all students and that helps students reach their full potential" (1).

Similarly, Bill 13 (Government of Ontario 2012) states that

> The people of Ontario and the Legislative Assembly … believe that a healthy, safe and inclusive learning environment where all students feel accepted is a necessary condition for student success; [and] Understand that students cannot be expected to reach their full potential in an environment where they feel insecure or intimidated.

Further, PPM 144 (Ontario Ministry of Education 2012b) identifies bullies in schools as barriers to others' academic success. Ontario school boards are required to develop a bullying prevention and intervention policy that states "Bullying adversely affects a student's ability to learn" (Ontario Ministry of Education 2012b, 6).

While we do not question the importance of keeping students safe at school, it is the framing and justification of addressing bullying because it compromises learning that we find troublesome. Westheimer (2010), similarly questions an Ontario school board's need to justify feeding hungry children in terms of supporting academic achievement rather than simply because they are hungry. Instead, he argues, that in Canada's contemporary education context, there is a "need for educational programmes to mould themselves in the image of test score improvement mechanisms" if they are to be valued (Westheimer 2010, 7).

Ontario's bullying policy, like England's behaviour policies, is "thoroughly subordinated to the standards agenda, that is, the pressure on schools, which is transmitted to and exerted on teachers and students, to raise achievements, measured in terms of examination performance" (Ball et al. 2011, 2). Thus, it reflects and promotes neoliberal and neoconservative values through the Ontario government's continued emphasis on raising provincial and international test scores and its focus on behaviour modification and regulation to help achieve those academic goals (Winton 2008). This emphasis is cause for concern because it perpetuates the narrowing of the focus of purposes and aims of schooling in favour of preparing students to become part of the workforce (Joshee 2012). Furthermore, bullying should be recognised as a cause for concern primarily because it is wrong to mistreat people. As a citizenry, we should prioritise teaching children how to treat one another (and themselves) with dignity and respect.

A standardised approach

Much like other policy responses to bullying (Walton 2011) and contemporary education policies more generally, Bill 13 (Government of Ontario 2012) and PPM 144 (Ontario Ministry of Education 2012b) advocate a "one size fits all" approach to defining and addressing bullying which is a hallmark of neoconservativism (Apple 2006). In general, standardised approaches in education marginalise and oppress people by treating everyone the same (Milner 2012).

First, the texts provide a definition of bullying which fails to recognise how bullying varies. For example, "homophobic bullying is not the same thing as all other types of bullying" (Loutzenheiser 2009). It does not look the same as other types of bullying; it does not involve the same issues, or require the same kinds of interventions and supports. In current bullying programmes, most often addressed are overt instances of bullying, such as physical altercations or verbal put-downs; policies much less frequently address more subtle forms of bullying such as emotional bullying, leveraging of power over other individuals, or homophobia (Walton 2004). Standard definitions of bullying also lead to narrow (hegemonic) notions of unacceptable and acceptable behaviour.

In addition, Bill 13 (Government of Ontario 2012) goes some way to standardise consequences for bullying by identifying circumstances under which students who bully must be suspended (although principals retain some discretion when determining whether or not to suspend a student). Policies that focus on preventing and addressing individual incidents of bullying in schools, support the decontextualisation of bullying discussed above. It also focuses attention largely on those incidents which are most highly visible (Walton 2011). Furthermore, "Generic strategies for increased safety in schools simply do not address forms of homophobic violence and, consequently, leave some of the most vulnerable students 'unsafe'" (Walton 2004, 29). Generic responses promote conformity and assimilation of student behaviour, disregarding the importance of multiple ways of being, thinking, knowing and acting.

Third, Bill 13 (Government of Ontario 2012) and PPM 144 (Ontario Ministry of Education 2012b) aim to standardise educators' responses to bullying incidents. Teachers and administrators are expected to follow standard protocols for reporting and investigating incidents of inappropriate behaviour (for which deviation or neglecting to follow is punishable). According to the Bill, "an employee of a board who becomes aware that a pupil of a school of the board may have engaged in an activity described in subsection 306 (1) or 310 (1) (*which list unacceptable/able behaviours*) shall report to the principal of the school about the matter. 2009, c. 17, s. 1; 2012, c. 5, s. 8 (1)" (Ontario Ministry of Education 2012b, 5). Principals are then required to investigate all such issues that have been reported to them.

"One size fits all" approaches that have strict codes of conduct perpetuate homogeneity of environments and advance sameness agendas (Milner 2012). Such policies constrain educator and administrator ability to take into consideration the individual and contextual knowledge, experience and needs of their students. They conform to historical hierarchies of power and privilege (Walton 2011). Further, much like accountability policies regarding standardised testing and curriculum, standardised bullying policies and programmes safeguard schools, and school boards from responsibility if bullying incidents occur, placing blame on individuals instead. Blame is placed on individual students for their actions (as bullies) or inactions (as bystanders) and on educators and administrators if they fail to report bullying to authorities and followed prescribed practices.

Components of Bill 13 (Government of Ontario 2012) and PPM 144 (Ontario Ministry of Education 2012b) that specify who is responsible and accountable for reporting and addressing incidents in specific manners, reinforce neoliberal and neoconservative interests in control and discipline. Law and order strategies involving strict discipline, regulation and punishment create strict regimes under which educators are expected to function. These regimes replace the welfare state with a punishing state (Giroux 2010) and contribute to the further deprofessionalisation and deskilling of the work of educators (Giroux 2010).

Constraints and possibilities in Ontario's bullying policy cycle

The points made above are not intended to undermine efforts to reduce bullying in schools nor to suggest that such endeavours are ill intended. We recognise that there are individuals committed to critical democracy in all contexts of Ontario's bullying policy cycle; however, some influences may be more powerful than their actions and intentions and lead to some of the detrimental effects outlined above. The findings highlight how the bullying "problem" in Bill 13 (Government of Ontario 2012) and PPM 144 (Ontario Ministry of Education 2012b) is constructed and connected to solutions that may ultimately achieve little positive effect. Walton (2011) describes this process as "wheel spinning" whereby "plenty of energy is consumed, power is leveraged and released, and a lot of noise results" but few results are achieved (131). In this final section, we suggest how Ontario educators might enact bullying policy in ways that move beyond Bill 13 (Government of Ontario 2012) and PPM 144's (Ontario Ministry of Education 2012b) constructions of the bullying problem and solution and promote critical democracy within their parameters.

First, rather conceptualising bullying as an individual problem and ignoring how larger systems of power and privilege that influence interactions (Loutzenheiser 2009; Walton 2011) educators can choose to define bullying more broadly and pay attention to how what occurs in schools may reflect social inequities. There are a number of texts and discourses within Ontario's bullying policy cycle that offer alternate conceptions of bullying and address the complexities of bullying that can be considered by educators as they appropriate Ontario's bullying policy.

Supporting Bias-free Progressive Discipline in Schools: Suggested Approaches and Practices for School and System Leaders, for example, written by the Ontario Ministry of Education in collaboration with Ontario's Human Rights Commission following the assent of Bill 13, deals explicitly with diverse factors affecting student behaviour, school climate, and discipline. It explains:

> When making decisions about intervention, supports, and discipline, successful leaders keep in mind that inappropriate behaviour on the part of students who belong to groups identified [in Ontario's Human Rights] Code may be in reaction to discrimination, and that being subjected to discrimination is likely to cause strong emotions and responses. (Ontario Ministry of Education & Ontario's Human Rights Commission 2013, 17)

The text encourages principals to use their discretion over whether or not to suspend a student for bullying and take a range of possible mitigating factors into account (although principals are not required to consider all of these factors by law). One factor is "whether the activity for which the student may be or is being suspended or expelled was related to any harassment of the student because of his or her race, ethnic origin, religion, disability, gender, or sexual orientation or any other harassment" (11). Principals can also use alternatives to out-of-school suspensions to ensure students are not at risk if an offending student is not excluded from school (e.g. in-school suspension and restorative practices). Excluding students contradicts critical democracy's commitments to inclusion and equity. Much research demonstrates that students who are excluded from school experience long-term consequences (Skiba et al. 2006). They have trouble returning to school, have poor relationships with teachers, suffer academically, develop negative attitudes towards adults in the education system and are less likely to complete high school than students who have not been suspended (Brown 2007; Cassidy 2005; Kajs 2006; Lee et al. 2011).

Supporting Bias-free Progressive Discipline in Schools (Ontario Ministry of Education & Ontario's Human Rights Commission 2013) also includes scenarios that can be used in professional development activities mandated by Bill 13 (Government of Ontario 2012). One scenario describes the case of a student who assaulted another student after months of being harassed due to his perceived sexual orientation. Educators are asked to consider what supports and consequences are appropriate under these circumstances. In addition to this text, the Ontario Ministry of Education publishes a list of resources on its website that are recommended for use in schools. Some of the resources link bullying to membership in marginalised groups in society more broadly.

Teachers can also engage students in critical analysis of the ways individuals' behaviour reflects social attitudes, practices and ideologies that advantage some groups while marginalising others. Examples of powerful individuals and groups bullying less powerful groups abound in movies, television shows, institutional procedures and political decisions. Staff and student discussions about bullying during mandatory Bullying Awareness and Prevention Week may include making connections between how people outside schools exercise power over others and how these processes are reflected and recreated in schools. They might focus on recent debates over gay marriage or whether Ontario's Catholic schools should be forced to permit clubs called gay–straight alliances. Bill 13's (Government of Ontario) Preamble provides support for such conversations as it states:

The people of Ontario and the Legislative Assembly ... Believe that students need to be equipped with the knowledge, skills, attitude and values to engage the world and others critically, which means developing a critical consciousness that allows them to take action on making their schools and communities more equitable and inclusive for all people, including LGBTTIQ (lesbian, gay, bisexual, transgender, transsexual, two-spirited, intersex, queer and questioning) people

In addition, PPM 144 (Ontario Ministry of Education 2012b) suggests that teachers can reinforce "Bullying prevention and awareness-raising strategies ... through curriculum-linked programmes" (2). The Ontario Language Curriculum for Grades 1–8 provides opportunities for consideration of relationships between bullying and social inequalities through media literacy. It explains: "Students must be able to differentiate between fact and opinion; evaluate the credibility of sources; recognize bias; *be attuned to discriminatory portrayals of individuals and groups, including women and minorities*; and question depictions of violence and crime. To develop their media literacy skills, students should have opportunities to view, analyse, and discuss a wide variety of media texts and relate them to their own experience" (emphasis added, Ontario Ministry of Education 2006, p 13).

Finally, critical democracy demands that bullying policies be subject to on-going re-examination, dialogue, and critique by affected and interested citizens. Mandatory Safe Schools Action Teams can facilitate these dialogues by collaborating with community organisations and encouraging staff, students and other community members to share their perspectives and experiences of bullying and anti-bullying initiatives. Indeed, the Teams are "encouraged to take on a leadership role in the school by planning activities that are relevant to bullying awareness and prevention and that engage the whole school community" (Ontario Ministry of Education 2012a). Such dialogues support critical democracy by enabling citizens to acquire new knowledge about policy issues, encounter perspectives that differ from dominant policy narratives, and encourage them to participate in policy processes (Winton and Evans 2014).

Note

1. Ball et al. (2011) refer to "policies, initiatives, procedures and strategies aimed at producing and sustaining positive behaviour for learning" (3). They both use the phrase themselves and refer to government documents and initiatives that use this phrase. We attribute the phrase to Ball et al. (2011) in this article while recognising that others use it as well.

References

American Psychological Association Task Force. 2008. "Are Zero Tolerance Policies Effective in the Schools? An Evidentiaty Review and Recommendations." *American Psychologist* 63 (9): 852–862.

Apple, M. W. 2006. *Educating the "Right" Way: Markets, Standards, God and Inequality.* 2nd ed. New York: Routledge.

Ayers, W., R. Ayers, and B. Dohrn. 2002. "Introduction: Resisting Zero Tolerance." In *Zero Tolerance: Resisting the Drive for Punishment in Our Schools*, edited by W. Ayers, B. Dohrn, and R. Ayers, xi–xvi. New York: New Press.

Bacchi, C. 2000. "Policy as Discourse: What Does It Mean? Where Does It Get Us?" *Discourse: Studies in the Cultural Politics of Education [Electronic Version]* 21 (1): 45–57.

Ball, S. J. 1994. *Education Reform: A Critical and Post-structural Approach.* Buckingham: Open University Press.

Ball, S. J. 1998. "Big Policies/Small World: An Introduction to International Perspectives in Education Policy." *Comparative Education* 34 (2): 119–130.

Ball, S. J., K. Hoskins, M. Maguire, and A. Braun. 2011. "Disciplinary Texts: A Policy Analysis of National and Local Behaviour Policies." *Critical Studies in Education* 52 (1): 1–14.

Baronov, D. 2007. "Global Capitalism and Urban Education." In *Urban Education: A Comprehensive Guide for Educators, Parents, and Teachers*, edited by J. L. Kincheloe, K. Heyes, K. Rose, and P. M. Anderson, 340–349. Lanham, MD: Rowman & Littlefield Education.

Bencze, L., and L. Carter. 2011. "Globalizing Students Acting for the Common Good." *Journal of Research in Science Teaching* 48 (6): 648–669.

Berger, K. S. 2007. "Update on Bullying at School: Science Forgotten?" *Developmental Review* 27: 90–126.

Bhattacharjee, K. 2003. "Ontario Safe Schools Act: School Discipline and Discrimination." Accessed December 1, 2009. http://www.ohrc.on.ca

Bowe, R., S. J. Ball, and A. Gold. 1992. *Reforming Education and Changing Schools: Case Studies in Policy Sociology.* London: Routledge.

Brown, W. 2006. "American Nightmare: Neoliberalism, Neoconservatism, and De-democratization." *Political Theory* 34 (6): 690–714.

Brown, T. M. 2007. "Lost and Turned out: Academic, Social, and Emotional Experiences of Students Excluded from School." *Urban Education* 42 (5): 432–455.

Carpenter, S., N. Weber, and D. Schugurensky. 2012. "Views from the Blackboard: Neoliberal Education Reforms and the Practice of Teaching in Ontario, Canada." *Globalisation, Societies and Education* 10 (2): 145–161.

Carroll, W. K., and M. Shaw. 2001. "Consolidating a Neoliberal Policy Bloc in Canada, 1796 to 1996." *Canadian Public Policy* 27 (2): 197–216.

Cassidy, W. 2005. "From Zero Tolerance to a Culture of Care." *Education Canada* 45 (3): 40–42.

Dake, J. A., J. H. Price, and S. K. Telljohann. 2003. "The Nature and Extent of Bullying at School." *Journal of School Health* 73 (5): 173–180.

Daniel, Y., and K. Bondy. 2008. "Safe Schools and Zero Tolerance: Policy, Program and Practice in Ontario." *Canadian Journal of Educational Administration and Policy* 70. http://www.umanitoba.ca/publications/cjeap/.

Davies, B., and P. Bansel. 2007. "Neoliberalism and Education." *International Journal of Qualitative Studies in Education* 20 (3): 247–259.

Dewey, J. 1966. *Democracy and Education*. Toronto: Collier-Macmillan Canada.

Dijkstra, J. K., S. Lindenberg, and R. Veenstra. 2008. "Beyond the Class Norm: Bullying Behavior of Popular Adolescents and its Relation to Peer Acceptance and Rejection." *Journal of Abnormal Child Psychology* 36: 1289–1299.

Dixon, R. 2011. *Rethinking School Bullying*. Cambridge: Cambridge University Press.

Edelman, M. 1988. *Constructing the Political Spectacle*. Chicago, IL: University of Chicago Press.

Fairclough, N. 2001. "Critical Discourse Analysis as a Method in Social Scientific Research." In *Methods of Critical Discourse Analysis*, edited by R. Wodak and M. Meyer, 121–138. Thousand Oaks, CA: Sage.

Farrington, D. P. 1993. "Understanding and Preventing Bullying." *Crime and Justice* 17: 381–458.

Furlong, M. J., J. D. Sharkey, E. D. Felix, D. Tanigawa, and J. G. Green. 2009. "Bullying Assessment: A Call for Increased Precision of Self-reporting Procedures." In *Handbook of Bullying in Schools: An International Perspective*, edited by J. R. Jimerson, S. M. Swearer, and D. L. Espelage, 329–345. New York: Routledge.

Gale, T. 1999. "Policy Trajectories: Tracing the Discursive Path of Policy Analysis." *Discourse: Studies in the Cultural Politics of Education* 20 (3): 393–407.

Gee, J. P. 2010. *How to Do Discourse Analysis: A Toolkit*. London: Routledge.

Giroux, H. 2010. "The University Debate: Public Values, Higher Education and the Scourge of Neoliberalism: Politics at the Limits of the Social November 2010." *Culture Machine*. Accessed March 19, 2014. http://www.culturemachine.net/index.php/cm/article/view/426/444GovernmentofAlberta

Goldberg, M. 2006. "Discursive Policy Webs in a Globalisation Era: A Discussion of Access to Professions and Trades for Immigrant Professionals in Ontario, Canada." *Globalisation, Societies and Education* 4 (1): 77–102.

Government of Alberta. 2012. "Bill 3: Education Act." Accessed March 29, 2014. http://www.assembly.ab.ca/ISYS/LADDAR_files/docs/bills/bill/legislature_28/session_1/20120523_bill-003.pdf

Government of Manitoba. 2013. "The Public Schools Amendment Act: Safe and Inclusive Schools." Accessed March 29, 2014. http://web2.gov.mb.ca/bills/40-2/b018e.php

Government of New Brunswick. 2012. "Bill 52: An Act to Amend the Education Act." Accessed March 29, 2014. http://www.gnb.ca/legis/bill/FILE/56/4/Bill-52-e.htm

Government of Ontario. 2012. "Bill 13: An Act to Amend the Education Act with Respect to Bullying and Other Matters." Accessed March 31, 2014. http://www.http://ontla.on.ca

Hamarus, P., and P. Kaikkonen. 2008. "School Bullying as a Creator of Pupil Peer Pressure." *Educational Research* 50 (4): 333–345.

Jacobs, A. K. 2008. "Components of Evidence-Based Interventions for Bullying and Peer Victimization." In *Handbook of Evidence-Based Therapies for Children and Adolescents*, edited by R. G. Steele, T. D. Elkin, and M. C. Roberts, 261–279. New York: Springer.

Joshee, R. 2012. "Challenging Neoliberalism through Gandhian Trusteeship." *Critical Studies in Education* 53 (1): 71–82.

Kajs, L. T. 2006. "Reforming the Discipline Management Process in Schools: An Alternative Approach to Zero Tolerance." *Educational Research Quarterly* 29 (4): 14–28.

Koyama, J. 2013. "Global Scare Tactics and the Call for US Schools to Be Held Accountable." *American Journal of Education* 120 (1): 77–99.

Larner, W. 2000. "Neo-liberalism: Policy, Ideology, Governmentality." *Studies in Political Economy* 63: 5–25.

Law, D. M., J. D. Shapka, S. Hymel, B. F. Olson, and T. Waterhouse. 2012. "The Changing Face of Bullying: An Empirical Comparison between Traditional and Internet Bullying and Victimization." *Computers in Human Behavior* 28 (1): 226–232.

Lee, T., D. Cornell, A. Gregory, and X. Fan. 2011. "High Suspension Schools and Dropout Rates for Black and White Students." *Education and Treatment of Children* 34 (2): 167–192.

Loutzenheiser, L. W. 2009. "When Theory and Practice Collide: The Case for Building Civic Capacity for Change." Paper Presented at the Queer Issues in the Study of Education and Culture, a 2009 Canadian Society for the Study of Education Pre-Conference, Ottawa, Ontario, May 22.

Milner, H. R. 2012. "Beyond a Test Score: Explaining Opportunity Gaps in Educational Practice." *Journal of Black Studies* 43 (6): 693–718.

Mishna, F., D. Pepler, C. Cook, W. Craig, and J. Wiener. 2010. "The Ongoing Problem of Bullying in Canada: A Ten-Year Perspective." *Canadian Social Work Review* 12 (2): 43–59.

Nevitte, N., and R. Gibbins. 1984. "Neoconservatism: Canadian Variations on an Ideological Theme?" *Canadian Public Policy* 10 (4): 384–394.

Nishina, A. 2004. "A Theoretical Review of Bullying: Can It Be Eliminated?" In *Bullying: Implications for the Classroom*, edited by C. Sanders and G. Phye, 36–62. San Diego, CA: Elsevier Academic Press.

Olweus, D. 1994. "Bullying at School: Basic Facts and Effects of a School Based Intervention Program." *Journal of Child Psychology and Psychiatry* 35 (7): 1171–1190.

Ontario Ministry of Education. 2004. McGuinty Government Acting to Protect Students. Accessed March 10, 2014. http://news.ontario.ca/archive/en/2004/12/14/McGuinty-government-acting-to-protect-students.html

Ontario Ministry of Education. 2006. "Language." Accessed July 2, 2014. www.edu.gov.on.ca

Ontario Ministry of Education. 2007. *Policy/Program Memorandum No. 144.*

Ontario Ministry of Education. 2009. *Policy/Program Memorandum No. 144.*

Ontario Ministry of Education. 2012a. *Bullying Awareness and Prevention Week.* Accessed July 2, 2014. http://www.edu.gov.on.ca/eng/safeschools/qsandas.html

Ontario Ministry of Education. 2012b. Policy/Program Memorandum No. 144.

Ontario Ministry of Education. 2014. *Policy/Program Memoranda.* Accessed March 14, 2014. http://www.edu.gov.on.ca/extra/eng/ppm/ppm.html

Ontario Ministry of Education & Ontario's Human Rights Commission. 2013. *Supporting Bias-Free Progressive Discipline in Schools.* Accessed July 2, 2014. www.edu.gove.on.ca

Pinto, L. 2012. *Curriculum Reform in Ontario: 'Common Sense' Policy Processes and Democratic Possibilities.* Toronto: University of Toronto Press.

Pinto, L. 2013. "The Case for Critical Democracy." In *Philosophy of Education: Introductory Readings*, edited by W. Hare and J. P. Portelli, 4th ed., 151–169. Edmonton, AB: Brush Education.

Pornari, C. D., and J. Wood. 2010. "Peer and Cyber Aggression in Secondary School Students: The Role of Moral Disengagement, Hostile Attribution Bias, and Outcome Expectancies." *Aggressive Behavior* 36 (2): 81–94.

Poyhonen, V., J. Juvonen, and C. Salmivalli. 2010. "What Does it Take to Stand up for the Victim of Bullying? The Interplay between Personal and Social Factors." *Merrill-Palmer Quarterly* 56 (2): 143–163.

Rizvi, F. 1., and B. Lingard. 2010. *Globalizing Education Policy.* New York, NY: Routledge.

Rogers, R., E. Malancharuvil-Berkes, M. Mosley, D. Hui, and G. Joseph. 2005. "Critical Discourse Analysis in Education: A Review of the Literature." *Review of Educational Research* 75 (3): 365–416.

Safe Schools Action Team. 2005. *Shaping Safer Schools: A Bullying Prevention Action Plan.* Ontario: Government of Ontario.

Salmivalli, C. 2010. "Bullying and the Peer Group: A Review." *Aggression and Violent Behavior* 15: 112–120.

Scheurich, J. J. 1994. "Policy Archaeology: A New Policy Studies Methodology." *Journal of Education Policy* 9 (4): 297–316.

Sherer, Y. C., and A. B. Nickerson. 2010. "Anti-bullying Practices in American Schools: Perspectives of School Psychologists." *Psychology in the Schools* 47 (3): 217–229.

Skiba, R. J., and M. K. Rausch. 2006. "School Disciplinary Systems: Alternatives to Suspension and Expulsion." In *Children's Needs III: Development, Prevention, and Intervention*, edited by G. G. Bear and K. M. Minke, 87–102. Bethesda, MD: National Association of School Psychologists.

Solomon, R. P., and J. P. Portelli. 2001. "Introduction." In *The Erosion of Democracy in Education: Critique to Possibilities*, edited by R. P. Solomon and J. P. Portelli, 15–27. Calgary: Detselig Enterprises.

Stone, D. 2002. *Policy Paradox: The Art of Political Decision Making*. 2nd ed. New York: W.W. Norton.

Taylor, S. 1997. "Critical Policy Analysis: Exploring Contexts, Texts and Consequences." *Discourse* 18 (1): 23–35.

Thomas, S. 2005. "The Construction of Teacher Identities in Educational Policy Documents: A Critical Discourse Analysis." *Critical Studies in Education* 46 (2): 25–44.

Tuters, S. 2014. "Neoliberal Influences: People Policies and Resources." Paper Presented at the Annual Meeting of the Canadian Society for Study of Education, St Catharines, Ontario, May 27.

US Department of Health and Human Services. n.d. *Policies and Laws*. Accessed March 29, 2014. http://www.stopbullying.gov/laws/index.html

Vidovich, L. 2007. "Removing Policy from Its Pedestal: Some Theoretical Framings and Practical Possibilities." *Educational Review* 59 (3): 285–298.

Walton, G. 2004. "Bullying and Homophobia in Canadian Schools." *Journal of Gay and Lesbian Issues in Education* 1 (4): 23–36.

Walton, G. 2005. "Bullying Widespread." *Journal of School Violence* 4 (1): 91–118.

Walton, G. 2011. "Spinning Our Wheels: Reconceptualizing Bullying beyond Behaviour-focused Approaches." *Discourse: Studies in the Cultural Politics of Education* 32 (1): 131–144.

Westheimer, J. 2010. "No Child Left Thinking: Democracy at Risk in Canada's Schools." *Education Canada* 50 (2): 5–8.

Winton, S. 2008. "The Appeal(s) of Character Education in Threatening times: Caring and Critical Democratic Responses." *Comparative Education* 44 (3): 305–316.

Winton, S. 2012a. *From Zero Tolerance to Progressive Discipline and Student Success in Ontario, Canada Educational Policy*. http://epx.sagepub.com/content/early/2012/07/23/0895904812453994

Winton, S. 2012b. "Positioning Ontario's Character Development Initiative in/through Its Policy Web of Relationships." *Alberta Journal of Educational Research* 58 (1): 1–16. http://www.ajer.ca/

Winton, S. 2013. "Rhetorical Analysis in Critical Policy Research." *International Journal of Qualitative Studies in Education* 26 (2): 158–177.

Winton, S., and M. P. Evans. 2014. "Challenging Political Spectacle through Grassroots Policy Dialogues." *Canadian Journal of Educational Administration and Policy* 156.

Working with schools in identifying and overcoming emotional barriers to learning

Poppy Nash[a] and Annette Schlösser[b]

[a]Department of Education, University of York, York, UK; [b]Department of Psychological Health and Wellbeing, University of Hull and N Lincs CAMHS, Hull, UK

This paper reports a case study on working closely with a secondary school, to enhance understanding of disruptive behaviour, through the use of bespoke Continuing Professional Development (CPD) materials. This project evolved from the researchers' previous research on the extent to which teachers believe disruptive pupils can control their behaviour. A notable finding was the sizeable minority of teachers in both primary and secondary schools who appear to be unaware of the psychological underpinnings of disruptive behaviour. That is, that such behaviour frequently communicates unresolved emotional needs, rather than wilful defiance. The current project aims to develop, implement and evaluate CPD resources developed by the researchers, for a one-day staff training day at a secondary school in north England. Prior to training, school staff completed a questionnaire to "audit" their perceptions of disruptive behaviour in school. Following evaluation, the CPD materials will be made available to other schools. It is anticipated that the materials will enable greater mutual understanding and respect for the ways in which disruptive behaviour is perceived by practitioners and school staff. Moreover, they will provide an urgently needed means of facilitating a shared knowledge base and a shared language for addressing emotional barriers to learning.

Introduction

Disruptive behaviour and pressure in schools surrounding Ofsted inspections, are cited as the most likely reasons for teachers to leave the profession (e.g. Chapman 2002; Wilson 2002; Kyriacou 2009). Ofsted refers to school inspections conducted by the Office for Standards in Education, which are required by law to undertake an independent assessment of school standards. Many teachers struggle with the current performativity culture in education, where constant testing of pupils is used to assess educational progress. Pupils who are disruptive in school, can challenge a teacher's attempts to deliver the desired learning outcomes. Most teachers manage pupil behaviour effectively by adhering to the behaviourist principles of the popular rewards and sanctions system (Rogers 2012), whereby desirable behaviour is rewarded and undesirable behaviour is punished. This practice is in line with school behavioural policies. However, research from Australia (Clunies-Ross, Little, and

Kienhuis 2008) tells us that teachers who use "reactive" strategies (i.e. responding to poor behaviour after it has occurred), tend to feel more stressed than those who use "proactive" strategies (i.e. preventing behavioural difficulties from occurring).

This paper reports on an ongoing project that aims to enhance understanding of the psychological underpinnings of challenging behaviour at school. It details the development, implementation and evaluation of bespoke Continuing Professional Development (CPD) resources developed by the researchers, for a one-day staff training day at a secondary school in north England. Prior to training, school staff completed a questionnaire also developed by the researchers, to "audit" their perceptions of disruptive behaviour in school.

Aim of research

This paper documents the researchers' close collaboration with a secondary school in north England, in developing, implementing and evaluating a training day for all staff at the school. In applying theory to policy and practice, the training day focused on attachment theory and adolescent development, and sought to explore the extent to which:

(1) Teachers viewed pupil behaviour as being under their own control.
(2) Teachers' knowledge of attachment theory and its applicability in education increased post training.
(3) Teachers' understanding of pupil's disruptive behaviour had increased after training.
(4) Teachers would consider altering their responses to student behaviour post-training.

Background

There is increased recognition that some of the most troubled pupils find it exception-ally difficult to regulate their behaviour, due to difficulties experienced in their home environment, historically and ongoing (Geddes 2006; Bombèr 2007; The Sutton Trust Report 2014). These pupils tend to benefit from various interventions in school and participating in a Nurture Group (Boxall 2002). Nurture Groups aim to "provide a restorative experience of early nurture in the children's neighbourhood school" (Boxall and Lucas 2010, xi). However, not all schools have access to a Nurture Group and a recent review by Hughes and Schlösser (2014), indicates that not all such interventions are set up along the lines of the classic Nurture Group as devised by Boxall (2002). In addition, the efficacy of Nurture Groups is highly varied, and the content and management of the groups can be inconsistent. The idea behind Nurture Groups that better teacher–pupil relationships will occasion better behaviour is derived from attachment theory (Bowlby 1969). This psychoanalytically derived theory has the potential to play a significant part in mainstream education in under-standing disruptive behaviour, but as yet it is currently much more familiar to those working in psychological and psychotherapeutic contexts than in Education.

Attachment theory is commonly drawn upon in understanding young people's behaviour within a clinical or therapeutic setting. Within schools, Geddes (2006) and Bombèr (2007) have highlighted the applicability of this approach, to help teachers appreciate the different behaviours pupils display. Geddes and Bombèr go beyond Boxall's Nurture Groups (Boxall 2002) as an intervention for targeted pupils, in that they show that an attachment-based approach can be used universally within education. Put simply, those pupils with secure attachment patterns find it easier to engage with teachers and the process of learning, than those who are insecurely attached (Bebbington 2008). The insecurely attached pupils, who have experienced, or are experiencing, either rejection/abandonment or inconsistent parenting, will struggle to pay attention or form a good relationship with teachers, or will have difficulty focusing on the materials presented in class. These situations can lead to low engagement, with disruptive behaviour as a possible consequence. If pupils are not engaged in class, they are more likely to seek stimulation and validation in a different way, resorting to clowning around, constantly demanding attention from teachers or peers, or occupying themselves in other distracting and off-task activities. Sustained attention is difficult for those with insecure attachment, so attentional difficulties and concomitant misbehaviour is likely to follow. There is a growing body of neuroscientific research findings which highlight the association between insecure attachment and learning difficulties (Gerhardt 2004; McCrory, De Brito, and Viding 2010).

Geddes (2006) identifies a continuum of disruptive behaviour, with low-level disruption (small, frequent hassles) at one end of the spectrum and dramatic, violent/abusive behaviour at the other end. All levels of disruption can be challenging for both teachers and class peers and may result in high levels of stress and tension for all concerned. This then has an impact on the willingness and ability of the whole class to concentrate and remain on task. Around a third of all metropolitan secondary school pupils experience classroom disruption and nearly half experience concentration difficulties due to peer behaviour (Layard and Dunn 2009). Like ripples in a pond, the systemic impact of even one challenging student can affect the learning potential of the whole class.

For most pupils, the behavioural principles which underpin the school's behaviour policy will result in improved behaviour, if used within a mutually respectful environment. The most challenging pupils, however, can appear "hard to reach" as their behaviour may be erratic and unpredictable and can escalate situations beyond what is manageable within schools. Often the last resort for these pupils is a fixed term or permanent exclusion, but this comes at a high cost, to the pupil, their family and the school itself. Exclusion is often viewed as failure by all involved (Greene 2009).

Paradoxically, the dominant behaviourist approach advocated in schools and enforced by behaviour policies has been criticised for itself escalating difficulties (Taylor 2010) and resulting in higher dropout rates (Greene 2009). It seems timely to re-address difficult behaviour in school using an attachment paradigm. It may be hard for teachers to imagine the detrimental home environments some of their pupils endure. Delaney (2009) outlines that challenging behaviour in the young person can be a direct consequence of not feeling safe in adult–child relationships, due to experiences of abuse, neglect or inconsistent caring. Young people build up an "internal working model" of adults as untrustworthy, unreliable and unsafe. They are therefore less likely to turn to other adults for support and help, and unlikely to show their vulnerability (whether that is emotional, cognitive or social). Their avoidant behaviour may serve them well at home, as it minimises danger and ensures survival, but at school this learned pattern of behaviour would be regarded as maladaptive and warranting disciplinary procedures.

Although secure attachment patterns are most common, insecure patterns are more prevalent than is perhaps expected at school (Bebbington 2008). Around 35–45% of the population are thought to be insecurely attached (Howe 2005), due to various experiences of rejection and loss. Bereavement would be universally understood as loss, but family breakdown, divorce, family conflict and frequent house moves are also included here (Delaney 2009). The trauma experienced by pupils can be "acted out" in schools, that is, the repercussions are evident in the pupil's behaviour. Sometimes, this is because the school is regarded as a "safe place" by the pupil, but for teachers such vehemence can be extremely difficult to deal with (Delaney 2009). The young person is unable to regulate themselves and appears out of control, due to the intensity of emotion (fear, panic, hopelessness), which may be suddenly triggered by some aspect of the school environment. Indeed, any aspect of school life can trigger associations of the pupil's early home environment. Teachers may not only be baffled by the behaviour, but also shocked by the depth of feeling and feel unable to control the situation, therefore potentially contributing to a downward spiral of behaviour. In these instances, adhering to behaviourist principles is unlikely to be successful (Greene 2009). A compassionate and collaborative stance is more likely to help uncover the reasons for the behaviour and to convey teachers' willingness to help and support the pupil. There is increasing interest in creating a "therapeutic presence" in schools, in which the emotional well-being of both pupils and staff are supported therapeutically when the need arises. This provision can also take the form of skills training for school staff, to enable them to take a more specialist role in supporting the troubled pupils (Solomon and Nashat 2010; Noor 2012).

Development and implementation of staff training resources

The researchers were given the opportunity to work on the current research project, with an average-sized secondary school in a large market town in northern England. The majority of the pupils were white and British, with English as their first language. The aims of the project align well with the school's focus on improving behaviour and attendance throughout the school.

Following close liaison with the school Senior Leadership Team, the research project comprises four stages, with the completion of Stage 4 at the end of the school year (July 2014).

Stage 1: All staff completed a questionnaire developed by the researchers, to obtain an "audit" of staff perceptions and experiences of disruptive behaviour in school (Summer 2013).

Stage 2: The researchers led a one-day staff training day, aimed at raising staff awareness of the psychological underpinnings of disruptive behaviour (Autumn 2013).

Stage 3: Evaluation of staff training day via staff feedback completed at the end of the training day (Autumn 2013).

Stage 4: Follow up of impact of training at 3 and 10 months post-training day (end of Autumn and Summer terms, respectively).

Stage 1: Completion of questionnaire by all members of school staff

The researchers developed a questionnaire for gathering information on the respondents' perceptions and experiences of disruptive behaviour at school. The 10-item

Table 1. To what extent can pupils control their own behaviour?

Extent of control	n	Valid %
No/some control over own behaviour	13	16.3
Mostly/totally in control of behaviour	67	83.8
Total	80	100.1

questionnaire was distributed to all members of staff during the second half of the Summer term. For the purpose of this paper, attention is focused on responses to the questions concerning the extent to which pupils are believed to control their own behaviour (Question 3) and possible factors related to disruptive behaviour (Question 8).

The underlying assertion is that pupils who are able to control their behaviour must be deliberately choosing to be disruptive at school. In view of this, it is thought that their misbehaviour warrants "punishment" and disciplinary procedures at school, in order for those concerned to learn the consequences of their behaviour. Table 1 shows that on this occasion, the majority of school staff believed that disruptive pupils could control most, if not all their behaviour (83.8%, $n = 67$). In contrast, a small minority of the respondents thought that such pupils had only some or no control over their behaviour (16.3%, $n = 13$).

With respect to the question concerning possible explanations for disruptive behaviour, the first six factors (8a–8f, for example, low engagement with learning) may be more familiar to school staff than the following six factors (8 g–8 l, for example, deep-seated anxiety), which tap into more psychological/psychodynamic aspects of behaviour. For this question, respondents were asked to rate each of the twelve possible factors on a four-point scale, Strongly Disagree – Disagree – Agree – Strongly Agree. In analysing the findings, the Strongly Disagree and Disagree categories were combined, as were the Strongly Agree and Agree response options. The findings show some striking areas of disagreement, especially concerning the more psychological factors. For example, it is notable that half of the participants did not agree that disruptive behaviour could be associated with deep-seated anxiety (50%, $n = 38$) or to low engagement with learning (50%, $n = 38$). In similar vein, but to a lesser extent, a sizeable minority of staff did not believe that disruptive behaviour may be attributable to a troubled home environment (38.5%, $n = 30$), feeling misunderstood (28%, $n = 21$), feeling disliked by others (38.5%, $n = 30$) or notably, that misbehaviour can signal emotional distress (25.3%, $n = 19$). A full breakdown of the findings can be seen in comparing pre-training and post-training follow-up responses to the questionnaire as discussed in a subsequent section (Table 4).

Stage 2: Staff training day "Identifying and overcoming emotional barriers to learning"

Staff training days are a statutory CPD requirement for schools, the purpose of which is to provide staff at all levels with training opportunities. Training days attended by all school staff offer a unique opportunity to impact upon the culture and ethos of the whole school. Grundy and Robison (2005) propose that CPD has three inter-related functions, namely, extension, renewal and growth. Whilst extension focuses on introducing teachers to new skills or knowledge, renewal is concerned with changing knowledge and practice and growth centres on enhancing expertise. The current project sought to foster these functions in developing CPD resources on the emotional barriers to learning, through the lens of attachment theory.

Objective of training day

The main objective for the staff training day was to raise staff awareness of the relevance of attachment theory in understanding and effectively managing disruptive behaviour.

Learning outcomes

The learning outcomes for the staff training day focused on raising staff awareness of other interpretations and perspectives of disruptive behaviour and to feel more informed about:

- Identifying "troubled" students.
- Overcoming emotional barriers to learning.
- Reflecting on staff perceptions and practices in relating to challenging students.
- Recognising choices in how staff respond to challenging students.

Programme for training day

- Welcome and introduction: What is today about?
  It is not about:
    o Applying techniques and recommending behaviour management strategies.
    o Urging staff to become therapists or counsellors in school.
  It is about:
    o Application of psychological theory to practice.
    o Understanding and working towards a strong whole school ethos.
    o Highlighting importance of systemic work in school.
    o Establishing a background of rapport in undertaking this research project.
- What are "emotional barriers to learning"?
- Identifying emotional barriers of learning.
- Overcoming emotional barriers of learning.
- Looking after ourselves.
- Where do we go from here?

Profile of participants attending training day

The Senior Leadership Team encouraged the whole school staff to attend the training day, whether they were a member of the teaching staff, support staff or involved in administration. In doing so, there were many opportunities for staff from different departments to discuss matters as they arose during the day. This joint occasion

Table 2.   Profile of participants attending staff training day.

Area of work in school	Female	Male	Total
Teaching (all levels)	21	28	49
	42.9%	57.1%	100.0%
Non-teaching/support	13	5	18
	72.2%	27.8%	100.0%
Administration	6	1	7
	85.7%	14.3%	100.0%
Total	40	34	74
	54.1%	45.9%	100.0%

enabled the whole school ethos on effective behaviour management to be strengthened, not least through sharing the same "language" and exploring potential ways forward. Table 2 shows the profile of the participants attending the day.

Stage 3: Evaluation of staff training day – feedback from staff at end of day

At the end of the training day, staff were asked to complete an evaluation feedback form relating to different aspects of the day. For example, they were asked if their ideas about disruptive behaviour had changed in the course of the training day, in response to what they had heard. From a total of 67 respondents, 76.1% ($n = 51$) replied Yes, 10.4% ($n = 7$) indicated No and the remaining 13.5% did not know ($n = 6$) or left this question blank ($n = 3$). These findings suggest that the majority of participants had changed their perspective on disruptive behaviour during the course of the training day. Where applicable, staff members were then asked to indicate how their ideas about disruptive behaviour had changed. The following responses are a sample of those received for this question, and suggest an enhanced awareness of the potential psychological underpinnings of misbehaviour.

- Have become more understanding towards pupils.
- More thought to my reactions.
- More sympathy and understanding of the lack of choice.
- Thinking more about the reasons behind the behaviours.
- To hear what the child is really telling us.
- Am reconsidering the idea of how much the child can control their behaviour and the way they react to things/staff.
- Children have even less control re behaviours than I thought.
- It has reminded me about the personal baggage students often carry around with them. Something that they are scared of and embarrassed by which plays a part in their disruptive behaviour.

When questioned about the content of the day, 77.6% ($n = 52$) of staff reported that 75% or more of the material was new and useful to them. They were subsequently asked to identify any positive outcomes or highlights of the day. The following responses suggest that they appreciated the links made during the training day between theory, policy and practice.

- I feel the whole day has given me a way forward in how I react to "all" students.
- Thank goodness "it" has hit school teachers! There's no such thing as bad behaviour – it got people talking!
- Very interesting to listen to, which opened up my views.
- Fascinating insights into brain development. Sharing ideas, having my assumptions challenged.
- Best training day I think I have ever had.
- The delivery – informative, helpful. Academic but with a common touch making it very accessible.
- I enjoyed the psychology as it provided a new way of looking at the students.

When participants were asked how the day's training could be improved in future, two particular "themes" emerged following thematic analysis of the data. The first of these was the wish for more time. Some staff suggested that it could be a two-day training in order for more discussion and small group activities to be included. The second recommendation was that the training should have a more practical focus, with more information on practical strategies related to the attachment perspective. Both of these suggestions are being considered for future training days, when the bespoke CPD resources developed for this research project will be made available to other schools.

Stage 4: Follow-up evaluation of training after three months

At the end of the Autumn term, staff were asked to complete the same pre-training "audit" questionnaire three months after the training event. For the purpose of this paper, attention is given to comparing the pre-training responses (Stage 1 outlined above) and those received for the same questions three months after the training (Stage 4). Table 3 compares responses for the question concerning the extent to which staff believed disruptive pupils can control their behaviour. At the three-month follow-up evaluation, there is a discernible shift in the percentage of respondents who believe that students may have less control over their behaviour, in line with attention given to the attachment perspective during the training day. That is, whilst 83.3% ($n = 67$) staff believed pre-training that disruptive pupils were mostly

Table 3. To what extent can pupils control their own disruptive behaviour?

Extent of control	n At pre-training ($n = 80$) At 3 month fu ($n = 30$)	Valid % At pre-training At 3 month fu
No/some control over own behaviour	13	16.3
	8	26.7
Mostly/totally in control of behaviour	67	83.8
	22	73.3
Total	80	100.1
	30	100.0

or in total control of their behaviour, this percentage reduced to 73.3% ($n = 22$) Three-month after attending the training day. It is anticipated that with continued involvement in the school over the next few months, a further reduction may be seen at the end of the school year.

Table 4 shows responses to the question regarding possible factors related to disruptive behaviour. Whilst it is disappointing that only 30 responses were received for the three month follow-up, the findings suggest a desirable shift from Disagree

Table 4. Possible factors related to disruptive behaviour.

			Pre-training [May 2013]		Three-month follow-up [December 2013]	
			n	Valid %	*n*	Valid %
a.	Low engagement with learning	*Agree*	38	50.0	30	100.0
		Disagree	38	50.0	0	0
		Total	76	100.0	30	100.0
b.	Learning difficulties	*Agree*	58	77.3	20	66.7
		Disagree	17	22.7	10	33.3
		Total	75	100.0	30	100.0
c.	Social and emotional difficulties	*Agree*	54	72.0	28	93.3
		Disagree	21	28.0	2	6.7
		Total	75	100.0	30	100.0
d.	Troubled home environment	*Agree*	47	60.3	27	93.1
		Disagree	30	38.5	2	6.9
		Undecided	1	1.3	–	–
		Total	78	100.1	29	100.0
e.	Difficulties with friendships/peer relationships	*Agree*	56	74.7	23	79.3
		Disagree	19	25.3	6	20.7
		Total	75	100.0	29	100.0
f	Difficulties relating to teacher(s) at school	*Agree*	38	50.0	20	66.7
		Disagree	38	50.0	10	33.3
		Total	76	100.0	30	100.0
g.	Deep-seated anxiety	*Agree*	38	50.0	20	71.4
		Disagree	38	50.0	8	28.6
		Total	76	100.0	28	100.0
h.	Feelings of shame/fear/anger/envy	*Agree*	58	77.3	22	73.3
		Disagree	17	22.7	8	26.7
		Total	75	100.0	30	100.0
i.	Sense of being misunderstood	*Agree*	54	72.0	20	66.7
		Disagree	21	28.0	10	33.3
		Total	75	100.0	30	100.0
j.	Sense that others don't like him/her	*Agree*	47	60.3	20	69.0
		Disagree	30	38.5	9	31.0
		Undecided	1	1.3	–	–
		Total	78	100.1	29	100.0
k.	Loyalty and commitment to peer group	*Agree*	56	74.7	26	86.7
		Disagree	19	25.3	4	13.3
		Total	75	100.0	30	100.0
l.	Disruptive behaviour communicates inner distress	*Agree*	56	74.7	25	89.3
		Disagree	19	25.3	3	10.7
		Total	75	100.0	28	100.0

to Agree in nine of the twelve factors. It is hoped that this movement will continue and be apparent in the final follow-up evaluation at the end of the school year. Amongst the most notable of the findings at three month follow-up compared with pre-training findings, is that all of the respondents agree that low engagement with learning is a possible factor related to disruptive behaviour (100%, $n = 30$), and the increased level of agreement that other possible factors are social and emotional difficulties (93.3.%, $n = 28$), a troubled home environment (93.1%, $n = 27$), deep-seated anxiety (71.4%, $n = 20$) and that disruptive behaviour communicates emotional distress (89.3%, $n = 25$). A full breakdown of the findings for each factor can be seen in Table 4.

Discussion and implications of findings to date

Most teachers attending the training day had some prior basic knowledge of attachment theory, either from teacher training or CPD events. When asked at the end of the training day if the material presented had changed their perception of disruptive behaviour, 76.1% of participants said that it had done so. The usefulness of attachment theory therefore extends well beyond the clinical setting and offers a framework for considering systemic interventions in school to support the most troubled and vulnerable pupils. Moreover, in reframing "difficult" pupils as "troubled" pupils, or pupils with emotional difficulties, new perspectives and energy can be brought to maintaining relationships from the teachers' point of view. Moving away from blaming and labelling young people as "troublesome", "challenging" or "disruptive", will provide space to reconsider the most conducive response to managing the behaviour of the most troubled and vulnerable pupils in school.

During the training day, teachers offered insights into the negative effects challenging behaviour had on them personally as professionals. However, with teachers more vigilant about student attachment behaviour, and encouraged to manage pupils' behaviour using this framework, there is a greater possibility for vulnerable learners to engage in school and, ultimately, to fulfil their individual potential. The better the relationships and mutual understanding between pupils and staff, the better the chance of effective teaching and learning for all concerned (Earl 2009).

Teacher concern was raised about how fellow pupils would engage with differentiation, as pupils have a strong sense of what is fair. Attachment theory highlights the importance of responding to individual need. Therefore, treating people fairly does not mean treating them the same or equally. In fact, treating all people the same, negates individual need. The challenge is to respond to individual need within the group (social) setting of the classroom. The onus is not on individual teachers to provide for every pupil's individual need, but for the school staff as a whole to respond to the individual's needs in a responsive and consistent fashion. Again, that requires systems thinking and collegial and leadership support (for example, Waters, Marzano, and McNulty 2004; Huber, Moorman, and Pont 2007).

In conclusion

The educational challenge for the future is how to embed performativity in a climate of participation and inclusion. For the current project, the support of the Senior Leadership Team has been invaluable and critical in exploring the psychological underpinnings of disruptive behaviour at school. Without leadership commitment, staff training in this area would not be possible or effective. A systemic, whole school approach is required, not only to ensure consistency in policy and management at all levels of staffing, but in developing a shared language and shared values (for example, Walters, Marzano, and McNulty 2004; Roby 2011). In future training and school-based interventions, the need for this systemic approach should be made explicit to effect the best possible outcome. A way forward is offered by Greene (2009), who views disruptive behaviour in terms of unsolved problems. His collaborative problem-solving approach is based on the language of inclusion, in forging helpful dialogues between the staff and students concerned. These problem-solving collaborations treat the students as partners in seeking solutions to the "unsolved problems" manifested by the disruptive behaviour. The approach is thus founded on a whole school ethos of mutual respect for all members of the school community.

Efforts made to bridge the worlds of Education and Psychology can result in school staff feeling better empowered to carry out their job as educators. This has been demonstrated by the enhanced understanding of staff following the training day regarding challenging behaviour at school (as suggested by staff feedback on the day). It is plausible that by highlighting the value of understanding disruptive behaviour through the lens of the attachment perspective, more teachers will feel enabled to remain in the profession. With greater insight into the psychological implications of disruptive behaviour, school staff may also be in a better position to understand and interpret challenging behaviour as a call for help. That is, a call for support from those whose history of emotional turbulence has equipped them poorly for the social and cognitive demands of school.

Following further evaluation, the CPD materials developed for the current project will be made available to other schools. It is anticipated that the materials will enable greater mutual understanding and respect for the ways in which disruptive behaviour is perceived by practitioners and school staff. Moreover, they will provide an urgently needed means of facilitating a shared knowledge base and a shared language for addressing emotional barriers to learning. Indeed, Delaney (2012, 122) encapsulates one of the fundamental challenges facing those who support the most troubled pupils at school, when she suggests that it may be the "lack of shared knowledge about each other's professions that can lead to unhelpful assumptions." There is much to do and urgently, to build a shared knowledge base, which is founded on mutual respect and mutual understanding concerning what the behaviour of the most troubled pupils is telling us.

References

Bebbington, E. 2008. *Stop Wasting My Time! Case Studies of Pupils with Attachment Issues in Schools with Special Reference to Looked after and Adopted Children*. Stirling: Post Adoption Central Support (PACS).

Bombèr, L. 2007. *Inside I'm Hurting: Practical Strategies for Supporting Children with Attachment Difficulties in Schools*. London: Worth.

Bowlby, J. 1969. *Attachment (Vol. 1 of Attachment and Loss)*. London: Hogarth Press.

Boxall, M. 2002. *Nurture Groups in School: Principles and Practice*. London: Sage.

Boxall, M., and S. Lucas. 2010. *Nurture Groups in School: Principles and Practice*. 2nd ed. London: Sage.

Chapman, C. 2002. "Ofsted and School Improvement: Teachers' Perceptions of the Inspection Process in Schools Facing Challenging Circumstances." *School Leadership & Management* 22 (3): 257–272.

Clunies-Ross, P., E. Little, and M. Kienhuis. 2008. "Self-Reported and Actual Use of Proactive and Reactive Classroom Management Strategies and their Relationship with Teacher Stress and Student Behaviour." *Educational Psychology* 28 (6): 693–710.

Delaney, M. 2009. "How Teachers Can Use a Knowledge of Attachment Theory to Work with Difficult-to-Reach Teenagers." Chap. 3 in *Teenagers and Attachment: Helping Adolescents Engage with Life and Learning*, edited by A. Perry, 63–96. London: Worth.

Delaney, M. 2012. "What Can Educational Psychotherapy Teach Teachers?" Chap. 10 in *Why Can't I Help This Child to Learn? Understanding Emotional Barriers to Learning*, edited by H. High, 121–136. London: Karnac.

Earl, B. 2009. "Exterior Fortresses and Interior Fortification: Use of Creativity and Empathy When Building an Authentic Attachment Relationship in School." Chap. 4 in *Teenagers and Attachment: Helping Adolescents Engage with Life and Learning*, edited by A. Perry, 97–121. London: Worth.

Geddes, H. 2006. *Attachment in the Classroom: The Links between Children's Early Experience, Emotional Well-Being and Performance in School: A Practical Guide for Schools*. London: Worth.

Gerhardt, S. 2004. *Why Love Matters: How Affection Shapes a Baby's Brain*. Abingdon: Taylor & Francis.

Greene, R. W. 2009. *Lost at School: Why Our Kids with Behavioral Challenges are Falling through the Cracks and How We Can Help Them*. New York: Scribner Book.

Grundy, S., and J. Robison. 2005. "Teacher Professional Development: Themes and Trends in the Recent Australian Experience." Chap. 6 in *International Handbook of Continuing Professional Development of Teachers*, edited by C. Day and J. Sachs, 119–145. Maidenhead: Open University Press.

Howe, D. 2005. *Child Abuse and Neglect: Attachment, Development and Intervention*. Basingstoke: Palgrave Macmillan.

Huber, S., R. H. Moorman, and B. Pont. 2007. *School Leadership for Systemic Improvement in England: A Case Study Report for the OECD Activity Improving School Leadership*. London: OECD Directorate for Education. http://www.oecd.org/edu/school/40673692.pdf.

Hughes, N. K., and A. Schlosser. 2014. "The Effectiveness of Nurture Groups: A Systematic Review." *Emotional and Behavioural Difficulties*, 1–24. doi:10.1080/13632752.2014.883729.

Kyriacou, C. 2009. *Effective Teaching Skills: Theory and Practice*. 3rd ed. Cheltenham: Nelson Thornes.

Layard, R., and J. Dunn. 2009. *A Good Childhood: Searching for Values in a Competitive Age. Report for the Children's Society*. London: Penguin.

McCrory, E., S. A. De Brito, and E. Viding. 2010. "Research Review: The Neurobiology and Genetics of Maltreatment and Adversity." *Journal Child Psychology & Psychiatry* 51 (10): 1079–1095.

Noor, L. 2012. "It's because of What We Did That I'm Going to University: A Qualitative Exploration of the Experience of Growing through a School's Therapeutic Programme." *European Journal for Qualitative Research in Psychotherapy* (5): 56–70. ISSN 1756–7599.

Roby, D. E. 2011. "Teacher Leaders Impacting School Culture." *Education* 131 (4): 782–790.

Rogers, B. 2012. *The Essential Guide to Managing Teacher Stress*. London: Pearson.

Solomon, M., and S. Nashat. 2010. "Offering a 'Therapeutic Presence' in Schools and Education Settings." *Psychodynamic Practice* 16 (3): 289–304.

The Sutton Trust Report. 2014. *Baby Bonds: Parenting, Attachment and a Secure Base for Children*. Report written by S. Moullin, J. Waldfogel, and E. Washbrook, March, London.

Taylor, C. 2010. *A Practical Guide to Caring for Children and Adolescents with Attachment Difficulties*. London: Jessica Kingsley.

Waters, J. T., R. J. Marzano, and B. McNulty. 2004. "Leadership That Sparks Learning." *Educational Leadership* 61 (7): 48.

Wilson, V. 2002. *Feeling the Strain: An Overview of the Literature on Teachers' Stress*. Edinburgh: University of Glasgow, Scottish Council for Research in Education.

Some possible effects of behaviour management training on teacher confidence and competence: evidence from a study of primary school teachers in Hong Kong

Paul Cooper[a] and Zi Yan[b]

[a]Department of Special Education and Counselling, The Hong Kong Institute of Education, Tai Po, Hong Kong; [b]Department of Curriculum and Instruction, The Hong Kong Institute of Education, Tai Po, Hong Kong

This study aims to explore the relationships between the extent and perceived quality of teachers' experience of training in behaviour management (BM), and their awareness of the nature and extent of behavioural problems among school students, and their confidence in their own competence to deal with such problems. Teachers ($n = 183$) from Hong Kong primary schools were surveyed. The results showed that gender, age and whether teachers have received training had no significant influence on teachers' awareness, conception and confidence regarding BM. A negative correlation was found between teachers' levels of satisfaction in relation to their training experiences and their perceptions of the level of problematic behaviours among students, and the impact of students' problematic behaviour on their teaching. A positive correlation was found between teachers' levels of satisfaction in relation to their training experiences and their confidence in their own competence to deal with students' problematic behaviour.

Introduction

Studies of the effects of training in behaviour management (BM) have tended to focus on the relatively short-term effects of specific training programmes. This study is concerned with exploring the novel question of the relationship between the cumulative experience of training in BM (or lack of training in BM) over time and the possible impact of this on teachers' perceptions of the nature and extent of classroom behavioural problems, and their self-confidence in dealing them. The study took place in Hong Kong.

Background

It has long been recognised that a positive social climate, characterised by good order as well as harmonious and supportive social relationships, is a key feature of successful schools. This is strongly reflected in the "school effectiveness" (Rutter et al. 1979; Purkey and Smith 1983; Mortimore et al. 1988) and "school improvement" (Hargreaves and Fullan 2012) research literatures. Successful schools are places where staff and students work together cooperatively and harmoniously on challenging and sometimes stressful academic tasks, success in which is defined by rigorous achievement indicators. Schools also tend to be relatively large social organisations which, by necessity, have to be carefully structured and routinized in complex ways. For example, in state-funded mainstream schools in Hong Kong, actual class sizes averaged 28 in primary schools and between 30 and 33 in secondary schools and it is not unusual for individual schools to cater for as many as 1000 pupils or more at any one time (EDB 2012).

This means that schools are highly complex communities requiring careful regulation that ensures, at the very least, the safety of all its members as well as the efficient and effective pursuit of its educational goals. This situation is made all the more challenging by the fact that the pupils in Hong Kong, in common with those in all parts of the developed world, are compelled by law to be present in school. Evidence from various sources suggests that, in general, this element of compulsion tends to be more or less acceptable to students depending on the extent to which they place value on the goals and/or experience of formal education (Cooper and McIntyre 1996; Cooper et al. 2000), and/or the extent to which the school attendance provides them with rewarding social experiences (Reid 1986; Patterson, Reid, and Dishion 1992). Where students do not regard schooling as valuable they are likely to become disaffected and respond in one of three ways: (1) to withdraw (i.e. avoid attending school); (2) to externalise their disaffection (i.e. become uncooperative and/or disruptive) or (3) to internalise their disaffection (i.e. to be cognitively disengaged and to be passively non-compliant) (Cooper and Jacobs 2011a; Cooper, Bilton, and Kakos 2013). Where students view school primarily as a social activity (i.e. as an opportunity to interact with their friends), there is a danger that they may view formal curricular activities as irrelevant and disruptive to their socialising activities and actively challenge this perceived intrusion. Schooling as a purely social activity may also give rise to a sense of ownership of the school setting as a territory to be defended against the intrusion of other groups and/or individuals (e.g. rival gangs; ethnic minorities; and persons with disabilities), resulting in gang violence and bullying (Eisenbraun 2007).

Added to these potential difficulties is the often perceived mismatch between traditional ways of measuring educational success, dominant in mainstream schools, and the broader social, emotional and learning needs of students in general, and particularly those who may experience delays in their development and/or learning difficulties of one kind or another. In spite of ongoing efforts to meet needs of an increasingly diverse range of students, the emphasis on summative judgments of student performance tend to produce high levels of academic failure, which in turn contribute to social exclusion and disaffection (Trust 2010; Cooper and Jacobs 2011a). This problem is amplified in an educational climate that is increasingly influenced by narrowly focused league tables of student performance, such as PISA, which are being shown to have a significant impact on the thinking and prescriptions of educational policy-makers (Baird et al. 2011; Alexander 2012). This suggests that the challenge of promoting educational engagement for all students will be made increasingly difficult as schools in Hong Kong pursue the Hong Kong legislative council's policy of "Integrated Education" (IE). Whereby mainstream schools are required to cater for the social and educational needs of an increasingly diverse range of students (CSENIE 2012).

It is not surprising, therefore, that prominent among Hong Kong teachers' concerns are issues of "order and discipline" in their schools. Pang's (2004) study of teachers in Hong Kong ($n = 554$ from 44 schools) found strong associations between their job satisfaction and their degree of satisfaction with levels of "order and discipline" in their schools. These factors were also associated, though to a lesser degree, with their levels of commitment to teaching. In short, this evidence suggests that teachers are happier and work harder when they believe that they are working in a well-ordered environment. A further highly significant factor identified by Pang was teacher perceptions of "sense of community".

Community is perhaps most usefully defined in terms of a shared vision of what a group of people have in common and what it is they need to do, individually and collectively, in order to promote their collective best interests. Traditionally, in Hong Kong, schools were designed to group students according to common characteristics, especially: age, gender and ability. It has been argued that Hong Kong is a country where such segregation has reduced considerably in recent years, but persists to a greater degree than in many other countries (Wiseman 2008). The cumulative evidence has been taken to suggest that Hong Kong's adoption of an IE agenda (Forlin 2007; Forlin and Rose 2010; Forlin and Cooper 2013) may be placing a significant strain on the climate of order and discipline in some schools (CSENIE 2012). It is not surprising, therefore, that there is evidence to show that teachers in Hong Kong, in common with their counterparts in other countries (e.g. MacBeath et al. 2006), have raised concerns about the practical feasibility of catering for students with disabilities in mainstream classrooms (Chen, Jin, and Lau 2006) and the impact of this policy on order and discipline in schools.

A key feature of this area of concern is the adequacy of teachers' skills in relation to classroom and BM. As Chan, Chong, and Ng (2011) indicate, powerful evidence exists to suggest that training has an important role to play in the development of mainstream teachers' and other education professionals' knowledge, understanding and skills in relation to student behaviour. Numerous studies of programmes designed to raise staff awareness of the nature of social, emotional and behavioural problems and provide training in intervention strategies show that such programmes can improve teacher confidence and competence and lead to measurable improvements in student behaviour and educational engagement (Frolich et al. 2002; Marzocchi et al. 2004; Schiff and BarGil 2004; Rossbach and Probst 2005; Zentall and Javorsky 2007).

This is important, not least because of powerful evidence showing that social, emotional and behavioural problems are dynamic. In school settings, serious problems of this type can often be seen to emerge from mild and minor discipline problems which intensify when mishandled by teachers (Patterson, Reid, and Dishion 1992; Cooper et al. 2000). The incidence of such escalation is likely to increase in settings where students with special educational needs associated with social, emotional and or behavioural vulnerabilities are present (DES 1989; Molnar and Lindquist 1989; Cooper et al. 2000). This means that the quality of teachers' skills and understanding of classroom and BM is of vital importance.

There is a long tradition of research showing an association between aversive relationships with teachers, social, emotional and behavioural difficulties (SEBD) and educational failure (Hargreaves, Hester, and Mellor 1975; Tattum 1982; Cooper 1993; Myers and Pianta 2008). Conversely, teachers who show warmth, empathy and respect for students and create a nurturing environment are likely to prevent the development of disruptive behaviour, and encourage positive self-regard and pro-social engagement among students; in contrast, teachers who do not possess these qualities are likely to provoke disruptive behaviour (Cooper et al. 2000; Lodge and Lynch 2003). However, as MacBeath et al. (2006) suggest teachers' good intentions have a limited impact in the absence of appropriate training and support.

Omoteso and Semudara (2011), in a paper on classroom management in Nigeria, claim that personal qualities may be sufficient to equip a teacher with the necessary abilities to be an effective classroom manager. They also refer to a "common belief" that "female teachers are less firm when it comes to management of classroom misbehaviours and may not be able to effectively manage the classroom as their male counterparts" (3). These authors also argue that teachers with longer service are likely to be more effective in classroom management than less experienced colleagues. It should be stressed, however, that the predominant view in the literature is that training is a major component in the development of teacher skills in this area.

The efficacy of behavioural, cognitive behavioural and systemic school-based interventions, for preventing and dealing with emotional and behavioural problems in schools is well evidenced (Poon-McBrayer and Lian 2002; Chan, Chong, and Ng 2011; Cooper and Jacobs 2011a, 2011b). Unfortunately, the use of such interventions in schools is limited. Results from a recent survey carried out in Hong Kong schools ($n = 226$) found that difficulties they experienced in dealing with emotional and behavioural problems in schools were cited by experienced teachers as making the implementation of a whole school approach to IE extremely difficult (Sin et al. 2011). The same study also noted concern among teachers about their lack of appropriate training in supporting learners presenting with the most challenging types of SEN, such as those associated with emotional, social and behavioural difficulties. Against this has to be placed a recent study which shows that some Hong Kong teachers, in both ordinary and special schools, whilst expressing concern at what they perceive to be an increase in the incidence of emotional difficulties, and challenging behaviour, consider themselves to be effective in dealing with it and exhibit a sense of confidence in this respect (Chan, Chong, and Ng 2011). Having said this, the evidence presented in this study refers only to teachers' claims and perceptions and not their actual classroom behaviour.

In Hong Kong, the Education Bureau is well aware of the importance of training in the area of classroom and BM, and devotes considerable resources to in-service training for teachers in this area. People who are currently teaching in Hong Kong schools are likely to have experienced a wide variety of training courses in classroom and BM and approaches to disruptive behaviour. These include block release courses, whereby teachers are released from their schools for varying periods of time to undertake short courses at The Hong Kong Institute of Education (HKIEd) and various of the seven Universities in Hong Kong. This topic is also included in the undergraduate Initial Teacher Training (ITT) curriculum at HKIEd and in the short postgraduate ITT programmes that are available in Hong Kong. Teachers are also able to study the topic at postgraduate Diploma level, at Master's degree level and at Doctoral level. Over the years certain aspects of the pattern of provision have changed, with older members of the teaching profession having experienced different training opportunities from the younger colleagues, both in terms of the nature of the design of certain training programmes as well as their contents (Poon-McBrayer and Lian 2002; Chan, Chong, and Ng 2011).

In spite of this extensive commitment of time and money, little is known of the medium to long-term effectiveness of these different training experiences. The purpose of this study was to explore practising teachers' perceptions of the impact of their training experiences in BM on their current levels of confidence and competence in relation to BM. In particular, teachers were asked about their satisfaction with their experiences and the impact of these experiences on their confidence in relation to BM. They were also asked about their preferred BM approaches.

Central to this study is the intention to test key assumptions regarding the value of formal training in BM in influencing teachers' understanding of student behavioural problems; their confidence in dealing with these problems and the quality of their strategic choices in relation to BM.

The present study

Study aims

This study set out to explore the relationships between the extent and perceived quality of teachers' experience of training in BM, and their awareness of the nature and extent of emotional, personal, physical and social behavioural problems among school students, and their confidence in their own competence to deal with such problems in classroom. In addition to exploratory statistical analysis involving multiple regression, the authors also set out with four hypotheses, based on the literature review.

Hypotheses

(1) There would be a positive relationship between perceived quality of training (i.e. satisfaction) and teacher confidence.
(2) There would be a positive relationship between perceived quality of training (i.e. satisfaction) and teacher awareness of the nature and awareness of the nature and extent of emotional, personal, physical and social behavioural problems among school students.
(3) There would be a positive relationship between the extent of training and teacher confidence.
(4) There would be a positive relationship between the extent of training and awareness of the nature and extent of emotional, personal, physical and social behavioural problems among school students.

Method

A convenience sample of teachers ($n = 183$) from Hong Kong primary schools was recruited via schools engaged in various in-service teacher education programmes being run by a Higher Education Institution in Hong Kong. Among the participants, there are 41 (22.4%) males, 141 (77.0%) females and 1 (.5%) without gender information. The majority of participants have undergraduate degree (129, 70.5%); 41 (22.4%) have master or above qualification; 12 (6.7%) with certificate or diploma; and only 1 (.5%) did not provide qualification information. As for teaching experience, 48 (26.2%) reported experience of 9 years or less; 62 (33.9%) have 10 to 19 years of experience; 43 (23.5%) report 20–29 years of experience; 10 (5.5%) have 30 years or more of experience; and 20 (10.9%) did not provide such information. It is important to note that the institution concerned is responsible for providing 80% of primary school teachers in Hong Kong and a high majority of the in-service training in BM.

Ethical approval for this study was granted by the HKIEd Research Ethics Committee. After informed consent was secured, these participants were surveyed with The Effects of BM Training Scale (adapted by the authors and colleagues) that is designed to collect data from eight domains: (1) demographic information; (2) experience of training related to BM (whether teachers have received training); (3) the level of their satisfaction with the training ranging from 1 (strongly dissatisfied) to 4 (strongly satisfied); (4) awareness of the nature of problematic behaviour of students (emotional, personal, physical and social) they experience in their classrooms (e.g. how often do the children they teach lack motivation to learn); (5) the perceived impact of problematic behaviour of students on teachers (that is, the extent to which teachers felt themselves to be negatively affected by student misbehaviour) (e.g. the extent to which the behaviour of the children they teach results in difficulty in maintaining the class programme); (6) their confidence in their own competence to deal with such problems in classroom (e.g. how much they can do to control disruptive behaviour in the classroom); (7) their BM strategies that we divided into positive and negative strategies, with positive strategies being defined as those with a substantial research evidence base (e.g. using praise and rewards), and negative strategies being defined as those often found in research studies to be associated with the exacerbation of classroom behavioural problems (e.g. using teacher's authority to threaten the child; and (8) further support they will seek when the behavioural problems are more than they can manage (e.g. seeking help from other professionals).

Data analysis

Rasch analysis (1960) was employed to calibrate the teachers' measures on the scales. Based on those Rasch-calibrated person measures, conventional analysis including t-test, ANOVA, correlation was then employed to address the research objective, i.e. to explore the relationships between the extent and perceived quality of teachers' experience of training in BM, their awareness of the nature and extent of behavioural problems among school students, and their confidence in their own competence to deal with such problems.

Rasch analysis is used before applying conventional analysis in order to avoid arriving at misleading conclusions by applying conventional analytical techniques directly to raw scores. Conventional analytical techniques based on classic test theory require interval scale data input (Wright 1997). However, raw data collected through Likert-type scales are usually ordinal, since the categories of Likert-type scales indicate only ordering without any proportional levels of meaning (Wright 1997; Bond and Fox 2007). The Rasch model can overcome this problem by converting ordinal data into interval measures and provide linear measurement from ordered category responses (Linacre 2006). Such interval measures can then be subjected to conventional analysis.

Results

Psychometric properties of the scales

The Rasch analysis was first employed to examine the psychometric properties of the scales. The criteria used to evaluate the quality of the scales included Rasch person/item reliability; item fit statistics; and the amount of variance explained by Rasch measures. Rasch reliability indicates the probability that persons (or items) estimated with high measures actually do have higher measures than persons (or items) estimated with low measures (Linacre 2006). Item fit statistics estimate the extent to which the empirical data match the model. Outfit and Infit mean squares (MNSQ) are widely used indices of item fit statistics. Researchers (e.g. Wright and Linacre 1994; Yan 2014) suggested that MNSQs falling in the range of .6–1.4 indicated a productive measurement for survey data with rating scales. This criterion was adopted as the cut-off value of MNSQ fit statistics in this study. Variance explained by Rasch measures refers to the proportion of variance in the observed data which can be explained by the item difficulties, person abilities and rating scale structures (Linacre 2006). The higher the proportion of variance explained, the better prediction the Rasch model provides. Table 1 summarises the psychometric properties of the nine scales used in the current study.

It can be seen from Table 1 that the nine scales have acceptable psychometric properties. Only three items, from APE, IMP and PMA, respectively, were removed due to misfitting to the Rasch model (MNSQ higher than 1.4). The Rasch item reliabilities for all scale are higher than .90 and the Rasch person reliabilities are all higher than .7 except NMA. A close investigation revealed that the five items in NMA were not well targeted at the respondents. Two items are too difficult to endorse by most of respondents, while the remaining three items did not separate the respondents in terms of their levels on the negative management skills very well. This scale could be improved in future studies by adding some items that are easier to endorse. The Rasch measures explained 45–65% of the variances in the data which is acceptable. The results indicate the appropriateness of the scales for use with the sample in the current study.

Table 1. Psychometric properties of measurement scales.

Scale	Abbr.	No. of Items	Rasch person/item reliability	Variance explained by measures (%)
Confidence in BM	CBM	4	.83/.93	65.2
Awareness of emotional misbehaviour	AEM	9	.78/.98	45.2
Awareness of physical misbehaviour	APH	8	.82/.98	53.4
Awareness of personal misbehaviour	APE	9	.84/.98	54.4
Awareness of social misbehaviour	ASO	6	.69/.96	52.7
Impact	IMP	4	.73/.97	56.2
Positive management	PMA	11	.75/.99	48.5
Negative management	NMA	5	.51/.99	53.0
Further support	FSU	5	.78/.93	50.8

The effects of demographic factors on teacher responses to scales

The first issue to be dealt with was the effects of gender and training experience on teachers' BM since they were proposed by Omoteso and Semudara (2011) as being potentially significant factors in teachers' BM competency. *T*-test was conducted on Rasch-calibrated person measures to examine the difference between male and female teachers; and between teachers with and without BM training on different dimensions in the scale. The results (see Table 2) show that gender and whether teachers have received training had no significant impact on teachers' responses to all scales.

ANOVA was conducted to check the effects of age, teaching experience and qualifications on teachers' responses to different scales. The results are presented in Table 3.

As shown in Table 3, teaching experience has no significant effect on any of the scales except NMA: that is, teachers with more teaching experience indicated a greater tendency to employ unproductive and exacerbating strategies than less experienced colleagues. The effect of age was statistically significant on IMP ($p < .05$) and NMA ($p < .05$). *Post hoc* comparisons indicated that the youngest group (aged between 20 and 29) had significantly lower measures on IMP than their older peers. The effect of qualifications was statistically significant on PMA ($p < .05$). *Post hoc* comparisons indicated that teachers with certificate or diploma had significantly lower measures on PMA than teachers with higher qualifications (degree, master or above).

The correlations between characteristics of training, teachers' satisfaction with training and teachers' responses to scales

Using the group of teachers who had received BM training as the sample ($N = 40$), correlations were calculated between the characteristics of their training experiences (e.g. the highest level of training (HLT); total length of training (TLT); the elapsed time since last experience of training (ETT); teachers' satisfaction with training (SAT)) and teachers' responses to the scales. The results are presented in Table 4.

Table 2. *T*-test between male and female teachers, and between teachers with and without BM training.

Scale	Gender			Training experience		
	Male ($N = 41$)	Female ($N = 141$)	p for t test	With training ($N = 40$)	Without training ($N = 143$)	p for t test
CBM	1.80	1.88	.848	2.53	1.67	.074
AEM	−2.85	−2.95	.697	−2.90	−2.95	.844
APH	−2.07	−2.29	.578	−2.58	−2.16	.293
APE	.41	.58	.624	.52	.53	.974
ASO	−1.33	−1.31	.967	−1.19	−1.37	.676
IMP	−2.34	−2.49	.741	−2.48	−2.48	.988
PMA	1.11	1.31	.316	1.46	1.21	.192
NMA	−.51	−.71	.219	−.56	−.69	.402
FSU	−.43	−.20	.526	.16	−.41	.129

Note: All measures are in logits.

Table 3. *p* values of the main effect of age, teaching experience, qualifications.

Scales	*p* value of ANOVA		
	Age	Teaching experience	Qualifications
CBM	.247	.619	.118
AEM	.647	.979	.239
APH	.915	.611	.516
APE	.571	.685	.069
ASO	.222	.926	.309
IMP	.047*	.061	.489
PMA	.398	.523	.013*
NMA	.048*	.033*	.251
FSU	.304	.655	.256

*$p < .05$.

As shown in Table 4, there is no significant correlation between the characteristics of training and teachers' responses to scales except a positive correlation ($r = .475$, $p < .05$) between TLT and teachers' responses to the scale FSU.

However, teachers' satisfaction with trainings they have received, SAT, is found to have significant relations with their responses to many scales. There is a significant positive correlation ($r = .458$, $p < .01$) between teachers' SAT and CBM. Negative correlations are found between teachers' SAT and teachers' awareness of misbehaviour of children including APH ($r = -.396$, $p < .05$) and APE ($r = -.391$, $p < .05$). Negative correlations are also found between teachers' satisfaction with training and their perceived impact of children's misbehaviour on themselves (IMP) ($r = -.448$, $p < .01$), and further support (FSU) ($r = -.326$, $p < .05$). In other words, the more satisfied teachers were with their training, the more confident they were about their BM competence; the less frequently they labelled students' physical and personal misbehaviour; the less they experienced negative impact from students' misbehaviour; and the less frequently they sought help from others due to students' misbehaviour.

Most challenging problems

Teachers were asked to identify five problems which they regard as the most difficult to manage from all misbehaviours listed in the scale. Table 5 presents the most challenging problems perceived by teachers with and without BM training.

There is substantial overlap between the choices of the two groups of teachers. Four out of five challenging problems are the same with slightly different order for the two groups. The problem "Make offensive noises (shouting, calling out, screaming, talking back)" ranked 4 for teachers with training is ranked six for teachers without training. There are, however, some special cases. For example, the "Has no friendships with peers", which is no. 4 challenging problems for teachers without training, is ranked as no. 20 by teachers with BM training.

Discussion

Gender and age

The finding that gender and teaching experience have no significant effect on nearly all the scales is consistent with the general trend in the literature which tends to emphasise the primacy of specific skills over such personal characteristics. The

Table 4. Correlations between the characteristics of training, teachers' SAT and teachers' responses to scales.

	A	B	C	D	E	F	G	H	I	J	K	L	M
A. HLT	—												
B. TLT	.442*	—											
C. ETT	.268	.373	—										
D. SAT	-.040	-.038	.107	—									
E. CBM	-.017	-.023	-.188	.458**	—								
F. AEM	-.199	.284	.324	-.168	.130	—							
G. APH	-.194	.213	.069	-.396*	-.073	.742**	—						
H. APE	-.068	.330	.166	-.391*	-.151	.680**	.777**	—					
I. ASO	-.168	-.076	.235	-.267	-.071	.384*	.660**	.707**	—				
J. IMP	-.074	.318	.197	-.448**	-.297	.525**	.537**	.536**	.297	—			
K. PMA	-.297	.120	.065	-.113	-.035	.259	.295	.538**	.331*	.218	—		
L. NMA	-.044	.379	.133	-.357*	-.186	.233	.360*	.469**	.310	.317*	.549**	—	
M. FSU	-.070	.475*	.328	-.326*	-.130	.260	.269	.407**	.101	.285	.532**	.541**	—

*$p < .05$; **$p < .01$.

Table 5. The most challenging problems perceived by teachers.

	% of participants who selected
Teachers with training (N=40)	
1. Lack motivation to learn	55
2. Refuse to follow instructions (disobey the class rules, challenge teachers' instruction, constantly tell the parents "No" etc.)	35
3. Lack ability to concentrate in the class/school	35
4. Make offensive noises (shouting, calling out, screaming and talking back)	30
5. Have angry outbursts or temper tantrums	30
Teachers without training (N = 143)	
1. Lack motivation to learn	52
2. Lack ability to concentrate in the class/school	43
3. Refuse to follow instructions (disobey the class rules, challenge teachers' instruction and constantly tell the parents "No" etc.)	26
4. Has no friendships with peers	22
5. Have angry outbursts or temper tantrums	21

finding that length of service is associated with "negative management" is, however, interesting. Whilst it is important to treat this finding with caution owing to low reliability of the negative management scale (see above), when considered in relation to the finding that age was also statistically significant ($p < .05$) in relation to the "Impact" of students' negative behaviour on teachers interesting possibilities emerge. This might be taken to suggest that teachers' emotional resilience, amongst this sample, had a tendency to diminish over time. This possibility is supported by the finding that the youngest group (aged between 20 and 29) experienced significantly lower levels of personal "Impact" than their older peers, indicating a higher level of emotional resilience. This may be an indication of the phenomenon of teacher "burnout" (Howard and Johnson 2004), which is characterised as severe psychological distress which often appears after prolonged exposure to highly stressful work environments. For teachers, high among the sources of stress are working with poorly motivated students and the strain of maintaining discipline (Kyriacou 2001; Behan and Blake 2014). It is highly likely that burnout can be a moderator of the effects of BM training, as well as being a possible source of impairment to the utilisation of skills. This suggests that where teacher burnout is an issue, the effectiveness of training in the absence of direct intervention for burnout is likely to be diminished.

Qualifications and training

The finding that level of qualifications was statistically significant on dimension "Positive management" ($p < .05$) and the finding that teachers with certificate or diploma had significantly lower measures on "Positive management" than teachers with higher qualifications (undergraduate, masters' degree, master or above) suggests the importance of continuous award-bearing professional development. This suggests the importance of high-level academic training and is consistent with concerns expressed by newly qualified teachers that pre-service training alone is, on its own, an inadequate preparation for challenges associated with BM and SEBD (Garner 2013). Whilst this argument is often used as a basis for arguing for better quality and more extensive pre-service training, it also draws attention to the developmental nature of professional learning.

It is widely agreed that professional, as opposed to purely theoretical learning emerges from reflection in and on practice (Schön 1983). One way of thinking about teaching from this perspective is through the lens of the concept of teachers' craft knowledge (Desforges and McNamara 1979; Brown and Donald 1993; Cooper and McIntyre 1996). This posits that teachers learn the "craft" of teaching over time through a cumulative process of practical problem-solving in which may draw on many sources including personal reflection, interaction with professional peers and formal teacher education programmes. This would appear to chime with the finding in the current study that there was a positive correlation ($r = .475$, $p < .05$) between "TLT" and teachers' responses to the scale "further support". This shows that teachers with the highest levels of training were more likely to seek the support of specialist colleagues, which implies knowledge of the limits to the scope of their skills as well awareness of the availability of appropriate support.

Teacher satisfaction

Teachers' satisfaction with the training they have received was found to have significant associations with their responses to many of the sub-scales, including "Confidence in BM" ($r = .458$, $p < .01$). This indicates a strong association between satisfaction and the effectiveness of training (from the teachers' perspectives). Furthermore, negative correlations were found between teachers' SAT and teachers' awareness (i.e. experience) of the misbehaviour of children including Physical ($r = -.396$, $p < .05$) and Personal ($r = -.391$, $p < .05$). This suggests that teachers who were satisfied with their BM training experienced fewer classroom behavioural problems than their less satisfied peers. Again, this may point to the effectiveness of the training in providing these teachers with necessary skills. Also, the negative correlations between teachers' satisfaction with training and their perceived impact of children's misbehaviour on themselves ($r = -.448$, $p < .01$), and their needs for further support ($r = -.326$, $p < .05$) also suggest a possible positive impact on their ability to manage behavioural problems effectively.

Most common BM challenges

The findings indicate substantial overlap between teachers with and without BM training when it comes to identifying the five most challenging BM challenges that they experience. A majority of teachers in both groups rate students' "lack of motivation to learn" as the common problem. Teachers without training cite students' lack of ability as the second most common problem, whilst this is third among teachers with BM training. "Refusal to follow instructions" is third among teachers without BM. Fourth among this group is "students without friendships with peers". Whilst fourth for the teachers with BM is "students making offensive noises". Both groups list students' behaviour "tantrums" as fifth most common problem. These differences appear negligible for the most part. However, a tentative observation might be that the inclusion of "students without friendships with peers" in the no-training group's list indicates the influence of the perceived negative student peer group being seen as creating difficulties. This might be taken to indicate problems with group management, which is a core skill of BM.

Conclusion

This is a relatively small-scale study, but the first of its kind to be carried out in Hong Kong. It is important to stress the fact that the study focuses solely on teachers' perceptions, and does not deal in detail with the content, quality and format of the training received by participants. In this sense, the study is best seen as a preliminary to more detailed investigation. With these limitations in mind the study can be claimed to provide some interesting findings that make a useful contribution to the literature on the management of behaviour in schools in Hong Kong that are likely to resonate and give rise to reflection on similar issues in other contexts.

Of general significance is the provision of evidence for the psychometric properties of the effects of BM training scale. We have shown that this scale, originally devised by Professor Chris Forlin at the HKIEd, has satisfactory psychometric properties from the perspective of Rasch measurement.

Substantive findings of the study have shown that, in the sample studied, there was a strong relationship between satisfaction with training received and perceptions of confidence. Clearly, satisfaction alone is not a sufficient effectiveness indicator in relation to course quality. In this study, however, it was shown that satisfaction with training, as well as extent of training was associated with the use of positive BM strategies and the perception of experiencing relatively lower levels of BM problems. Lack of training, on the other hand, indicated possible deficiencies in group management skills. Satisfaction was also associated with confidence in relation to BM. This is a very important finding, since lack of confidence in relation to BM is in itself a negative obstacle to effective BM. Having said this, the relationship between age/length of service on the use of negative (i.e. problem promoting) strategies and personal impact of BM problems may indicate that teacher burnout is a moderating factor in the effectiveness of BM training, and that the emotional well-being of teachers, especially those who are more further along in their careers, has to be taken into account when addressing their needs in relation to BM.

This study paves the way for more detailed studies of the relationship between teachers' specific experience of BM training and the classroom performance of teachers. An important way forward would be to explore teacher perceptions in greater depth through interviews, and to triangulate these perceptions with observational data.

References

Alexander, R. 2012. "International Evidence, National Policy and Educational Practice: Making Better Use of International Comparisons in Education." Keynote Presentation at the Third Van Leer International Conference on Education, Jerusalem.

Baird, J., T. Isaacs, S. Johnson, G. Stobart, G. Yu, T. Sprague, and R. Daugherty. 2011. *The Policy Effects of PISA*. Oxford: Oxford University Centre for Educational Assessment.

Behan, D., and B. Blake. 2014. "Does Teacher Training Prepare Teachers for the Challenge of Students Experiencing Emotional/Behavioral Disorders?" In *The Sage Handbook of Emotional and Behavioural Difficulties*, edited by P. Garner, J. Kauffman, and J. Elliott, 401–414. London: Sage.

Bond, T. G., and C. M. Fox. 2007. *Applying the Rasch Model: Fundamental Measurement in the Human Sciences*. 2nd ed. Mahwah, NJ: Lawrence Erlbaum.

Brown, S., and M. Donald. 1993. *Making Sense of Teaching*. Buckingham: Open University Press.

Chan, A., S. Chong, and K. Ng. 2011. "Perception of What Works for Teachers of Students with EBD in Mainstream and Special Schools in Hong Kong." *Emotional and Behavioural Difficulties* 16 (2): 173–188.

Chen, S., M. Jin, and K. Lau. 2006. "Preservice and Inservice Teachers' Attitudes Toward Teaching Students with Disabilities in Regular Physical Education Settings in Hong Kong and Mainland China." *Research Quarterly for Exercise and Sports (Abs)* 77 (1): A-91.

Cooper, P. 1993. *Effective Schools for Disaffected Students*. London: Routledge.

Cooper, P., M. Drummond, S. Hart, C. McLaughlan, and J. Lovey. 2000. *Positive Alternatives to Exclusion*. London: Routledge.

Cooper, P., and B. Jacobs. 2011a. *From Inclusion to Engagement: Promoting the Educational Engagement of Young People through Policy and Practice*. Chichester: Wiley-Blackwell.

Cooper, P., and B. Jacobs. 2011b. *Evidence of Best Practice Models and Outcomes in the Education of Children with Emotional Disturbance/Behavioural Difficulties: An International Review*. Report for the National Council for Special Education. Ireland.

Cooper, P., and D. McIntyre. 1996. *Effective Teaching and Learning: Teachers' and Students' Perspective*. Buckingham: Open University.

Cooper, P., K. Bilton, and M. Kakos. 2013. "The Importance of a Biopsychosocial Approach to Interventions for Students with Social, Emotional and Behavioural Difficulties." In *The Routledge International Companion to Emotional and Behavioural Difficulties*, edited by T. Cole, H. Daniels, and J. Visser, 89–95. London: Routledge.

CSENIE (Centre for Special Educational Needs and Inclusive Education). 2012. *Study on Equal Learning Opportunities for Students with Disabilities under the Integrated Education System*. Report for Equal Opportunities Commission. Hong Kong.

DES (Department of Education and Science). 1989. *Discipline in Schools*. The Elton Report. London: Dept. Ed & Sci.

Desforges, C., and D. McNamara. 1979. "Theory and Practice: Methodological Procedures for the Objectification of Craft Knowledge." *British Journal of Teacher Education* 5 (2): 145–152.

EDB (Education Bureau of Hong Kong). 2012. *Press Releases and Publications*. Accessed June 3, 2013. http://www.edb.gov.hk/index.aspx?nodeID=1039&langno=1

Eisenbraun, K. 2007. "Violence in Schools: Prevalence, Prediction, and Prevention." *Aggression and Violent Behaviour* 12 (4): 459–469.

Forlin, C. 2007. "A Collaborative, Collegial and More Cohesive Approach to Supporting Educational Reform for Inclusion in Hong Kong." *Asia-Pacific Education Review* 8 (2): 1–11.

Forlin, C., and P. Cooper. 2013. "Student Behaviour and Emotional Challenges for Teachers and Parents in Hong Kong." *British Journal of Special Education* 40 (2): 58–64.

Forlin, C., and R. Rose. 2010. "Authentic School Partnerships for Enabling Inclusive Education in Hong Kong." *Journal of Research in Special Education Needs* 10 (1): 13–22.

Frolich, J., J. Rolich, M. Dopfner, H. Biegert, and G. Lehmkuhl. 2002. "Teacher Training in the Management of Children with Attention Deficit Hyperactivity Disorder." *Praxis Der Kinderpsychologie Und Kinderpsychiatrie* 51 (6): 494–506.

Garner, P. 2013. "Teacher Education: Dilemmas and Tensions for School Staffworking with Pupils with EBD." In *The Routledge International Companion to Emotional and Behavioural Difficulties*, edited by T. Cole, H. Daniels, and J. Visser, 330–339. London: Routledge.

Hargreaves, A., and M. Fullan. 2012. *Professional Capital: Transforming Teaching in Every School*. New York: Teachers' Press.

Hargreaves, D., S. Hester, and F. Mellor. 1975. *Deviance in Classrooms*. London: Routledge.

Howard, S., and B. Johnson. 2004. "Resilient Teachers: Resisting Stress and Burnout." *Social Psychology of Education* 7: 399–420.

Kyriacou, C. 2001. "Teacher Stress: Directions for Future Research." *Educational Review* 53: 28–35.

Linacre, J. M. 2006. *A User's Guide to WINSTEPS/MINISTEP: Rasch-model Computer Programs*. Chicago, IL: Winsteps.

Lodge, A., and K. Lynch. 2003. "Young People's Equality Concerns: The Invisibility of Diversity." In *Encouraging Voices: Respecting the Rights of Young People who have been Marginalised*, edited by M. Shevlin and R. Rose, 15–35. Dublin: Dublin National Disability Authority.

MacBeath, J., M. Galton, S. Steward, A. Macbeath, and C. Page. 2006. *The Costs of Inclusion*. Cambridge: University of Cambridge.

Marzocchi, G. M., M. D. Pietro, C. Vio, E. Bassi, G. Filoramo, and A. Salmaso. 2004. "Management of Classroom Hyperactivity and Opposition Behavior: A Teacher Training Study." *Psicoterapia Cognitiva E Comportamentale* 10 (2): 83–96.

Molnar, A., and B. Lindquist. 1989. *Changing Problem Behavior in School*. San Francisco: Jossey-Bass.

Mortimore, P., P. Sammons, L. Stoll, D. Lewis, and R. Ecob. 1988. *School Matters: The Junior Years*. Chicago, IL: Open Books.

Myers, S. S., and R. C. Pianta. 2008. "Developmental Commentary: Individual and Contextual Influences on Student–Teacher Relationships and Children's Early Problem Behaviors." *Journal of Clinical Child and Adolescent Psychology* 37 (3): 600–608.

Omoteso, B., and A. Semudara. 2011. "The Relationship between Teachers' Effectiveness and Management of Classroom Misbehaviours in Secondary Schools." *Psychology* 2 (9): 902–908.

Pang, S. K. N. 2004. "The Effects of Schools on Teachers' Feelings about School Life: A Multilevel Analysis." *Hong Kong Teachers' Centre Journal* 2: 64–84.

Patterson, G., J. Reid, and T. Dishion. 1992. *Anti-social Boys*. Vol. 4. Eugene, OR: Casralia.

Poon-McBrayer, K. F., and M. J. Lian. 2002. *Special Needs Education: Children with Exceptionalities*. Hong Kong: Chinese University Press.

Purkey, S. C., and M. S. Smith. 1983. "Effective Schools: A Review." *The Elementary School Journal* 85: 427–452.

Rasch, G. 1960. *Probabilistic Models for Some Intelligence and Achievement Test*. Expanded ed. Copenhagen: Danish Institute for Educational Research. (1980, Chicago, IL: The University of Chicago Press.)

Reid, J. B. 1986. "Social-interactional Patterns in Families of Abused and Nonabused Children." In *Altruism and Aggression*, edited by C. Zahn-Waxler, M. Cummings, and M. Radke-Yarrow, 238–255. New York: Cambridge University Press.

Rossbach, M., and P. Probst. 2005. "Development and Evaluation of an ADHD Teacher Group Training." *Praxis Der Kinderpsychologie Und Kinderpsychiatrie* 54 (8): 645–663.

Rutter, M., B. Maughan, P. Mortimore, and J. Ouston. 1979. *Fifteen Thousand Hours: Secondary Schools and Their Effects on Children*. Cambridge, MA: Harvard University Press.

Schiff, M., and B. BarGil. 2004. "Children with Behavior Problems: Improving Elementary School Teachers' Skills to Keep These Children in Class." *Children and Youth Services Review* 26 (2): 207–234.

Schön, D. 1983. *The Reflective Practitioner: How Professionals Think in Action*. New York: Basic Books.

Sin, K., C. Forlin, M. Au, and F. Ho. 2011. *Review of Inclusive Practices in Hong Kong*. Hong Kong: Hong Kong Institute of Education.

Tattum, D. P. 1982. *Disruptive Pupils in Schools and Units*. Chichester: Wiley.

Trust, Sutton. 2010. *Education and Social Mobility in England*. London: The Sutton Trust.

Wiseman, A. 2008. "A Culture of (in) Equality?: A Cross-national Study of Gender Parity and Gender Segregation in National School Systems." *Research in Comparative and International Education* 3 (2): 179–201.

Wright, B. D. 1997. "A History of Social Science Measurement." *Educational Measurement: Issues and Practice* 16 (4): 33–45.

Wright, B. D., and J. M. Linacre. 1994. "Reasonable Mean-square Fit Values." *Rasch Measurement Transactions* 8: 370.

Yan, Z. 2014. "Predicting Teachers' Intentions to Implement School-based Assessment Using the Theory of Planned Behaviour." *Educational Research and Evaluation* 20 (2): 83–97.

Zentall, S. S., and J. Javorsky. 2007. "Professional Development for Teachers of Students with ADHD and Characteristics of ADHD." *Behavioral Disorders* 32 (2): 78–93.

Promoting resilience through adversity: increasing positive outcomes for expelled students

Nadia Coleman

Educational Leadership and Policy Studies, University of Denver, Denver, USA

This article endeavours to increase educators' understanding of the experiences of students who have been expelled from school in order to represent this critical stakeholder group in future policy development and programme implementation. Students' perspectives are presented through thick description in this narrative case study. Findings indicate that expulsion from school can alter the trajectory of a student's life – for better or for worse. Without thoughtful intervention from caring educators, this interruption in students' education may have an irreparable destructive impact on students' futures. Educators must develop interventions focused on bringing forth protective factors that are documented to increase resilience, thus making students less susceptible to the risks inherent in removing them from school.

Introduction

Expulsion from school is life changing. Along with no longer attending school, expulsion has many additional consequences. Serious negative consequences of expulsion have been documented over the past several decades. Students who have been expelled from school have lower grades and show poorer achievement on standardised tests than do their peers (Davis and Jordan 1994; Morrison and D'Incau 2000; Skiba and Rausch 2006). Expelled students also graduate from high school at lower rates than do their peers (DeRidder 1991; Morrison and D'Incau 2000; Skiba and Peterson 1999). Expelled students may also have a lack of access to appropriate educational alternatives (American Academy of Paediatrics 2003; Burns 1996; Morrison and D'Incau 2000). Exclusion from school has been documented to lead to long-term social exclusion (Ball, Maguire, and Macrae 2000; Macrae, Maguire, and Milbourne 2003) and increased involvement in illegal activity (Skiba and Peterson 1999). Excluded students also experience increased mental, physical and emotional problems (American Academy of Paediatrics 2003; Brooks, Schiraldi, and Ziedenberg 2000).

Since expulsion has a significant effect on a student's day-to-day life and has many negative consequences, closer examination of students' expulsion experiences is warranted. Two research questions were developed to explore the lived experiences of students who had experienced expulsion from school:

(1) What is the expulsion experience from the perspective of expelled students?

(2) What are the contextual, organisational and personal issues that emerge from the voices of expelled students?

With a better understanding of expelled students' experiences, educators may take steps to increase students' resilience to the risks inherent in removing students from school.

Previous research

A large body of research exists on the demographics of students who are suspended and expelled, excluded students' low academic achievement and high dropout rate, the increased risk of social exclusion, mental, physical and emotional problems for expelled students, and the consequences of zero tolerance. However, much less research has been conducted on students' experiences and perceptions of exclusionary discipline.

Experts in the field have stated that there is a need for a better understanding of excluded students' experiences and perceptions. Morrison et al. (2001) called to action experts in the field to expand research on the expulsion process and its impacts. Gordon Rouse (2001, 69) argued for the need for such research. He wrote, "More attention should be given to the opinions and ideas of the excluded children themselves in the search for a solution to young people's disaffections with education and England's high rates of exclusion". Moses (2001) also discussed how impacted students' voices have been silenced and called for redress. This research was an opportunity to act on the recommendations of prior studies and to understand the experiences and perceptions of the stakeholders most impacted by exclusionary discipline – the expelled students themselves.

Although many previously expelled students struggle in one or many facets of life later in adolescence or as adults, others thrive and experience great success. Researchers studying resilience attempt to explain why some individuals have far more success than others in similar situations in overcoming obstacles and recovering from trauma. Two conditions are inherent in the construct of resilience: exposure to significant adversity, stress or trauma, and positive adaptation despite this adversity (Luthar, Cicchetti, and Becker 2000). Although discrepancies exist in definitions of resilience, most recent constructs of resilience define resilience as a process vs. a personal trait.

A person's level of resilience is impacted by the risk factors and the protective factors that they experience. Protective factors protect individuals from harmful effects, decreasing the likelihood of negative outcomes, while risk factors put individuals at increased risk of experiencing harmful effects, increasing the likelihood of negative outcomes.

Feyl-Chavkin and Gonzalez (2000) identified five key categories of protective factors:

(1) Supportive relationships, particularly encouragement from school personnel and other adults,

(2) Student characteristics, such as self-esteem, motivation and accepting responsibility,

(3) Family factors such as parental support/concern and school improvement,
(4) Community factors such as community youth programmes,
(5) School factors such as academic success and pro-social skills training (2).

Interventions developed through resilience research may improve educational outcomes for expelled students. Resilience-building strategies may be utilised as a preventive measure for at-risk students prior to expulsion, during the expulsion term to mitigate risk factors or after expulsion to help students to recover from the trauma of the experience.

Method

Qualitative methods, specifically narrative inquiry, were an ideal vehicle for empowering students to contribute to the debate surrounding exclusionary discipline. As Creswell (2007) states, "We conduct qualitative research when we want to empower individuals to share their stories, hear their voices, and minimise the power relationships that often exist between a researcher and participants in a study". Narrative inquiry facilitated the addition of students' experiences and perspectives to the body of knowledge regarding expelled students. Narrative techniques are techniques in which participants are invited to reflect on particular events or particular periods in their lives through telling stories, often in relation to a specified theme or themes (Wengraf 2001). "Narrative inquiry gives us a research methodology for engaging in the study of people's experiences", Clandinin explains (2006, 51).

The primary method of data collection in this study was in-depth, unstructured narrative interviews with students who experienced expulsion from school. Non-directive questioning strategies were utilised to authentically capture students' voices and to diminish the power differential between the researcher and young participants (Heath 2009).

Students shared their stories verbally, as well as through art and writing. Heath (2009) notes that one major weakness of the narrative approach is that some young people are simply more able to tell stories about their lives than others. To respond to this potential weakness, analysis of students' writing and artwork was also employed as a means for collecting participants' stories. Students' creative representations of the expulsion experience took the form of poetry, song lyrics, rap, cartoons and drawings. Data included descriptions of *what* individuals experienced and *how* they experienced it (Moustakas 1994).

Participants attended an alternative educational programme for expelled students in one metropolitan school district in Colorado. Invitations to participate were mailed to the homes of a random sample of 38 students who attended during the 2009–2010 and 2010–2011 school years. Eight students between the ages of 13 and 19 volunteered to participate. Three participants were female and five were male. Three Black, three White and two Latino students participated.

As a result of expulsion, participants lost access to class offerings, seat time, graduation credit and extracurricular activities. During their expulsion term, their education was limited to attending the district's part-time educational programme. Taking responsibility for one's actions in his or her expulsion incident and addressing and correcting behaviours and thinking processes which led to students' expulsion was a cornerstone of the alternative programme they attended.

Moustakas' (1994) procedures provided detailed, specific, systematic steps for distilling the essence of the experience. Moustakas' procedure is based on extracting significant statements describing an experience from interview transcripts and then identifying fundamental, universal elements of the experience.

First, participant's statements that were relevant to the phenomenon of interest were identified. Statements were organised into themes. Clusters of themes were checked against the original interview protocols for validation using lines of questioning suggested by Colaizzi (1978). After validation a structural description of what each participant experienced was written. Each participant's experience was contextualised in textural description by describing the setting and conditions which affected the participants' experiences. Structural descriptions and textural descriptions were combined to create an all-encompassing description of each participant's experience. Confirmation interviews with the original participants were conducted to allow participants to confirm or to question preliminary data analysis. After being reviewed by participants, all the participants' experiences were integrated into one description which represented the experiences of the group as a whole. Finally, the unifying experiences and views of the participants that formed the essential, invariant structure of the experience were identified.

Participants' writing, poetry, song lyrics and rap are presented as originally written. Fidelity to students' writing was maintained in order to present students' actual words in their own voices. Pseudonyms were assigned to people and locations to preserve participants' anonymity.

Findings

Although other students may have far more negative experiences, for students in this study, expulsion was life changing in a positive way. Their experience during the expulsion term was a transformative experience that had positive impact on the trajectory of their lives. Although expulsion itself was a traumatic and stressful event, expulsion was a catalyst for personal transformation.

Needing peer approval was a precursor to expulsion

All participants cited gaining acceptance or approval from peers as the primary motivating factor in engaging in expellable behaviour. No participants cited any other rationale for engaging in these behaviours. Participants stressed the importance they placed on being accepted by their peers before their expulsion incidents.

Participants' comments revealed that they believed that engaging in rebellious behaviour would increase their "coolness". Rebellious behaviours included distributing drugs and alcohol, using drugs and alcohol, fighting, taking dares, carrying knives, guns and other weapons, and defying authority figures. Participants explained that they presumed that they would be seen as "cool", "a big shot" and "popular" for engaging in expellable behaviours. Students shared that engaging in these activities was their attempt to demonstrate conformity to a group's norms and to gain acceptance into that group by engaging in behaviours that were valued by its members. For example, Gabriela brought alcohol to school to be accepted by "the popular girls". She felt that she was able to become "cool" too after providing alcohol to the group. "I was trying to fit in with everybody. Everybody thought it was funny to get drunk at school. I brought it [alcohol] and they were like, 'You're so cool to hang around with'", she explained.

Students' comments revealed that the need to be accepted by peers overwhelmed their concern of potential consequences. Participants discussed the conflict of their own morals and their desire to be accepted by their peer group. Their participation in their expulsion incidents indicated that their sense of right and wrong was often overridden by the need to be accepted by their peer group.

Looking for validation, approval and recognition from peers was not new for students in this study. They shared that their expulsion incidents were a single event in an established pattern of acceptance-seeking behaviours. "My attitude and behaviour I couldn't explain when adults or teachers asked me about it. I didn't care what they thought. I was only interested in what me and my friends thought was cool", Jose said. His statement captured participants' mind set and need for external approval prior to expulsion.

Intense trauma of expulsion was a catalyst for change

Although expulsion itself was a traumatic and stressful event, expulsion was a catalyst for personal transformation. In fact, it may have been the immensity of trauma that created conditions in which individuals previously resistant to change became open to learning and growth.

At the time of their expulsion, participants conceptualised expulsion as a life-ending event. They shared that they saw no future for themselves and viewed expulsion as impending death. "It feels like I've been put on death row", Deon said. He also concluded his "entire life would end up in the trash". "It was over for me", Jose stated. Destiny said expulsion felt like a man standing on a bridge, just about to jump, pondering how badly it would hurt and how quickly death would come. Deon drew a picture a person hanging by a noose around his neck. The character had EXP, short for expulsion, written on his chest. "CONDEMNED" was written above the picture.

Participants reported experiencing intense sadness, depression and suicidal ideation at the time of their expulsion. Participants visualised expulsion itself as "a dark cloud" or "a dark situation". They reported that a sense of isolation intensified the negative emotions they experienced. Jose stated, "We are treated like we don't exist". "We are nowhere kids – no names, no faces, no prayers, no hope", he wrote.

Participants emphasised the trauma they experienced as a result of expulsion. Tanisha said she was "in shock" and compared the trauma of being expelled to being in a bad car crash. Destiny sketched a picture of a teenager with a look of shock and horror on her face. The inscription at the bottom of the drawing read, "Sometimes we have to go a bit insane and go through something we never imagined before we can learn from our mistakes and find out who we are". Jose also noted that, "Expulsion isn't for everybody because some people would lose their minds".

Although participants reported high levels of distress, they conceptualised expulsion as a needed interruption in their lives. Students perceived that they would have continued engaging in detrimental, risky behaviours had they not been expelled and received intervention through the alternative educational programme they attended. Being removed from school, the social setting that fuelled their peer-centred thinking and behaviour provided an opportunity to evaluate their priorities and to rebuild their lives. "I learned what I should do in the future, which I probably wouldn't have learned if I didn't get expelled", Jerome explained.

Participants cited expulsion as an eye-opening experience that served as a catalyst in taking control of their lives. Deon explained that expulsion was a horrifying event, but he also recognised an opportunity to rebuild his life and to transform himself into a better person. He wrote:

> Being expelled is being damned. But from the ashes a phoenix will rise. Life suddenly has a new meaning and a new purpose. The phoenix will rise, but not yet. First it needs to die, to hit the bottom. The phoenix is all of us. The few who made a mistake and paid for it with our everything. Some will fall into old habits, but the strong will rise from the ashes and change.

They noted that they had become more thoughtful in their decision-making process. Michael said, "Life is like driving. If your eyes are closed you aren't going to go the way they should. My eyes were closed "cause I wasn't thinking about the future". Participants discussed the life-changing power of the expulsion experience. As Jose put it, "Getting expelled helped me out. It changed me". "I have changed as a person from a boy into a young man planning his future", Deon asserted.

Students' need for external approval contributed to perceived stigmatisation

Students believed that they were stereotyped and stigmatised due to their expulsion. Participants seemed to take negative interactions to heart, internalising others' negative comments. They presumed that others made a plethora of upsetting assumptions about them. Students perceived that others viewed them as "trouble-makers", "drug-users", "gang members", "thugs", "monsters", "violent people", "thieves", "criminals", "losers", "idiots", "dropouts", "burnouts", "nobodies", "pariahs", "sinners", "delinquents", "social rejects" and "society's rejects". They shared that they were hurt by the judgements that others, especially school officials, had made about them. Deon described his sense of how others saw him and his expelled peers:

We are nowhere kids,

No names, no faces, no prayers, no hope.

Society has thrown us away, spit in our faces,

Labelled us sinners, pariahs, criminal nobodies.

We see them stare,

Stare in fear and disdain,

Fear of what they don't know-

What they don't want to know.

But there's more to us than just that

8 letter word.

We are people

But they don't see that.

When they look at us they see only

Our demons,

Not the angels in our hearts.

Students shared worries that the stigmatisation they felt would follow them into the future limiting future opportunities and the likelihood of success later in life. They perceived that they would have to work harder than their classmates to repair the damage caused by their expulsions. "Being expelled puts you ten steps behind when you were three steps ahead in your game", Jose stated.

Participants cited concerns of the potential negative repercussions expulsion could have on their reputations. Deon drew a comic strip labelled "My rep". The first scene was a frowning cartoon face, a gun next to it, bullet discharged, moving toward the head. The second box contained shards of the cartoon face broken apart and jumbled beyond recognition. He explained his cartoon:

> When I was expelled it was like taking a bullet to the head. I felt so bad because I knew that all of my teachers that really liked me would be disappointed in me. I also thought that my entire life would end up in the trash. It was over for me. I thought that getting expelled would make all my future teachers have a very bad picture of me before they got to know me. That's why expulsion is a bullet to the head. Once you are shot in the face you'll never look the same. Your appearance to others will be forever altered.

Participants appealed to educators to support future students in overcoming adversity by suspending judgement and treating all students as normal people who make mistakes. The perception of educators seeing them as nothing more than "just an expelled kid" was prominent and several participants used this exact phrase to describe how they believed educators viewed them. Jerome said, "A lot of people at the school I'm at think I'm just an expelled student. That's it". Deon wrote, "There is more to us than just that 8-letter word". Speaking directly to educators Jose said:

> I honestly don't know how to convince you with words that were not bad because there are so many stigmas. I guess the only way for you to find out is by coming to meet us. If you were to come down here, you would see that we aren't bad people or dangerous.

Although participants felt that others saw them as bad people as a result of their expulsion, participants did not see themselves as bad people. All participants talked about being "human" or "normal people who make mistakes". Jose explained, "We are all only human and humans make mistakes all the time". They noted that expulsion programme staff made the distinction between bad people and bad decisions. They explained that this distinction was important in helping them to feel good about themselves, although they had made poor choices that lead to expulsion.

Perception of increased success in school

Participants perceived increased success in school following expulsion. They cited increased discipline, improved attendance, decreased truancy, increased focus, better student skills, better relationships with teachers, increased willingness to seek out help, less rule-breaking, fewer discipline referrals, improved grades and improved student skills. They attributed their increased success to the interventions they experienced through the alternative programme they attended.

Participants reported an increased focus on academic achievement after expulsion. Even though some students did not always like school, they saw education as key in their future success. Maria explained that before her expulsion she went to school to socialise. After her expulsion her priorities changed. "I realised that going to school is *to learn*. If I don't learn, I have nothing", she stated. Students experienced a shifting sense of risk and reward. Students shared that, during their expulsion term, they realised how much they risked in making a poor choice. "Being expelled is the easy way out of achieving your dreams", Destiny stated. Students saw the realisation of the high cost of their poor decisions was a first step in re-evaluating their priorities in life.

Although participants experienced positive outcomes as a result of expulsion, they shared a conviction that the traditional school is the best environment for students. They equated the lack of options available to them to "a drought" and felt they were "being left behind". They still felt that missing out on the opportunities afforded to them by traditional school caused irreparable harm. "There's just so much more you can experience in normal school that'll help you later in your life. You miss out on it and you ain't ever gonna make it up", Jerome explained. All participants desired more learning opportunities for themselves while expelled, and shared a conviction that expelled students should have access to more educational opportunities.

Participants insisted that expelled students could inform leaders and policy-makers in improving outcomes for students expelled in the future. They appealed to adults who make decisions pertinent to expelled students' lives to take the time to get to know the population their decisions impact. "We're people, not numbers, and they need to see that", Jose explained. They argued that educators must recognise expelled students as a critical stakeholder group and to take their experiences into consideration in decision-making, programme development and policy-making.

Relationships with supportive adults improved student outcomes

Students did not gain approval or recognition from their peers; however, in the end, they did acquire the support and affirmation they were searching for – but from adults. Participants highlighted the importance of supportive adults in overcoming adversity. Participants cited expulsion programme staff as key players in helping students to rebuild themselves and their lives. Deon wrote:

> Being expelled is a building crumbling down, and expulsion teachers are architects. When I was in school I was making a building that would let me climb to success, but then something bad happened and it crumbled down to little pieces. When something interferes with your plans and they crumble you're gonna need help building back up. Expulsion teachers are architects because they helped me design and rebuild from scratch what got destroyed.

When asked what recommendations he had for how to best help expelled students Jerome replied, "Care. Care about the kids". Similarly, all participants shared that they were able to be successful in their academic pursuits due to the support of caring adults who believed they were capable.

Students gleaned messages about their worth from the resources their educational programmes lacked. They perceived that a lack of resources and programme funding was evidence that the educational system had given up on them. "We need new chairs because a lot of the ones we had were broken and cracked, basically trash. Is all we really deserve is trash?" Deon asked. However, the perception that the system had given up on them was in sharp contrast with their perception of their worth to the educators they worked with at the programme. Students perceived that their

teachers at the programme worked to overcome the shortcomings of the physical setting and resources allocated to the programme to improve conditions for students.
Students perceived the staff's efforts to obtain additional resources as evidence that
their teachers valued them and believed that they could be successful if given the
tools and opportunity. They also shared a conviction that investing resources into
expelled students is worthwhile. "We're good kids; we're worth it!" Tanisha argued.

Participants repeatedly appealed to educators to help them and their expelled
peers to experience success. "Our future is in your hands", Jose wrote. "Please help
us receive the education we want and deserve", Destiny pleaded. They shared a conviction that potential lies dormant within expelled students, waiting to be awakened
by educators. In a letter directed to educators, Jose wrote,

> Many of us will go on to do great things, but we need help. If you don't give it to us,
> we might end up in jail, or worse. I am appealing to *you*, the district administrators,
> the principals, the teachers: Help us!

Students demonstrated resilience through adversity

All participants reported increased resilience and perseverance following expulsion.
At the time of their expulsion, participants conceptualised expulsion as a life-ending
event, but, in time, they saw expulsion as an obstacle on their path to success. They
described expulsion as "a big old rock in the road" and "speed bumps on the road
of life". Jose wrote:

> Expulsion is an obstacle waiting for redemption to tear it down. I find expulsion to be
> nothing but a limit for students, sort of like a delay. I chose the word obstacle, instead
> of delay, because some students just can't get over the fact that they're expelled and
> give up. Most students, however, find a way to overcome their expulsion and prove to
> the district and to the public that no one should be judged on their mistakes, but on
> what they do to recover from their mistakes.

Students' resilience was visible in their conceptualisation of themselves as survivors. Several students specifically used the term "survivors" to refer to themselves.
Explaining expulsion, Michael wrote, "It's like exile or death. I choose exile over
death to show that I will survive". Destiny compared the hardiness of expelled students to that of dandelions, in that they both display incredible levels of resilience
through the adversity they experience. Destiny wrote:

> Dandelions can be kicked, stepped on, cut down and blown away, but they still con-
> tinue to come right back, no matter what happens. Expulsion may have blown our old
> life away, but part of us still remains inside and will start off new. We can be stepped
> on, crushed and blown away, but as long as we want to, we can get right back up and
> we will have that new lesson learned that makes us a brand new person, but at the
> same time, still a branch off of the old us. A dandelion is the only plant that can sur-
> vive through a drought. Just like expelled kids.

Participants shared accounts of persevering though their struggles. Deon said, "I
see my life as a journey to be accomplished at all costs. In other words, I will not
go down without a fight!" When asked what advice he would impart upon other
expelled students, he simply stated, "Don't give up".

Participants discussed the belief that, although expulsion would make their future
more difficult, they had the drive and the tools to be successful. Deon recalled how
he had successfully navigated through adversity in the past and felt confident that he

had "learned what it takes". Jose shared that he was also confident in his ability to persevere through hard times:

> It's a long road ahead that will take a lot of work, but I feel expulsion school has set me right for that. I am ready and willing to take that road ahead. I don't have many chances left and I don't want to throw my future away, so I'll do whatever it takes to turn my life around.

Participants explained that they saw success after expulsion as a means to redeeming themselves to others, as well as to themselves. "I made myself a better person. I redeemed myself", Jordan stated. Participants' comments revealed that they viewed attending the expulsion programme as a second chance and saw their expulsion term as a period of rebuilding their lives and recreating themselves. Although participants conceptualised expulsion itself as something negative, like a "dark storm cloud" or a "dark situation", they utilised positive imagery to represent the new opportunities and growth that were born out of their expulsion. They viewed attending expulsion school as a second chance. Jose wrote:

> Being expelled is like being shot, then getting a second life. Expulsion was like a bullet because it killed me as soon as I heard it. Then I got a second life because going to the expulsion program is a second chance. It is going to help me get back into school again.

Development of an internal locus of control

Expulsion was a critical incident that moved students' decision-making from an external to an internal locus of control. As their need for validation for peers decreased, their internal locus of control grew, and they become more confident in making their own decisions. "I see myself as an individual now. I want anyone who knows me to see me and remember me as me", Jose said. Being distanced from their classmates facilitated their ability to look critically at their own behaviour and was a catalyst in helping them to think for themselves. "I am okay with myself now instead of needing my friends and other kids to be cool with me", Destiny said. An internal locus of control allowed them to put their own well-being over the whims of others and to avoid risk-taking behaviours that would endanger their well-being "It's had me think of the future ahead of me and how I want to make it", Jose remarked.

Participants developed awareness of how involvement with their peers had impacted their lives. Students determined that what their peers thought of them was not as important as they had once believed. After her expulsion Tanisha re-evaluated the importance of gaining and maintaining extrinsic approval and recognition from her peers.

> I was putting my energy to being around the cool kids and not putting it into my school work. So that got me off track, because I was trying to be the cool kid and I could have been the book-smart kid, and then been cool to myself,

she explained.

Participants reported that, although they lost respect for themselves at the time of their expulsion, they not only regained but also increased their self-respect as they rebuilt their lives after expulsion. As they lost self-respect, their self-concept became more negative and then became increasingly positive after surviving expulsion. Jose said:

I lost my self-respect and gained it back, all through my expulsion. I lost it by giving in to what people said to me about being a loser because I got kicked out of school. Then I gained it back by not caring what people say about me at all, because I redeemed myself and proved that I could have a lot more successes being kicked out of school than a lot of people can being in school. I have a lot more self-respect now than I ever did before, because I actually had to do something to prove that I deserve it.

Participants shared that they believed they were capable of achieving their dreams as long as they exhibited the same perseverance that they had demonstrated during their expulsion experience. They articulated a new-found realisation that they had control over their lives and their ability to achieve their goals. As they cared less about their peers' perceptions of them, they focused more on their own goals and dreams. Their narratives indicated that they had developed a positive outlook on the future. Students perceived their success in surviving expulsion as evidence that they were the masters of their own destiny and would find success in the future. Jerome wrote:

Master of destiny

No matter the difficulty

You have to challenge yourself

And unleash your full potential

Expulsion is a side effect of bad choices

Made by you and only you can change it.

The past has past

The future is ahead of you

The future keeps going

The world keeps turning

Life goes on

Never forget

Your actions shape you and your future.

Discussion

Although other students may have far more negative experiences, for students in this study, expulsion was life changing in a positive way. Their experience during the expulsion term was a transformative experience that had positive impact on the trajectory of their lives. Although expulsion itself was a traumatic and stressful event, expulsion was a catalyst for personal transformation.

Before expulsion participants' behaviour and decision-making was fuelled by a desire to be accepted by their peers, demonstrating an external locus of control and little autonomy. Individuals with external locus of control attribute outcomes to circumstances or other people (Gurin, Gurin, and Morrison 1978). An external locus of control may have also been a factor in students' expulsions since external locus of control has been linked to negative outcomes such as aggression (Halloran et al. 1999), depression (Rotheram-Borus et al. 1990) and sexual offending (Parton and Day 2002).

Affiliation with peers was critical in participants' decision to engage in risk-taking behaviours that led to expulsion. This is not surprising since adolescents' affiliation with friends is a strong predictor of adolescents' own risk-taking behaviour (Keenan et al. 1995). One explanation may be that, over time, affiliation with peers who engage in risky behaviours increases teens' risk-taking behaviour (Keenan et al. 1995). It was not possible to determine if students' reasons for engaging in expellable behaviour were reflective of students at large, since no research was found which documented students' motivation for engaging in expellable behaviours.

Students' need for external approval contributed to the belief that they were stigmatised due to their expulsion. It is not surprising that participants perceived stigmatisation, since adolescents tend to overestimate the extent to which others evaluate them (Lapsley and Murphy 1985). An increased focus on others' opinions may be related to the "imaginary audience" in which people believe that others are constantly observing and evaluating them, even if this isn't reality (Frankenberger 2000).

Since students were driven by an extrinsic locus of control, they may have been especially sensitive to the messages they believed they received from others. Students' comments suggested that their feelings of sadness, embarrassment and shame seemed to be greatly exacerbated by their awareness of the disapproval they received from extrinsic sources. Their statements illustrated the negative impact that others' disappointment had on their emotional state and self-concept. The negative emotions students experienced during their expulsion term may have been exacerbated by their need for external approval since a higher incidence of mental health problems occurs in individuals who are more sensitive to criticism of others, more dependent on others' approval and more accepting of negative feedback (Campbell 1990).

Surprisingly, participants reported an extensive list of positive changes as a result of expulsion. These findings are inconsistent with the large body of existing literature that documents a plethora of negative outcomes associated with expulsion. Positive changes reported by participants include: improved attendance, increased focus and motivation, higher grades, increased persistence, better student skills, improved relationships with teachers, increased willingness to seek out help, positive outlook on the future, improved relationships with peers, increased mental and emotional strength, fewer discipline referrals, increased respect of authority figures, decreased law breaking, and decreased drug and alcohol use. The fact that participants experienced far more positive outcomes than their peers suggests that participants may have encountered more protective factors than their peers who experienced more negative outcomes.

The programme participants attended may have provided these protective factors. Four types of protective factors are those that reduce exposure to and impact of risk, diminish negative consequences that follow a traumatic event, nurture self-efficacy and self-esteem through accomplishments, and foster positive relationships and experiences that provide new resources or directions in life (Howard, Dryden, and Johnson 1999). Participants' narratives indicated that they experienced: support from caring adults (Higgins 1994; Howard, Dryden, and Johnson 1999), support in meeting teachers' high expectations (Bernard 1993), increased self-efficacy

(Brooks 1994), development of a more positive self-concept (Werner 1993), development of an internal locus of control (Gordon 1996; Werner 1993), increased autonomy (Gordon 1996; Masten and Garmezy 1985) and a positive outlook on the future (Werner 1993). As a result of targeted intervention, participants may have experienced desirable outcomes including improved self-concept, increased self-efficacy, increased autonomy, increased resilience and development of an internal locus of control. Each of these desirable outcomes has been documented to have a positive impact on individuals' well-being (Clausen 1991; Werner and Smith 1989).

Positive interactions with caring adults transformed the negative experience of being expelled into an opportunity for growth and improving oneself. Supportive relationships with caring adults may have protected students from some of the negative outcomes associated with expulsion, since positive relationships with caring adults are documented to facilitate resilience in children and adolescents (Garmezy 1991; Howard, Dryden, and Johnson 1999; Rak and Patterson 1996; Werner 1993; Werner and Smith 1989). Findings were consistent with studies by Garmezy (1991), Werner and Smith (1989) and Howard, Dryden, and Johnson (1999), in that participants specifically identified teachers in this supportive role. Participants' strong external locus of control may have made positive support from caring adults who believed they were capable, especially significant to this population. Students' experiences conform to Jordan's (1992) theory of resilience as a transformational process in which a person is able to navigate adversity by developing connections and relationships with others.

Before expulsion participants' self-concept depended on their success in being accepted by peer groups they deemed desirable. Their self-concept was built primarily on reflected appraisals of how they perceived others viewed them, as opposed to direct appraisals. Direct appraisal results from our own evaluations of what we are like based on our own reactions to past life experiences. Reflected appraisal results from our perceptions of how we are seen by others (Gallagher 2000). Participants' narratives indicated that after they were distanced from their peers, their self-concept became increasingly based on direct appraisals.

Participants' stories indicate that, through their experience, students may have developed a more positive self-concept, increased self-efficacy and adopted an optimistic outlook on the future. These changes may have protected students from some of the negative consequences of expulsion, since these traits are common in resilient individuals, (Brooks 1994; Gordon Rouse 2001; Werner 1993).

Participants' report of increased resilience is surprising since traumatic events and stressors, like expulsion, have been documented as risk factors that decrease resilience (Doll and Lyon 1998; Garmezy 1991; Rak and Patterson 1996). The trauma of expulsion could have caused additional difficulties for participants in social functioning. Adolescents may be especially vulnerable to social learning effect from peers who engage in risk-taking behaviours when experiencing high levels of social or psychological distress (Prinstein, Boergers, and Spirito 2001). This suggests that expulsion could act as a catalyst for students' risk-taking behaviours to increase. This may not only make expulsion ineffective in decreasing expellable behaviour but also may actually increase students' participation in risky behaviours. An increase in risk-taking behaviours after expulsion is consistent with findings that students who are excluded from school have more suspensions after expulsion than their peers (Arcia 2006).

The experiences of students in this study are not representative of individuals who choose not to attend alternative programmes for expelled students. Unfortunately, existing research indicates that many expelled students and their parents opt out of alternative programmes (Burns 1996; Morrison et al. 2001). Students who do not participate in alternative programmes miss opportunities during the expulsion term that participants found to be meaningful. Participants who attended the district's expulsion programme received the support necessary to take advantage of this opportunity. Had students opted out of attending the expulsion programme or had they lacked support during the expulsion term, this opportunity for growth may have been wasted.

The large body of existing literature documenting the negative social, emotional, physical, psychological and academic effects of expulsion must be taken into consideration when assessing the utility of expulsion. Although students experienced growth and maturation while attending the district's alternative educational programme, being barred from the diverse opportunities afforded to them by traditional school caused them to miss out on learning experiences that could never be re-created. Educators' focus must be on keeping students in school because whenever a student is removed from the school setting, there is potential for harmful outcomes (American Academy of Paediatrics 2003). Preventing expulsion is the first step in limiting the risks and potential negative outcomes associated with expulsion.

This study must be understood as a window that provides a glimpse into the lives of one small group of students who have been expelled from school. It should not be used independently from the larger body of research about expelled students in developing policy which impacts young people's lives. The findings of this research provide one snapshot of the expulsion experience, and many others must be taken to construct the collage of what it means for students at large to be expelled from school.

While this study does add the voices of eight young people to this discussion, more research on expelled students' experiences is needed to truly include students in the debate surrounding the use of exclusionary discipline. Topics for further inquiry include: possible interventions for preventing expulsion, triggers for developing an internal locus of control, experiences of students who do not attend alternative educational programmes, experiences of students who perceive the impact of expulsion to be primarily negative, and the reasons why students and their families opt out of alternative educational programmes.

Recommendations for facilitating resilience

Resilience-building strategies can be implemented in school-wide efforts or as targeted interventions for at-risk students. Expulsion may be prevented by implementing targeted intervention for at-risk students. Programmes servicing expelled students might utilise resilience-building strategies for the entire student population to mitigate harmful consequences during the expulsion term. Resilience strategies may also be implemented after expulsion to help students to recover from the trauma of the experience.

Schools can foster students' resilience by fostering the common personal traits shared by resilient individuals. These include high self-esteem (Brooks 1994; Masten and Garmezy 1985) self-efficacy (Brooks 1994), high intelligence and cognitive ability (Gordon 1996), excellent social skills (Gordon 1996; Gordon Rouse 2001), positive self-concept (Werner 1993), internal locus of control (Gordon 1996; Werner 1993) and autonomy (Gordon 1996; Masten and Garmezy 1985). Although some personal traits such as IQ are fixed, educators can facilitate development of other personal traits, including strong social skills, positive self-concept, internal locus of control, high self-esteem, self-efficacy and autonomy.

Another powerful avenue for increasing students' resilience is hiring caring, supportive adults and encouraging them to develop meaningful relationships with students. Rak and Patterson (1996) found that enduring relationships with adults, such as teachers, school counsellors, coaches, neighbours, clergy, supervisors of extra-curricular activities and mental health professionals mitigated the negative effects of adversity. Howard, Dryden, and Johnson (1999) found that children who recovered from adversity believed that their teachers took a personal interest in their well-being both within and outside of school.

Fostering school belongingness is another powerful tool in developing students' resilience. School belongingness refers to the extent to which a student feels personally included, accepted, respected and supported by others at school (Goodenow 1993). Bernard (1993) found that providing a school environment that is caring, supportive, positive and provides many opportunities for participation facilitates resilience in children. Resilience was also fostered by schools that set high expectations for all learners and provided support for all learners in reaching high expectations.

Conclusions

The risk factors and protective factors at play in each individual student's case are unique to the student and context. The interplay of risk factors and protective factors impact an individual student's resilience determining the level of positive or negative outcomes experienced as a result of expulsion. Outcomes of expulsion become increasingly positive as more protective factors are in play. Educators must develop interventions focused on bringing forth protective factors that have been documented to increase resilience and to make students less susceptible to the risks inherent in excluding students from school.

The experiences of these eight students are evidence that, when students receive appropriate intervention, the expulsion experience can change students' lives in a positive way. Knowing this, responsible educators must develop socio-emotional and academic interventions for expelled students that channel the positive life-changing potential of this experience. This study is proof that expulsion from school does not have to be a tragic event. Instead, educators can harness the trauma of expulsion and utilise this interruption in students' education to intervene in patterns of counter-productive behaviour. Through thoughtful targeted intervention by educators, expulsion can be the first step in students' journeys to achieve their goals and to live their dreams.

References

American Academy of Pediatrics. 2003. "Out-of-School Suspension and Expulsion." *Pediatrics* 112: 1206–1209.

Arcia, E. 2006. "Achievement and Enrollment Status of Suspended Students: Outcomes in a Large, Multicultural School District." *Education and Urban Society* 38: 359–369.

Ball, S. J., M. Maguire, and S. Macrae. 2000. *Choice, Pathways, and Transitions Post-16: New Youth, New Economies in the Global City.* London: Routledge/Falmer.

Bernard, B. 1993. "Fostering Resilience in Children." *Educational Leadership* 51 (3): 44–46.

Brooks, R. 1994. "Children at Risk: Fostering Resilience and Hope." *American Journal of Orthopsychiatry* 64: 545–553.

Brooks, K., V. Schiraldi, and J. Ziedenberg. 2000. *School House Hype: Two Years Later.* Washington, DC: Justice Policy Institute and the Children's Law Center.

Burns, L. V. 1996. "Metro Regional Alternative Education Program for Expelled Youth: An Outcome-Based Program Evaluation." PhD diss., James Madison University.

Campbell, J. 1990. "Self-esteem and Clarity of the Self-concept." *Journal of Personality and Social Psychology* 59: 538–549.

Clandinin, D. J. 2006. "Narrative Inquiry: A Methodology for Studying Lived Experience." *Research Studies in Music Education* 27 (1): 44–54.

Clausen, J. 1991. "Adolescent Competence and the Shaping of the Life Course." *American Journal of Sociology* 96 (4): 805–842.

Colaizzi, P. F. 1978. "Psychological Research as the Phenomenologist Views It." In *Existential Phenomenological Alternatives for Psychology*, edited by R. S. Valle and M. King, 58–62. New York, NY: Oxford University Press.

Creswell, J. W. 2007. *Qualitative Inquiry and Research Design.* London: Sage.

Davis, J., and W. Jordan. 1994. "The Effects of School Context, Structure, and Experiences on African American Males in Middle and High School." *The Journal of Negro Education* 63 (4): 570–587.

DeRidder, L. M. 1991. "How Suspension and Expulsion Contribute to Dropping out." *Educational Digest* 56 (6): 44–47.

Doll, B., and M. A. Lyon. 1998. "Risk and Resilience: Implications for the Delivery of Educational and Mental Health Services in Schools." *School Psychology Review* 27: 348–363.

Feyl-Chavkin, N., and J. Gonzalez. 2000. "Mexican Immigrant Youth and Resiliency: Research and Promising Programs." *ERIC Digest*, October.

Frankenberger, K. 2000. "Adolescent Egocentrism: A Comparison among Adolescents and Adults." *Journal of Adolescence* 23: 343–354.

Gallagher, S. 2000. "Philosophical Conceptions of the Self: Implications for Cognitive Science." *Trends in Cognitive Sciences* 4: 14–21.

Garmezy, N. 1991. "Resilience in Children's Adaptation to Negative Life Events and Stressed Environments." *Pediatrics* 20: 459–466.

Goodenow, C. 1993. "The Psychological Sense of School Membership among Adolescents: Scale Development and Educational Correlates." *Psychology in the Schools* 30: 79–90.

Gordon, K. 1996. "Resilient Hispanic Youths' Self-concept and Motivational Patterns." *Hispanic Journal of Behavioral Sciences* 18: 63–73.

Gordon Rouse, K. A. 2001. "Resilient Students' Goals and Motivation." *Journal of Adolescence* 24: 461–472.

Prinstein, M. J., J. Boergers, and A. Spirito. 2001. "Adolescents' and Their Friends' Health-risk Behavior: Factors that Alter or Add to Peer Influence." *Journal of Pediatric Psychology* 26 (5): 287–298.

Gurin, P., G. Gurin, and B. M. Morrison. 1978. "Personal and Ideological Aspects of Internal and External Control." *Social Psychology* 41: 275–296.

Halloran, E. C., D. M. Doumas, R. S. John, and G. Margolin. 1999. "The Relationship between Aggression in Children and Locus of Control Beliefs." *The Journal of Genetic Psychology* 160: 5–21.

Heath, S. 2009. *Researching Young People's Lives.* Los Angeles, CA: Sage.

Higgins, G. 1994. *Resilient Adults: Overcoming a Cruel past.* San Fransisco, CA: Jossey-Bass.

Howard, S., J. Dryden, and B. Johnson. 1999. "Childhood Resilience: Review and Critique of Literature." *Oxford Review of Education* 25: 307–323.

Jordan, J. 1992. *Relational Resilience*. Working Paper Series. Wellesley, MA: Stone Center.

Keenan, K., R. Loeber, Q. Zhang, M. Stouthamer-Loeber, and W. B. van Kammen. 1995. "The Influence of Deviant Peers on the Development of Boys' Disruptive and Delinquent Behavior: A Temporal Analysis." *Development and Psychopathology* 7: 715–726.

Lapsley, D. K., and M. N. Murphy. 1985. "Another Look at the Theoretical Assumptions of Adolescent Egocentrism." *Developmental Review* 5: 201–217.

Luthar, S. S., D. Cicchetti, and B. Becker. 2000. "The Construct of Resilience: A Critical Evaluation and Guidelines for Future Work." *Child Development* 71 (3): 543–562.

Macrae, S., M. Maguire, and L. Milbourne. 2003. "Social Exclusion: Exclusion from School." *International Journal of Inclusive Education* 7 (2): 89–101.

Morrison, G. M., S. Anthony, M. H. Storino, J. J. Cheng, M. J. Furlong, and R. L. Morrison. 2001. "School Expulsion as a Process and an Event: Before and after Effects on Children at Risk for School Discipline." *New Directions for Youth Development* 2001 (92): 45–71.

Masten, A., and N. Garmezy. 1985. "Risk, Vulnerability, and Protective Factors in Developmental Psychopathology." In *Advances in Clinical Child Psychology*, edited by B. Lahey and A. Kazdin, Vol. 8, 1–52. New York: Plenum Press.

Morrison, G. M., and B. D'Incau. 2000. "Developmental and Service Trajectories of Students with Disabilities Recommended for Expulsion." *Exceptional Children* 66 (2): 257.

Moses, B. F. 2001. "The Impact of Public School Suspension/Expulsion on Students and Their Families." PhD diss., The Union Institute.

Moustakas, C. 1994. *Phenomenological Research Methods*. London: Sage.

Parton, F., and A. Day. 2002. "Empathy, Intimacy, Loneliness and Locus of Control in Child Sex Offenders: A Comparison between Familial and Non-familial Child Sexual Offenders." *Journal of Child Sexual Abuse* 11 (2): 41–57.

Rak, C., and L. Patterson. 1996. "Promoting Resilience in at-Risk Children." *Journal of Counseling and Development* 74: 368–373.

Rotheram-Borus, M. J., P. D. Trautman, S. C. Dopkins, and P. E. Shrout. 1990. "Cognitive Style and Pleasant Activities among Female Adolescent Suicide Attempters." *Journal of Consulting and Clinical Psychology* 58: 554–561.

Skiba, R., and R. Peterson. 1999. "The Dark Side of Zero-Tolerance." *Phi Delta Kappan* 80 (5): 372.

Skiba, R., and M. Rausch. 2006. "Zero-Tolerance, Suspensions, and Expulsions: Questions of Equity and Effectiveness." In *Handbook for Classroom Management: Research, Practice and Contemporary Issues*, edited by C. M. Everson and C. S. Weinstein, 87–102. Mahwah, NJ: Earlbaum.

Wengraf, T. 2001. *Qualitative Research Interviewing*. London: Sage.

Werner, E. E. 1993. "Risk, Resilience, and Recovery: Perspectives from the Kauai Longitudinal Study." *Development and Psychopathology* 5: 503–515.

Werner, E. E., and R. S. Smith. 1989. *Vulnerable but Invincible: A Longitudinal Study of Resilient Children and Youth*. New York: Adams-Bannister-Cox.

Factors affecting successful reintegration

David Vittle Thomas

Pembrokeshire Behaviour Support Service, Pembroke, Wales

This study explores the perspectives of education practitioners towards the process of reintegrating pupils (many of whom display social, emotional and behavioural difficulties), from a pupil referral unit (PRU) to mainstream educational provision in a rural bilingual Welsh authority, and examines the barriers and facilitators they identified as evident within their individual schools and catchment area served with regards to reintegrating and including pupils. The study locates the process within a specific geographical context and discusses whether there are specific reintegration barriers and facilitators inherent within the setting. Patterns of pupil referral and reintegration between the PRU and mainstream schools were examined and analysed from "pupil tracking data" which tracked pupils throughout an academic year from their arrival at the PRU before the perspectives of education practitioners towards potential reintegration barriers and facilitators were gathered through an initial expert sample and a second landscape sample postal questionnaire. Interviews were subsequently conducted with respondents from Primary, Secondary and PRU settings to drill down into the influence of specific barriers and facilitators identified earlier. This study suggests that although generic reintegration barriers and facilitators may be evident within all settings, there were specific factors inherent within this geographical context identified by education practitioners, which acted in the most part as barriers to successful reintegration and inclusion.

Identification of the issue

The concept of inclusion has been a dominant ideology underlying educational policy having strong links to social justice where inclusion may be viewed as an attempt to eradicate educational inequality. Numerous policies have been introduced in England and Wales in an attempt to embed inclusion within practice, including in recent years, the Every Child Matters legislation (DFES 2003).

Campbell, Gold, and Lunt (2003) described the key aspect of the inclusion debate as concern over balancing individual needs against those of the majority's, where pupils have a right to receive their education within a mainstream setting including pupils identified as displaying special educational needs (SEN). Within the diverse spectrum of SEN, there is one group of pupils deemed the most difficult to include – those labelled as displaying social, emotional and behavioural difficulties (SEBD). Whilst policy encourages all SEN pupils to be included within mainstream

188

education, teacher responses to a survey by Goodman and Burton (2010) indicated the experience of pupils with SEBD in mainstream schools is far from consistent with SEBD pupils categorised as the most difficult to include due to their challenging behaviour, yet some schools successfully include such pupils.

In many cases, challenging behaviour will have resulted in the removal of the pupil from mainstream education and placement at a pupil referral unit (PRU). PRUs are neither planned nor designed to provide a long-term setting for pupils and should not be regarded by local authorities as filling this role. Under section 19 of the Education Act 1996, local authorities have a statutory duty to make arrangements to provide education for pupils who are excluded from school and not on the roll of a school. PRU placements should not be viewed as part of the range of SEN provision, rather should be adopted for relatively short time frames whilst a more appropriate provision is found or the pupil reintegrates to mainstream school as soon as such a transition is deemed appropriate. However, evidence (Wilkin, Gulliver, and Kinder 2005) suggests that significant numbers of pupils remain at a PRU in the long term rather than the placement offering a fixed short-term respite from mainstream education.

Research aims

The aim of the research was to discern and explain patterns of pupil reintegration at KS1-KS3 from a PRU to mainstream education. Within the study area, there are a wide range of schools and communities supported by a single PRU. I believed there to be factors inherent within the specific rural bilingual geographical context impacting (both positively and negatively) pupils and the likelihood of attempting a reintegration transition and of achieving a successful outcome. Factors included transport issues, school size and availability of specialist staff to support pupils and schools, for example. Within this area of Wales are specific issues of concern, for example, relatively low socio-economic levels, language of school, pupils and community which may impact upon habitus. Habitus (Bordieu 1977) refers to the lifestyle, values and expectations of particular social groups, acquired and reproduced through everyday life experiences. The habitus of some communities may not match mainstream school expectations and there are marked differences between a predominantly English speaking, relatively more urban south compared to traditionally Welsh speaking more rural north.

Previous research has focused upon a pupil's individual characteristics in relation to the success of reintegration and interventions. The focus of the present study rests upon the situation of the individual rather than the aspects of that individual's personality. It is the individual's situation which I believe to be of greater importance in the reintegration process which will inform participant perspectives. I believe through gaining an understanding of systems and how they operate to be instrumental in the identification of key influences upon the success of specific pupil transitions. In particular, I wished to focus upon factors identified by educational practitioners as influencing the success of reintegration transitions. Within the spirit of inclusion, the views of all participants including pupils and families should be sought (Allan 2011). The present study focuses specifically on the perspectives of education practitioners, and a follow-up study canvassing perspectives of other groups would be beneficial in producing a fuller inclusive picture.

Inclusion and integration

Evans and Lunt (2002) highlighted that inclusion had become a dominant ideology underpinning social and educational policy whilst Campbell (2002) noted the key aspect of the inclusion debate being balancing the needs of the individual with those of the majority's. Loreman (2007) believed the literature to be supportive of inclusion through provision of social, academic and financial benefits to education systems and pupils allied to moral, ethical and social justice origins of the ideology.

The Code of Practice (DfES 2001) confirmed acceptance of an inclusive ideology, in that a pupil's SEN would normally be met in mainstream education yet, it appears (Hodkinson and Vickerman 2009) that in practice inclusion is not universally achieved – it has limits. Hodkinson (2010) asserted the drive towards inclusive education to be an example of a situation where policy, development and philosophy had outpaced practice. The end point for inclusion is the school controlled by staff and communities served. Clough and Garner (2003) noted inclusion in practice is not achieved for all pupils as some educational establishments are not "fit for purpose" to include all children due to lack of knowledge, vision, will and resources.

Inclusion appears dependent upon staff attitude and competencies to deliver the ideology in practice. Croll and Moses (2000) determined the majority of teachers to be supportive of inclusion generally but not in all cases for pupils labelled SEBD or displaying challenging classroom behaviour. Cole, Daniels, and Visser (2003) suggested a need for reform of attitudes, ethos and curriculum within schools and development of staff skill to increase the likelihood of pupils displaying SEBD and disaffection having their needs addressed within mainstream education.

In 2002, Cole, Visser and Daniels were unable to identify a single approach which could be transplanted to all schools to address the needs of pupils with SEBD. They did however suggest that school policy and practice underpinned by values, attitudes and beliefs of staff and governors forge a school's approach to meeting needs which would be context specific.

Integration is used within education to describe a commitment to educating children with SEN in mainstream schools wherever possible, whilst inclusion describes the process of ensuring equality of learning opportunity for all. Inclusion involves the adaptation of policies and practices to remove barriers to learning so that no learner is marginalised; inclusion concerns the creation of appropriate learning environments for all children (for example Corbett and Norwich 1999; Norwich and Lewis 2007; Tomlinson 2001). Ainscow (2000) suggested the movement to place children with SEN within mainstream education to be increasingly driven by the notion of inclusion rather than integration. Integration has been viewed as placing pupils in mainstream school without additional organisational accommodation whilst inclusion (Ainscow 2000) concerns altering the system to accommodate those who are "different" with Ainscow, Booth, and Dyson (2004) viewing inclusion as identifying and minimising barriers to learning and participation.

Warnock (2005) refuted that inclusion be about placement or location advocating a learning concept of inclusion through including children in the common educational enterprise of learning, wherever they learn best. Gillinson and Green (2008) concluded inclusion to concern treating everybody equally rather than the same.

Whilst the concept of inclusion may have superseded that of integration it is interesting to note the language of returning pupils to mainstream education to focus upon reintegration. If pupils are to have their needs met in mainstream school following a transition after a period of time away, the term "reinclusion" could possibly be coined to reflect a willingness on behalf of the school to accommodate the pupil which I believe to be a basic precursor to success.

In 1997, Thomas argued that reintegration rested upon what Lipsky and Gartner (1996) termed a readiness model. Children need to prove their readiness to return to a mainstream setting rather than the mainstream setting being expected to prove a readiness to accommodate and accept the child. Thomas (1997) believed reintegration to describe the assimilation by mainstream schools of particular labelled children whilst the key aspect of inclusion is that children who are at disadvantage for whatever reason are not excluded from mainstream education.

Lindsay (2003) noted that inclusive education had been established as the main policy imperative with respect to children with SEN in England and Wales yet although inclusion had been championed as a means to remove barriers and reduce discrimination it remained a contested concept. McSherry (2012) believed inclusion to be especially contested with pupils attending a PRU or displaying SEBD. For such pupils, McSherry believed schools operated a predominantly assimilationist stance citing examples of schools offering trial placements whilst retaining the option to remove the pupil if their behaviour was deemed unacceptable rather than accepting pupils without additional caveat and displaying a willingness to adapt their policies and procedures to increase the likelihood of a successful outcome.

Pupil labelling

Farrell and Tsakalidou (1999) suggested evidence within England and Wales that mainstream schools were becoming openly hostile to the inclusion of certain groups of SEN pupils. McSherry (2012) suggested schools were particularly reluctant to take on pupils displaying challenging behaviour especially those labelled SEBD.

Lauchlan and Boyle (2007) suggested labelling may be advantageous to a child leading to treatment not otherwise forthcoming or provision of additional resources to meet need and increased awareness and understanding of difficulties. Norwich (1999) and Phelan (2002) believed the act of labelling in reality led to stigmatisation and ostricisation of the child which may not otherwise have occurred. Evidence suggests that the SEBD label carries many negative connotations and a damaging effect upon preconceptions of education practitioners dealing with a such labelled pupil.

SEBD and staff perspectives

Students labelled SEBD have not been included as successfully as pupils displaying other SEN. Pupils with SEBD have always presented a challenge to schools and teachers, yet some schools appear better equipped to meet these pupils' needs than others (Cole, Visser, and Daniels 1999).

What is evident is that the perspectives of professionals working with SEBD pupils influences the course of action followed and subsequently impacts upon the pupil. Croll and Moses (1985) reported teachers ascribed the majority of causes (82%) of challenging behaviour as emanating from within the child (38%) and to parental/home factors (44%) with Shapiro et al. (1999) suggesting similar figures of 46% of cause emanating within the child and 33% from the home. Both studies suggest a sense of powerlessness or willingness to intervene from teachers as they ascribed the majority of causation factors as being outside of their locus of control.

Miller, Ferguson, and Moore (2002), however, suggested that parents believed teacher behaviour especially perceptions regarding unfair labelling to be an equally major cause of difficulties. It appears therefore that labels attached to pupils may contribute to their difficulties and lead to pupil disaffection with education.

Swinson, Woof, and Melling (2003) focused upon mainstream school staff perspectives towards pupils with SEBD. Their study highlighted a reluctance to accept pupil return from a PRU due to preconceived notions they would be disruptive and challenging to manage. Over time as pupils settled and behaviour compared favourably with their peers staff perception became increasingly positive suggesting that as staff become increasingly empowered to deal with challenging behaviour, their own attitude becomes increasingly positive resulting in the forging of positive relationships between pupils and staff.

Jull (2008) expressed concern that SEBD is perhaps the only form of SEN which exposes a child to increased risk of exclusion due to the identification and labelling of their SEN and that these children are at greater risk of becoming marginalised and excluded from mainstream education than peers. SEBD pupils can, as a result, miss out on opportunities afforded to peers and lack access to support they need. The Statistics for Wales First Release (SDR 164/2011) reported some 13,006 pupils across Wales were labelled as SEBD.

Pupil referral units

Local authorities have a duty of care for all children within their remit to provide a suitable education supportive of their welfare, health and education. Provision outside mainstream education is deemed alternative provision an example of which is a PRU.

Garner (1996) explored PRU provision in the mid-1990s comparing them to the "disruptive units" he viewed as their precursor common in England and Wales in the 1970s–1980s. Whilst conceding improvements in PRU provision had been made Garner (2000) viewed their existence as contrary to the spirit of inclusion suggesting that PRUs stood as confirmation that in the case of SEBD pupils inclusive thinking was yet to be established in practice. In contrast, the 2005 ESTYN survey of PRUs in Wales complimented their work and highlighted positive features including offering access to the curriculum for all pupils, effective discipline and behaviour policies accepted and understood by pupils, effective individually tailored programmes of study and strong positive links with schools and home.

Reintegration

GHK Consulting (2004) following a survey of 150 LEAs in England viewed reintegration as the efforts made by schools, LEAs and other agencies to return pupils who are absent, excluded or otherwise missing from mainstream school provision. Reintegration could be attempted for a diverse range of pupils groups each displaying a range of distinct reintegration needs. Tootill and Spalding (2000) suggested the likelihood of successful reintegration be increased through, for example, offering a pupil a fresh start at a new school to break a cycle of negative experience and that the process be planned and promoted as a positive experience to which the pupil has earned the opportunity to participate.

Visser (2000) noted schools hold an important role in enabling a successful outcome and needed to promote a commitment from a majority of staff to inclusion and ability to access additional resources and services as required. Within schools demonstrating such qualities was an increased likelihood of teachers having a clear definition of SEBD, a professional commitment to these pupils and a flexible skilled response to match pupil need. Visser (2005) concluded schools successfully promoting reintegration viewed all pupils as part of the school community, were open and shared practice and aimed to reduce barriers to SEBD pupil participation.

Research methods

I followed a mixed methods approaching beginning with a review of historical quantitative pupil tracking data which tracked pupil transitions into, out of and within the PRU over a historical time frame to identify potential variables and relationships impacting upon reintegration. This was followed by postal questionnaire of first an expert sample and a subsequent landscape sample gathering both qualitative and quantitative data and finally, semi-structured face-to-face interviews were conducted with an expert sample gathering qualitative data based on school experience of reintegration. The study included both within stage and across stage mixed methods.

Results and analysis

The data was subjected to two analyses. The first involved grouping and comparing responses based upon respondent job title. Three categories were identified – Head teacher (including head of unit), SENCO and classroom practitioner (teacher and LSA). I considered this to be a valuable categorisation of respondents as I believed that respondents' duties and role may influence their perspective towards reintegration believing that Head teachers and SENCOs to have greater concern for reintegration process with classroom practitioners concern for reintegration outcome.

For the second analysis, respondents were grouped by education sector as I believed that respondents across different sectors would display differing perspectives towards reintegration. The categories were infant/primary (IPS), secondary (SS) and non-mainstream (NMS). I believed IPS respondents where reintegration appears to be more successful to display more positivity towards reintegration than SS respondents from where many PRU pupils do not attempt reintegration and, expected NMS respondents to appear more positive than mainstream colleagues. Staff attitude towards reintegration and pupils I believe helps explain patterns of successful reintegration within the county and that schools which have experienced success are more likely to display positive attitudes increasing the likelihood of establishing positive cycles of future success.

Potential reintegration barriers and facilitators

Table 1 indicates average rating scores calculated per respondent category to variables offered by the questionnaire as potentially influencing successful reintegration. Respondents rated relative importance of variables on a scale of 1 (not important/influential) to 5 (important/influential). It is important to note that the numbers of respondents within each group were not equal which may impact upon the comparativeness of results. During analysis, participant rating scores were grouped, with average scores calculated for each participant group.

Table 1.   The average ratings given to variables influencing reintegration.

Response	Head	SENCO	Classroom practitioner	IPS	SS	NMS	Overall average
Pupil age	2.86	2.90	3.67	2.68	3.43	3.63	3.20
Key stage	3.00	3.00	3.00	2.77	3.43	3.25	3.08
Exclusion reason	4.24	4.50	3.33	4.09	4.57	3.88	4.10
Time out	4.33	4.60	5.00	4.50	4.29	4.75	4.58
Pupil SEN	3.38	3.40	3.17	3.50	2.71	3.50	3.28
Pupil literacy	3.14	2.90	2.17	3.09	2.71	2.63	2.77
Pupil numeracy	3.05	3.00	2.17	3.00	2.86	2.63	2.79
Pupil perception	4.52	4.30	4.33	4.45	4.71	4.13	4.41
Staff perception	3.90	3.70	4.50	3.73	4.00	4.50	4.06
Pupil reputation	3.67	3.00	3.67	3.41	3.57	3.63	3.49
School size	3.00	3.00	3.17	3.00	2.59	3.50	3.04
Class size	3.24	2.90	4.00	3.09	2.86	4.13	3.37
School ethos	4.33	4.50	5.00	4.64	4.43	4.75	4.61
Staff training	4.19	4.70	4.67	4.45	4.14	4.50	4.44
Available resources	4.24	4.70	3.67	4.33	4.57	4.00	4.25
Curriculum	3.52	3.40	3.50	3.14	4.29	3.75	3.60
Funding	3.95	4.10	4.17	4.22	4.00	3.50	3.99
Parental support	4.95	4.60	5.00	4.82	4.86	5.00	4.87
Outside support	4.19	4.60	3.50	4.14	4.71	3.88	4.17
BSS support	4.48	4.50	4.17	4.41	4.57	4.38	4.42
LSA support	4.24	4.70	4.70	4.45	4.43	4.13	4.35
LEA support	3.90	4.30	3.83	3.95	4.43	3.75	4.03
Protocol	3.52	4.10	3.50	3.59	4.14	3.50	3.73
Top 8 variables	1st	2nd	3rd	4th	5th	6th	7th	8th

Variables rated as most important/influential were largely located within the sphere of control and influence of the education system suggesting schools hold a potentially large influence over reintegration success. However, it is important to consider the reintegration process of individual pupils and schools are unique and therefore difficult to suggest whether there is sufficient flexibility within the school or education system to individually tailor the reintegration package to each pupil. It is also important to consider the relative influence of variables within the process as even though school-based influences appear large, do these influences carry equal or greater significance than the lesser amount of pupil, home or environment-located factors i.e. if a pupil is determined not to make a move to a particular school and there is no parental support for the move even with all the variables apparently under school control can they be offset or overcome (Table 2)?

Table 2. Top 8 Variables influencing reintegration (grouped by job title and education sector).

Rank	Head	SENCO	Classroom practitioner	IPS	SS	NMS
1	Parental support	Staff training	Time out	Parental support	Parental support	Parental support
2	Pupil perception	Resources	School ethos	School ethos	Pupil perception	School ethos
3	BSS support	LSA support	Parental support	Time out	Outside support	Time out
4	School ethos	Parental support	Staff training	Pupil perception	Exclusion reason	Staff perception.
5	Time out	Outside support	Staff perception	LSA support	Resources	Staff training
6	Resources	Time out	Pupil perception	Staff training	BSS support	BSS support
7	Exclusion reason	BSS support	BSS support	Resources	LSA support	LSA support
8	LSA support	Exclusion reason	LSA support	BSS support	LEA support	Class size

Some agreement existed across participant groups as to which variables exert the greatest influence upon reintegration. Grouping categories of participants' average scores evidence that parental support was deemed of greatest importance (average score 4.87, range 4.60–5.00). Both classroom practitioners and NMS participants assigned this variable an average score of 5.00.

School ethos ranked second (average score 4.61, range 4.33–5.00) although not across all participants. A school with an inclusive ethos, I believe, is more likely to achieve successful reintegration in that a pupil feeling they were valued members of the school community would have a more positive perception of the school. This was of greatest importance to classroom practitioners.

Thirdly, length of time the pupil had been away from mainstream school prior to attempting reintegration received an average score of 4.58 (range 4.29–5.00). The longer a pupil had been away from mainstream, the harder it becomes to reintegrate successfully. A PRU is a very different environment especially to a mainstream secondary school and the longer a pupil spends in a PRU environment the more difficult it would be to cope with a return to mainstream school. This was of greatest importance to classroom practitioners.

Staff training rated fourth (average score 4.44, range 4.14–4.70). Staff appropriately trained to deal with challenges a reintegrating pupil may bring are likely to feel confident in dealing with, and less threatened by, the pupils' arrival and, therefore, have a more positive perception than an untrained member of staff who may be reluctant to work with the pupil and consciously or otherwise make the pupil feel less welcome. This was of greatest importance to SENCOs.

Support from the PRU rated fifth (average score 4.42, range 4.17–4.57). This could be support for the pupil, parents and mainstream school and was important before transition commenced and during the process and continued support should be available as appropriate after the pupil had returned to mainstream school. This was of greatest importance to secondary schools.

Pupil perception ranked sixth (average score 4.41, range 4.13–4.71). I believed this may have rated of greater importance by respondents in that the pupil must want to return to mainstream school and be positive towards the transition, school and staff before there is any possibility of success, the pupil must want to be at the school before being willing to abide by school rules and guidelines. This was of greatest importance to secondary schools.

LSA support ranked seventh (average score 4.35, range 4.13–4.70). This was of equal greatest importance to SENCOS and classroom practitioners. Availability of resources to support the reintegration process ranked eighth (average score 4.25, range 3.67–4.70). This was of greatest importance to SENCOS.

There was also agreement as to which variables exerted the least amount of influence upon reintegration. Grouping the six categories of participants, average scores evidence that pupil literacy was deemed of least importance (average score 2.77, range 2.17–3.14). Classroom practitioners deemed this least important. Research by Fletcher-Campbell and Wilkin (2003) identified delays in pupil literacy levels as having a detrimental impact upon reintegration through making it increasingly difficult for the pupil to cope with work within the mainstream school environment. Pupil numeracy was ranked of second least importance (average score 2.79, range 2.17–3.05). This was deemed of least importance to classroom practitioners. It was expected that this variable would have rated of greater importance particularly to this group, as it would be classroom practitioners who would be working to combat these difficulties on a daily basis.

Deemed third least important was school size (average score of 3.04, range 2.59–3.50). This was deemed of least importance to secondary schools. I had expected that this variable would have rated of greater importance as within the literature, for example Wallace (2010), school size is deemed to influence sustained reintegration success rates, with smaller schools offering a more personal environment to pupils and being able to tailor disciplinary approaches to meet individual need.

A review of literature had been unsuccessful in locating data relating pupil exclusion and reintegration to school size. Research for the Local Government Association suggested the optimum size for a secondary school to be 900 pupils and a primary school to be 300 pupils. Measured in this context, six of the eight secondary schools within the county would have pupil rolls above optimum size whilst 54 of the 61 primary schools would be below the optimum limit. Research by Howley and Howley (2004) suggested optimum school size could not be measured using pupil number, rather related to school leadership, ethos and quality of teaching and learning and will be dependent upon the relative poverty or affluence of the pupil cohort and school catchment area.

Research by Stevenson (2006) suggested although optimum school size is as yet undetermined there is evidence that pupils from poorer socio-economic backgrounds achieve greater progress in smaller schools. This is in accordance with earlier research in the USA published in the 1999 Research Roundup of the National Association of Elementary School Principles which suggested that smaller schools offered advantages to pupils related to a caring ethos and sense of nurture.

In 2010 Wallace (who advocates a "schools within schools" approach to large secondary schools) concluded that smaller schools led to decreased exclusion due to more positive pupil–staff relationships. This was in contrast to Day et al. (2008) who cited that larger schools provide better quality teaching, leadership and management and a wider range of diverse learning and curriculum opportunities which may mitigate against challenging behaviour and exclusion.

Pupil key stage rated as fourth least importance (average score 3.08, range 2.77–3.43). This was of least importance to IPS participants and closely related to pupil age which rated of fifth least importance (average score 3.20, range 2.68–3.67). This was of least importance to IPS participants.

Pupil SEN ranked sixth least important (average score 3.28, range 2.71–3.50). This was of least importance to secondary schools. Research by Broomhead (2013) suggested that pupil SEN may, in some cases, increase the risk of pupil exclusion and decrease the likelihood of successful reintegration or inclusion.

Class size ranked seventh least importance (average score 3.37, range 2.90–4.13). This was of least importance to SENCOS. Pupil reputation ranked eighth least important (average score 3.49, range 3.00–3.67). This was of least importance to SENCOS. Research by Wilkin, Gulliver, and Kinder (2005) suggested that informal pupil reputation may impact upon reintegration either positively or negatively depending upon the reputation.

Following initial individual variable analysis, variables were grouped into four categories and participants were asked to rate and compare their relative influence. The categories were "within pupil" variables i.e. sphere of influence located within the reintegrating pupil, for example, attitude; secondly, "at home" variables (sphere of influence radiated from pupil's home/family, for example, parental attitude); thirdly, "environmental" variables (located within the wider environment the pupil lived in, for example, peer attitudes and aspiration). The fourth category consisted of "within school" variables (sphere of influence located within mainstream school, PRU or alternative provision and wider education system, for example, staff training or government policy).Participants rated the influence/importance of these variables on the same 1–5 rating scale as individual variables (Table 3).

The overall average score across all participants to all categories was 4.26. There were, however, three categories namely pupil, home and school-based factors identified as more influential recording an above-average score and a further category of wider environment factors receiving below-average scores, therefore, of lesser importance.

Scores were remarkably similar (range of 0.22 between first and third most important variable). Within pupil factors were ascribed most importance (4.52 average score), followed by "at home" factors (4.47) with school-based factors ranking

Table 3.   The average rating given to groups of factors influencing reintegration.

	Highest ranked variable as identified by participants						
Variable	Head	SENCO	Classroom practitioner	Infant/Primary school	Secondary school	Non-main school	Overall average
Pupil	4.55	4.80	4.17	4.59	4.86	4.14	4.52
Home	4.55	4.40	4.33	4.41	4.71	4.43	4.47
Environ.	3.55	3.60	4.00	3.45	4.14	3.71	3.74
School	4.30	4.20	4.33	4.23	4.43	4.29	4.30
Average	4.24	4.25	4.21	4.17	4.54	4.14	4.26

third (4.30). Participants deemed the largest influences upon reintegration to be located within the pupil and home environment i.e. factors outside the control or sphere of influence of the school and, therefore, the key to reintegration success lay outside their control. Finally, "environmental" factors were viewed of lesser importance although an average score of 3.74 suggests factors were still of significance.

IPS participants assigned the second overall lowest average score of 4.17 to the four categories with "within pupil" factors receiving the highest average score of 4.59 and, environmental factors received their lowest average score of 4.23, assigning the lowest average score to environmental factors of any participant group.

SS participants assigned the highest overall average score of 4.54 to the four categories with "within pupil" factors receiving the highest average score of 4.86. These participants assigned the highest average score across the four categories.

NMS participants assigned the lowest average score of 4.14 to the four categories. Unlike mainstream colleagues they displayed differing perceptions as to relative influence of factors, assigning the greatest level of influence to "at home" factors with a score of 4.43 and again, environmental factors last. These participants assigned the lowest average score to both within pupil and school-based factors of the three participants. It is possible to suggest that colleagues who work within NMS work not just with pupils who are disaffected and disenfranchised by experiences within mainstream education, but also with equally disaffected parents, often negative about and confrontational towards mainstream schools attempting to reintegrate their children following previous breakdowns in provision. Parental negativity filters down to pupils and influences perceptions they form of schools, negative parental attitude is likely to foster negative pupil attitude and increase the chance of negative outcomes. Within the literature, Rieser (2010), PRU staff, noted negative parental attitudes and the relative importance of forging positive links with parents before any change in pupil attitude towards mainstream school could be shaped.

Head teachers gave the second highest overall average score of 4.24 to the four categories with both "within pupil" and "at home" variables jointly receiving the highest score of 4.55, with environmental factors lagging some way behind with 3.55. Head teachers assigned the highest average score to "home" factors and lowest to "environmental" factors.

SENCOs gave the highest overall average score of 4.25 to the four categories with "within pupil" factors receiving the highest average score of 4.80, with environmental factors again ranked fourth. SENCOs assigned the highest average score to "within pupil" factors and the lowest to "school"-based factors.

Classroom practitioners gave the lowest overall average score of 4.21 to the four categories. They held a differing perception of the influence of variables to SMT colleagues in that school and home-based factors were of equal greatest influence (average score 4.33) and again environmental factors ranked fourth. Classroom practitioners assigned the highest average score to school- and environmental-based factors of the three groups and, the lowest average score to within pupil factors. I felt classroom practitioners would have greater experience of working with pupils on a daily basis than SMT and, therefore, able to view the impact of school-based variables such as the success of strategies employed. Mather and Goldstein (2001) suggested that as classroom practitioners see positive results from strategies they implement they become increasingly confident and positive about working with "difficult" pupils and of the amount of influence they can exert within their classroom.

Discussion – factors educational practitioners identified as influencing reintegration success

A general consensus emerged from questionnaires with participants exhibiting a remarkable consistency concerning factors they believed to exert an influence upon success of reintegration and upon factors exerting a lesser influence. The relative importance of other variables varied according to the position and school type of the participant.

Across both questionnaire stages participants indicated that pupil age, gender, SEN, literacy and numeracy ability were of little importance to reintegration, neither was the size of the class nor school to which the reintegration would occur. Pupil reputation was viewed as important by expert respondents but deemed of lesser importance in the broader landscape sample, which may be related to lack of direct experience within the landscape sample set.

Prior to commencing the study I believed that each of these variables may have been important, a view confirmed by analysis of historical data in that the above-mentioned variables appeared at least to be potential driving forces governing referral to the PRU and accounted for variations in reintegration patterns to mainstream school. For example, girls are referred in far lower numbers to the PRU but are reintegrated in proportionately greater numbers to mainstream settings. The majority of referred pupils displayed literacy difficulties through reading and spelling delays with, in general, reintegrating pupils displaying lesser difficulties and the majority of referrals were from larger schools which in the majority of cases would be the same schools to which pupils would return.

These variables may not be the main driving forces of referral and reintegration which I believe to be unique to each individual pupil and school rather than generic, but at the very least are contributory factors and may be determinants as to where future intervention may be focused such as targeting resources to families of schools or upon meeting the needs of boys in particular in mainstream schools.

School factors

Participants considered ethos to be the most important school-based reintegration factor. Reintegration appears to be successful within schools which demonstrate a nurturing whole school ethos within which a critical mass of staff are committed to an inclusive ideology, are appropriately trained and in which provision is offered which matches the needs of the reintegrating pupil. Schools should seek to reduce barriers to the participation of reintegrating pupils through ensuring that the philosophy of inclusion is embedded within school practice and accepted by students, parents, staff, governors and the local community.

Many pupils at the PRU studied, attempt reintegration following an extended period of time away from mainstream education. This may act as a barrier to reintegration. Research by Grandison (2011) concurs with this view as does the study carried out in 2000 by Tootill and Spalding which suggested that reintegration is increasingly successful if all parties expect the reintegration to occur as soon as possible, strong links are forged with the PRU or alternative provision setting, flexible patterns of attendance are possible and curriculum offered is flexible to match pupil need. The length of time in which the pupil has been away from the mainstream education setting may have an impact upon the success of reintegration with a shorter time period of attendance at a PRU likely to foster success provided the pupil is deemed to be ready and able to make a return.

Not all pupils will reintegrate nor is a mainstream education placement the most appropriate provision for all pupils as noted by the Welsh Assembly Government "mainstream education is not always right for every child" (WAG 2006).

Teacher factors

Having caring skilled members of staff in place was viewed as a key component to ensuring successful reintegration with a member of staff willing to advocate on behalf of the pupil and be someone whom the pupil trusts to listen to their side viewed as crucial.

Many participants noted the importance of training being made available to staff prior to commencement of reintegration in that training in and awareness of issues may help encourage greater acceptance of the pupil by at least a critical mass of staff. The competency which teachers feel in dealing with pupils with challenging behaviour and EBD may be related to the success or otherwise of reintegration with mainstream teachers receiving little training in dealing with such pupils (indeed as a teacher within the PRU training in this area is also scarce).

School staff can create barriers to reintegration. Schools as appropriate need to take into account the circumstances behind challenging behaviour such as learning difficulties; continue improvements to the quality of teaching and ensure that all staff be given behaviour-management training and ongoing support.

Many participants noted the importance of staff building relationships, in particular with the pupil. The teacher needs to be willing to connect with the pupil on a personal level and build relationships, with pupils needing to feel the teacher is genuinely interested in them and concerned with their progress and success (Barr and Parrett 1993).

Parental/home factors

Research by Leyser and Kirk (2004) suggests that although many parents believe in the goal of including pupils within mainstream schools, there is reluctance on the part of many parents towards the reintegration of their own children with only 14–36% of parents favouring such a move.

Pupil factors

Participants believed that the reintegrating pupil was largely responsible for a successful outcome and, in particular, needed to display a desire to reintegrate as well as positive attitude, an acceptance of school rules, a willingness to take advantage of opportunities offered by the school and the acceptance of support offered and use of strategies given to them prior to their return.

Factors specific to the rural bilingual setting

A number of factors were identified by interviewees pertaining to the specific issues of attempting reintegration within the study area. What emerged was a view that factors inherent to the county relating to geography, language and culture, socio-economic issues and poverty and deprivation impacted not only upon pupils at the PRU attempting a reintegration but upon all pupils. There was a belief that many pupils were at disadvantage due to the area in which they resided and it could be argued that potentially those pupils referred/reintegrated were impacted upon more than the general school population.

Historically, many pupils who have attended the PRU have been from families, from poorer socio-economic backgrounds and broken homes, for example, and are suffering increased levels of disadvantage within an already disadvantaged area. Negative factors relating to the county were largely based within the realms of geography – rurality, culture, family issues, socio-economic issues and outside agencies whilst there were issues relating to differences in Welsh language speaking and transport difficulties which could make the reintegration process more difficult.

Any success factors based within the county were largely, according to participants, located within schools themselves and to a lesser extent within the families of pupils who have historically reintegrated successfully.

This research unearths similarities in issues and educational practitioner perspectives concerning reintegrating pupils from a PRU to mainstream school within a largely rural education authority in Wales, to findings by Lawrence (2011) researching reintegration within a large urban English context.

This would indicate that reintegration is difficult to successfully promote regardless of the setting in which it is attempted and despite the reintegration experience being unique to individual pupils and schools entering into the process there appear to be common generic barriers and facilitators located within national guidance and legislation, schools and staff, PRUs, local education authorities, local communities, reintegrating pupils and their families.

However, this research suggests that these issues are compounded and exacerbated by factors within the county and these factors relate in the main to geography (rural nature, lack of transport, etc.), culture (Welsh language prevalent in some areas, narrow world view and lack of family aspiration) and an apparent lack of willingness by schools to entertain transfers of pupils to allow reintegration to take place within a new setting offering the pupil a fresh start.

A consensus emerged from questionnaire respondents who exhibited consistency concerning factors they believed to exert influence upon reintegration success and, those factors which did not. The relative influence attributed to variables varied according to position and school type of respondents.

Respondents indicated pupil age, gender, SEN, Literacy, Numeracy and pupil reputation exerted limited influence upon reintegration as did class or school size in which reintegration would be attempted. Analysis of the historical tracking data suggested these variables may potentially have been driving forces governing referral to PRU and to account for subsequent reintegration patterns to mainstream school. Respondents suggested these variables may contribute to a lesser extent rather than act as the principal drivers of referral and reintegration which are unique to each pupil and school attempting a transition yet, may merit further study as to where future interventions be focused including targeted support for families of schools.

Following questionnaire analysis, interviews were conducted with an expert sample who had experience of reintegration transitions. Analysis of responses suggests the following to exert influence upon reintegration success.

School factors

Interviewees considered ethos to be of paramount importance and most influential school located reintegration variable. Reintegration appears successful within schools which demonstrate a nurturing whole school ethos within which a critical mass of staff are committed to an inclusive ideology, are appropriately trained and in which provision is offered matching the needs of the reintegrating pupil. Schools should seek to reduce barriers to participation through ensuring an inclusive philosophy is embedded within school practice and accepted by pupils, parents, staff, governors and local community.

Many pupils attending the PRU studied, attempt reintegration following an extended period of time outside mainstream education. This may act as a reintegration barrier as suggested by Tootill and Spalding (2000) and Grandison (2011) who viewed successful reintegration as being increasingly likely if all participants expect the transition to occur as soon as possible, strong links are forged with the alternative provider, flexible attendance is possible as is a flexible tailored curriculum. Although successful reintegration appears to occur when a transition is made as soon as the pupil is deemed able to do so there was a suggestion that

In some schools there is a view that pupils should maybe not go back to the school

Primary interviewee 1

And, it should be recognised that not all pupils will reintegrate nor is a mainstream placement the most appropriate provision for all pupils

Mainstream education is not always right for every child

Welsh Assembly Government (2006)

Availability of caring skilled staff was also viewed as key to ensuring successful reintegration, with a staff member willing to advocate on behalf of the pupil and be trusted by the pupil to listen to their concerns vital. Interviewees noted the importance of availability of staff training prior to the commencement of reintegration in that increased awareness of issues may foster greater acceptance of the pupil and

A positive attitude about accepting the pupil from the whole school

Primary interviewee 1

The competency with which teachers deal with challenging behaviour and SEBD is related to training and through appropriate training

The staff were up for the challenge and accept that SEBD problems are very much as big a problem as numeracy

Primary interviewee 1

An interviewee from the behaviour support service believed that although ongoing training was important more should be done during initial teacher training

I tend to find teachers are experts in their subjects but not necessarily experts in child development, they have not been taught about how children will deal with situations in the classroom

Behaviour support interviewee 1

School systems can produce barriers to reintegration, for example, through set time-tables, uniform expectations and behaviour norms with attention needed to ensure flexibility in delivery to meet pupil need. Schools need to consider circumstances underlying challenging behaviour such as learning difficulties; continue to improve quality of teaching and ensure all staff are appropriately trained

> Barriers include what goes on in the classroom, content of lessons, teacher delivery and how you organise your groups and sets

> Secondary interviewee 2

Interviewees noted the importance of positive relationships being forged between staff and pupil which may be difficult especially when a pupil is reintegrating to the school which referred them to the PRU. There may be staff reluctance to contemplate their return

> Once a child has been removed from school there will be a stigma attached. It can be very difficult for some staff to accept a child coming back without some concern in the back of their mind

> Primary interviewee 2

Some schools were aware of such difficulties and were seeking to overcome them

> There is a prejudice in teachers' minds about these pupils and we work really hard to overcome that; we have a policy of no revenge, no raking over the past ... we make a great effort if pupils do return to welcome them

> Secondary interviewee 1

Parental/home factors

Leyser and Kirk (2004) suggested that many parents believed in the goal of including pupils within mainstream schools. One interviewee praised the parents of the reintegrating pupil in that

> A very positive aspect was the attitude of the parents. They were excellent and were genuinely pleased and grateful for the opportunity for their child to attend here

> Primary interviewee 1

There can be reluctance on the part of many parents towards the reintegration of their own children with only 14–36% of parents favouring such a transition. This was noted here, for example,

> Parents have their part to play, we often hear comments like "why is my son going back to that bloody school?" this negative attitude filters down to the children

> Behaviour support interviewee 1

Parents of other pupils can also impact upon reintegration success and can feel concerned about pupils with known behaviour issues impacting upon the education of their own child

> There have been incidents of some very misinformed parents being quite forthright with their views at the school gates

> Primary interviewee 1

There was also a suggestion that parents could inadvertently hamper reintegration success by

> Not handing down coping strategies or installed resilience within their children … the children are only aware of a very narrow slice of life
>
> Secondary interviewee 1

Pupil factors

Interviewees believed the reintegrating pupil to have a large responsibility for achieving a successful outcome and needed, in particular, to display a desire to reintegrate as well as exhibit a positive attitude, acceptance of school rules, willingness to take advantage of opportunities offered by the school and acceptance of support offered and use of strategies given to them prior to return. This can prove difficult in practice in that

> The pupil point of view is that they are being sent back to a situation where they have previously failed
>
> Behaviour support interviewee 1

And

> The children we attempt to reintegrate lack the necessary coping strategies to deal with what is going on in their lives both within and outside of school
>
> Secondary interviewee 2

Context specific factors

When discussing barriers to and facilitators of successful reintegration specific to the area, interviewees were pessimistic identifying triple the number of barriers to facilitators. What emerged was a view that factors inherent to the study area relating to geography, language and culture, socio-economic issues, poverty and deprivation had a negative impact not only upon pupils attempting a reintegration from the PRU to mainstream education but upon all pupils. There was a belief that pupils were at a disadvantage due to where they resided and it could be argued these factors had a greater impact upon pupils referred to the PRU than the general population.

Historically, many pupils attending the PRU have been from poorer socio-economic backgrounds and suffer from increased levels of disadvantage within what can be an already disadvantaged area. There was a sense that many families were rooted in a very small geographic area for generations and that through a lack of skill or aspiration they had failed to prosper and achieve their potential. This had led to a collective low self-esteem and a lack of resilience had become the norm within families with negative beliefs being reinforced across generations becoming trapped in a negative spiral which was increasingly difficult for schools to overcome. Pupils in many instances had experienced a very narrow and negative world view and allied to a lack of well-paid job opportunities had limited aspirations for their future

There are so few job opportunities and a lack of multiplicity of roles for children to see in their home lives or town or local area. This mitigates against aspiration ... it's hard to pin aspiration to them of striving to achieve in the future as they don't see success around them

Secondary interviewee 1

Further issues identified as making reintegration difficult included the spread of Welsh language in some schools and communities compared to others, a marked difference between rural and urban areas within the county compounded by poor transport links especially public transport allied to lack of personal transport within many families of PRU pupils.

Conclusion

This study unearths similar issues and educational practitioner perspectives concerning the reintegration of pupils from a PRU to mainstream education within a largely rural, bilingual Welsh setting to findings by Lawrence (2011) researching reintegration within a large urban authority in England. Both studies suggest that reintegration is difficult to promote successfully regardless of the setting in which it is attempted and despite the reintegration experience being unique to the pupil and school involved, there are common generic barriers to and facilitators of reintegration located within schools and staff, national legislation, PRUs, local authorities, communities and wider environment, reintegrating pupils and their families.

This study suggests that educational practitioners believed there to be barriers to reintegration inherent within and exacerbated by the geography (largely rural and poor transport networks), culture (Welsh and non-Welsh speaking communities, narrow world view and experience, perceived lack of aspiration) and an apparent unwillingness by schools to entertain transfers of pupils to allow reintegration to take place in a new setting affording the pupil a fresh start and opportunity to break negative cycles of behaviour.

References

Ainscow, M. 2000. "The Ron Gulliford Lecture: The Next Step for Special Education: Supporting the Development of Inclusive Practices." *British Journal of Special Education* 27 (2): 76–80.

Ainscow, M., T. Booth, and A. Dyson. 2004. "Understanding and Developing Inclusive Practices in Schools: A Collaborative Action Research Network." *International Journal of Inclusive Education* 8 (2): 125–139.

Allan, J. 2011. "Complicating, Not Explicating: Taking Up Philosophy in Learning Disability Research." *Learning Disability Quarterly* 34 (2): 153–161.

Barr, R., and W. Parrett. 1993. *Hope at Last for At-riskyouth.* Needham Heights, MA: Allyn and Bacon.

Bourdieu, P. 1977. *Outline of a Theory of Practice, Cambridge Studies in Social and Cultural Anthropology.* Cambridge: Cambridge University Press.

Broomhead, K. E. 2013. "Preferential Treatment or Unwanted in Mainstream Schools? The Perceptions of Parents and Teachers with Regards to Pupils with Special Educational Needs and Challenging Behaviour." *Support for Learning* 28 (1): 4–10.

Campbell, C. 2002. "Conceptualizations and definitions of inclusive schooling." In *Developing Inclusive Schooling: perspectives, policies and practices*, edited by C. Campbell. London: Institute of Education, University of London.

Campbell, C., A. Gold, and I. Lunt. 2003. "Articulating Leadership Values in Action: Conversations with School Leaders." *International Journal of Leadership in Education* 6 (3): 203–221.

Clough, P., and P. Garner. 2003. "Special Educational Needs and Inclusive Education: Origins and Current Issues." In *Education Studies*, edited by S. Bartlett and D. Burton, 72–93. London: Sage.

Cole, T., H. Daniels, and J. Visser. 2003. "Patterns of Provision for Pupils with Behavioural Difficulties in England: A Study of Government Statistics and Behaviour Support Plan Data." *Oxford Review of Education* 29 (2): 187–205.

Cole, T., J. Visser, and H. Daniels. 1999. "A Model Explaining Effective Ebd Practice in Mainstream Schools." *Emotional and Behavioural Difficulties* 4 (1): 12–18.

Corbett, J., and B. Norwich. 1999. "Learners with Special Educational Needs." In *Understanding Pedagogy and Its Impact on Learning*, edited by P. Mortimore, 115–136. London: Paul Chapman Publishing.

Croll, P., and D. Moses. 1985. *One if Five*. London: Routledge and Kegan Paul.

Croll, P., and D. Moses. 2000. "Ideologies and Utopias: Education Professionals' Views of Inclusion." *European Journal of Special Needs Education* 15 (1): 1–12.

Day, C., P. Sammons, D. Hopkins, K. Leitherwood, and A. Kingston. 2008. "Research into the Impact of School Leadership on Pupil Outcomes: Policy and Research Contexts." *School Leadership and Management* 28 (1): 5–25.

DfES (Department for Education and Skills). 2001. *Special Educational Needs Code of Practice*. London: DfES.

DfES (Department for Education and Skills). 2003. *Every Child Matters*. Annesley: DfES.

Education Act. 1996. ©. London: HMSO.

Evans, J., and I. Lunt. 2002. "Inclusive Education: Are There Limits?" *European Journal of Special Needs Education* 17 (1): 1–14.

Farrell, P., and K. Tsakalidou. 1999. "Recent Trends in the Re-integration of Pupils with Emotional and Behavioural Difficulties in the United Kingdom." *School Psychology International* 20 (4): 323–337.

Fletcher-Campbell, F., and A. Wilkin. 2003. *Review of the Research Literature on Educational Interventions for Pupils with Emotional and Behavioural Difficulties*. Slough: National Foundation for Educational Research.

Garner, P. 1996. "A la Recherché du Temps Perdu: Case-study Evidence from Off-site and Pupil Referral Units." *Children and Society* 10 (3): 187–196.

Garner, P. 2000. "The Range and Impact of LEA Behaviour Support Plans." *Emotional and Behavioural Difficulties* 5 (1): 3–11.

GHK Consulting, Holden McAllister Partnership, and IPSOS Public Affairs. 2004. *The Reintegration of Children Absent, Missing or Excluded from School*. Research Report 598. London: The Stationery Office.

Gillinson, S., and H. Green. 2008. *Beyond Bricks and Mortar – An Alternative Approach to the SEN Debate*. London: Royal National Institute for the Deaf.

Goodman, R. L., and D. M. Burton. 2010. "The Inclusion of Students with BESD in Mainstream Schools: Teachers' Experiences of and Recommendations for Creating a Successful Inclusive Environment." *Emotional and Behavioural Difficulties* 15 (3): 223–237.

Grandison, K. J. 2011. "School Refusal and Reintegration from Short Stay School to Mainstream." Doctoral diss., The University of Birmingham.

Hodkinson, A. 2010. "Inclusive and Special Education in the English Educational System: Historical Perspectives, Recent Developments and Future Challenges." *British Journal of Special Education* 37 (2): 61–67.

Hodkinson, A. and P. Vickerman. 2009. *Key Issues in Special Educational Needs and Inclusion*. London: Sage.

Howley, C. B., and A. A. Howley. 2004. "School Size and the Influence of Socioeconomic Status on Student Achievement: Confronting the Threat of Size Bias in National Data Sets." *Education Policy Analysis Archives* 12 (52): 1–35.

Jull, S. K. 2008. "Emotional and Behavioural Difficulties (EBD): The Special Educational Need Justifying Exclusion." *Journal of Research in Special Educational Needs* 8 (1): 13–18.

Lauchlan, F., and C. Boyle. 2007. "Is the Use of Labels in Special Education Helpful?" *Support for Learning* 22 (1): 36–42.

Lawrence, N. 2011. "What Makes for a Successful Re-integration from a Pupil Referral Unit to Mainstream Education? An Applied Research Project." *Educational Psychology in Practice* 27 (3): 213–226.

Leyser, Y., and R. Kirk. 2004. "Evaluating Inclusion: An Examination of Parent Views and Factors Influencing Their Perspectives." *International Journal of Disability, Development and Education* 51 (3): 271–285.

Lindsay, G. 2003. "Inclusive Education: A Critical Perspective." *British Journal of Special Education* 30 (1): 3–12.

Lipsky, D. K., and A. Gartner. 1996. "Inclusion, School Restructuring, and the Remaking of American Society." *Harvard Educational Review* 66 (4): 762–797.

Loreman, T. 2007. "Seven Pillars of Support for Inclusive Education: Moving from 'Why?' to 'How?'." *International Journal of Whole Schooling* 3 (2): 22–38.

Mather, N. and Goldstein, S. 2001. "Behavior Modification in the Classroom." In *Learning Disabilities and Challenging Behaviors: A Guide to Intervention and Classroom Management*, 96–117. Baltimore, MD: Paul H Brookes.

McSherry, J. 2012. *Challenging Behaviour in Mainstream Schools: Practical Strategies for Effective Intervention and Reintegration*. London: Routledge.

Miller, A., E. Ferguson, and E. Moore. 2002. "Parents' and Pupils' Causal Attributions for Difficult Classroom Behaviour." *British Journal of Educational Psychology* 72 (1): 27–40.

Norwich, B. 1999. "The Connotation of Special Education Labels for Professionals in the Field." *British Journal of Special Education* 26 (4): 179–183.

Norwich, B., and A. Lewis. 2007. "How Specialized is Teaching Children with Disabilities and Difficulties?" *Journal of Curriculum Studies* 39 (2): 127–150.

Phelan, A. 2002. "Inclusion through ICT: The Wider View". In *Special Educational Needs and the Internet: Issues for the Inclusive Classroom*, edited by C. Abbott, 146–163. London: Routeledge Falmer.

Rieser, R. 2010. "Building Teacher Confidence and Competence to Include Children with Disabilities."

Shapiro, E. S., D. N. Miller, M. Sawka, M. C. Gardill, and M. W. Handler. 1999. "Facilitating the Inclusion of Students with EBD into General Education Classrooms." *Journal of Emotional and Behavioral Disorders* 7 (2): 83–93.

Stevenson, K. R. 2006. "School Size and Its Relationship to Student Outcomes and School Climate." *National Clearinghouse for Educational Facilities* 1–8.

Swinson, J., C. Woof, and R. Melling. 2003. "Including Emotional and Behavioural Difficulties Pupils in a Mainstream Comprehensive: A Study of the Behaviour of Pupils and Classes." *Educational Psychology in Practice* 19 (1): 65–75.

Thomas, G. 1997. "Inclusive Schools for an Inclusive Society." *British Journal of Special Education* 24 (3): 103–107.

Tomlinson, S. 2001. "Sociological Perspectives on Special and Inclusive Education." *Support for Learning* 16 (4): 191–192.

Tootill, R., and B. Spalding. 2000. "How Effective can Reintegration be for Children with Emotional and Behavioural Difficulties?" *Support for Learning* 15 (3): 111–117.

Visser, J. 2000. "What Schools Need for EBD Pupils to be Included." In International Special Education Congress (ISEC), University of Manchester, Manchester, NH, July 24−28.

Visser, J. 2005. "Working with Children and Young People with Social and Emotional Behavioural Difficulties: What Makes What Works, Work?" *Handbook of Emotional and Behavioural Difficulties* 225–244.

Wallace, W. 2010. Schools within Schools: Human Scale Education in Practice. London: Calouste Gulbenkian Foundation.

Warnock, M. 2005. *Special Educational Needs: A New Look*. London: Philosophy of Education Society of Great Britain.

WAG (Welsh Assembly Government). 2006. *Welsh Government Circular 47/2006: Inclusion and Pupil Support.*

Wilkin, A., C. Gulliver, and K. Kinder. 2005. *Serious Play: A Study of Arts Activities in Pupil Referral Units and Learning Support Units*. London: Calouste Gulbenkian Foundation.

The relationship between ethnic diversity and classroom disruption in the context of migration policies

Gert-Jan M. Veerman

Department of Sociology and Anthropology, University of Amsterdam, Amsterdam, The Netherlands

This paper studies the relationship between ethnic school composition and classroom disruption in secondary education in the context of migration policies. We measured classroom disruption using students' reports from 3533 schools in 20 countries provided by cross-national PISA (Programme for International Student Assessment) 2009 data. We employ the migrant share and the ethnic diversity net of the native share as indicators of the ethnic composition of a school. The MIPEX (Immigrant Integration Policy indEX) is used as an indicator of migration policies. Our results show a positive association between ethnic school diversity net of the migrant share and classroom disruption. Furthermore, we show a negative interaction term of the migration policy and ethnic diversity. Consequently, our results indicate that students in countries with a more inclusive migration policy are at least less harmed by influence of ethnic school diversity regarding classroom disruption. Findings partly support the "contact hypothesis" and reject the "threat hypothesis" in an educational context.

1. Introduction

One of the founders of sociology, Emile Durkheim, considered school discipline as an important research field, and argued that school discipline is a key to the process of youth socialisation and an instrument for moral education (Durkheim 2002 [1961]). More recently, sociologists also recognise school discipline as potentially playing a "critical role in children's and adolescents" internalisation of conventional social expectations and norms' (Arum, Ford, and Velez 2012, 2). Moreover, a better disciplinary climate associates with higher cognitive school performances (Arum, Ford, and Velez 2012).

Recent studies on school discipline measure the economic and ethnic homogeneity of school networks (Arum, Ford, and Velez 2012; van de Werfhorst, Bergstra, and Veenstra 2012). Although these recent studies on school behaviour use "the share of immigrants" or "ethnic diversity" (Stefanek et al. 2012) in a school or class as an indicator of homogeneity, these studies lack to separate the influence of the *share* of children with a migration background and the *diversity* among this group of children. *Ethnic share* refers to the proportion of immigrant children in a class (independent of which specific ethnic group children are identified with), whereas *ethnic diversity* refers to the composition in the class in terms of the number and size of different ethnic groups. Although a higher proportion of immigrant students might refer to a higher ethnic heterogeneity of a school, a high proportion of immigrants might also refer to a lower ethnic homogeneity due to a strong concentration of one specific immigrant group in a school. Therefore, the proportion of immigrants and the ethnic diversity isolates different processes concerning diversity (Veerman, van de Werfhorst, and Dronkers 2013). A few recent studies on student achievement have distinguished the share and diversity (Braster and Dronkers 2013; Dronkers and van der Velden 2013; Maestri 2011; Van Houtte and Stevens 2009; Veerman, van de Werfhorst, and Dronkers 2013), although primarily predicting student achievement or other student-level outcomes. We investigate whether diversity is related to classroom disorder. A lack of school discipline may emerge in schools with high diversity, but might differ between destination countries. We study this using Programme for International Student Assessment (PISA) 2009 data from 20 different countries for which data are available on the origin countries of the parents of the students.

This study, therefore, aims to contribute to the literature in three ways. First, we measured classroom disruption using the reports of the students' reports instead of the reports from school staff. Second, we distinguished both the proportion of immigrants and ethnic diversity in our model using two distinct conceptualizations of ethnic school composition. Finally, we distinguished how differences in migration policies between countries might influence the association between the ethnic composition and school climate.

2. Theory and hypotheses

2.1. *Ethnic diversity and school climate*

Why does ethnic diversity of schools relate to school climate? Ethnic diversity refers to ethnic composition in school in terms of the number and size of different ethnic groups and consequently, to the relative number of possible interethnic contacts (Veerman, van de Werfhorst, and Dronkers 2013). A number of recent studies show a negative association between ethnic diversity and school performance for immigrant students in secondary education in a large number of European destination countries (Dronkers and van der Velden, 2013; Veerman and Dronkers 2013). A part of this negative relation is explained by pointing to mechanisms of problems of adapting the teaching to the different needs of students (Veerman, van de Werfhorst, and Dronkers 2013) or of problems of understanding the instruction (Maestri 2011) due to fewer incentives to adapt to the culture of the destination country. Furthermore, as Esser (2004) argues, increased interethnic contact may lead to increased interethnic tension. These tensions may negatively influence academic performance (Hoxby 2000). Moreover, these interethnic tensions might lead to more disordered incidents.

Although cross-country studies find a significant relation between ethnic diversity and student performance, studies in specific contexts show no significant or even positive relations between ethnic diversity and school performances. These positive relations are explained by the idea of enrichment due to more cultures in a class (Lazear 1998; Maestri 2011), the urban context (Braster and Dronkers 2013) or the country context (Veerman and Dronkers 2013).

Recent studies on school discipline use both economic variation and proportion of ethnic students to explain differences between school climates (Arum, Ford, and Velez 2012). These researchers have found a higher proportion of (children of) immigrants to be related to disciplinary problems. Single-country studies, however, show no significant results (Arum and Velez 2012). Furthermore, a qualitative study in the English context indicates no relationship between the share of migrants and classroom disruption (Lupton 2005). Although Arum, Ford, and Velez (2012) show that while disruption and victimisation are negatively related to school performance, these indicators asked directly to the teacher can measure only one impression of disruptive behaviour. However, the classroom disruption concept might refer to a combination of different student behaviours. For instance, classroom disruption might refer to whether or not students can work and whether or not they listen to instructions during the lessons alongside classroom disorder. Especially, in the more common cases, where there is no classroom disorder all the time, a combination of disorder and work behaviour covers a range of student disruptive behaviour through-out the entire lesson.

Although the proportion of immigrants strongly correlates to ethnic diversity, a school with a high proportion of immigrants does not necessarily lead to more possible interethnic contacts (Veerman, van de Werfhorst, and Dronkers 2013). For instance, a school with 100% Turkish immigrant students is ethnically homogenous and consequently results in no interethnic contacts. Therefore, following the idea of more interethnic tensions due to more interethnic contacts, our *classroom disruption hypothesis* states that:

A higher ethnic diversity is associated to more classroom disruption.

2.2. Ethnic diversity and school climate in different contexts

Although we expect overall, a positive relationship between ethnic diversity and classroom disruption, recent studies show opposed relationships between ethnic diversity and school performances between countries (Veerman and Dronkers 2013) and different relationships between ethnic diversity and tolerance (Janmaat 2012) in different countries. Consequently, different contexts might influence the tensions between different ethnic groups.

Positive attitudes about dealing with diversity are explained in the "contact hypothesis" of Allport (1954) and negative attitudes between ethnic groups by the "threat hypothesis" in recent debate about interethnic contacts (Gijsberts, Van der Meer, and Dagevos 2012; Keating and Benton 2013; Putnam 2007). From the threat hypothesis perspective, it is argued that natives may feel threatened by migrants in their position (Blalock 1957). The threat hypothesis, therefore, explains the possible ethnic tensions between natives and migrants due to natives' notions of possible domination by migrants in political or economic positions.

Allport (1954) stressed, from the contact perspective, the importance of conditions that must be fulfilled in the contacts. He mentioned "equal status within the situation" and "authority support" as two of the four conditions for optimal contact between different ethnic groups. Pettigrew and Tropp (2006) revealed in their meta-analysis the overall positive effect of intergroup contact on intergroup attitudes, but they found that Allport's conditions are not essential for positive outcomes. Janmaat (2012) and Pettigrew (1998) mentioned the possible influence of the society on the contacts of different ethnic groups. Pettigrew argued that the contacts and conditions between different ethnic groups are structured and formed by institutional and societal norms (Pettigrew 1998). Consequently, we expect from a "contact hypothesis" perspective that countries with more inclusive migration policies support with their authority the positive intergroup contacts on institutional levels. Furthermore, the rights that a country provides its immigrants, is an indication of the dominant norms regarding equality between ethnic groups in that country. The findings of Veerman and Dronkers (2013) seem to support this contact perspective on a country level, because they show for Turkish students a positive relationship between ethnic diversity and school performance in a country with a more inclusive migration policy and opposed relationships in countries with less inclusive migration policies. Janmaat (2012) revealed a positive relationship between ethnic diversity and tolerance in Sweden and Germany and no relation in England. Nevertheless, England is the country that is in the ranking of inclusive migration policies a country between Sweden and Germany (Koopmans, Michalowski, and Waibel 2012). Moreover, a comparative study on immigrant educational attainment in Britain, Canada and the United States found comparable results between the destination countries (Rothon, Heath, and Lessard-Phillips 2009). Consequently, these studies indicate no influence of the migration policy. However, a more recent study shows a smaller ethnic inequality in test scores in countries with more inclusive migration policies, using 10 destination countries (van de Werfhorst, van Elsas, and Heath 2014).

Besides these studies, in the context of education, other studies are more sceptical about the integration force of more inclusive migration policies. Three arguments are typically given in this critical literature. First, multiculturalism policies may lead to social and economic marginalisation (Koopmans 2010). Second, Duyvendak et al. (2013) argue that an aggregation of indicators cannot measure a coherent integration model. Finally, more rights for migrants might induce feelings of threat of the natives (Wagner et al. 2006). Overall, the literature shows mixed findings with a number of arguments for the "threat hypothesis" that might reduce but not necessarily eliminate the influence from the perspective of the "contact hypothesis" especially in the case if we compare a higher number of destination countries. Our migration policy hypothesis therefore states that:

A higher ethnic diversity results in a weaker association to classroom disruption in countries with a regime of more inclusive migration policy.

3. Data and variables

3.1. Data

The analyses have been carried out using the cross-national PISA 2009. The cross-national PISA contains both social economic background and classroom disruption information of 15-year-old students from a high number of countries (OECD 2012). Unfortunately, a number of countries – including the United States – that participated in PISA did not indicate the countries of origin. Because we measured the influence of ethnic diversity,[1] information about more than three specific countries of origin countries is essential.[2] Consequently, we only focused on the European countries that have included the country of origin data in PISA and Australia and New Zealand. We split our analysis for Belgium in two sections as PISA allows the possibility of nationwide analysis alongside data selection for the Flemish region and the Walloon region.[3] Thus, our data-set contains information on 3729 schools in

20 destination countries. We omitted 4.2% of our schools due to student numbers lower than 8 per school. Moreover, 1.1% of these schools show no data regarding classroom disruption. Consequently we use the data of 3533 schools.

3.2. Variables

3.2.1. Dependent variables

The dependent variable in this study is the *classroom disruption of the school*. PISA 2009, contains five possible questions that could measure the classroom disruption with the following topics: "students don't listen to teacher", "the teacher has to wait a long time for quiet", "students cannot work well", "students don't start working for a long time after the lesson begins" and "there is noise and disorder". The questionnaire for students contains four possible answers: "never or hardly ever", "some lessons", "most lessons" or "all lessons". If the classroom disruption variable forms no adequate scale in some countries, we should remove these countries from cross-country analysis (André, Dronkers, and Fleischmann 2009) or possibly remove indicators. Categorical Principal Components Analysis (CATPCA) in both cross-national data and country data show factor loadings of 0.7^4 or more for all questions except for "the teacher has to wait for quiet". The factor loading of "the teacher has to wait for quiet" is approximately 0.7 in most countries except for Greece where a 0.4 value is shown in the data. Consequently, we created a variable for classroom disruption for our cross-national analysis that contains all selected countries and possible questions from PISA except "wait for quiet", using the listwise deletion setting of CATPCA. Although the answers of students refer to their experience and interpretation of the question, we refer to classroom disruption, in this paper, to make the text more readable.

3.2.2. School-level variables

Percentage of immigrants. We computed the percentage of immigrants using the number of immigrant students in schools.

Origin diversity residual. Using the number of students per country of origin involved in each school, we computed an inverted Herfindahl index of country of origin diversity. We calculated the index as follows: $1 - ((\text{proportion ethnic group 1})^2 + (\text{proportion ethnic group 2})^2 + \dots + (\text{proportion ethnic group } n)^2)$. Although earlier studies showed that the proportion of immigrants in a school and country of origin diversity are concepts that we should distinguish both theoretically and empirically, Veerman, van de Werfhorst, and Dronkers (2013) showed that in an empirical model the use of both variables may lead to problems of multicollinearity, due to the strong Pearson correlation between proportion of immigrants and the country of origin diversity. Using the method applied by Veerman, van de Werfhorst, and Dronkers (2013), we estimated a quadratic regression model at school level, predicting diversity to be a function of the percentage of immigrants controlled with dummies for the different destination countries. We then took the residuals of this regression model, thereby measuring the difference between origin diversity as is observed in a school relative to the predicted diversity (see Appendix C for a visualisation of the correlation between the percentage of migrants and ethnic diversity). This measurement thus does establish the level of diversity, given a particular percentage of immigrant students. The residualized diversity indicator is independent of the percentage of immigrant students, because residuals are assumed independent of the X-variables in ordinary least squares regression.

The *mean ESCS* was calculated using the ESCS score of all students in school.

Variation in ESCS. We computed the coefficient of variation in ESCS by dividing the standard deviation in ESCS within the school by the school-level mean ESCS.

Percentage of females. We computed the percentage of females using the number of female students in the school.

3.2.3. Educational system level

We use the Gross Domestic Product (GDP) per capita 2009 based on purchasing power parity in constant 2005 international dollars from the World Bank (World Bank 2013). The GDP provides an indication of living standards across different countries. For Scotland, we calculated a GDP comparable to the World Bank using information concerning the difference in GDP between the United Kingdom and Scotland (McLaren, Armstrong, and Gibb 2013). Regional GDP data for Belgium could have been included, but Walloon and Flemmish students both live in the Brussels region.[5] This region shows the highest GDP in Belgium. It is for this reason that GDP data for Belgium was set at a national level.

The MIPEX (Immigrant Integration Policy indEX) is a composite index of policy areas that measures the integration policy of destination countries (Niessen, Huddleston, and Citron 2007). The MIPEX II distinguishes six integration policy areas: labour market access, family reunion, long-term residence, political participation, access to nationality and anti-discrimination. The MIPEX is based on expert interviews and policy assessments, using 140 indicators. A high MIPEX refers to a more inclusive integration policy. We use the MIPEX index as an indication of whether the destination country has a more or less inclusive migration policy. We use the MIPEX II data that was collected in 2007 because this is the MIPEX data that was collected before, rather than after the PISA data collection took place. Unfortunately, information concerning Croatia was first collected after 2011 and was only available with the categories of recent MIPEX III from 2010. Although MIPEX II and MIPEX III are not completely comparable, we use the MIPEX III data for Serbia and Croatia in our analysis. We underpin that the MIPEX index of Croatia may show some bias due to changes over time and the composition of the index[6].

3.3. Descriptive statistics

Table 1 shows the mean values and standard deviations of our dependent variables per destination country.

The classroom disruption scores vary from –0.26 in Germany to 0.36 in Greece. These countries differ more than a standard deviation. Alongside Germany also Latvia scores a mean disruptive score under –0.20. Furthermore, Table 1 shows also for Luxembourg a classroom disruption above 0.20.

Tables 2a and 2b show that the difference in means and standard deviations is small between the cross-national data and the cross-national data MIPEX countries selected. Table 2b shows that the MIPEX values range from 30 to 78. Consequently, our data-set contains a wide range of the countries where MIPEX is measured,

Table 1. Descriptive statistics of classroom disruption by destination country.

	N	Mean	SD
Australia	351	0.05	0.35
Austria	230	−0.04	0.45
Belgium (Flemish)	143	0.02	0.35
Belgium (Walloon)	107	−0.01	0.34
Czech Republic	236	0.13	0.52
Croatia	156	0.10	0.40
Denmark	276	−0.11	0.31
Finland	188	0.18	0.37
Germany	209	−0.26	0.33
Greece	159	0.36	0.33
Latvia	174	−0.29	0.33
Liechtenstein	12	−0.19	0.36
Luxembourg	38	0.25	0.30
Montenegro	47	−0.25	0.23
Netherlands	178	0.16	0.29
Norway	189	0.13	0.35
New Zealand	161	0.03	0.29
Portugal	206	−0.19	0.28
Scotland	97	−0.06	0.29
Switzerland	376	−0.10	0.34
Total	3533	−0.00	0.36

Source: PISA 2009. Own computation.

Table 2a. Descriptive statistics of variables in cross-national data

	Minimum	Maximum	Mean	SD
Classroom disruption	−1.02	1.77	−0.01	0.39
School level				
Proportion immigrants*	0.00	100.00	25.46	21.01
Residuals Origin diversity	−0.61	0.21	0.00	0.03
Mean ESCS	−1.80	1.61	0.11	0.48
Variation ESCS	0.04	0.28	0.13	0.030
Proportion of female*	0.00	100.00	50.00	17.62
N countries	20			
N school	3533			

*Grand mean centred in analyses.
Source: PISA 2009. Own computation

because our data contains the country with the lowest MIPEX score and the second highest MIPEX score (Niessen, Huddleston, and Citron 2007).

4. Models and results

4.1. Analytical design

We employed a multilevel model, in which schools are nested in countries. We estimated our models using Markov Chain Monte Carlo (MCMC) estimation techniques, because this approach is likely to reduce bias in comparison to Maximum Likelihood estimation in a model with 16 countries and cross-level interactions (Stegmueller 2013).

Table 2b. Descriptive statistics of variables in cross-national data MIPEX countries selected.

	Minimum	Maximum	Mean	SD
Classroom disruption	−1.02	1.77	−.01	0.40
School level				
Proportion immigrants*	0.00	100.00	23.75	20.95
Residuals Origin diversity	−0.62	0.20	0.00	0.03
Mean ESCS	−1.80	1.61	0.09	0.49
Variation ESCS	0.04	0.28	0.13	0.03
Proportion of female*	0.00	100.00	49.9290	16.43
Country level				
GDP	12,902	67,915	31067.02	9463.64
MIPEX2007*	30	78	53.42	13.19
N countries	16			
N school	2962			

*grand mean centred in analyses.
Source: PISA 2009. Own computation.

Because MCMC is a Bayesian estimation technique, we estimated the confidence (i.e., credibility intervals) that measure the uncertainty of the parameter estimates. The confidence interval indicates a 95% probability that the parameter estimate will lie between two values of the interval.

Our first Model 1a contains all explaining variables at school level and country level using classroom disruption as dependent variable. At school level, this first model is largely comparable to the research model of Arum, Ford and Velez (2012). Our Model 1b contains only the 16 countries with MIPEX data available. We have added in our second Model, the GDP and MIPEX at country level, as Akiba et al. (2002) revealed an influence of GDP on victimisation. Finally, we have added the cross-level interaction term in our third Model. As a result, we could test our *disruption hypothesis* using Model one and we test our *migration policy hypothesis* with Model 3.

Although our dependent variables may seem to be observable, the student answers might be influenced by cross-national interpretation differences. Gerber (2012) mentions – for instance – that speaking out of turn, might be interpreted by the teacher as classroom disorder in Russia, while it might be interpreted otherwise in other countries. Furthermore, the answers might be influenced by cross-national (van Herk, Poortinga, and Verhallen 2004) and cross-cultural response styles (Fischer et al. 2009). In a supplement found in Appendix A, we checked for the possible influence of cross-national response styles using an additional model that contains dependent variables with grand mean-centred values on national level. Consequently, we removed all country influences and assumed in this model that all differences in scores between countries are not due to actual differences in classroom disruption, but due to differences in response styles.

In Appendix B, we included a weighting factor on school level in all models to control for accuracy of measurement of the mean school disruption as reported by students. We calculated the weighting factor as follows: 1/school-level variance. Thereafter, we divided the individual weighting factor by the mean of our weighting factor to get a mean weighting factor of one. Consequently, we give schools with a

Table 3. Bayesian results of the school origin compositions on classroom disruption in cross-national PISA data.

	Model 1a		Model 1b		Model 2		Model 3	
	B	95% CI	B	95% CI	B	95% CI	B	95% CI
Constant	-0.07	-0.18 0.04	-0.01	-0.12 0.10	-0.20	-0.58 0.19	-0.20	-0.56 0.12
School level								
Percentage immigrants of school	-0.01	-0.00 0.00	0.00	0.00 0.00	0.00	0.00 0.00	0.00	-0.00 0.00
Residuals Origin diversity of school	0.67*	0.33 1.01	0.82*	0.43 1.20	0.82*	0.44 1.20	0.81*	0.43 1.17
Mean ESCS	-0.13*	-0.16 -0.10	-0.09*	-0.12 -0.06	-0.09*	-0.13 -0.07	-0.09*	-0.12 -0.07
Variation ESCS	0.55*	0.03 1.06	0.45	-0.12 1.00	0.45	-0.11 1.00	0.46	-0.12 1.01
Percentage females of school	-0.00*	-0.00 -0.00	-0.00*	-0.01 -0.00	-0.00*	-0.01 -0.00	-0.00*	-0.01 -0.00
Educational system level								
GDP					0.00	-0.00 0.00	0.00	-0.00 0.00
MIPEX					0.00	-0.01 0.01	0.00	-0.01 0.01
MIPEX*Resid. Diversity							-0.04*	-0.08 -0.01
Variance								
Country level	0.04*	0.02 0.08	0.04*	0.02 0.09	0.04*	0.02 0.09	0.04*	0.02 0.09
School level	0.12*	0.11 0.12	0.12*	0.12 0.13	0.12*	0.12 0.13	0.12*	0.12 0.13
DIC	2.458.17		2.181.90		2.182.07		2.178.71	
N countries	20		16					
N schools	3533		2962					

*0 not in 95% CI.
Source: PISA 2009. Own computation.

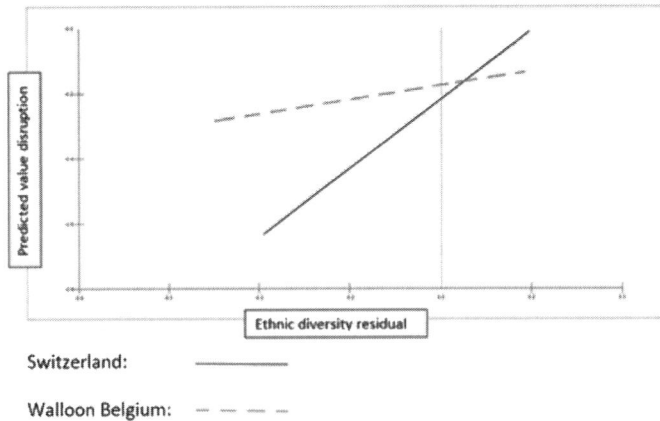

Switzerland: ―――――

Walloon Belgium: ― ―― ― ―

Figure 1. Ethnic diversity (residualised) on classroom disruption in cross-national PISA data and the MIPEX scores of Walloon Belgium (66) and Switzerland (42) (based on Table 3, model 3).

lower variance (i.e. less heterogeneity of the students' judgments) a higher weighting factor. We use in our control for accuracy of measurement, a Maximum Likelihood estimation technique, because weighting factors are ignored in MCMC (Centre for Multilevel Modelling 2011).

4.2. Results

Table 3 model 1a and 1b show for ethnic diversity significant parameter estimates of 0.7 (95% CI: 0.3–1.0) and 0.8 (95% CI: 0.4–1.2). Consequently, we confirmed our *classroom disruption hypothesis*.

Using Model 3, we test our *migration policy hypothesis* which predicts that the association between classroom disruption and ethnic diversity is weaker in countries with more inclusive migration policies. Consequently, we expected a significant negative association between the cross-level interaction between the MIPEX data and ethnic diversity. The results for Model 3 in Table 3 confirmed the *migration policy hypothesis*.

Figure 1 shows that for a country with a higher MIPEX, a higher ethnic diversity residual can lead to a decrease of the classroom disruption.

Appendix A shows results that are corrected for between-country variation using the grand mean-centred values of the disruption score. Results are comparable to our results in Table 3, of course the between-country variance disappears. Therefore, if all differences between countries are due to cross-national response styles, the findings still confirm both the classroom disorder hypothesis and the migration policy hypothesis. Finally, Appendix B shows results that are corrected for accuracy of measurement. Although our results of ethnic diversity are comparable to our results in Table 3, the significant negative association between the cross-level interaction between the MIPEX data and ethnic diversity becomes non-significant.

5. Conclusion and discussion

In this paper, we investigated the relation between the ethnic composition of schools, and school discipline at secondary schools using PISA 2009 data. School discipline is one of the indicators of the internalisation of conventional social expectations and norms.

Besides the influence of ethnic composition on non-cognitive school performance, we explored the country-level influence of migration policies on this relation. We underpinned the importance of both the conceptual and methodological differences between ethnic share and ethnic diversity. Furthermore, we developed an indicator that measures classroom disruption as mentioned by the students. Finally, we introduced the MIPEX index in our discussion concerning school discipline and country comparisons, as we expected migration policy differences between countries to explain a part of the differences in the association between ethnic school composition and school discipline between countries.

Our results demonstrated that ethnic diversity significantly associates with the classroom disruption. Consequently, students at schools with more possible interethnic contacts than we expect due to the proportion of immigrants show increased classroom disruption. Our non-significant associations for share of migrants and classroom disruption are in line with the results by Arum and Velez (2012) and Lupton (2005) for individual countries regarding the share of migrants, but it also underpins the importance to control both for the share of migrants and ethnic diversity in a single research model.

Our results indicate differences between countries with different migration policies. Our data demonstrated that immigrants in countries with a higher MIPEX showed a lower association between ethnic diversity and classroom disruption. Nevertheless, the association becomes non-significant when we control for the variability between schools in the accuracy of school variables based on student data. The significant results in this study suggest that the non-significant results regarding migration policies in the context of education in earlier studies are caused by the low number of destination countries included in these other studies, as both the studies conducted by van de Werfhorst, van Elsas, and Heath (2014) and the current study show significant results for migration policies that include multiple destination countries.

The results indicate that immigrants in countries with a more inclusive migration policy are at least less harmed by influence of ethnic school diversity regarding classroom disruption. These findings partly support the "contact hypothesis" and reject the "threat hypothesis" in an educational context. Countries with more inclusive migration policies possibly support the positive intergroup contacts with their authority (Pettigrew 1998) at school level. Consequently, these results show that we should take into account, the institutional context when we refer to the influence of ethnic diversity, on classroom disruption. Although our research design is cross-sectional, the results indicate that changes in migration policies are not only possibly related to migration, but also exert influence on interactions between students on school level. Consequently, migration policy-makers should be aware of this possibly perverse effect of more restrictive migration policies. Furthermore, teachers should be aware of political changes regarding migration as they could lead to increased tension in the classroom, which in turn could lead to increased classroom disruption.

5.1. *Limitations and directions for future research*

Our research design with a cross-country comparison has its limitations. For instance, Manatschal (2011) shows sub-national variation in integration policy for Swiss cantons. Although a research design that measures at sub-national level for all countries might be preferable, a model with sub-national information for all countries is impossible as sub-national information is not accessible for Germany (Prokic-Breuer and Dronkers 2012) in the current PISA data. Second, we recognise that nationality and culture may have influenced individual interpretation and experience of students regarding their perception of school climate and that this may not reflect actual behaviour in the classroom. However, an analysis that controlled for such national differences indicate comparable results. Third, because our students are all in secondary education, the results might differ for students in different age stages (Veerman, van de Werfhorst, and Dronkers 2013). Finally, claims about causal effects of school composition or country migration policy on students' school classroom disruption should be made with caution, due to the cross-sectional character of the data used. Cohort study data, sub-national data from future studies or studies with students in different age stages can enrich and develop the findings of this study.

Acknowledgements

The author would like to thank Professor Herman G. van de Werfhorst of the University of Amsterdam and Professor Jaap Dronkers of the Maastricht University for their helpful advice. Gert-Jan M. Veerman received support from the Doctoral Grant for Teachers funded by the Netherlands Organization for Scientific Research [grant number 023.001.120].

Notes

1. Although our indicator refers to country of origin diversity instead of ethnic diversity in our data, we used the concept ethnic diversity because this term is more common in our research field.
2. PISA data only contains information about the country of origin and – for some destination countries – the migrant's language. Consequently, we cannot refer to a broader concept of student ethnicity (Hutchinson and Smith 1996), but only to country of origin.
3. We split Belgium in two regions due to the language difference between the regions and due to the regionally organised educational system.
4. Only Greece shows a factor loading of 0.6 for "long time to start".
5. The Walloon data and the Flemmish data contain both students from the Brussels region, because these students are assigned to a region based on the teaching language of their school.
6. We checked our results using the MIPEX III or excluding Croatia and found comparable results. Results available on request.

References

Akiba, M., G. K. LeTendre, D. P. Baker, and B. Goesling. 2002. "Student Victimization: National and School System Effects on School Violence in 37 Nations." *American Educational Research Journal* 39: 829–853.
Allport, G. W. 1954. *The Nature of Prejudice*. Cambridge: Perseus Books.

André, S., J. Dronkers, and F. Fleischmann. 2009. "Verschillen in groepsdiscriminatie zoals waargenomen door immigranten uit verschillende herkomstlanden in veertien lidstaten van de Europese Unie." [Perception of in-group Discrimination among Immigrants in 14 Member States of the European Union.] *Mens En Maatschappij* 84: 448–482.

Arum, R., K. Ford, and M. Velez. 2012. "School Discipline, Student Achievement and Social Inequality." In *Improving Learning Environments in Schools: School Discipline and Student Achievement in Comparative Perspective*, edited by R. Arum and M. Velez, 1–41. Stanford, CA: Stanford University Press.

Arum, R., and M. Velez. 2012. *Improving Learning Environments in Schools: School Discipline and Student Achievement in Comparative Perspective*. Stanford, CA: Stanford University Press.

Blalock, H. M. 1957. "Per Cent Non-White and Discrimination in the South." *American Sociological Review* 22: 677–682.

Braster, J. F. A., and J. Dronkers. 2013. "De positieve effecten van etnische verscheidenheid in de klas op de schoolprestaties van leerlingen in een multi-etnische metropool." [The Positive Effects of Ethnic Diversity of Classes on the Educational Performance of Pupils in a Multi-ethnic Metropolitan City.] *Sociologie* 9: 3–20.

Centre for Multilevel Modelling. 2011. *Weighting in MLwiN*. Bristol: University of Bristol.

Dronkers, J., and R. van der Velden. 2013. "Positive but Also Negative Effects of Ethnic Diversity in Schools on Educational Performance? An Empirical Test Using Cross-national PISA Data." In *Integration and Inequality in Educational Institutions*, edited by M. Windzio, 71–98. Dordrecht: Springer.

Durkheim, E. 2002[1961]. *Moral Education a Study in the Theory and Application of Sociology of Education*. Mineolla, NY: Dover.

Duyvendak, J. W., R. van Reekum, F. El-Hajjari, and C. Bertossi. 2013. "Mysterious Multiculturalism: The Risks of Using Model-based Indices for Making Meaningful Comparisons." *Comparative European Politics* 11: 599–620.

Esser, H. 2004. "Does the 'New' Immigration Require a 'New' Theory of Intergenerational Integration." *International Migration Review* 38: 1126–1159.

Fischer, R., J. Fontaine, F. Vijver, and D. A. van de Hemert. 2009. "An Examination of Acquiescent Response Styles in Cross-cultural Research." In *Proceedings Eighteenth International Congress of the International Association for Cross-cultural Psychology*, 137–147. Accessed October 17, 2013. http://iaccp.org/drupal/sites/default/files/spet ses_pdf/16_Fischer.pdf

Gerber, Th. P. 2012. "School Discipline, Math and Science Achievement, and College Aspirations in Contemporary Russia." In *Improving Learning Environments in Schools: School Discipline and Student Achievement in Comparative Perspective*, edited by R. Arum and M. Velez, 222–250. Stanford, CA: Stanford University Press.

Gijsberts, M., T. van der Meer, and J. Dagevos. 2012. "Hunkering Down' in Multi-ethnic Neighbourhoods? The Effects of Ethnic Diversity on Dimensions of Social Cohesion." *European Sociological Review* 28: 527–537.

van Herk, H., Y. Poortinga, and Th. M. M. Verhallen. 2004. "Response Styles in Rating Scales: Evidence of Method Bias in Data from 6 EU Countries?" *Journal of Cross Cultural Psychology* 35: 346–360.

Hoxby, C. 2000. "Peer Effects in the Classroom: Learning from Gender and Race Variation." *NBER Working Paper,7867.*

Hutchinson, J., and A. D. Smith, eds. 1996. *Ethnicity*. Oxford: Oxford University Press.

Janmaat, J. G. 2012. "The Effect of Classroom Diversity on Tolerance and Participation in England, Sweden and Germany." *Journal of Ethnic and Migration Studies* 38: 21–39.

Keating, A., and T. Benton. 2013. "Creating Cohesive Citizens in England? Exploring the Role of Diversity, Deprivation and Democratic Climate at School." *Education, Citizenship and Social Justice* 2: 165–184.

Koopmans, R. 2010. "Trade-offs between Equality and Difference: Immigrant Integration, Multiculturalism and the Welfare State in Cross-national Perspective." *Journal of Ethnic and Migration Studies* 36: 1–26.

Koopmans, R., I. Michalowski, and S. Waibel. 2012. "Citizenship Rights for Immigrants: National Political Processes and Cross-national Convergence in Western Europe." *American Journal of Sociology* 117: 1202–1245.

Lazear, E. P. 1998. "Diversity and Immigration." NBER Working Paper, 6535.

Lupton, R. 2005. "Social Justice and School Improvement: Improving the Quality of Schooling in the Poorest Neighbourhoods." *British Educational Research Journal* 5: 589–604.

Maestri, V. 2011. "Een nadere beschouwing van de samenstelling van etnische minderheden op Nederlandse basisscholen. Diversiteit en leerprestaties." [A further examination of the composition of ethnic minorities in Dutch primary schools. Diversity and learning performance.] In Goede bedoelingen in het onderwijs: Kansen en missers [Good Intentions in Education: Opportunities and Misses], edited by J. Dronkers, 155–178. Amsterdam: Amsterdam University Press.

Manatschal, A. 2011. "Taking Cantonal Variations of Integration Policy Seriously – or How to Validate International Concepts at the Subnational Comparative Level." *Swiss Political Science Review* 17: 336–357.

McLaren, J., J. Armstrong, and K. Gibb. 2013. *Measuring an Independent Scotland's Economic Performance*. Glasgow: Centre for Public Policy for Regions.

Niessen, J., T. Huddleston, and L. Citron. 2007. *Migrant Integration Policy Index*. Brussels: British Council and Migration Policy Group.

OECD. 2012. *PISA 2009 Technical Report*. Paris: Organisation for Economic Co-operation and Development.

Pettigrew, T. F. 1998. "Intergroup Contact Theory." *Annual Review Psychology* 49: 65–85.

Pettigrew, T. F., and L. R. Tropp. 2006. "A Meta-analytic Test of Inter-group Contact Theory." *Journal of Personality and Social Psychology* 90: 751–783.

Prokic-Breuer, T., and J. Dronkers. 2012. "The High Performance of Dutch and Flemish 15-year-old Native Pupils: Explaining Country Differences in Math Scores between Highly Stratified Educational Systems." *Educational Research and Evaluation* 18: 749–777.

Putnam, R. 2007. "E Pluribus Unum: Diversity and Community in the Twenty-first Century the 2006 Johan Skytte Prize Lecture." *Scandinavian Political Studies* 30: 137–174.

Rothon, C., A. Heath, and L. Lessard-Phillips. 2009. "The Educational Attainments of the 'Second Generation': A Comparative Study of Britain, Canada, and the United States." *Teachers College Records* 111: 1404–1443.

Stefanek, E., D. Strohmeier, R. Van de Schoot, and C. Spiel. 2012. "Bullying and Victimization in Ethnically Diverse Schools." In *Migrations: Interdisciplinary Perspectives*, edited by M. Messer, R. Schroeder, and R. Wodak, 79–88. Vienna: Springer Vienna.

Stegmueller, D. 2013. "How Many Countries for Multilevel Modeling? A Comparison of Frequentist and Bayesian Approaches." *American Journal of Political Science* 57: 748–761.

Van Houtte, H., and P. A. J. Stevens. 2009. "School Ethnic Composition and Students' Integration outside and inside Schools in Belgium." *Sociology of Education* 82: 217–239.

Veerman, G.-J. M., and J. Dronkers. 2013. "Ethnic Composition of Schools and School Performances in Secondary Education of Turkish Migrant Students in 7 Countries and 19 European Educational Systems." CReAM Discussion Paper Series, 13/14.

Veerman, G.-J. M., H. G. van de Werfhorst, and J. Dronkers. 2013. "Ethnic Composition of the Class and Educational Performance in Primary Education in the Netherlands." *Educational Research and Evaluation* 19: 370–401.

Wagner, U., O. Christ, T. F. Pettigrew, J. Stellmacher, and C. Wolf. 2006. "Prejudice and Minority Proportion: Contact instead of Threat Effects." *Social Psychology Quarterly* 69: 380–390.

van de Werfhorst, H. G., M. Bergstra, and R. Veenstra. 2012. "School Disciplinary Climate, Behavioral Problems, and Academic Achievement in the Netherlands." In *Improving Learning Environments in Schools: School Discipline and Student Achievement in Comparative Perspective*, edited by R. Arum and M. Velez, 196–221. Stanford, CA: Stanford University Press.

van de Werfhorst, H. G., E. van Elsas, and A. Heath. 2014. "Educational Disadvantages of Second Generation Immigrants in Ten Nations." In *Unequal Attainments: Ethnic Educational Inequalities in Ten Western Countries*, edited by A. Heath and Y. Brinbaum. Oxford: British Academy/Oxford University Press.

World Bank. 2013. *GDP per Capita, PPP (Constant 2005 International $)*. Washington, DC: World Bank. http://data.worldbank.org/indicator/NY.GDP.PCAP.PP.KD

Appendix A

Table B1. Bayesian results of the school origin compositions on country grand classroom disruption in cross-national PISA data.

	Model 1a			Model 1b			Model 2			Model 3		
	B	95% CI		B	95% CI		B	95% CI		B	95% CI	
Constant	-0.03	-0.10	0.03	-0.03	-0.10	0.04	-0.06	-0.15	0.04	-0.06	-0.16	0.05
School level												
Percentage immigrants of school	-0.00	-0.00	0.00	0.00	0.00	0.00	0.00	-0.00	0.00	0.00	-0.00	0.00
Residuals Origin diversity of school	0.68*	0.33	1.02	0.83*	0.45	1.21	0.83*	0.46	1.21	0.82*	0.41	1.20
Mean ESCS	-0.12*	-0.15	-0.09	-0.09*	-0.12	-0.05	-0.09*	-0.12	-0.06	-0.09*	-0.12	-0.06
Variation ESCS	0.36	-0.12	0.34	0.32	-0.21	0.83	0.31	-0.23	0.84	0.31	-0.24	0.85
Percentage females of school	-0.00*	-0.00	-0.00	-0.00*	-0.01	-0.00	-0.00*	-0.01	-0.00	-0.00*	-0.01	-0.00
Educational system level												
GDP							0.00	-0.00	0.00	0.00	-0.00	0.00
MIPEX							0.00	-0.00	0.00	0.00	-0.01	0.00
MIPEX*Resid. Diversity										-0.04*	-0.08	-0.01
Variance												
Country level	0.00	0.00	0.00	0.00	0.00	0.00	0.00	0.00	0.00	0.00	0.00	0.00
School level	0.12*	0.11	0.12	0.12*	0.12	0.13	0.12*	0.12	0.13	0.12*	0.12	0.13
DIC	2.447.10			2.172.15			2.170.05			2.170.34		
N countries	20			16								
N schools	3533			2962								

0 not in 95% CI.
Source: PISA 2009. Own computation.

Appendix B

Table B2. Maximum Likelihood results of the school origin compositions on classroom disruption in weighted cross-national PISA data.

	Model 1a		Model 1b		Model 2		Model 3	
	B	SE	B	SE	B	SE	B	SE
Constant	−0.35**	0.09	−0.31**	0.10	−0.48**	0.14	−0.48**	0.14
School level								
Percentage immigrants of school	−0.00	0.00	0.00	0.00	0.00	0.00	0.00	0.00
Residuals Origin diversity of school	0.64**	0.22	0.69**	0.24	0.69**	0.24	0.64**	0.22
Mean ESCS	−0.10**	0.04	−0.08*	0.04	−0.08*	0.04	−0.08*	0.04
Variation ESCS	1.32**	0.50	1.21*	0.52	1.21*	0.51	1.21*	0.50
Percentage females of school	−0.00**	0.00	−0.01**	0.00	−0.01**	0.00	−0.01**	0.00
Educational system level								
GDP					0.00	0.00	0.00	0.00
MIPEX					0.00	0.00	0.00	0.00
MIPEX*Resid. Diversity							−0.03	0.02
Variance								
Country level	0.04**	0.01	0.04**	0.01	0.03**	0.01	0.03	0.01
School level	0.10**	0.01	0.10**	0.01	0.10**	0.01	0.10	0.01
Log Likelihood	2.975.21		2.584.44		2.581.94		2.578.60	
N countries	20		16					
N schools	3533		2962					

**p<0.01; *p<0.05.
Source: PISA 2009. Own computation.

Appendix C

Correlation ethnic diversity and percentage immigrants

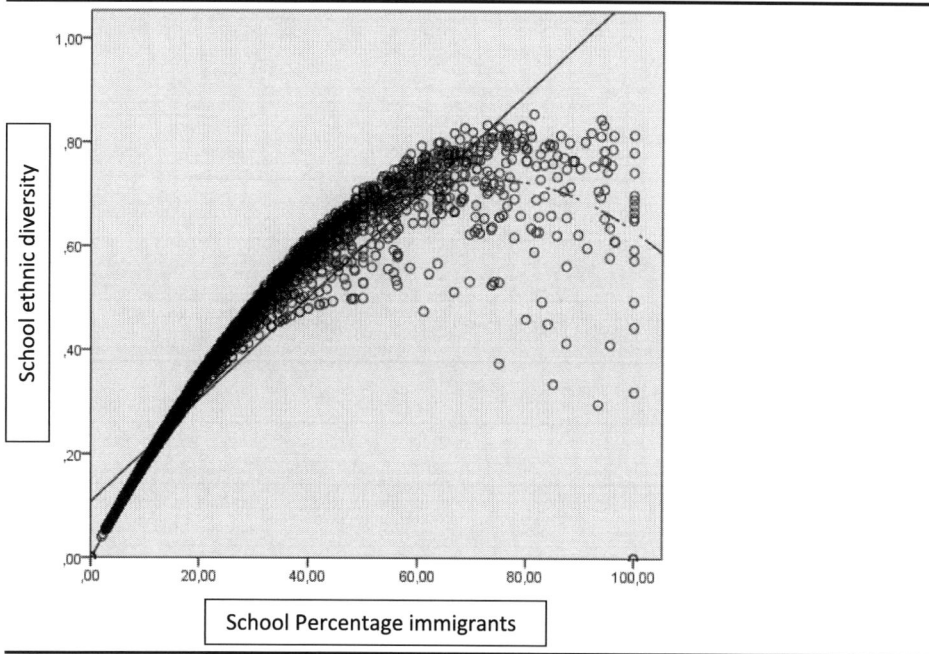

Index